BEHAVIORAL ASSESSMENT OF SEVERE DEVELOPMENTAL DISABILITIES

Michael D. Powers

Jan S. Handleman

AN ASPEN PUBLICATION®
Aspen Systems Corporation
Rockville, Maryland
Royal Tunbridge Wells
1984

Library of Congress Cataloging in Publication Data

Powers, Michael D.
Behavioral assessment of severe developmental disabilities.

Includes bibliographies and index.
1. Developmentally disabled children. 2. Behavioral assessment in children.
I. Handleman, Jan S. II. Title. [DNLM: 1. Austism. 2. Child Behavior.
3. Child Development Disorders. 4. Mental Retardation. WS 350.6 P888b]
RJ506.D47P69   1984   618.92'89   84-16878
ISBN: 0-89443-863-8

Publisher: John R. Marozsan
Associate Publisher: Jack W. Knowles, Jr.
Editorial Director: Margaret Quinlin
Executive Managing Editor: Margot G. Raphael
Managing Editor: M. Eileen Higgins
Editorial Services: Ruth McKendry
Printing and Manufacturing: Debbie Collins

Library of Congress Catalog Card Number: 84-16878
ISBN: 0-89443-863-8

Printed in the United States of America

1 2 3 4 5

To JoLynn, Elaine, and Lauren

Table of Contents

Foreword

Behavioral Assessment of Severe Developmental Disabilities is a book that grew from prolonged, intensive interdisciplinary exchange between an educator and a psychologist who were grappling with challenges in the assessment and education of children with autism, mental retardation, and other severe developmental disabilities. Their fruitful collaboration highlights an exciting aspect of work with the severely developmentally disabled—there has been substantial movement across traditional disciplinary boundaries. Special education, psychology, nursing, and speech therapy have had an especially happy collaboration in developing treatment approaches for this population. Perhaps the pervasive nature of these handicapping conditions has humbled professionals and made it clear to us that we must draw from many sources to generate the broad-based treatment plans so essential to our clients.

It has been my privilege to work closely with Michael Powers and Jan Handleman at the Douglass Developmental Disabilities Center, our university-based center for the education of children with autism. I have come to know them as educators, scholars, and skilled, sensitive clinicians. I can share with the reader, therefore, the assurance that these two men have extensively field-tested the strategies they describe in this book. It is a book not of speculation, but of integrated practice and research.

Drs. Powers and Handleman are among a relatively small group of researchers in the field of developmental disabilities whose work is conducted in a setting dedicated to service. As a consequence, the questions they address are consistently pragmatic and important, not minor or academic issues addressed in an isolated fashion. It is relatively easy to do research on developmental disabilities when one has no ongoing educational and clinical responsibilities to one's subjects. It is quite another challenge to design research to be done in the context of service delivery. Drs. Powers and Handleman have been able to meet the real needs of their clients while making a substantial contribution to professional practice.

The reader can expect to find in this book a highly useful distillation of the clinical and educational experiences of two very fine practitioners. Their words will speak for themselves!

Sandra L. Harris, PhD
Rutgers, The State University

Preface

This is a book for psychologists, educators, and human service personnel who work with severely developmentally disabled children and adults. These clients—variously described as autistic, severely or profoundly retarded, or multihandicapped—present a significant challenge to workers in the field. Fortunately, a substantial treatment literature has emerged over the past twenty years, greatly facilitating the habilitation of these clients. However, in the rush to treat identified behavioral excesses and deficits, methods of assessment to be used before intervention have been less comprehensively described. Our own clinical experience with treatment failures with these individuals has sensitized us to the need for comprehensive, multidimensional behavioral assessment before intervention efforts are begun. This book is an attempt to address that need.

In *Behavioral Assessment of Severe Developmental Disabilities* we have applied the specificity of behavioral assessment principles and methods to a variety of functional behavioral excesses, deficits, and strengths exhibited by severely developmentally disabled clients. Throughout, we have emphasized an approach to behavioral assessment that integrates research and practice. This approach includes (1) target behavior identification, (2) determination of controlling variables, (3) development of a treatment plan, and (4) evaluation of the effects of intervention.

The behavior of a severely developmentally disabled person does not exist in a vacuum. Because of this, we believe that a comprehensive behavioral assessment calls for the consideration of multiple sources of data. These include family interviews, DSM-III diagnosis, and information from "standard" psychological evaluations. When multiple sources of data are considered, treatment efforts become more individualized—the ultimate goal of behavioral assessment.

M.D.P.
J.S.H.

Acknowledgments

There are many people whose support and guidance have contributed to the completion of this book. Most important are the children and families we have worked with at the Douglass Developmental Disabilities Center and elsewhere over the past twelve years. The many lessons they have taught us provided the content for these pages. Many thanks must be given to Sandra Harris for her unbounded support, critical eye, and nurturance in shaping our professional careers as well as her useful comments on the entire manuscript. Kenneth C. Schneider and Charles A. Maher read portions of the manuscript and made many useful comments. Joan B. Chase was—and continues to be—a valued friend and colleague in our work with severely developmentally disabled infants and children. Appreciation is expressed to Maria Arnold, Ray Romanczyk, and the many staff members of the DDDC, and to Virginia C. Bennett, Linda R. Hay, and S. Ruth Schulman of the Graduate School of Applied and Professional Psychology at Rutgers for their support. Thanks are also due to Helen Bajusz for her formidable word processing skills, and to Lori Aks and Linda Hoffman for typing portions of the book.

While others gave much to this book, our families provided the support, encouragement, and tolerance for our task-oriented behavior that ultimately made it possible. It is to JoLynn Powers, and Elaine and Lauren Handleman, that we owe a most special thanks.

M.D.P.
J.S.H.

Chapter 1

Nature and Needs of Severely Developmentally Disabled Clients

INTRODUCTION

Clinicians practicing in today's social service agencies are faced with the complex task of assessing severely developmentally disabled clients. Varied diagnoses, combined with the input from interdisciplinary professionals, create an atmosphere of confusion regarding the boundaries of this condition with other handicaps. The following pages contain discussions of specific handicapping conditions; severe developmental disabilities are not viewed as a diagnostic entity, but rather as a constellation of common characteristics shared by a particular group of clients. Within this framework, assessment can assume a more functional form as attention is directed toward intervention and treatment.

AN OVERVIEW

Prominent contemporary views on developmental disabilities suggest that the disorders include cognitive or physical handicapping conditions that originate early in life and interfere with developmental progress. Such conditions often result in multiple handicaps that require comprehensive special education services to ensure maximum growth and development.

Our current conceptualizations of these conditions can be traced historically to President Kennedy's Panel on Mental Retardation, appointed on October 17, 1961 (Thompson & O'Quinn, 1979). The panel was charged with making recommendations on personnel, treatment programs, and governmental participation regarding the care and treatment of retarded persons. The panel's activity in the 1960s resulted in the passing of federal legislation creating funds for the construction of centers and facilities for the mentally retarded; in addition, personnel training programs were initiated at American colleges and universities. This political and professional involvement eventually gave rise to people who possessed a broader interest in children with other developmental disabilities.

The term developmental disabilities was legitimized in 1974 with federal legislation, Public Law No. 94–103. While this law originally defined a developmental disability as a disorder attributable to autism, cerebral palsy, epilepsy, and mental retardation, changes in the 1978 federal definition (Pub. L. No. 95–602) described developmental disabilities in terms of functional limitations as opposed to specific categories. According to the 1978 definition, developmental disabilities refer to a severe, chronic disability that:

- is attributable to a mental or physical impairment or combination of mental and physical impairments;
- is manifested before the person attains age 22;
- is likely to continue indefinitely;
- results in substantial functional limitations in three or more of the following areas of major life activity: (i) self care, (ii) receptive and expressive language, (iii) learning, (iv) mobility, (v) self-direction, (vi) capacity for independent living, and (vii) economic sufficiency; and
- reflects the person's need for special services that are of lifelong or extended duration and are individually planned and coordinated. (Pub. L. No. 95–602)

As the result of the legislative activity and parent advocacy of the 1970s, many states have loosely grouped a population of developmentally disabled individuals referred to as the severely and profoundly handicapped. The Bureau of Education for the Handicapped (BEH) of the Federal Office of Education (USOE, 1974, Section 121.2) offers the following definition:

> Severely handicapped children are those who, because of the intensity of their physical, mental, or emotional problems or a combination of such problems, need education, social, psychological, and medical services beyond those which are traditionally offered by regular and special education programs, in order to maximize their full potential for useful and meaningful participation in society and for self-fulfillment. Such children include those classified as seriously emotionally disturbed (schizophrenic and autistic), profoundly and severely mentally retarded, and those with two or more serious handicapping conditions such as the mentally retarded-blind and the cerebral palsied-deaf.
>
> Such severely handicapped children may possess severe language and/or perceptual cognitive deprivations and evidence a number of

abnormal behaviors including: failure to attend to even the most pronounced social stimuli; self-mutilation, self-stimulation, manifestation
of durable and intense temper tantrums, and the absence of even the
most rudimentary of forms of verbal control, and may also have an
extremely fragile physiological condition. (Pub. L. No. 95–602, §121.2)

The broad sense of the term severely and profoundly handicapped has been
employed to describe individuals excluded from public programs as a result of
their extensive handicaps. The term severely and profoundly handicapped has
been developed for educational purposes (Van Etten, Arkell, & Van Etten, 1980).
It differs from the term developmental disabilities in that no age limit is established
and no prognosis is required (Van Etten et al., 1980). The close similarity between
the two terms suggests that the label severely developmentally disabled is more
descriptive.

HISTORICAL PERSPECTIVE ON SEVERE DEVELOPMENTAL
   DISABILITIES

Confusion over the terminology regarding the severely developmentally disabled can be traced to the development of professional thinking about the
condition identified as infantile autism. Originally discussed by Leo Kanner in
1943, the term autism, along with mental retardation and multiple handicaps, has
been expanded and included under the umbrella of developmental disabilities.

The behaviors of children labeled as autistic appear to be influenced by different
organic and/or environmental factors than do the behaviors of nondevelopmentally disabled children. These factors, currently unspecified, produce a set of
deviant behaviors that originally was recognized by Kanner (1943) and delineated
as the syndrome of early infantile autism. Kanner (1974) described four main
characteristics shared by autistic children: (1) extreme inability to relate to other
people, (2) delayed acquisition of speech, (3) obsessive desire to maintain
environmental sameness, (4) good cognitive potential. Since this original description, numerous other diagnostic criteria have been proposed. The variety evident
in such characterizations reflects the behavioral heterogeneity of those children
labeled autistic. Diagnosis is complicated further because some characteristics of
early infantile autism can be seen in the development of both normal children and
children with other psychological and cognitive disorders. It has been suggested
that autistic children differ mainly in the severity and patterning of their abnormalities (Kanner, 1958; Lovaas, 1981; Rutter, 1966, 1979; Rutter & Lockyer,
1967).

Examination of the more prominent views of autism (Kanner, 1974; Lovaas,
Koegel, Simmons, & Long, 1973; Rutter, 1979; Ornitz, 1971; Wing, 1966)

indicates two common diagnostic criteria: retarded language development and disturbed interpersonal relationships. Rutter and Lockyer (1967) define disturbed interpersonal relationships as marked by aloofness, avoidance of eye contact, apparent lack of interest in people, and minimal demonstration of feelings. Lack of interest in and noninvolvement with people are also described by Dupont (1969) and postulated by O'Gorman (1970) to be due to a preference by these children to ". . . relate to neutral objects which they can control, which unlike people, make no demands on them" (p. 92).

Rutter (1971) describes three other characteristics exhibited by autistic children more often than nondevelopmentally disabled groups: (1) ritualistic behavior, such as strong attachment to unusual objects; (2) stereotyped and repetitive mannerisms involving body movement; and (3) an attentional deficit. Ritualistic and compulsive behaviors can be characterized by the following forms: a morbid attachment to unusual objects; peculiar preoccupations; a resistance to change; obsessive rituals; arm flapping; rocking; facial grimaces; and masturbation (O'Gorman, 1970). Lovaas et al. (1973) incorporate Rutter's (1971) description under the more behavioral categories of apparent sensory deficit, severe affect isolation, self-stimulatory behavior, self-mutilating behavior, and language abnormalities. The lack, or minimal demonstration, of social and self-help behaviors is additionally cited by Lovaas et al. (1973).

There have been major changes in the concept of autism since Kanner's (1943) description. There appears to be a shift from viewing the condition within the social and emotional realm to attributing it to a cognitive disorder with a neurological origin (Rutter, 1974). Some researchers postulate that autistic children have a dysfunctional reticular formation (Hermelin & O'Connor, 1968; Ornitz, 1973). Sander, Stechler, Burns, and Julia (1970) discuss many autistic characteristics in terms of soft neurological signs. In addition, the work of Goldfarb (1961) supports the notion of organic involvement as a contributing factor in autism. Recent research is pursuing a physiological as opposed to an emotional etiology of the condition (Cohen & Shaywitz, 1982).

Biomedical research is expanding our understanding of autism and other severe developmental disabilities (Cohen & Shaywitz, 1982). Like severe mental retardation, the etiology of autism is probably multifactorial (Coleman, 1976; Fish & Ritvo, 1978) and includes factors such as viral infections, metabolic diseases, and pre- and postnatal trauma (Ciaranello, Vandenberg, & Anders, 1982). It has been suggested that many of the characteristics of autistic and other multiply handicapped children may be expressive of central nervous dysfunction (Ciaranello et al., 1982; Maurer & Damasio, 1982). In addition, the detection of hyperserotonemia in autistic and retarded children has created research optimism (Campbell, Friedman, DeVito, Greenspan, & Collins, 1974; Partington, Tu, & Wong, 1973; Young, Kavanagh, Anderson, Shaywitz, & Cohen, 1982). In the last decade, there also has been growing interest in the possibility of genetic and congenital factors in severe developmental disabilities (Folstein & Rutter, 1977; Ritvo, Ritvo, & Brothers, 1982; Spence, 1976; Stubbs, 1977). A recent finding is the identification of the fragile X syndrome in some autistic males (Folstein & Rutter, 1977; Meryash, Szymanski, & Gerald, 1982).

Although the conceptualization of autism cited above spans the most frequently given characteristics, different investigators may emphasize one feature more strongly than others. This heterogeneity underscores the fact that autism may be a hypothetical construct, not an entity, and only reflects the researcher's observation of certain similarities among a particular group (Lovaas, 1981, Lovaas et al., 1973). In addition, autism and other severe developmental disabilities, such as early childhood schizophrenia and severe mental retardation, share many of the cited behaviors of autism (Creak, 1969; Mahler, 1965). The current preference by professionals to describe these children as severely developmentally disabled seems to offer a reasonable solution to the labeling confusion.

DIAGNOSIS AND DIFFERENTIAL DIAGNOSIS

Controversy has arisen over the definition of autism in recent years (Schopler, 1978). Specifically, concerns exist with regard to the boundaries of autism with other conditions. Confusion over the terminology originated with Kanner's (1943) choice of the same word that Bleuler (1911/1950) used to discuss schizophrenia. While Kanner (1943) focuses his description on a failure to develop interpersonal relationships, Bleuler (1911/1950) suggests a withdrawal from relationships as characteristic of schizophrenia.

The development of professional concern about autism is marked by varied opinions regarding primary diagnostic criteria. For example, Schain and Yannet (1960) omit maintenance of sameness from their description and Tinbergen and Tinbergen (1972) emphasize avoidance of eye contact. Ornitz and Ritvo (1968) focus on disturbances of perception as a primary factor. This confusion is evidenced further in numerous clinical accounts of different problems attributed to the same condition (Rutter, 1979).

Assessment of autistic children is an intricate task and this further complicates diagnosis. While the lack of speech associated with autism presents a major difficulty, the reported negativism many children demonstrate contributes to the difficulties of testing (Cowan, Hoddinott, & Wright, 1965). Alpern (1967) also describes the problem of noncompliant behavior interfering with assessment.

There have been many attempts to differentiate autism from other conditions. With regard to etiology, reports indicate that it is difficult to diagnose autism in terms of the absence of organic brain dysfunction (Rutter, 1979). Others suggest that the etiology of the condition is not attributable to a single physiological cause but rather to a variety of disease states, such as tuberose sclerosis (Lotter, 1974) and congenital rubella (Chess, Korn, & Fernandez, 1971).

Examination of the diagnostic variable of general intelligence seems to suggest that IQs in autistic children are similar to IQs in other groups of individuals (Wing, 1979). While there are reports that autism and mental retardation coexist, Hermelin and O'Connor (1970) suggest that the differentiation between the two conditions seems to be a valid and meaningful one. Numerous reports indicate close similarity between mental retardation and autism (Gillies, 1965; Lockyer & Rutter, 1969; Tubbs, 1966; Schopler, 1966).

While somewhat more distinct, autism's historical place in the realm of severe developmental disabilities parallels the history of severe mental retardation. For example, diagnosis with the mentally retarded population is also problematic (Snell & Renzaglia, 1982). Like autistic children, severely retarded youngsters exhibit a wide variety of psychological and physical characteristics (Snell, 1982) that include self-stimulatory behavior (Landesman-Dwyer & Sackett, 1978) and self-injury (Baumeister, 1978). Moreover, few retarded persons have a single handicap (Van Etten et al., 1980). The following description of a severely retarded child by Sontag, Burke, and York (1973) highlights numerous similarities with the characteristics of an autistic child.

> Those who are not toilet trained: aggress toward others; do not attend to even the most pronounced social stimuli; self-mutilate; ruminate; self-stimulate; do not walk, speak, hear or see; manifest durable and intense temper tantrums; are not under even the most rudimentary forms of verbal control; do not imitate; manifest minimally controlled seizures; and/or have extremely brittle medical existences. (p. 21)

As with autism, it is impossible to identify the precise etiology of many cases of severe mental retardation (Snell & Renzaglia, 1982). Some of the known biological causes of the condition include metabolic disorders and chromosomal abnormalities (Abromowitz & Richardson, 1975).

The coexistence of autism and mental retardation under the 1974 federal definition of developmental disabilities has created a close clinical relationship. Examination of the literature reveals numerous similar needs and treatment considerations. Kirk (1962) describes the moderately to severely retarded child as in need of services outside the typical special education mainstream and in need of a curriculum focusing on social and language development. The segregation of the severely mentally retarded from the public schools has been suggested because needed specialized services have not been provided (Anderson & Greer, 1976). Also, the importance of language deficiency as a primary characteristic of mental retardation is stated by Bricker and Bricker (1970). The similarity of professional thinking regarding the mentally retarded and the autistic is evidenced further by Kolstoe's (1970) discussion of the controversies over both etiology and classification and the suggestion that mentally retarded children are more heterogeneous than homogeneous.

Further attempts to clarify diagnosis are noted in the literature regarding the differences between autism and schizophrenia. Rutter (1974) reports that as a result of the many differences between the two conditions (e.g., age of onset, presence or absence of hallucinations), they should be regarded as separate conditions. Also, distinctions have been made between autism, sensory deficits, and aphasia (Rutter, 1979).

While the literature is marked by discussions regarding the accurate diagnosis of autism, mental retardation, and other severe developmental disabilities, concerns have been reduced somewhat by including these conditions under the more general category of severe developmental disabilities. Lovaas (1981) writes that severely developmentally disabled children share a number of characteristics that include retarded functioning, difficulty with self-help, inability to play appropriately, and problems with communication. This focus on functional characteristics allows diagnosis, assessment, and treatment planning to be linked in a meaningful way.

DIAGNOSTIC CRITERIA AND CHARACTERISTICS

Unlike the diagnosis of severe mental retardation, the diagnosis of autism has been partially simplified by the criteria established by the American Psychiatric Association (1980) and the National Society of Autistic Children (Schopler, 1978). Exhibit 1–1 presents a description of these two diagnostic systems. While the two systems differ with regard to the component of disturbances of developmental rate and sequence, close examination reveals an agreement with regard to four basic criteria that, in their broad sense, can be applied to the severely developmentally disabled population: (1) language deficiency; (2) disturbed interpersonal relationships; (3) inconsistent response to sensory stimulation; and (4) developmental delays and associated cognitive disorders.

Exhibit 1–1 Synopsis of Diagnostic Criteria of Autism

*DSM-III**	*NSAC***
1. Severe language deficiency	1. Language deficiency
2. Pervasive lack of interpersonal responsiveness	2. Disturbed interpersonal relationships
3. Bizarre responses to environmental stimulation	3. Inconsistent responses to sensory stimulation
4. Absence of hallucinations and delusions	4. Developmental delays
5. Age of onset prior to 30 months of age	5. Onset prior to 30 months

   * *Diagnostic and Statistical Manual* (3rd ed.)
   ** National Society for Autistic Children

Language Deficiency

It is widely recognized that difficulty with language is a primary characteristic of autism and other severe developmental disabilities (Carr, 1979; Halpern, 1970; Harris, 1975; Hermelin, 1971; Hermelin & Frith, 1971; Lovaas, 1981; Rutter, 1968; Tager-Flusberg, 1981; Wing, 1966, 1979). Such children have difficulty with the acquisition and use of language (Litt & Schreibman, 1981; Menyuk, 1978). When they develop language, it is usually abnormal in quality (Rutter, 1968).

Kanner (1943) originally described a variety of disturbances that marked the language of autistic children. Cited characteristics include: complete absence of speech; echolalic speech; singsong speech patterns; word order reversals; pronoun reversals; delayed echolalia; and extreme literalness of content. Provonost (1966) reported on the speech behavior and language comprehension of 14 children diagnosed as autistic according to Kanner's (1943) description. Eight of the children did not produce intelligible words and were referred to as the vocalization group. Provonost (1966) noted in the children a characteristic looseness of the musculature in all areas of oral functioning; extensive use of prolonged monotonal vocalizations with many occurrences of high-pitched sounds; and extreme variations of voice quality. The speech of the other group (the talking group) consisted of words, phrases, and sentences with the most characteristic utterance being immediate echolalic reproductions of statements made by adults. Much of the speech of the talking group was linguistically inappropriate to the situation in which it was used; the dependence was on situational clues rather than linguistic content.

Reports of delayed echolalia and pronoun reversals are consistent in the literature (Hinerman, Jenson, Walker, & Petersen, 1982; Rutter & Lockyer, 1967). Also, defects in the form of neologisms and metaphorical usage commonly are reported in the language of many severely developmentally disabled children (Cunningham & Dixon, 1961; Wolff & Chess, 1965; Tubbs, 1966). In addition, many of these children demonstrate problems with both the semantics and syntactic elements of language (Cromer, 1981).

Many severely developmentally disabled children who develop speech demonstrate language disorders in such areas as speech delivery, emotional expression, and inflection (Rutter, 1970). Such children also are described as demonstrating language-related dysfunctions in verbal understanding, abstraction, and sequencing (Rutter, 1979). Bartak, Rutter, and Cox (1975) showed that autistic children have difficulty in understanding gesture and written language. Hermelin and O'Connor (1970) report that autistic children also have difficulty in associating words semantically and with memory of verbal items. In addition, these children tend to perform poorly on tests that require verbal skills (Lockyer & Rutter, 1970).

Autistic and mentally retarded children have been reported to demonstrate similar language difficulties (DeMyer, 1976; Wing, 1981). Like autistic children, the mentally retarded have difficulty generalizing language from one stimulus situation to another (Hamilton, 1966) and with conversational speech forms (Garcia, 1974). In addition, the reported difficulty that severely developmentally disabled children demonstrate with generative language has been reported repeatedly across several language classes (Welch, 1981); descriptive adjectives (Hart & Risley, 1968); productive and receptive plurality (Guess, 1969; Guess & Baer, 1973); past and present tense verb inflections (Shumaker & Sherman, 1970); generative use of "is" in descriptive sentences (Fygetakis & Gray, 1970); adjectival inflections (Baer & Guess, 1971); generative use of "is" and "the" (Bennett & Ling, 1972); generative use of plural allomorphs (Sailor, 1971); and the use of singular and plural sentences (Garcia, Guess & Byrnes, 1973).

The increasing interest in alternative systems of communication further highlights the professional concern for the pervasive difficulty that severely developmentally disabled children have with communication. It has been documented that autistic (Carr, 1979) and profoundly retarded children (Poulton & Algozzine, 1980) can be taught to use manual signs to express basic needs and wants.

In summary, the severely developmentally disabled may demonstrate varied degrees of speech, language, and communication difficulties. Areas of specific difficulty include the mechanics of speech and gesture; the acquisition of speech and language; and the comprehension of language and language-related material. Exhibit 1–2 presents a summary of speech and language difficulties.

Exhibit 1–2 Speech and Language Deficiencies of Severely Developmentally Disabled Children

Nonverbal
  Complete absence of speech
  Absence of or difficulty with gestural communication

Verbal deficiencies
  Volume disorders
  Echolalia
  Singsong intonation
  Monotonal vocalizations
  High-pitched vocalizing
  Pronoun reversal
  Improper emotional inflection
  Limited generalization
  Extreme literalness
  Poor word recall
  Inconsistent imitation

Disturbed Interpersonal Relationships

It is not unusual for severely developmentally disabled children to demonstrate numerous aberrant behaviors (Johnson, Baumeister, Penland, & Inwald, 1982). Difficulty with social interaction and insistence on environmental sameness commonly are reported characteristics of many of these children (Kanner, 1946; Baumeister, 1978; Birnbrauer, 1979). Avoidance of eye contact has been described as a primary demonstration of disturbed interpersonal interactions (Howlin, 1978). There are numerous reports of such children being withdrawn or aloof (O'Gorman, 1967; Rimland, 1964; Kanner, 1943). Also, autistic and other severely developmentally disabled children have been reported as preferring objects to people (O'Gorman, 1967), and they may engage in prolonged tantrums (Johnson & Koegel, 1982). Perhaps the most striking underlying interpersonal problem regards the low motivation displayed by many of the children (Egel, 1980).

Many severely developmentally disabled children do not appear to be interested in socially appropriate activities (Johnson & Koegel, 1982). They may exhibit little curiosity (Koegel & Schreibman, 1976) and may engage in self-stimulatory behavior to effect social reaction (Devany & Rincover, 1982). In addition, self-injurious behavior (SIB), a behavior of great concern to professionals working with these clients, can be linked to interpersonal attention (Lovaas & Simmons, 1969) or avoidance (Carr, Newsom, & Binkoff, 1976). Carr (1977) describes the motivational components of SIB in considerable detail.

The problem of SIB in severely developmentally disabled children has been discussed widely (Cataldo & Harris, 1982; Johnson & Baumeister, 1978; Russo, Carr, & Lovaas, 1980). It is probably the most dangerous type of psychopathology, with client symptoms ranging from self-hitting to head banging, biting, and scratching. It has been estimated that 17% of institutionalized retarded clients engage in some form of self-injury (Ross, 1972; Smeets, 1971). While the exact causes of self-injury are unknown (Cataldo & Harris, 1982), operant psychology has offered effective strategies designed to decrease the frequency and severity of the behavior in many cases (Frankel & Simmons, 1976; Romanczyk & Goren, 1975; Schroeder, Schroeder, Rojahn, & Mulick, 1981).

Inconsistent Response to Sensory Stimulation

Considerable attention has been directed toward the unresponsiveness of severely developmentally disabled children to complex environmental stimuli (Hermelin & O'Connor, 1970; Koegel, Dunlap, Richman, & Dyer, 1981). Inconsistent response to sensory stimulation has been suggested as a primary characteristic of autism and other severe developmental disabilities (Kanner, 1943; Rimland, 1964; Schopler, 1978). Often, many children are described as having dysfunctional peripheral sensory systems; however, after closer examination, hearing, for example, is within normal limits. One difficulty these children have in responding to environmental stimuli is evidenced by the phenomenon of stimulus overselectivity (Kolko, Anderson, & Campbell, 1980; Lovaas, Koegel, & Schreibman, 1979; Lovaas, Schreibman, Koegel, & Rehm, 1971). Many severely developmentally disabled clients have difficulty in adequately responding and attending to multiple sensory input (Lovaas, Schreibman, Koegel, & Rehm, 1971; Varni, Lovaas, Koegel, & Everett, 1979) and tend to respond to a narrow range of informational input. In addition, many children respond or perseverate on a single stimulus to the exclusion of others (Boucher, 1977; Hermelin & Frith, 1971). Both these difficulties interfere greatly with learning.

One of the most pervasive behaviors of the severely developmentally disabled is self-stimulation (Devany & Rincover, 1982; Berkson & Davenport, 1962; Eason, White, & Newsom, 1982). Self-stimulatory behavior interferes with a variety of abilities: observational learning (Varni, et al., 1979); mastered behaviors (Lovaas, Litrownik, & Mann, 1971); and attention (Koegel & Covert, 1972). Some authors suggest that self-stimulatory behavior may be controlled by sensory consequences (Rincover, 1978; Rincover, Newsom, & Carr, 1979). Also, self-injurious behavior has been described as a form of sensory stimulation (Baumeister & Forehand, 1973; Favell, McGimsey, & Schell, 1982; Rutter, 1966). The difficulty severely developmentally disabled children display with processing sensory information is also evidenced by reports of some of these children being insensitive to pain (Johnson & Koegel, 1982).

Inconsistent responding also is exemplified by the pervasive problem severely developmentally disabled children demonstrate with generalization of behavior (Hamilton, 1966; Handleman, 1979a; Rincover & Koegel, 1975). The situational specificity of many of the responses of these children often interferes with their transfer of responding to novel persons (Garcia, 1974), to new settings (Rincover & Koegel, 1975), or to the home environment (Handleman, 1979a).

Developmental Delays and Associated Cognitive Disorders

Since Kanner's original description in 1943, researchers have questioned the cognitive capacity of severely developmentally disabled children (Curtiss, 1981). It has been postulated that these children demonstrate difficulty in integrating perceptual and cognitive processes (Carter, Alpert, & Stewart, 1982). Many severely developmentally disabled children have been described as having information processing deficits as demonstrated on paired associate tasks, in short term memory, and in concept formation (Carter et al., 1982; Ellis et al., 1982; Hermelin & O'Connor, 1970). Also, autistic and other severely developmentally disabled children frequently are described as demonstrating developmental discontinuity (Donnellan, Gossage, LaVigna, Schuler, & Traphagan, 1977). While developmental disabilities are typically associated with retarded functioning, splinter skills in various areas may be evident (Donnellan et al., 1977).

Severely developmentally disabled children have been described as being deficient in many skill areas (Johnson & Koegel, 1982), and in general they demonstrate little goal-directed behavior (Dunlap & Egel, 1982). Many children fail to develop appropriate play (Johnson & Koegel, 1982), and many school age children are not toilet trained, nor do they demonstrate appropriate self-help skills. In addition, many of these children demonstrate impairments of motor organization and have difficulty with such skills as spatial relations and motor planning (Kanner, 1958). As severely developmentally disabled children grow older, the discrepancy between developmental level and chronological age increases (Brown, Branston, Hamre-Nietupski, Pumpian, Certo, & Gruenwald, 1979).

NEEDS OF SEVERELY DEVELOPMENTALLY DISABLED CHILDREN

The needs of the severely developmentally disabled are varied and extend into numerous areas. Most often the educational needs of these children are addressed. In addition, concern for their home life is relevant to the extent that it helps to provide comprehensive intervention. Recently, as a result of federal legislation, attention has been directed toward the community needs of the children as plans are made for their social integration into less restrictive environments. Examination of these three interrelated domains will serve to highlight the complex service needs of severely developmentally disabled clients.

Educational Needs

One of the original approaches to the education and treatment of the severely developmentally disabled is based on psychodynamic theory (Achenbach, 1974). Techniques such as play therapy (Axline, 1974) characterize the psychodynamic approach. The basic assumption of this approach is that the parental environment is responsible for limiting vital experiences of early life (Bettelheim, 1967). According to this assumption, it is the therapists' or teachers' role to establish an emotional bond with the child through both support and acceptance.

Kanner and Eisenberg's (1955) report on the failure of psychodynamic treatment to effect change in severely developmentally disabled children initiated interest in the behavioral treatment of such children, along with Brown's (1960) supporting study indicating that these children were unaffected by psychotherapy. The first comprehensive attempt to analyze the behavior of severely developmentally disabled children within a behavioral framework was accomplished by Ferster (1961), who relates the very impoverished behavioral development seen in such clients to a general deficiency in acquired reinforcers. Ferster's theoretical contention of the relationship between learning principles and behavioral development is viewed as a primary contribution to the education and treatment of the severely developmentally disabled.

Ferster and DeMyer (1962) were the first to indicate that the behaviors of the severely developmentally disabled could be related to certain explicit environmental manipulations. Wolf, Risley, and Mees (1964) systematically employed behavioral procedures to teach socially practical behaviors to such children. Since Skinner's (1957) affirmation of the operant nature of language, considerable attention has been directed toward the application of behavioral principles in the development or remediation of speech and language skills among populations of severely developmentally disabled children (Hollis & Sherman, 1967; Isaac, Thomas, & Goldiamond, 1960; Lovaas, 1968; Lovaas, Berberich, Perloff, & Schaffer, 1966). Interest has expanded to include the increasing of free vocalizations (Jellis & Grainger, 1972) and the teaching of complex morphological and transformational rules (Wheeler & Sulzer, 1970; Stevens-Long & Rasmussen, 1974; Howlin, 1981). Also, the use of sign language as an alternative form of communication has received increasing attention (Bonvillian, Nelson, & Rhyne, 1981; Walker, Hinerman, Jenson, & Peterson, 1981).

Autistic and other severely developmentally disabled children require special attention in order to learn (Wing & Wing, 1971). Behavior therapists have documented that such children can learn and develop through active and structured programming (Schreibman & Koegel, 1981; Lovaas & Newsom, 1976). A structured approach frequently is suggested (Rutter, 1970; Wing, 1976), emphasizing curricular content areas of language, self-help, and maladaptive behaviors (Rutter & Bartak, 1973; Hemsley & Howlin, 1976). The elimination of self-stimulatory behavior and other behaviors that compete with learning (Devany & Rincover, 1982), along with the establishment of basic instructional control (Harris, 1975), is a prerequisite to educating these children. Also, a specific focus of behavior management has been to motivate these children to learn by the use of systematic reinforcement (Egel, 1980; Koegel & Williams, 1980). Exhibit 1–3 summarizes major curricular content areas and skills appropriate to each area.

The effectiveness of operant techniques for teaching responsive interactions and communication to severely developmentally disabled children is well documented (Harris, 1975). Less widely recognized are the limitations of these programs for teaching spontaneous behavior (Bricker & Bricker, 1970; Stremel, 1972). Programs designed to increase a child's spontaneity attempt to reduce the child's reliance on verbal prompts from others and focus on enhancing the child's awareness of the physical environment as containing the cues for speech and other behaviors (Sosne, Handleman, & Harris, 1979).

A particular educational concern involves the difficulty that many severely developmentally disabled children have with generalization. These children are

Exhibit 1-3 Curriculum Content for Early Educational Programming

Instructional control
Sitting
Attending
Following directions
Discrimination
Elimination of interfering behaviors

Communication
Nonverbal imitation
Verbal/sign imitation
Functional communication

Daily living
Self-help
Independent play
Cooperative play
Prevocational/work oriented activities

reported as possibly being bound to the stimulus situation and, as a result, are limited in their ability to transfer learning from one situation to another (Hamilton, 1966). While generalization cannot be expected as a consequence of teaching (Handleman, 1979a), it can be programmed. For example, exposing a child to a variety of teachers has resulted in increased generalization to novel instructors (Garcia, 1974; Kale, Kaye, Whelan, & Hopkins, 1968). Exposure to a variety of teaching settings also can facilitate transfer of learning to extratherapy settings (Griffiths & Craighead, 1972; Jackson & Wallace, 1974; Rincover & Koegel, 1975). In addition, recent investigations indicate that teaching in a variety of settings can facilitate generalization to the natural environment (Handleman, 1979a, 1981; Handleman & Harris, 1980, 1983).

As the basic educational needs of severely developmentally disabled children are being met, attention has been directed toward more comprehensive planning. A recent concern raised by clinicians and administrators is whether severely developmentally disabled children require a longer school year than their non-handicapped peers. Recent legal decisions have argued that there is a compelling need for a year-round school experience for these youngsters (*Armstrong v. Klien,* 1979; *Battle v. Commonwealth,* 1980). Numerous authors have reviewed both the legal and ethical issues involved in reaching a decision about the need for an extended school year (Larsen, Goodman, & Glean, 1981; Leonard, 1981; Makuck, 1981; Stotland & Mancuso, 1981). Larsen and colleagues (1981) effectively summarize these arguments and state: "It is an article of faith in special education that during the summer hiatus some students—and particularly the more severely handicapped—lose many of the skills they acquired during the regular school year. . . ." (p. 258).

Home Needs

Extending education into the home provides for optimal intervention (Wing, 1972; Schopler & Reichler, 1971) and facilitates the transfer of treatment gains (Handleman, 1979a). Training parents to work with their children at home enables the direct reinforcement of school programming, in addition to teaching self-help and independent living skills (Kozloff, 1975; Lovaas et al., 1973).

Parents provide a valuable clinical resource that can result in the intensive repetition, review, and reinforcement of behavior crucial to the education of severely developmentally disabled children (Baker, Brightman, Heifetz, & Murphy, 1976; Harris & Milch, 1981; McClannahan, Krantz, & McGee, 1982). Effective parent teachers can provide extended programming in all curricular content areas. In addition, home programming can provide the variety necessary for facilitating generalization to other settings (Handleman, 1979a).

Home needs also extend beyond the severely developmentally disabled child to include the entire family (Harris, 1983). The disruption to normal family functioning caused by the severely handicapped child creates a need for more comprehensive family intervention. Education, training, and support services provide a framework for meeting the complex needs of the family.

Community Needs

As the result of Public Law No. 94–142 and the call for education and treatment in the "least restrictive" environment, attention has been directed toward the mainstreaming of severely developmentally disabled children. Mainstreaming as a philosophy toward education is as important for the developmentally disabled as it is for any other individual. While attempts at mainstreaming such children may be problematic (Poorman, 1980), modifications of the concept are crucial. Adopting a normalization principle (Wolfensberger, 1975), in addition to strategies designed to facilitate transition to more normal environments (Handleman, 1979b), can improve chances for success. Preparation of severely developmentally disabled children for placements that were previously deemed inappropriate due to the nature of the children's problems must be well organized and systematically planned. A team consisting of the school, parents, and community professionals should coordinate the effort. Transition of severely developmentally disabled children to more "normal" settings must be a goal of programming. Most individuals involved with these children maintain this goal but are frustrated by the primitive state of the art. Now, with the push to provide services to such children within the mainstream of public education, the need to obtain this goal is heightened.

More community-based services that have enhanced the quality of life for the severely developmentally disabled have been witnessed in recent years (Menolascino & McGee, 1980). There appears to be increasing consensus that community-based residential settings for such clients are more appropriate than institutional placements (Ferleger & Boyd, 1979; Gilhool, 1978). Also, in an attempt to continue community living options for the severely developmentally disabled, respite care services have grown (Upshur, 1982). The temporary relief that respite care can provide for families can often support community participation and possibly avoid institutionalization (Townsend & Flanagan, 1976).

REFERENCES

Abromowitz, H. K., & Richardson, S. A. (1975). Epidemiology of severe mental retardation in children: Community studies. *American Journal of Mental Deficiency, 80,* 18–39.

Achenbach, T. R. (1974). *Developmental psychopathology.* New York: Ronald Press.

Alpern, G. D. (1967). Measurement of "untestable" autistic children. *Journal of Abnormal Psychology, 72,* 478–496.

American Psychiatric Association. (1980). *Diagnostic and statistical manual of mental disorders* (3rd ed.). Washington, DC: Author.

Anderson, R. M., & Greer, J. G. (1976). *Educating the severely and profoundly retarded.* Baltimore: University Park Press.

Armstrong v. Kline, 476 F. Supp. 583 (F.D. Pa. 1979).

Axline, V. (1974). *Play therapy.* Boston: Houghton Mifflin.

Baer, D. M., & Guess, D. (1971). Receptive training of adjectival inflections in mental retardates. *Journal of Applied Behavior Analysis, 4,* 129–139.

Baker, B. L., Brightman, A. J., Heifetz, L. J., & Murphy, D. M. (1976). *Behavior problems.* Champaign, IL: Research Press.

Bartak, L., Rutter, M., & Cox, A. (1975). A comparative study of infantile autism and specific developmental receptive language disorder. I. The children. *British Journal of Psychiatry, 126,* 127–145.

Battle v. Commonwealth, 79-2158, 79-2188-90, 79-2568-70 (3rd Cir. July 18, 1980).

Baumeister, A. A. (1978). Origins and control of stereotyped movements. In C. E. Meyers (Ed.), *Monographs of the American Association on Mental Deficiency.*

Baumeister, A. A., & Forehand, R. (1973). Stereotyped acts. In N. R. Ellis (Ed.), *International review of research in mental retardation* (Vol. 6). New York: Academic Press.

Bennett, C. W., & Ling, D. (1972). Teaching a complex verbal response to a hearing-impaired girl. *Journal of Applied Behavior Analysis, 5,* 321–328.

Berkson, G., & Davenport, R. K. (1962). Stereotyped movements in mental defectives: I. Initial survey. *American Journal of Mental Deficiency, 66,* 849–852.

Bettelheim, B. (1967). *The empty fortress.* New York: Free Press.

Birnbrauer, J. S. (1979). Applied behavior analysis, service, and the acquisition of knowledge. *The Behavior Analyst, 2,* 15–21.

Bleuler, E. (1950). Dementia praecox in a group of schizophrenic clients. (J. Zinkin, Trans.). New York: International University Press. (Original work published in Deutiche, 1911)

Bonvillian, J. D., Nelson, K. E., & Rhyne, J. M. (1981). Sign language and autism. *Journal of Autism and Developmental Disorders, 11,* 125–138.

Boucher, J. (1977). Alternation and sequencing behavior, and response to novelty in autistic children. *Journal of Child Psychology and Psychiatry, 18,* 67–72.

Bricker, W. A., & Bricker, D. D. (1970). A program of language training for the severely handicapped child. *Exceptional Children, 37,* 101–111.

Brown, J. L. (1960). Prognosis from presenting symptoms of preschool children with atypical development. *Journal of Orthopsychiatry, 30,* 382–390.

Brown, L., Branston, M. B., Hamre-Nietupski, S., Pumpian, I., Certo, N., & Gruenwald, L. (1979). A strategy for developing chronological age appropriate and functional curricular content for severely handicapped adolescents and young adults. *Journal of Special Education, 13,* 81–90.

Campbell, M., Friedman, E., Greenspan, L., & Collins, P. J. (1974). Blood serotonin in psychotic and brain-damaged children. *Journal of Autism and Childhood Schizophrenia, 4,* 33–41.

Carr, E. G. (1977). The motivation of self-injurious behavior: A review of some hypotheses. *Psychological Bulletin, 84,* 800–816.

Carr, E. G. (1979). Teaching autistic children to use sign language: Some research issues. *Journal of Autism and Developmental Disorders, 9,* 345–359.

Carr, E. G., Newsom, C. D., & Binkoff, J. A. (1976). Stimulus control of self-destructive behavior in a psychotic child. *Journal of Abnormal Child Psychology, 4,* 139–153.

Carter, L., Alpert, M., & Stewart, S. M. (1982). Schizophrenic children's utilization of images and words in performance of cognitive tasks. *Journal of Autism and Developmental Disorders, 12,* 279–293.

Cataldo, M. F., & Harris, J. (1982). The biological basis for self-injury in the mentally retarded. *Analysis and Intervention in Developmental Disabilities, 2,* 21–40.

Chess, S., Korn, S. J., & Fernandez, P. B. (1971). *Psychiatric disorders of children with congenital rubella.* New York: Brunner/Mazel.

Ciaranello, R. D., Vandenberg, S. R., & Anders, T. F. (1982). Intrinsic and extrinsic determinants of neuronal development: Relation to infantile autism. *Journal of Autism and Developmental Disorders, 12,* 115–146.

Cohen, D. J., & Shaywitz, B. A. (1982). Preface to special issue on neurobiological research in autism. *Journal of Autism and Developmental Disorders, 12,* 103–108.

Coleman, M. (Ed.). (1976). *The autistic syndromes.* Amsterdam: North Holland.

Cowan, P. A., Hoddinott, B. A., & Wright, B. A. (1965). Compliance and resistance in the conditioning of autistic children: An explanatory study. *Child Development, 36,* 913–923.

Creak, M. (1969). Clinical and E.E.G. studies on a group of thirty-five psychotic children. *Developmental Medicine and Child Neurology, 11,* 218–227.

Cromer, R. F. (1981). Developmental language disorders: Cognitive processes, semantics, pragmatics, phonology and syntax. *Journal of Autism and Developmental Disorders, 11,* 57–74.

Cunningham, M. A., & Dixon, C. (1961). A study of the language of an autistic child. *Journal of Child Psychology and Psychiatry, 2,* 193–202.

Curtiss, S. (1981). Dissociations between language and cognition: Cases and implications. *Journal of Autism and Developmental Disorders, 11,* 15–30.

DeMyer, M. (1976). Motor, perceptual-motor and intellectual disabilities of autistic children. In L. Wing (Ed.), *Early Childhood Autism.* Oxford: Pergamon Press.

Devany, J., & Rincover, A. (1982). Self-stimulatory behavior and sensory reinforcement. In R. L. Koegel, A. Rincover, & A. L. Egel (Eds.), *Educating and understanding autistic children.* San Diego: College Hill Press.

Donnellan, A., Gossage, L. D., LaVigna, G. W., Schuler, A., & Traphagen, J. (1977). *Teaching makes a difference.* Sacramento: California State Department of Education.

Dunlap, G., & Egel, A. (1982). Motivational techniques. In R. L. Koegel, A. Rincover, & A. L. Egel (Eds.), *Educating and understanding autistic children*. San Diego: College Hill Press.

Dupont, R. (1969). *Education of the emotionally disturbed child*. Englewood Cliffs, NJ: Prentice-Hall.

Eason, L. J., White, M. J., & Newsom, C. (1982). Generalized reduction of self-stimulatory behavior: An effect of teaching appropriate play to autistic children. *Analysis and Intervention in Developmental Disabilities, 2*, 157–169.

Egel, A. L. (1980). The effects of constant versus varied reinforcer presentation on responding by autistic children. *Journal of Experimental Child Psychology, 30*, 455–463.

Ellis, N. R., Deacon, J. R., Harris, L. A., Poor, A., Angers, D., & Diorio, M. S. (1982). Learning, memory, and transfer in profoundly, severely and moderately retarded persons. *American Journal of Mental Deficiency, 87*, 186–196.

Favell, J. E., McGimsey, J. F., & Schell, R. M. (1982). Treatment of self-injury by providing alternate sensory activities. *Analysis and Intervention in Developmental Disabilities, 2*, 83–104.

Ferleger, D., & Boyd, A. (1979). Anti-institutionalization: The promise of the Pennhurst case. *Stanford Law Review, 3*, 717–752.

Ferster, C. B. (1961). Positive reinforcement and behavioral deficits of autistic children. *Child Development, 32*, 437–456.

Ferster, C. B., & DeMyer, M. K. (1961). The development of performance in autistic children in an automatically controlled environment. *Journal of Chronic Diseases, 13*, 312–345.

Fish, B., & Ritvo, E. R. (1978). Psychoses of childhood. In J. D. Noshpitz & I. Berlin (Eds.), *Basic handbook of child psychiatry*. New York: Basic Books.

Folstein, S., & Rutter, M. (1977). Infantile autism: A genetic study of 21 twin pairs. *Journal of Child Psychology and Psychiatry, 18*, 297–321.

Frankel, F., & Simmons, J. Q. (1976). Self-injurious behavior in schizophrenic and retarded children. *American Journal of Mental Deficiency, 80*, 512–522.

Fygetakis, L., & Gray, B. B. (1970). Programmed conditioning of linguistic competence. *Behavior Research and Therapy, 8*, 153–163.

Garcia, E. (1974). The training and generalization of a conversational speech form in nonverbal retardates. *Journal of Applied Behavior Analysis, 1*, 137–149.

Garcia, E., Guess, D., & Byrnes, J. (1973). Development of syntax in a retarded girl using procedures of imitation, reinforcement and modeling. *Journal of Applied Behavior Analysis, 6*, 299–310.

Gilhool, T. (1978). Habilitation of developmentally disabled persons in a small group community setting versus a large group institutional setting. Philadelphia: PILCOR, N.D.

Gillies, S. M. (1965). Some abilities of psychotic children and subnormal controls. *Journal of Mental Deficiency Research, 9*, 89–101.

Goldfarb, W. (1961). *Childhood schizophrenia*. Cambridge: Harvard University Press.

Griffiths, H., & Craighead, W. E. (1972). Generalization in operant speech therapy for misarticulation. *Journal of Speech and Hearing Disorders, 37*, 485–494.

Guess, D. (1960). A functional analysis of receptive language and productive speech: Acquisition of the plural morpheme. *Journal of Applied Behavior Analysis, 2*, 55–64.

Guess, D., & Baer, D. M. (1973). An analysis of individual differences in generalization between receptive and productive language in retarded children. *Journal of Applied Behavior Analysis, 6*, 311–329.

Halpern, W. I. (1970). Schooling of autistic children. *American Journal of Orthopsychiatry, 40*, 665–671.

Hamilton, J. (1966). Learning of a generalized response class in mentally retarded individuals. *American Journal of Mental Deficiency, 71,* 100–108.

Handleman, J. S. (1979a). Generalization by autistic-type children of verbal responses across settings. *Journal of Applied Behavior Analysis, 12,* 273–282.

Handleman, J. S. (1979b). Transition of autistic-type children from highly specialized programs to more "normal" educational environments. *Journal for Special Educators, 15,* 273–279.

Handleman, J. S. (1981). Transfer of verbal responses across instructional settings by autistic-type children. *Journal of Speech and Hearing Disorders, 46,* 69–76.

Handleman, J. S., & Harris, S. L. (1980). Generalization from school to home with autistic-type children. *Journal of Autism and Developmental Disorders, 10,* 323–333.

Handleman, J. S., & Harris, S. L. (1983). Generalization across instructional settings by autistic children. *Child & Family Behavior Therapy, 5,* 73–83.

Harris, S. L. (1975). Teaching language to nonverbal children with emphasis on problems of generalization. *Psychological Bulletin, 82,* 565–580.

Harris, S. L. (1983). *Families of the developmentally disabled: A guide to behavioral interventions.* Elmsford, NY: Pergamon Press.

Harris, S. L., & Milch, R. E. (1981). Training parents as behavior therapists for their autistic children. *Clinical Psychology Review, 1,* 49–63.

Hart, B. M., & Risley, T. R. (1968). Establishing use of descriptive adjectives in the spontaneous speech of disadvantaged preschool children. *Journal of Applied Behavior Analysis, 1,* 109–120.

Hemsley, R., & Howlin, P. (1976). Managing behavior problems. In M. P. Everard (Ed.), *An approach to teaching autistic children.* Oxford: Pergamon Press.

Hermelin, B. (1971). Rules of language. In M. Rutter (Ed.), *Infantile autism: Concepts, characteristics and treatment.* London: Churchill Livingstone.

Hermelin, B., & Frith, U. (1971). Psychological studies of childhood autism: Can autistic children make sense of what they see and hear? *Journal of Special Education, 5,* 107–117.

Hermelin, B., & O'Connor, N. (1968). Measures of the occipital alpha rhythm in normal, subnormal and autistic children. *British Journal of Psychiatry, 114,* 603–610.

Hermelin, B., & O'Connor, N. (1970). *Psychological experiments with autistic children.* Oxford: Pergamon Press.

Hinerman, P. S., Jenson, W. R., Walker, G. R., & Petersen, P. B. (1982). Positive practice overcorrection combined with additional procedures to teach signed words to an autistic child. *Journal of Autism and Developmental Disorders, 12,* 253–263.

Hollis, J. H., & Sherman, J. A. (1967). *Operant control of vocalizations in profoundly retarded children with normal hearing and moderate bilateral loss (#167).* Lawrence, KS: Parsons Research Center.

Howlin, P. (1978). The assessment of social behavior. In M. Rutter & E. Schopler (Eds.), *Autism: A reappraisal of concepts and treatment.* New York: Plenum Press.

Howlin, P. (1981). The effectiveness of operant language training with autistic children. *Journal of Autism and Developmental Disorders, 11,* 89–106.

Isaac, W., Thomas, R., & Goldiamond, I. (1960). Application of operant condition to reinstate verbal behavior in psychotics. *Journal of Speech and Hearing Disorders, 25,* 8–12.

Jackson, D. A., & Wallace, R. F. (1974). The modification and generalization of voice loudness in a fifteen-year-old retarded girl. *Journal of Applied Behavior Analysis, 7,* 461–471.

Jellis, T., & Grainger, S. (1972). The back projection of kaleidoscopic patterns as a technique for eliciting verbalizations in an autistic child. *British Journal of Disorders of Communication, 7,* 157–162.

Johnson, J., & Koegel, R. L. (1982). Behavioral assessment and curriculum development. In R. L. Koegel, A. Rincover, & A. L. Egel (Eds.), *Educating and understanding autistic children*. San Diego: College Hill Press.

Johnson, W., & Baumeister, A. (1978). A self-injurious behavior: A review and analysis of methodological details of published studies. *Behavior Modification, 2,* 465–484.

Johnson, W. L., Baumeister, A. A., Penland, M. J., & Inwald, C. (1982). Experimental analysis of self-injurious, stereotypic, and collateral behavior of retarded persons: Effects of overcorrection and reinforcement of alternative responding. *Analysis and Intervention in Developmental Disabilities, 2,* 44–66.

Kale, R. J., Kaye, J. H., Whelan, P. A., & Hopkins, B. L. (1968). The effects of reinforcement on the modification, maintenance and generalization of social responses of mental patients. *Journal of Applied Behavior Analysis, 1,* 307–314.

Kanner, L. (1943). Autistic disturbances of affective contact. *Nervous Child, 2,* 217–250.

Kanner, L. (1946). Irrelevant and metaphorical language in early childhood autism. *American Journal of Psychiatry, 103,* 242–246.

Kanner, L. (1958). The specificity of early infantile autism. *Acta Paedo Psychiatry, 25,* 108–115.

Kanner, L. (1974). *Childhood psychosis: Initial studies and new insights*. New York: Wiley.

Kanner, L., & Eisenberg, I. (1955). Notes on the follow-up studies of autistic children. In P. H. Hock & J. Zulin (Eds.), *Psychopathology of childhood*. New York: Grune & Stratton.

Kirk, S.A. (1962). *Educating exceptional children*. Boston: Houghton Mifflin.

Koegel, R., & Covert, A. (1972). The relationship of self-stimulation to learning in autistic children. *Journal of Applied Behavior Analysis, 5,* 381–388.

Koegel, R. L., Dunlap, G., Richman, G. S., & Dyer, K. (1981). The use of specific orienting cues for teaching discrimination tasks. *Analysis and Intervention in Developmental Disabilities, 1,* 187–198.

Koegel, R. L., & Schreibman, L. (1976). Identification of consistent responding to auditory stimuli by a functionally "deaf" autistic child. *Journal of Autism and Childhood Schizophrenia, 6,* 147–156.

Koegel, R. L., & Williams, J. A. (1980). Direct vs. indirect response reinforcer relationships in teaching autistic children. *Journal of Abnormal Child Psychology, 8,* 537–547.

Kolko, D. J., Anderson, L., & Campbell, M. (1980). Sensory preference and overselective responding in autistic children. *Journal of Autism and Developmental Disorders, 10,* 259–271.

Kolstoe, O. P. (1970). *Teaching educable mentally retarded children*. New York: Holt, Rinehart & Winston.

Kozloff, M. A. (1975). *Reaching the autistic child: A parent-training program*. Champaign, IL: Research Press.

Landesman-Dwyer, S., & Sackett, G. P. (1978). Behavioral changes in nonambulatory profoundly mentally retarded individuals. In C. E. Meyers (Ed.), *Quality of life in severely and profoundly mentally retarded people*. Washington, DC: American Association on Mental Deficiency.

Larsen, L., Goodman, L., & Glean, R. (1981). Issues in the implementation of extended school year programs for handicapped students. *Exceptional Children, 47,* 255–263.

Leonard, J. (1981). 180 day barrier: Issues and concerns. *Exceptional Children, 47,* 246–253.

Litt, M. D., & Schreibman, L. (1981). Stimulus-specific reinforcement in the acquisition of receptive labels by autistic children. *Analysis and Intervention in Developmental Disabilities, 1,* 171–186.

Lockyer, L., & Rutter, M. (1969). A five to fifteen year follow-up study of infantile psychosis. III. Psychological aspects. *British Journal of Psychiatry, 115,* 865–882.

Lockyer, L., & Rutter, M. (1970). A five to fifteen year follow-up study of infantile psychosis. IV. Pattern of cognitive ability. *British Journal of Social and Clinical Psychology, 9,* 152–163.

Lotter, V. (1974). Factors related to outcome in autistic children. *Journal of Autism and Childhood Schizophrenia, 4,* 263–277.

Lovaas, O. I. (1968). A program for the establishment of speech in psychotic children. In H. N. Sloane & B. D. MacAulay (Eds.), *Operant procedures in remedial speech and language training.* Boston: Houghton Mifflin.

Lovaas, O. I. (1981). *Teaching developmentally disabled children. The Me Book.* Baltimore: University Park Press.

Lovaas, O. I., Berberich, J., Perloff, B., & Schaefer, B. (1966). Acquisition of imitative speech by schizophrenic children. *Science, 151,* 705–707.

Lovaas, O., Koegel, R., & Schreibman, L. (1979). Stimulus overselectivity in autism: A review of research. *Psychological Bulletin, 86,* 1236–1254.

Lovaas, O. I., Koegel, R., Simmons, J. Q., & Long, J. (1973). Some generalization and follow-up measures on autistic children in behavior therapy. *Journal of Applied Behavior Analysis, 6,* 131–166.

Lovaas, O. I., Litrownik, A., & Mann, R. (1971). Response latencies to auditory stimuli in children engaged in self-stimulatory behavior. *Behaviour Research and Therapy, 9,* 34–49.

Lovaas, O. I., & Newsom, C. D. (1976). Behavior modification with psychotic children. In H. Leitenberg (Ed.), *Handbook of behavior modification and behavior therapy.* Englewood Cliffs, NJ: Prentice-Hall.

Lovaas, O., Schreibman, L., Koegel, R., & Rehm, R. (1971). Selective responding of autistic children to multiple sensory input. *Journal of Abnormal Psychology, 77,* 211–222.

Lovaas, O. I., & Simmons, J. Q. (1969). Manipulation of self-destruction in three retarded children. *Journal of Applied Behavior Analysis, 2,* 143–157.

Mahler, M. (1965). On early infantile psychosis: The symbiotic and autistic syndromes. *Journal of Child Psychiatry, 4,* 213–242.

Makuch, G. J. (1981). Year-round special education and related services: A state director's perspective. *Exceptional Children, 47,* 272–274.

Maurer, R. G., & Damasio, A. P. (1982). Childhood autism from the point of view of behavioral neurology. *Journal of Autism and Developmental Disorders, 12,* 195–206.

Menolascino, F. J., & McGee, J. J. (1981). The new institutions: Last ditch arguments. *Mental Retardation, 19,* 215–220.

Menyuk, P. (1978). Language: What's wrong and why. In M. Rutter & E. Schopler (Eds.), *Autism: A reappraisal of concepts and treatment.* New York: Plenum Press.

Meryash, D. L., Szymanski, L. S., & Gerald, P. S. (1982). Infantile autism associated with the fragile X syndrome. *Journal of Autism and Developmental Disorders, 12,* 295–302.

McClannahan, L. E., Krantz, P. J., & McGee, G. G. (1982). Parents as therapists for autistic children: A model for effective parent training. *Analysis and Intervention in Developmental Disabilities, 2,* 223–252.

O'Gorman, G. (1967). *The nature of childhood autism.* New York: Appleton-Century-Crofts.

Ornitz, E. (1971). *Infantile autism.* London: Churchill Livingstone.

Ornitz, E. (1973). Childhood autism: A review of the clinical and experimental literature. *California Medicine, 118,* 21–47.

Ornitz, E. M., & Ritvo, E. R. (1968). Perceptual inconstancy in early infantile autism. *Archives of General Psychiatry, 18,* 76–98.

Partington, M. W., Tu, J. B., & Wong, C. Y. (1973). Blood serotonin levels in severe mental retardation. *Developmental Medicine and Child Neurology, 15,* 616–627.

Poorman, C. (1980). Mainstreaming in reverse with a special friend. *Teaching Exceptional Children, 12,* 136–142.

Poulton, K. T., & Algozzine, B. (1980). Manual communication and mental retardation: A review of research and implications. *American Journal of Mental Deficiency, 85,* 145–152.

Provonost, W. (1966). A longitudinal study of the speech behavior and language comprehension of fourteen children diagnosed as atypical or autistic. *Exceptional Children, 33,* 19–26.

Rimland, B. (1964). *Infantile autism.* New York: Appleton-Century-Crofts.

Rincover, A. (1978). Sensory extinction: A procedure for eliminating self-stimulatory behavior in psychotic children. *Journal of Abnormal Child Psychology, 6,* 299–310.

Rincover, A., & Koegel, R. (1975). Setting generality and stimulus control in autistic children. *Journal of Applied Behavior Analysis, 8,* 235–246.

Rincover, A. Newsom, C. D., & Carr, E. G. (1979). Using sensory extinction procedures in the treatment of compulsive-like behavior of developmentally disabled children. *Journal of Consulting and Clinical Psychology, 47,* 695–701.

Ritvo, E. R., Ritvo, E. C., & Brothers, A. M. (1982). Genetic and immunohematologic factors in autism. *Journal of Autism and Developmental Disorders, 12,* 109–114.

Romanczyk, R. G., & Goren, E. R. (1975). Severe self-injurious behavior: The problem of clinical control. *Journal of Consulting and Clinical Psychology, 43,* 730–739.

Ross, R. T. (1972). Behavioral correlates of levels of intelligence. *American Journal of Mental Deficiency, 76,* 545–549.

Russo, D. C., Carr, E. G., & Lovaas, O. I. (1980). Self-injury in pediatric populations. In J. Ferguson & C. B. Taylor (Eds.), *Comprehensive handbook of behavioral medicine.* Holliswood, NY: Spectrum.

Rutter, M. (1966). Prognosis: Psychotic children in adolescence and early adult life. In J. K. Wing (Ed.), *Early childhood autism: Clinical educational and social aspects.* London: Pergamon Press.

Rutter, M. (1968). Concepts of autism. *Journal of Child Psychology and Psychiatry, 9,* 1–15.

Rutter, M. (1970). Autistic children: Infancy to adulthood. *Seminars in Psychiatry, 2,* 435–450.

Rutter, M. (1971). The description and classification of infantile autism. In D. M. Churchill, G. D. Alpern, & M. K. DeMyer (Eds.), *Infantile autism: Proceedings of Indiana University colloquium.* Springfield, IL: Charles C. Thomas.

Rutter, M. (1974). The development of infantile autism. *Psychological Medicine, 4,* 147–163.

Rutter, M. (1979). Diagnosis and definition. In M. Rutter and E. Schopler (Eds.), *Autism: A reappraisal of concepts and treatment.* New York: Plenum Press.

Rutter, M., & Bartak, L. (1973). Special educational treatment of autistic children: A comparative study. II. Follow-up findings and implications for services. *Journal of Child Psychology and Psychiatry, 14,* 241–270.

Rutter, M., & Lockyer, L. (1967). A five to fifteen year follow-up study of infantile psychosis: Social and behavioral outcome. *British Journal of Psychiatry, 113,* 1183–1199.

Sailor, W. (1971). Reinforcement and generalization of productive plural allomorphs in two retarded children. *Journal of Applied Behavior Analysis, 4,* 305–310.

Sander, L. W., Stechler, G., Burns, P., & Julia, H. (1970). Early mother-infant interaction and 24-hour patterns of activity and sleep. *Journal of the American Academy of Child Psychiatry, 9,* 103–123.

Schain, R. J., & Yannet, H. (1960). Infantile autism: An analysis of 50 cases and a consideration of certain relevant neurophysiologic concepts. *Journal of Pediatrics, 57,* 560–567.

Schopler, E. (1966). Visual versus tactual receptor preference in normal and schizophrenic children. *Journal of Abnormal Psychology, 71,* 108–114.

Schopler, E. (1978). National Society for Autistic Children definition of the syndrome of autism. *Journal of Autism and Childhood Schizophrenia, 8,* 162–169.

Schopler, E., & Reichler, R. J. (1971). Parents as co-therapists in the treatment of psychotic children. *Journal of Autism and Childhood Schizophrenia, 1,* 87–102.

Schreibman, L., & Koegel, R. L. (1981). A guideline for planning behavior modification programs for autistic children. In S. M. Turner, K. S. Calhoun, & H. E. Adams (Eds.), *Handbook of clinical behavior therapy.* New York: John Wiley & Sons.

Schroeder, S. R., Schroeder, C. S., Rojahn, J., & Mulick, J. A. (1981). Self-injurious behavior: An analysis of behavior management techniques. In J. L. Matson & J. R. McCartney (Eds.), *Handbook of behavior modification with the mentally retarded.* New York: Plenum Press.

Schumaker, J., & Sherman, J. A. (1970). Training generating verb usage by imitation and reinforcement procedures. *Journal of Applied Behavior Analysis, 3,* 273–287.

Skinner. B. F. (1957). *Verbal behavior.* New York: Appleton-Century-Crofts.

Smeets, P. M. (1971). Some characteristics of mental defectives displaying self-mutilation behavior. *Training School Bulletin, 68,* 131–135.

Snell, M. E. (1982). Characteristics of the profoundly mentally retarded. In P. Cegelka & H. Prehm (Eds.), *Mental retardation: From categories to people.* Columbus, OH: Charles E. Merrill.

Snell, M. E., & Renzaglia, A. M. (1982). Moderate, severe and profound handicaps. In N. G. Harring (Ed.), *Exceptional children and youth* (3rd ed.). Columbus, OH: Charles E. Merrill.

Sontag, E., Burke, P. J., & York, R. (1973). Considerations for serving the severely handicapped in the public schools. *Education and Training of the Mentally Retarded, 8,* 20–26.

Sosne, J. B., Handleman, J. S., & Harris, S. L. (1979). Teaching spontaneous-functional speech to autistic-type children. *Mental Retardation, 17,* 241–245.

Spence, M. A. (1976). Genetic studies. In E. R. Ritvo (Ed.), *Autism: Diagnosis, current research and management.* New York: Spectrum.

Stevens-Long, J., & Rasmussen, M. (1947). The acquisition of simple and compound sentence structure in an autistic child. *Journal of Applied Behavior Analysis, 7,* 473–480.

Stotland, J. F., & Mancuso, E. (1981). U.S. court of appeals decision regarding Armstong vs. Kline: The 180 day rule. *Exceptional Children, 47,* 266–270.

Stremel, K. (1972). Language training: A program for retarded children. *Mental Retardation, 10,* 47–49.

Stubbs, E. G. (1977). Autistic children exhibit undetectable hemagglutination-inhibition antibody titers despite previous rubella vaccination. *Journal of Autism and Childhood Schizophrenia, 6,* 269–274.

Tager-Flusberg, H. (1981). On the nature of linguistic functioning in early infantile autism. *Journal of Autism and Developmental Disorders, 11,* 45–56.

Tinbergen, E. A., & Tinbergen, N. (1972). Early childhood autism: An etiological approach. In *Advances in ethology. Journal of Comparative Ethology, 10*(Suppl.), Berlin & Hamburg: Verlag Paul Parry.

Thompson, R. J., & O'Quinn, A. N. (1979). *Developmental disabilities: Etiologies, manifestations, diagnoses and treatment.* New York: Oxford University Press.

Townsend, P. W., & Flanagan, J. J. (1976). Experimental preadmission program to encourage home care for severely and profoundly retarded children. *American Journal of Mental Deficiency, 80,* 562–569.

Tubbs, V. K. (1966). Types of linguistic disability in psychotic children. *Journal of Mental Deficiency Research, 10,* 230–240.

United States Office of Education for the Handicapped, Pub. L. No. 95–602, 45 U.S.C. §121.2 (1974).

Upshur, C. C. (1982). Respite care for mentally retarded and other disabled populations: Program models and family needs. *Mental Retardation, 20,* 2–7.

Van Etten, G., Arkell, C., & Van Etten, C. (1980). *The severely and profoundly handicapped: Programs, methods, and materials.* St. Louis: C.V. Mosby.

Varni, J. W., Lovaas, O. I., Koegel, R. L., & Everett, N. L. (1979). An analysis of observational learning in autistic and normal children. *Journal of Abnormal Child Psychology, 7,* 31–43.

Walker, G. R., Hinerman, P. S., Jenson, W. R., & Peterson, P. B. (1981). Sign language as a prompt to teach a verbal "yes" and "no" discrimination to an autistic boy. *Child Behavior Therapy, 3,* 77–86.

Welch, S. J. (1981). Teaching generative grammar to mentally retarded children: A review and analysis of a decade of behavioral research. *Mental Retardation, 19,* 277–284.

Wheeler, A. J., & Sulzer, B. (1970). Operant training and generalization of a verbal response form in a speech deficient child. *Journal of Applied Behavior Analysis, 3,* 139–147.

Wing, J. K. (1966). *Early childhood autism: Clinical, educational and social aspects.* London: Pergamon Press.

Wing, L. (1972). *Autistic children: A guide for parents and professionals.* New York: Brunner/Mazel.

Wing, L. (1976). The principles of remedial education for autistic children. In L. Wing (Ed.), *Early childhood autism* (2nd ed.). Oxford: Pergamon Press.

Wing, L. (1979). Social, behavioral, and cognitive characteristics: An epidemiological approach. In M. Rutter & E. Schopler (Eds.), *Autism: A reappraisal of concepts and treatment.* New York: Plenum Press.

Wing, L. (1981). Language, social and cognitive impairments in autism and severe mental retardation. *Journal of Autism and Developmental Disorders, 11,* 31–44.

Wing, L., & Wing, J. (1971). Multiple impairments in early childhood autism. *Journal of Autism and Childhood Schizophrenia, 1,* 256–266.

Wolf, M. M., Risley, T. R., & Mees, A. I. (1964). Application of operant conditioning procedures to the behavior problems of an autistic child. *Behavior Research and Therapy, 2,* 305–312.

Wolfensberger, W. (1975). *Normalization.* Toronto: National Institute on Mental Retardation.

Wolff, S., & Chess, S. (1965). An analysis of the language of fourteen schizophrenic children. *Journal of Child Psychology and Psychiatry, 6,* 29–41.

Young, J. G., Kavanagh, M. E., Anderson, G. M., Shaywitz, B. A., & Cohen, D. J. (1982). Clinical neurochemistry of autism and associated disorders. *Journal of Autism and Developmental Disorders, 12,* 147–166.

General Issues in the Behavioral Assessment of Severe Developmental Disabilities

INTRODUCTION

Severely developmentally disabled clients pose particular assessment problems that require careful consideration. Clinicians must be sensitive to a multitude of factors in order to determine where to begin intervention. Chapter 1 describes the nature and needs of severely developmentally disabled clients. A framework for conceptualizing this group was presented. Chapter 2 identifies those aspects of behavioral assessment that have particular relevance to the severely developmentally disabled, and provides a framework for understanding behavioral assessment as it can be used with this population.

ADVANTAGES OF BEHAVIORAL ASSESSMENT

While traditional (psychodynamic) methods of assessment with the severely developmentally disabled were prevalent in the 1950s, they are far less emphasized today. The advent and demonstrated efficacy of behavior therapy techniques with severely developmentally disabled clients have resulted in a primary dependence upon behavioral assessment methods with this population.

Behavioral assessment suggests that individual actions are only a sample of that person's behavior in a specific situation. In addition, an emphasis is placed on present behavior and functioning, rather than on past "causes" of the handicapping condition. Using behavioral assessment techniques, clinicians assess behavior directly, taking specific measures of many variables. This specificity ensures high face validity; that is, individuals observing the client are likely to agree that the technique appears to measure the target behavior for which it is intended. Data gathered by the behavioral assessor are used to (1) describe the target behavior; (2) select a treatment protocol; and (3) evaluate and revise that treatment protocol (Goldfried & Kent, 1972; Kanfer & Saslow, 1969).

Because behavioral assessment facilitates the use of program evaluation methods, it is useful for programs serving severely developmentally disabled clients. Program evaluation specifically seeks to measure the goals of human intervention programs through the use of field research methods in combination with behavioral assessment techniques (Jones, 1979). There is a particular emphasis on single-case research methodologies. (See Hersen and Barlow, 1976.) Evaluation of programs serves several purposes, including accounting for funds, answering external requests for information, making administrative decisions, and discovering unintended effects (Posavac & Carey, 1980). In this current age of consumerism and accountability, data related to these purposes can be most useful and should be sought whenever possible.

Parents can make use of behavioral assessment techniques (Harris & Milch, 1982), effectively broadening the treatment team for the client. Other potential human resources include paraprofessionals, students in practicums and internship roles, older nonhandicapped children (McLaughlin & Mallaby, 1975), foster grandparents (Fabry & Reid, 1978), and mentally retarded people (Craighead, Mercatoris, & Bellack, 1974). When clinicians consider the need for maintenance and generalization of learned adaptive behavior, the availability of additional human resources takes on added meaning. With severely developmentally disabled adults, and also to a large extent with children similarly afflicted, parents and paraprofessionals assume responsibility for the bulk of contact time. Professionals (with the possible exception of teachers of the handicapped) often serve in a consulting role, limiting their on-the-line contact. Because of this reality, all who are in contact with a given client assume a position on the habilitation team. As behavioral assessment stresses clarity of description, reliability, and face validity and is devoid of untestable inferences, it lends itself to staff and parent training. To the extent that such training achieves the goals set forth, a consistent assessment and intervention strategy can be maintained. Not only will a therapeutic milieu of this type facilitate client habilitation, it will also increase the competence and sense of self-efficacy of parent and paraprofessional alike. With burnout looming as an ever-present problem for these two groups, behavioral assessment represents a strategy that we can ill afford to ignore.

In the main, data gathered through behavioral assessment methods assist in the decision-making process while the program is in progress, as well as in determining the efficacy of the program after it ends. To the extent that treatment decisions are guided by observable behavior, and those data are recorded and preserved, accountability to clients is increased. Questions concerning the appropriateness of a target of intervention (e.g., head banging) can be answered more conclusively and authoritatively with the support of systematic and reliable data rather than subjective perceptions. In addition to protecting staff from reprisals for unwarranted intervention, this preserves the rights of clients. Clients no longer need to be subjected to the often well-meaning but inconsistent treatment efforts of staff members. In a litigation-conscious society, the inherent rewards in pursuing an accountable course are powerful indeed, surpassed only by a client's right to ethical and responsible treatment.

MAJOR ISSUES IN BEHAVIORAL ASSESSMENT

Although behavior therapists working with severely developmentally disabled children have for many years been attempting to understand and change behavior by identifying meaningful response units and their controlling variables, the emphasis frequently has been on the development of treatment strategies. This phenomenon is easier to comprehend when the state of clinical intervention with autistic and/or mentally retarded clients before the mid-1960s is considered. The early experimental successes of Ferster (1961) and Ferster and DeMyer (1961, 1962) with autistic children and of Orlando and Bijou (1960) and Birnbauer and Lawler (1964) with mentally retarded individuals provided a ray of hope where little hope existed previously. The explication of applied behavior analysis techniques in the years following this pioneering work offered new directions for the habilitative efforts of professionals working with these two populations.

As so often happens with the description of a powerful therapeutic intervention in professional literature, the rush to replicate, expand, and further develop the technique itself far surpasses the diagnostic and assessment procedures that typically precede the clinical use of that technique. The net results of such activity are techniques that, in many cases, have been used to expand the behavioral repertoire of numerous autistic and retarded clients. But professionals still are faced with clients for whom their best procedures succeed only minimally, if at all. They find that their successes in classrooms or clinics do not generalize to extratherapeutic environments, or if they do generalize, they are not maintained. The clinical picture becomes far more confusing and complex as clinicians search for those variables that may help them to explain why a purportedly effective procedure has failed to produce the results they expected. In addition, unsuccessful treatment programs left professionals vulnerable to ethical and social questions about the acceptability of their interventions from parents, other professionals, and the public.

It was within such a treatment-focused environment that the interest in behavioral assessment grew. Practicing professionals soon began to focus on improving the identification and measurement of dependent variables as well as on increasing the probability that those strategies would succeed. In addition, they sought to determine better methods to evaluate interventions employed (Nelson & Hayes, 1979). Ethical questions inherent in the selection of target behaviors were addressed (Myerson & Hayes, 1978), as were those questions related to the social validity of treatment techniques (Schreibman, Koegel, Mills, & Burke, 1981; Wolf, 1978).

Behavioral assessment of severely developmentally disabled persons has four objectives: (1) identification of the target behavior(s), (2) identification of controlling variables, both organismic and environmental, (3) development of a treatment plan, and (4) evaluation of the treatment program (Nelson & Hayes, 1981). Such an assessment is idiographic in application. That is, response covariations, controlling variables, and treatment strategies are understood as being particular to the individual client. In contrast, nomothetic assessment leads to generalizations about groups of individuals. For example, a nomothetic assessment of language skills with a group of autistic children would probably identify their serious verbal communication deficiencies. It would not tell, however, specific conditions under which one particular child emits vocalizations, or the type, frequency, intensity, or duration of those vocalizations. Nomothetic assessment, then, is best conceived of as a starting point in that it summarizes clinically relevant data, facilitates communication among clinicians, and helps clinicians to narrow treatment options (Nelson & Barlow, 1981). Proceeding on to treatment without further (idiographic) assessment would be fallacious. To continue the example above, it would be akin to prescribing language training to each and every autistic child encountered, without regard for specific situational determinants. Exhibit 2–1 describes issues to consider before setting priorities for intervention.

Identification of the Target Behavior

The task of identifying target behaviors for clinical intervention is often considered to be a relatively straightforward one. Indeed, there may be consensus among several professionals working with a developmentally disabled client that a speech, social skill, or self-injury problem exists. However, treatment programs initiated on the basis of such global, trait-bound assessments are often doomed to less than desirable outcomes. This is so because the behavior of developmentally disabled persons, like all human behavior, is notoriously idiosyncratic. Particular responses co-vary with settings, teachers, parents, other developmentally disabled persons, siblings, and so on. Moreover, each of these interactive agents brings a particular set of expectations and conditions to bear on the client.

To reduce confusion and impose a sense of structure on the task of identifying a target behavior, three criteria should be met when defining behavior. The response definition should be objective, clear, and complete (Hawkins & Dobes, 1975). A definition is considered to be objective when it refers to behavioral or environmental events that are observable. Observable events can be seen, touched, or heard and can range from a pupillary orienting response to a light stimulus to self-biting of the left wrist whenever the handicapped person is asked to sit down. Inferences have no place here; they refer to traits that are often construct bound and value laden. Moreover, the inclusion of inferences greatly undermines criterion number two, clarity.

Exhibit 2–1 Issues to Consider Before Setting Priorities for Intervention

---

1. Does a behavior problem exist?
   a. Have several people sought assistance for the problem? _____
   b. Does the person or group function very differently from the way that "typical" people or groups function? _____
   c. Have there been dramatic behavior changes? _____
2. Have direct or informal solutions been attempted?
   a. Physical examination? _____
   b. Changes in assignments and responsibilities? _____
   c. Changes in physical environment? _____
   d. Direct requests for behavior change? _____

(Negative responses to any of these questions suggest that informal methods should be considered before instituting a systematic applied behavior-analysis program, but if answers are affirmative or not applicable, one is justified in proceeding.)

3. Does the proposed behavior-analysis program have sufficiently high priority and level of support to justify proceeding?
   a. Is there adequate evidence that it is likely to succeed? _____
   b. Is the problem critical? _____
   c. Will the community support the program? _____
   d. Will the program receive administrative support? _____
   e. Does the behavior analyst have the competence to conduct the program successfully? _____
   f. Are there adequate funds, space, materials, and motivated personnel to conduct the program, or can reasonable substitutes be found? _____
   g. Are other community organizations unable to handle the problem adequately? _____

Affirmative responses to most of the items on this check list suggest that the most appropriate decision is to go ahead and begin selecting behavioral goals. We shall consider steps that should be followed in refining goals and planning the program later.

Source: Sulzer-Azaroff, B., and Mayer, G.R. (1977). *Applying behavior analysis procedures with children and youth.* New York: Holt, Rinehart & Winston. Copyright 1977 by Holt, Rinehart & Winston. Reprinted by permission.

A response definition must be clear enough that other individuals working with the client can discriminate occurrences of the target behavior from nonoccurrences. In addition, observation of the target behavior should be possible after reading the definition and before conferring with a colleague.

Finally, the definition of the target behavior must be complete. Emphasis is placed upon six key areas—unity, duration, interresponse time, latency, intensity, and topography—all of which should be accounted for before a final definition is formulated (Doke, 1976). *Unity* refers to the notion that behavior can be defined in terms of behavior onsets and offsets that occur sequentially, while *duration* refers to the period of time covered by a response. *Interresponse time* refers to the amount of time separating one response from another, while *latency* represents the amount of time that passes between a request for a behavior (or other discriminative stimulus) and the actual occurrence of that behavior. *Intensity* is more difficult to assess. With physical movements, it represents the distance a response moves × the mass that is moved. But when assessing the intensity of a bite, for example, more subjective measures must be relied upon. *Topography* refers to the type of movements seen, and the parts of the body involved in the response. Determining the topography of a response generally involves careful observation. For example, wrist mouthing may well be motivated by different controlling stimuli than wrist biting, but to the average observer they may look remarkably similar. When defining such a behavior, it would be important to specify whether teeth-to-wrist contact constitutes an occurrence of the target behavior or not. Failure to do so will invariably lead to the clients' confusion during treatment as to what exactly is expected of them, evidenced by a lack of progress with the treatment program.

In addition to delimiting response topography, the conditions under which the response occurs must be described specifically. As a rule of thumb, basic *wh* questions (who, what, where, with whom, when) must be answered. Consider, for example, clients who have been taught to kiss their parents, with the rationale that in so doing these clients become exposed to the natural community of reinforcers available in the family. Within the correct setting (family members/parents), this behavior can be both functional and socially valid. With strangers, however, the best approximation of this otherwise reasonable response may be unacceptable. If the writer of the response definition did not include "with whom" information as an integral part of the definition, independent observers may well differ as to the occurrence of "appropriate kissing." While the example is an oversimplification of this principle, omissions such as these often lead to confusion on the part of the professional and client alike.

Behavioral assessment of severely developmentally disabled clients should be based upon observations of well-defined target behaviors that are reliably observed. This last point is possible only when the above criteria have been met. Duly armed with a sound definition of the target behavior, independent observers can view a client's behavior and ascertain the absence or presence of the target response. On the basis of each rater's score, a ratio of interrater reliability (usually a percentage of agreement) is determined. Convention suggests that rates of agreement greater than or equal to .80 are acceptable (Kazdin, 1980). Rates below this figure suggest the presence of ambiguity in the definition of the target behavior that need to be addressed. Chapter 3 provides both an expanded rationale and specific methods of measuring reliability.

A nomothetic assessment of an individual's behavior, yielding a global description of the problem, is the first step in the chain of assessment decisions leading to intervention. While the identification of an objective, clear, and complete target behavior (Hawkins & Dobes, 1975) is the ultimate assessment goal, an intermediate step is often warranted. To this end, observation of the client informally in as many settings as is feasible for the purpose of generating an anecdotal record of behavior is helpful to the clinician. Anecdotal recordings are running descriptions of behavior in progress. Although decidedly molar in nature, they allow molecular patterns and particular behavioral sequences to be observed. In fact, their utility lies primarily in the behavioral "chunking" (breaking down sequences of behavior into discrete units or chunks) that does not take place in more molecular assessments. The net result is the accumulation of a great deal of data, not all of it useful for future programming, that permit situational analyses to be conducted post hoc.

This procedure can best be conceptualized as a funnel strategy (Hawkins, 1979) where large areas of client behavior are sampled initially until target areas evidence themselves more clearly. Eventually, more specific information is sought, and tangential areas discarded, in an attempt to better delimit the target behavior. Finally, the target behavior is defined operationally according to the criteria described above. This funnel procedure continues through the identification of organismic and environmental controlling variables, the development of a treatment program, and the evaluation of that program. Exhibit 2–2 provides a schematic representation of this strategy.

Exhibit 2–2 Funnel Model of Behavioral Assessment

Parents, teachers, additional related personnel screen
the client for behavioral excesses and deficits.

Anecdotal recordings of client behavior

Identification of the target behavior

Prioritization and selection of
treatment goals

Operational definitions of the
target behaviors
developed

Determination of antecedent
and consequent controlling
variables

Intervention

Evaluation

Because one of the goals of treatment is the maintenance and generalization of therapeutic gains, ongoing assessment should evaluate these gains across a variety of settings and with a variety of significant other people (parents, professionals, and so on). Conceivably, stimulus as well as response generalization would be assessed, with the assessment of maintenance effects conducted separately (cf. Koegel & Rincover, 1977). The funnel model is depicted more accurately as an hourglass when the responsibility for ongoing assessment is accepted. Exhibit 2–3 illustrates the addition of this emphasis.

Exhibit 2–3 The Hourglass Model of Behavioral Assessment

Parents, teachers, additional related personnel screen the
client for global behavioral excesses and deficits.

Anecdotal recordings of client behavior

Identification of the target behavior

Prioritization and selection of
target behaviors

Operational definitions of target
behaviors developed

Determination of antecedent
and controlling variables

Design and intervention
with a treatment plan

Evaluation of the
treatment plan

Ongoing assessment of
maintenance of treatment gains
in therapeutic environment

Ongoing assessment of maintenance of treatment
gains in the extratherapeutic environment

Ongoing assessment of the generalization of the treatment
plan in the extratherapeutic environment

Ongoing assessment of collateral effects

Selecting Targets for Intervention

Where to Begin: Selection of Target Behaviors

The selection of a target behavior where several potential ones exist is a problem that must be addressed by the clinician before proceeding with intervention. The foremost issue is essentially a matter of pragmatics: severely developmentally disabled clients almost invariably are referred to professionals by parents, teachers, or other significant people, increasing the likelihood that prospective targets for intervention will reflect the biases and values of persons other than the client (Evans & Nelson, 1977). While experience and social convention (as well as a person's perception of reality) suggest that parents and other caretakers usually act with the best interests of the client in mind, violations of this convention do occur. To the extent that clients' behaviors pose dangers to themselves or others, decisions are more clear cut; other targets, prioritized accordingly, will follow. In the event that discrimination among target behaviors is more ambiguous, however, several guidelines have been offered. Clients, parents, and therapists might select target behaviors that allow clients greater access to social and individual reinforcers (Myerson & Hayes, 1978). This guideline can be expanded to include target behaviors that have a greater likelihood of giving clients access to their natural community of reinforcers. For example, an appropriate smiling response might be a reasonable target behavior for the professional working with a severely mentally retarded child to the extent that such a behavior makes it likely that others will interact more frequently with that child.

Because one strength of behavioral interventions is that behavior can be shaped, Goldiamond (1974) suggests that clients and therapists target desirable behaviors that can be increased rather than unwanted behaviors that must be decreased. The rationale for this is twofold. First, behavior that is rewarded—allowing that successive approximations are determined realistically—is by definition more likely to occur. In contrast, behavior that is punished often elicits escape or avoidance responses from clients, removing them even further from these situations. Second, if a behavior has been extinguished through punishment or extinction, there is no guarantee that an appropriate substitute will appear in its place. In short, removing or reducing a target behavior teaches clients what *not* to do; it tells them nothing about what to do instead. It certainly can be argued that with a particular client and a specific behavior, decreasing that behavior is the only viable option. For example, Sajwaj, Libet, and Agras (1974) describe the use of lemon juice as a punishment for chronic ruminative vomiting. In this study, a severely developmentally disabled child who persisted in vomiting had a small quantity of lemon juice squirted into his mouth contingent upon the occurrence of the target behavior. Because the vomiting led to severe weight loss and placed the client in a life-threatening situation, punishment procedures were employed to bring about rapid change.

Cases of severe aggression also fall within the realm described above. If this course is mandated, however, the professional must accept the added responsibility of identifying and teaching a target behavior that will take the place of the inappropriate behavior just reduced. Behavior taught in such cases should be directed at helping clients acquire sensory, social, or primary reinforcement in an acceptable manner rather than in the maladaptive fashion to which they had become accustomed.

It has further been suggested that optimal levels of performance be sought when planning for treatment outcomes (Van Houten, 1979). In contrast to accepting average gains, striving for optimal levels requires a more careful, particular, and extended task analysis of the target behavior, facilitating initial learning and maintenance at each level of successive approximation to the goal. Moreover, as optimal levels are meant to be sought after but are rarely achieved, setting sights high may bring about a greater posttreatment level of behavior than would be expected with less stringent criteria. While this last point may appear to condone chance treatment gains, it is not intended to offer such gains as a primary objective of behavioral intervention. Rather, the implication is that more specific and elaborate criteria increase the potential for learning, generalization, and maintenance, serendipitous treatment gains notwithstanding.

Finally, it has been suggested that target behaviors that maximize the salient reinforcers of a particular client should be chosen over those that will impact minimally on available and preferred rewards (Ullman & Krasner, 1969). Within the context of developmental disabilities, this guideline provides for (a) access to reinforcers as an important factor in selecting a target behavior and (b) the creative manipulation of the response-reinforcer relationship so that better outcomes will be accrued from the careful use of reinforcers (see Egel, 1981; Shafer & Egel, 1981; Williams, Koegel, & Egel, 1981).

Where to Intervene: Some Guidelines

The prioritization of several possible target behaviors must be construed as a value judgment on the part of the professional, client, and any other significant person involved in the decision (Myerson & Hayes, 1978). As such, the inclusion or exclusion of certain behaviors is not based upon scientific principles but upon philosophical attitudes. That value judgments affect decisions regarding the treatment of the developmentally disabled should come as no surprise. But for clinicians to intervene solely on the basis of personal preference undermines not only a basic tenet of behavioral assessment—empiricism—but also the expected course of treatment, outcome, generalization, and maintenance of intervention.

O'Leary (1972) suggests that intervention begin with a behavior that is relatively easy to modify. In its most successful form, such an approach will contribute greatly to professionals', parents', and clients' feelings of achievement and self-efficacy. Further, a behavior that is relatively discrete (i.e., topographically obvious with clear functional determinants) affords an excellent "training ground" for the often misunderstood principles and techniques of behavioral assessment and intervention. Parents and teachers have the opportunity to observe their own affective and motor responses because the target behavior chosen requires relatively straightforward assessment and intervention procedures. Such opportunities augur well for the continued appropriate and sensitive use of the techniques with other more difficult behaviors.

Another alternative is to begin intervention with the behavior that causes the most distress to others involved with the client (Tharp & Wetzel, 1969). An advantage of this approach is that the target behavior represents a significant stress to others; hence its amelioration is highly valued. Further, parents and teachers often initially seek consultative services for this type of problem. Addressing their most pertinent needs facilitates cooperation and follow-through. Seductive as it seems, however, this alternative also has a major disadvantage. Consider the family seeking professional assistance in reducing their autistic daughter's screaming for attention. The initial interview reveals this to be a problem of long standing as well as one that has been resistant to change in the past. While the parents are motivated to work, they also have experienced a good deal of failure in their past attempts to modify this behavior. Their feelings of little control, past failure, and expected failure weigh heavily and likely will affect the treatment effort. In situations such as these, professionals must strike a delicate balance between long- and short-term goals, and between giving the parents what they want immediately or developing their competencies with more malleable behavior. Unfortunately, there are no easy answers to this dilemma; each situation warrants careful attention to the potential benefits and liabilities of starting at too high a level.

Behavior often exists not as a discrete unit but as part of a constellation of behaviors. To the extent that a potential target behavior can be linked reliably to a series of other behaviors, that target can be described as part of a behavior chain. When chaining of this type occurs, behavior just prior to another behavior acts as a discriminative stimulus for the second behavior. For example, the authors once worked with a child who reliably would emit the following behavior chain before attempting to bite another person: (1) vocalization of single syllable sounds, (2) agitated hand flapping while bouncing up and down in his seat, (3) mouthing of his own left wrist, (4) lunging forward in an attempt to bite. Angle, Hay, Hay, and Ellinwood (1977) investigated a similar phenomenon in another client and found that the alteration of an early response in the behavioral chain would interfere with the production of the target, terminal response. The results of their investigation suggest that behavioral assessment with severely developmentally disabled persons must focus on whether the target behavior is relatively discrete or whether it is the terminus for a reliably emitted sequence of behavior. In so doing, professionals may find themselves (as did the authors) able to intervene and stop the child's hand flapping and bouncing in the seat, rather than waiting until biting occurs.

Finally, behavior intervention that will facilitate response generalization could be chosen. Hay, Hay, and Nelson (1977) investigated the effects of reinforcement on accuracy with academic tasks and task behavior. Their results indicate that reinforcing accuracy resulted in a higher percent correct responding to academic tasks as well as in an on-task behavior increase. The converse was not found to be true. Thus, it behooves professionals working with severely developmentally disabled clients to attempt to identify those pivotal behaviors that may facilitate collateral growth in other, nontraining areas as well. This does not imply a cure or a "magic bullet" that, when isolated and treated, will have a curative effect on the clients under care. The sobering conclusion drawn by Lovaas, Koegel, Simmons, and Long (1973) that pivotal responses leading to profound changes in personality were not found in their sample of autistic children should not be construed as a deterrent to seeking target behaviors that will facilitate response generalizations. Rather, it should serve as a signal that the focus must shift from the global to the specific when issues of learning with the severely developmentally disabled are addressed.

Determination of Controlling Variables

Once a target behavior has been selected, contextual information related to the occurrence of that response must be obtained. While it is true that professionals often treat behavior as if it were discrete and unencumbered by the complexities of life, it is only for the purposes of scientific observation that they do so. Indeed, whatever intervention is utilized must be implemented contextually, because behavior does not exist in a vacuum, but rather within a complex social and environmental network. Because behavior is determined reciprocally, each response functions as both a stimulus to future behavior and a response to prior behavior. This in turn necessitates an attempt to determine which variables may be controlling the behavior that is targeted for intervention. Armed with such information, professionals will have several options to consider when deciding where to intervene.

To assist the behavioral assessor in determining controlling variables, the acronym SORKC (stimulus-organismic-response-contingencies of reinforcement-consequence) has been proposed by Kanfer and Saslow (1969), expanding upon a model originally proposed by Lindsley (1964). This model represents a deviation and improvement from the earlier ABC (antecedent-behavior-consequence) paradigm. The SORKC analysis allows for a multisituational, multidimensional assessment of behavior. The contingencies of reinforcement, while less frequently assessed with nonhandicapped children and adults, have been found to have an impact on the behavior of the severely developmentally disabled (Egel, 1981; Egel, 1980; Koegel, Schreibman, Britten, & Laitinen, 1979; Dunlap & Egel, 1982) and warrant inclusion and attention with this population. Finally, the ABC analysis does not address the schedule of reinforcement (K) maintaining the behavior. Several other advantages exist. The addition of the organismic (O) variable has special relevance to the severely developmentally disabled client because it allows for individual physiological conditions and prior learning histories to be considered in assessment and treatment planning.

Because the SORKC analysis provides a useful model for assessing the behavior of severely developmentally disabled clients, it will be presented in detail. However, while it greatly facilitates behavioral assessment with this population, the SORKC analysis is an insufficient paradigm for outcome evaluation (Bijou & Peterson, 1971). For this latter purpose a functional analysis (Peterson, 1968) is required. This is described in detail later in Chapter 2 under "Evaluation of the Treatment Program."

There are three major classes of controlling variables: current environmental variables (stimuli and consequences), organismic variables, and contingencies of reinforcement. Moreover, temporal and contextual bases exist within which these controlling variables operate (Mash & Terdal, 1981). While earlier approaches to behavioral assessment focused on present behavior and its controlling conditions (Ullman & Krasner, 1965), this restricted emphasis is no longer warranted (Mash & Terdal, 1981). Each of these factors will be considered below.

Current Environmental Variables: Stimuli (S)

An environmental condition that precedes a target behavior and is presumed to exert some degree of control over responding is referred to as a stimulus antecedent. These precursors of the target behavior can be categorized either as discriminative stimuli or as elicitors (Goldfried & Sprafkin, 1974). When past learning has taught an individual that a particular consequence will follow a certain response when that response is performed in the presence of a specific stimulus, that stimulus is termed an S^D (for discriminative stimulus). In short, the discriminative stimulus sets the stage for the performance of a particular response. Traffic lights are discriminative stimuli with which most adults are familiar. When the light is red, stopping will be negatively reinforced (i.e., a summons will not be issued for stopping). When the light is green, however, a different response has been learned. Amber requires still another response, this time involving the choice of whether to proceed with caution or to stop.

While useful for illustrative purposes, the above example is much simpler than those that usually are confronted with the severely developmentally disabled. A more relevant example might be of greater use. One of the authors (MDP) once worked with an autistic child who would tantrum each morning as soon as his bus made the turn into the school's driveway. For the earlier part of his ride to school each day, Alan presented few problems. After some consideration, it became clear that the turn into the driveway had become a discriminative stimulus for Alan, "alerting" him that he was once again about to enter a highly demanding situation. During the course of assessment, it was noted that Alan had been experiencing difficulties with compliance for some time (not following task-related directions and/or classroom rules), and was involved in the initial phases of intervention for that behavior. As so often happens, this target behavior had escalated—compared to baseline rates—when a contingent simple correction procedure was implemented. When discussing Alan's behavior with the bus driver, it became clear that his tantrums had begun three to four days after the implementation of the program to increase compliance in the classroom. It was hypothesized that (1) turning into the driveway functioned as an S^D for the anticipation of the negative consequences for noncompliance in the classroom and, (2) that the tantrums would decrease as noncompliance decreased in the classroom. This in fact was the case, for seven days later Alan ceased his tantrums on the bus, and consequations for noncompliance were down to one third of the baseline rate. Conceptualizing the bus turning as a discriminative stimulus prompted the authors to search for and identify what Alan perceived as so punishing. The treatment decision that followed differed radically from other conceptualizations that might have dictated the tantrums to be discrete behavior and, as such, something to be reduced in an isolated context.

Stimulus antecedents also can be classified as elicitors if, through classical conditioning, they evoke automatic emotional responses. For example, the contingent use of a water squirt from a plant mister as punishment for moderate forms of self-injurious behavior (Dorsey, Iwata, Ong, & McSween, 1980) might well bring about a negative emotional response to the sight of plant misters, even in the absence of self-injurious behavior. Because the client associates plant misters with sudden unpleasant wetness on the face, the mister takes on the properties of an eliciting stimulus.

The process of determining whether a stimulus is functioning as a discriminative cue or as an elicitor does not always lead to a clear-cut decision. But to the extent that professionals are able to make such a determination, both the course of assessment and the parameters of intervention can be more specific.

Antecedent stimuli come in many forms. While interactions with other people and social stimuli account for a large percentage of the events that influence behavior (Kazdin, 1980), physical and/or environmental conditions also play an important role. Included in this latter category are variables such as time of day, place, and environmental conditions (temperature or physical space, for example). When attempting to identify these variables, it is useful to generate an anecdotal record of all events and interactions that precede the target behavior (Bijou, Peterson, & Ault, 1968). A rule of thumb here is to be overinclusive, as the determination regarding which data are unimportant has yet to be made. Following the generation of these descriptive notes, patterns are identified and hypotheses are generated concerning which of these antecedent events may be controlling the target behavior. These hypotheses can be tested and, if correct, used to guide intervention.

Current Environmental Variables: Consequences (C)

The behavior of severely developmentally disabled clients is often maintained by reinforcing and aversive consequences. While most parents and professionals have a subjective sense of the relative valence of a consequence, sole reliance upon this mode of determining the effect of a particular consequence with a specific client often leads to misattribution. For this reason, consequences are defined functionally and according to two basic principles: (1) positive consequences increase or maintain behavior over time, and (2) aversive consequences decrease behavior over time. While this conceptualization may seem reductionistic, it underscores a basic issue of assessment with severely disabled clients: empirical, objective assessment is a prerequisite to intervention. Such an assessment may be augmented by social validation (Schreibman et al., 1981), but empirical validation always must be at the base.

The functional properties of a consequence must be distinguished from consequent events that have no demonstrated ability to control responding (Mash & Terdal, 1976). This caution is not intended to preclude creative hypothesis testing, but rather to emphasize the crucial need for *demonstration* of the functional properties of a consequence as a prior condition to intervention. An example from clinical practice will serve to illustrate these issues.

Eric is an autistic child who attended a day school for severely developmentally disabled children. During academic sessions with two other students and an undergraduate tutor, Eric would push his chair away from the table and refuse to return when asked. This behavior occurred from 5 to 14 minutes during a 20-minute teaching session and, despite the tutor's efforts, continued to escalate over an eight-day period. An assessment of consequent variables indicated that the tutor's consistent response was to call Eric back to his seat once (to which Eric always replied, "No"), to allow 5 seconds for compliance, and then to engage in a positive practice overcorrection procedure during which Eric would ask the tutor for permission to move away from the table. Notably, during the positive practice procedure Eric would laugh, act playfully, and sometimes get up from the chair and run away laughing, with the tutor following close behind.

As would be expected, the tutor grew to become disenchanted with this child. What was not yet clear to the tutor, however, was that the positive practice consequation and verbal attention to Eric (albeit perceived as aversive by the tutor) was functioning as a reinforcer. In short, Eric appeared to enjoy the attention and worked at maintaining it at high levels.

As was their practice when faced with the phenomenon of negative attention as a reinforcer, the staff assessed the approval/disapproval ratio for Eric during those work sessions. In general, percent approvals/percent disapprovals was approximately 20%/80%, indicating that Eric was receiving reinforcement for appropriate behavior only about 20% of the time. The tutor was not catching Eric being good! On the basis of these data it was hypothesized (1) that Eric's behavior was being maintained by the tutor and (2) that ignoring Eric's misbehavior while concurrently reinforcing his appropriate behavior would eventually reverse this trend, at which time the approval/disapproval ratio would rise accordingly.

An intervention was implemented that (1) discontinued positive practice overcorrection, (2) set as the *tutor's* criterion an approval/disapproval ratio of 70/30 or higher, and (3) utilized modeling to further attenuate the effects of reinforcement for appropriate work behavior (e.g., when Eric ran away from the table during work sessions the other two students were reinforced verbally for a variety of appropriate behaviors). This intervention succeeded in reducing the duration of time that Eric spent away from the table to 1 to 2 minutes per teaching session and in increasing the approval/disapproval ratio to criterion level within seven school days. Eric's appropriate task behavior in a small group continued to improve. He maintained this appropriate behavior for more than two and one-half years. He has since left the school for a less restrictive educational placement.

Response-Reinforcer Relationships: Several researchers have investigated procedures that are designed to bring about more rapid acquisition and generalization of responses by autistic children. The particular methods employed involve the manipulation of consequent stimuli. Because they involve conditions of reinforcement that are set by clinicians, they are described below.

Koegel and Williams (1980) compared direct versus indirect response-reinforcer relationships on the acquisition of target behaviors. Direct relationships were those where the target behavior was part of the response chain required to obtain the consequent reward (e.g., for the target behavior drinking from a cup, the reinforcer—juice—would be in the cup). In contrast, indirect response-reinforcer relationships were those where the target behavior was not a part of the response chain to obtain the reinforcer. They found that direct response-reinforcer relationships led to rapid acquisition of the target behavior and suggested that increased attention to task may be fostered by utilizing direct response-reinforcer relationships (Koegel & Williams, 1980).

In a related study, Williams, Koegel, and Egel (1981) compared the effectiveness of arbitrary versus functional response-reinforcer relationships on learning. Arbitrary relationships were defined as those in which no specific relationship existed between the reinforcement and the target behavior. Functional relationships, however, evidenced a specific relationship between the reinforcer and the target behavior. If, for example, the target behavior involved touching a cup, the reinforcer would be located in that cup. In this way, touching the cup became a functional step toward obtaining the reward.

Williams and colleagues (1981) found that functional response-reinforcer relationships led to improved rates of learning and rapid acquisition of the criterion. Moreover, when the arbitrary condition was reinstated after the children had succeeded with the functional phase, the responses were maintained. These authors hypothesize that attention to task was increased because a contingent relationship existed between the reinforcement and the target behavior.

Expanding these findings, Shafer and Egel (1981) investigated the nature of generalization with functional response-reinforcer relationships. They found that increased generalization to extratherapeutic settings was related to the use of functional response-reinforcer relationships.

Taken together, these three studies suggest at least two considerations for assessment. First, an assessment of attention to task should be undertaken if the client has a history of low rates of responding or has problems with a particular task. Second, if the above results are construed as a function of novelty, the client should be assessed for a wide variety of reinforcing events/objects. In so doing, clinicians ensure the availability of many potential reinforcers that may have a direct or functional relationship to the particular tasks being taught.

Organismic Variables (O)

Organismic variables represent a frequently neglected class of variables of interest to the behavioral assessor. Included here are self-statements and feelings (Goldfried & Sprafkin, 1974); expectations of reward or punishment (Franzini, 1970); expectations of personal efficacy (Bandura, 1977); biological states, such as fatigue, hunger, health, and visual acuity (Nelson & Hayes, 1979); and genetic, biochemical, or neurological variables (Mash & Terdal, 1981) that influence behavior.

Such information is of special importance when assessing clients with severe developmental disabilities. Conditions that have a specific effect upon the form and function of behavior, such as Down's syndrome or phenylketonuria (PKU), must be accounted for during assessment so that the ensuing intervention reflects the particular excesses and deficits under the control of "internal" factors. To the extent necessary to confirm or disconfirm an organic basis for specific kinds of behavior, medical information should be included and considered before implementation of a treatment plan. For example, Realmuto and Main (1982) reported a case of Gilles de la Tourette syndrome in a 13-year-old autistic boy. In the absence of the diagnosis of Tourette's syndrome, this client's nonpurposeful, repetitive movements and incomprehensible utterances might well have been the target of a rather straightforward behavioral intervention. The diagnosis of Tourette's, however, suggests the efficacy of one of the neuroleptic drugs, such as haloperidol

(Carter, 1975), as an adjunctive therapy. That problematic behavior is often a function of biological and psychological variables presents no hindrance to intervention; treatment can be administered in both areas (Davison, 1969).

While the interaction of biological and social variables in the behavioral assessment of the severely developmentally disabled is often less clear than for clients with seizure disorders (Balaschack & Mostofsky, 1981) or juvenile diabetes (Melamed & Johnson, 1981), the specific or inferred organicity often found with severely developmentally disabled clients should be accounted for as well as possible.

The assessment and identification of organic factors presents clinicians with the choice of intervening with either a goal of habilation or of compensation. Organismic variables that can be altered suggest goals of a habilitative nature. The hypothesis here is that by manipulating the controlling variables, one can change the problem behavior. For example, the identification of a conductive hearing loss in a severely handicapped child would necessitate the prescription of hearing aids before commencement of a simultaneous communication program (Handleman, Arnold, Veniar, Kristoff, & Harris, 1982). In contrast, variables that cannot be altered (e.g., congenital cataracts or known lesions in the cerebral cortex) require compensatory treatment goals.

In either case, the identification of salient biological factors in no way predicts outcome. As these variables have been a part of the client's behavioral repertoire for a long time, brief interventions, no matter how comprehensively assessed, are unlikely to effect lasting change alone. Rather, maintenance and generalization of treatment gains must be programmed systematically (Stokes & Baer, 1977) within multiple environments and with multiple clinicians (Handleman, 1979; Koegel & Rincover, 1977). This approach will offer the greatest utility within either a habilitative or compensatory framework.

Contingencies of Reinforcement (K)

These variables refer to the schedules of reinforcement (Ferster & Skinner, 1957) and the contingencies, or particular conditions, of reinforcement (Kanfer & Saslow, 1969) that influence the topography, rate, correctness, durability, and potency of a client's response. Both schedules and contingencies of reinforcement are ultimately under the control of clinicians.

Until recently, contingencies of reinforcement have been among the least emphasized of the components of the SORKC analysis. It was assumed that in order for behavior to be established, a continuous reinforcement schedule (CRS) was initially necessary (Harris, 1975). Over time, the clinician would gradually "thin out" the schedule of reinforcement (Drash, Caldwell, & Leibowitz, 1970) to a variable schedule (e.g., one reinforcer for every two, then three, four . . . correct responses) until it approximated the natural environment. McReynolds

(1970) further suggested that during the initial phases of learning, primary reinforcers were most effective. Once the behavior was learned, however, secondary reinforcers could maintain the response. Problems in learning could be expected if the initial schedule was too weak, if it was thinned out too quickly, or if inappropriate reinforcers were employed. With the exception of these relatively broad guidelines, little heed was paid to the relationship between numerous important reinforcement parameters (e.g., intertrial interval, specificity, and so on) and the behavior of the client. Fortunately, this state of affairs has changed in the last several years due to the efforts of Koegel and his colleagues, whose work will be summarized briefly.

Schedule of Reinforcement. Koegel and Rincover (1974) investigated the effects of systematically increasing group size while thinning out the reinforcement schedule with a group of severely developmentally disabled children. In so doing, they sought to reduce the teacher-child ratio to one that more closely approximated other classes for severely handicapped children (1:8). The success of the training program was facilitated by the assessment of various preparatory skills. All of these skills should be considered when the target behavior is larger group instruction. Thus, clinicians should first assess the baseline group-size performance rate for each student. Holding the teaching task constant across all group-size situations and using a child not being assessed as a confederate, clinicians could assess percent correct responding in one-to-one, two-to-one, three-to-one, and so on student-teacher settings. The setting for which the client fell below the response criterion (typically 80% to 85% correct responses to task) would be the first training setting. Subsequent movement upward would depend upon the attainment of criterion levels.

In systematically describing the relationship between the schedule of reinforcement and response to large group instruction, Koegel and Rincover (1974) clearly refute the notion that severely developmentally disabled clients can be brought together into a less restrictive educational setting without *first* assessing the schedule of reinforcement and its role in maintaining behavior.

Koegel, Schreibman, Britten, and Laitinen (1979) analyzed the effects of altering the schedule of reinforcement during training on stimulus overselectivity. Their results indicate that a variable schedule of reinforcement led to less overselective responding than did a continuous schedule. Stimulus overselectivity is often a serious problem for autistic clients (Lovaas, Koegel, & Schreibman, 1979) and only slightly less so for other developmentally disabled learners (Bilsky & Heal, 1969; Lovaas, Koegel, Schreibman, & Rehm, 1971). Clinicians working with these populations should assess a client's ability to attend to multiple cues present within a stimulus situation before proceeding with instruction. Further, assessment of the impact of a continuous versus a variable schedule of reinforcement should be conducted in order to determine the optimal conditions for instructional success.

Variation of Reinforcement. Because motivating developmentally disabled persons can be difficult, it becomes critically important to assess clients across this domain. Extrinsic motivation, or those outside events that shape responding in a desired direction, will be considered here. Intrinsic motivation requires an inferential process that relies on indirect measures, and is beyond the scope of this book.

Egel (1980, 1981) has addressed reinforcer variation in his work with autistic children. In one study, he found an increase both in the total number of responses emitted and in the speed of responding when several reinforcers were available to a client, as opposed to the exclusive use of a single type of reinforcer (Egel, 1980). In another investigation (Egel, 1981), the varied presentation of reinforcers led to an increase in correct responding as well as in on-task behavior. Taken together, these results provide evidence for the need to assess the functionality of various reinforcers when clinicians plan interventions for severely developmentally disabled clients. Factors to be considered include salience (potency), availability, and appropriateness of use. These last two factors illustrate philosophical rather than empirical issues because the proposed use of certain reinforcers (e.g., edibles or the use of a client's lunch throughout the morning session) sometimes leads to value conflicts with teachers and/or administrators and supervisors. Thus, irrespective of their past or future utility, the use of certain rewards may be forbidden. Short of such restrictions, however, clinicians must determine which reinforcers are appropriate and assure novelty through reinforcer variation. Over the course of treatment, ongoing assessment of the client's behavior will either validate those choices or refute them, signaling reassessment and change.

While assessment is often initiated prior to intervention, a change in client response during the course of treatment should immediately alert clinicians to the possibility of satiation. An assessment for reinforcer salience would then follow.

Stimulus-Specific Reinforcement. Recent authors have hypothesized that correct task performance of severely developmentally disabled clients increases as a function of how closely and clearly the reinforcer and the discriminative stimulus are linked (Saunders & Sailor, 1979; Litt & Schreibman, 1981). Termed stimulus-specific reinforcement (Litt & Schreibman, 1981), this process refers to reinforcement that is given only when a particular response is provided. For example, in a language task designed to train the client's discrimination among in, out, over, and under, a piece of cookie might be given for all correct "in" responses, a drink of juice for all correct "out" responses, and so on. Litt and Schreibman (1981) investigated this phenomenon and found that stimulus-specific reinforcement led to greater percentages of correct responding than did either salient reinforcers (a single, consistently employed, highly desirable reinforcer) or varied reinforcers (random consequation of correct responses with one of a variety of functional reinforcers). These authors note, however, that the specific reinforcers utilized must be of equal desirability to the client.

This research identifies an important area for assessment. In order to facilitate training and increase motivation, clinicians must assess for a variety of functional reinforcers. This is necessary in order to provide for the range of discriminations that might be made within a given teaching task. These reinforcers then must be "graded" by the client so that a reinforcer hierarchy can be generated. This latter process can be accomplished through a free-choice assessment in which the client is provided with a reinforcement menu from which to choose only after responding correctly to task. Data would be kept regarding frequency of item selection with the assessment repeated across several tasks and settings. Gathering similar information from parents, teachers, or cottage staff would expedite this process. Any preferences reported by others that are not confirmed by data are questionable and should be investigated further.

Variation of Intertrial Interval. Intertrial interval refers to the elapsed time between the consequation in Trial 1 and the presentation of the discriminative stimulus (S^D) in Trial 2 of a teaching task. Consider, for example, the steps involved in teaching eye contact to a developmentally disabled child. The clinician would: (1) present the S^D, "Look at me"; (2) the client would respond/not respond; (3) the clinician would consequate that response with a reinforcer or correction; and (4) the clinician would wait a brief period of time before commencing with Trial 2. This fourth step represents the intertrial interval.

Koegel, Dunlap, and Dyer (1980) investigated the effects of long versus short intertrial intervals on rate of correct responding in autistic children. They found that for the particular child/task combinations investigated, relatively short intertrial intervals (1–4 seconds) were superior to long intervals (4–26 seconds).

The implications of these findings for assessment are important. Because the duration of the intertrial interval serves as a functional variable (Koegel et al., 1980), its manipulation by the clinician, planned or inadvertent, affects client responding and subsequent reinforcement. Thus, a low rate of client responding would suggest the need for an assessment of intertrial intervals. This could be done by recording the duration of a representative sample of intertrial intervals using time sampling methods. Once this baseline is established, systematic manipulation of the interval duration will allow a statement of the effect of the interval on the response to be made.

This post hoc style of assessment differs from a priori assessment espoused in this book. However, the unique interactions of child variables—such as mental age, distractibility, and/or chronological age—with task variables—such as complexity or prior experience (Koegel et al., 1980)—that are possible within any given child/task situation are large indeed. An attempt to anticipate, assess, and plan for these interactions prior to intervention will doubtless be a time-consuming and unwieldy task. As a result, a quick dose of the cure is more feasible than attempts at prevention, contrary to the popular maxim.

Stimulus Variation: Constant Versus Varied Task. Dunlap and Koegel (1980) investigated the effects of presenting a single task versus presenting a variety of tasks during a training session on the rate of autistic children's correct responding. They found that the varied task condition not only produced increased rates of correct responding, but also led to more interested and enthusiastic behavior on the part of the children.

As with the assessment of intertrial interval duration, post hoc assessment may be the most expedient. Thus, tasks for which a low rate of responding occurs should be assessed for a "boredom factor" that may well be the result of low stimulus novelty due to repetitious presentation (Berlyne, 1960). This assessment could be done by systematically alternating the presentation of training stimuli during one teaching session, then holding it constant for the next session. More ambitious clinicians might wish to evaluate these effects using an alternating treatment design (Barlow & Hayes, 1979). In either case, the results of the assessment for stimulus variation may uncover a novelty effect in responding, leading to adjustment of the training protocol.

Responses (R)

While a client's response may appear to be a relatively straightforward event, comprehensive assessment would attend to at least five response dimensions: duration, pervasiveness, frequency, magnitude (Goldfried & Sprafkin, 1974), and topography. Duration refers to the period of time between the onset and offset of each instance of behavior. A measure of pervasiveness provides an indication of the form and type of environments within which the response occurs. Frequency refers to how often a behavior occurs, and magnitude represents the degree of positive or negative valence attached to the behavior (Goldfried & Sprafkin, 1974). Topography refers to the motor characteristics of a behavior (i.e., how it looks). While seemingly a straightforward dimension, the topographical assessment of complex, interrelated behavior can be difficult indeed.

Early conceptualizations of behavioral assessment typically stressed observable behavior and its controlling variables. However, a broader view has been espoused recently. This *triple response mode* reconceptualization calls for the assessment of motor, physiological, and verbal/cognitive behavior present in the circumstance under scrutiny (Lang, 1968). In many cases, these modes may covary. Such covariance should not be assumed, however (Lang, 1968; Jones, 1979). This point is particularly salient with regard to the developmentally disabled to the extent that discordance between behavior and affect is endemic. For example, the authors have observed children engaging in high rates of self-injurious behavior while smiling or laughing. Doubtless, issues of intensity, situational specificity, and the attention-seeking or avoidance function of the self-injurious behavior (Carr, 1977) are relevant here. But to the unwitting observer who expects agreement between affective and motor behavior, this discordance can be puzzling indeed. Thus, the prima facie acceptance of only one response mode could lead to an erroneous assumption concerning the function of the response in question. While it is expected that many types of behavior emitted by severely developmentally disabled persons will resist triple response mode assessment, the attempt should nonetheless be made before intervention strategies are initiated. Should such an assessment be possible, the availability of triple response mode data will facilitate ongoing assessment during all phases of treatment.

Development of a Treatment Plan

Once the SORKC analysis has been conducted on the target behavior, information relevant to the development of an effective treatment plan must be gathered. Here the goal is to place the target behavior within situational contexts that are specific to the client. In so doing, clinicians individualize the treatment plan.

Kanfer and Saslow (1969) describe in detail several domains to be assessed in this phase. Their approach includes:

A. Assess the problem situation for:
  1. Behavioral excesses.
  2. Behavioral deficits.
  3. Nonproblematic behavioral assets.
B. Clarify the problem situation:
  1. Who objects to the behavior(s)?
  2. Who supports the behavior(s)?
  3. Specify the conditions within which the behavioral excesses or deficits occur.
  4. Would amelioration of the target behavior lead to new problems in living for the client? If so, how?
C. Assess for motivation:
  1. Survey reinforcers.
  2. Specify the conditions under which various reinforcers are salient.
  3. Determine those persons or groups who have been effective in reinforcing the client's behavior in the past.
  4. Survey punishers.
  5. Specify the conditions under which various punishers are salient.
  6. Determine those persons or groups who have been effective in punishing the client's behavior in the past.
D. Assess the client's developmental status:
  1. Assess biological/physical changes that might limit functioning and/or treatment, as well as the natural history of biological/physical limitations.

    2. Assess social status for affiliations; for community perceptions of the client and his or her disability; availability of community reinforcers for change. Can these factors be brought to bear on the treatment plan?

    3. Assess changes in behavior for the emergence of new behaviors, absence of previously emitted behaviors, and changes in the intensity or frequency of ongoing behavior. Can biological and social status be related to the observed changes in behavior?

E. Assess self-control:

    1. Assess the limitations of self-control.

    2. Assess for the necessary conditions required for self-control.

    3. Assess for those methods of self-control presently in the client's behavioral repertoire.

    4. Which situations (persons, places, events) cause a breakdown in self-control?

    5. Can the client's available self-control skills be used in a treatment plan? If so, how?

F. Assess social relationships for:

    1. Significant others who influence the client's behavior.

    2. Persons who facilitate appropriate behavior.

    3. Persons who elicit inappropriate behavior.

    4. Which reinforcers are operative in the social sphere (i.e., verbal, physical, overt, subtle)?

    5. Do those involved with the client *clearly* signal the cessation of reinforcement and the onset of punishment? When does this break down?

    6. How can the influential persons in a client's life be incorporated into the treatment plan?

G. Assess the sociocultural and physical correlates of a client's behavior:

    1. Assess the prevailing cultural norms related to the problem behavior.

    2. Assess these norms across the various environments in which the client interacts. Are these norms similar or discrepant? Can these similarities or discrepancies be addressed in the treatment plan? If so, how?

    3. How do environmental limitations reduce the client's opportunities for reinforcement?

    4. In which physical environments are client problems most pronounced?

    5. Which physical environments foster appropriate behavior in the client?

6. In what ways can these sociocultural and physical correlates be addressed in the treatment plan? (pp. 429–437)

The foregoing assessment framework is not intended to be exhaustive. Indeed, several items may well be inappropriate for particular clients and could be excluded without invalidating the entire procedure. It is important, however, to keep the multisituational, multidimensional framework intact because failure to do so would increase the risk of obtaining treatment results that do not generalize across persons, settings, or events.

Evaluation of Treatment Plan

Once the first three goals of behavioral assessment have been addressed (identification of the target behavior; determination of organismic and controlling variables; development of a treatment plan) the last goal—evaluation of the treatment plan—begins. In order for this evaluation to be conducted properly, clinicians must plan for two principal elements: (1) choice of an appropriate experimental design and (2) selection of appropriate and practical dependent measures.

Once chosen, these two elements form the core of the functional analysis of behavior. As described by Peterson (1968), the functional analysis proceeds from (1) systematic observation of the target behavior in order to obtain a baseline (pretreatment) rate; (2) analysis of the antecedent and consequent variables; (3) experimental manipulation of a condition that is hypothesized to be related functionally to the target behavior; and (4) systematic observation to record changes subsequent to that manipulation. Each of the "B" phases in the experimental designs described in Chapter 3 constitutes manipulation of functionally related conditions. As such, statements of effectiveness of a given treatment are based upon the degree of demonstrated causality or functionality. Even the best hypothesis as to the cause of a target behavior falls below acceptable standards if a functional analysis proves inconclusive.

Selection of the Experimental Design

Single-subject designs are more useful for the purposes of behavioral assessment than are group experimental designs utilizing statistical analyses (Hersen & Barlow, 1976). Increased utility stems from the greater internal validity (Campbell & Stanley, 1966) available with these designs, as well as the increased ability of single-case designs to pinpoint causal relationships between the treatment plan and the client's behavior. These designs are described in detail in Chapter 3.

Selection of Dependent Measures

Dependent measures are those measures obtained for the variable that is expected to change as a result of the intervention. In short, they are obtained for the dependent variable. Examples of dependent variables include eye contact, time on task, amount of food consumed, instances of pica, and so on. The measures for these and other dependent variables must be both practical and valid, and should lead to high rates of interrater reliability (Nelson & Hayes, 1981).

There are numerous dependent measures that can be used to evaluate treatment effectiveness. Included here are self-report measures by staff, frequency counts, duration measures, permanent product data, problem checklists, and archival data (such as incident reports, nursing notes, attendance reports, and weekly weight checks). Techniques for the use of these and others are described in detail in Chapter 3.

SUMMARY

The utility of behavioral assessment for clients with severe developmental disabilities was described and a framework for assessment was presented. Clinicians must first identify the target behavior. Considerations for prioritizing target behaviors, as well as guidelines for intervention, were presented. The variables controlling the target behavior must then be determined. To this end, the utility of the SORKC analysis was described, with special reference to organismic variables and contingencies of reinforcement. A multisituational, multidimensional treatment plan is then developed. This activity expands the behavioral assessment from a molecular to a more molar level of analysis. Finally, considerations for the evaluation of the treatment plan were presented, including the selection of dependent measures and experimental designs.

REFERENCES

Angle, H. V., Hay, L. R., Hay, W. M., & Ellinwood, E. H. (1977). Computer assisted behavioral assessment. In J. D. Cone & R. P. Hawkins (Eds.), *Behavioral assessment: New directions in clinical psychology*. New York: Brunner/Mazel.

Balaschak, B. A., & Mostofsky, D. I. (1981). Seizure disorders. In E. J. Mash & L. G. Terdal (Eds.). *Behavioral assessment of childhood disorders*. New York: Guilford.

Bandura, A. (1977). Self-efficacy: Toward a unifying theory of behavioral change. *Psychological Review, 84*, 191–215.

Barlow, D. H., & Hayes, S. C. (1979). Alternating treatments design: One strategy for comparing the effects of two treatments in a single subject. *Journal of Applied Behavior Analysis, 12*, 199–210.

Berlyne, D. E. (1960). *Conflict, arousal, and curiosity*. New York: McGraw-Hill.

Bijou, S. W., & Peterson, R. F. (1971). Functional analysis in the assessment of children. In P. McReynolds (Ed.), *Advances in psychological assessment* (Vol. 2). Palo Alto, CA: Science and Behavior Books.

Bijou, S. W., Peterson, R. F., & Ault, M. H. (1968). A method to integrate descriptive and experimental field studies at the level of data and empirical concepts. *Journal of Applied Behavior Analysis, 1*, 175–191.

Bilsky, L., & Heal, L. W. (1969). Cue novelty and training level in the discrimination shift performance of retardates. *Journal of Experimental Child Psychology, 8,* 503–511.

Birnbauer, J. S., & Lawler, J. (1964). Token reinforcement for learning. *Mental Retardation, 2,* 275–279.

Campbell, D. T., & Stanley, J. C. (1966). *Experimental and quasi-experimental designs for research.* Chicago: Rand-McNally.

Carr, E. G. (1977). The motivation of self-injurious behavior: A review of some hypotheses. *Psychological Bulletin, 84,* 800–816.

Carter, C. H. (1975). *Handbook of mental retardation syndromes* (3rd ed.). Springfield, IL: Charles C. Thomas.

Craighead, W. E., Mercatoris, M., & Bellack, B. (1974). A brief report on mentally retarded residents as behavioral observers. *Journal of Applied Behavior Analysis, 7,* 333–340.

Davison, G. C. (1969). Appraisal of behavior modification techniques with adults in institutional settings. In C. M. Franks (Ed.), *Behavior therapy: Appraisal and status.* New York: McGraw-Hill.

Doke, L.A. (1976). Assessment of children's behavioral deficits. In M. Hersen & A. Bellack (Eds.), *Behavioral assessment: A practical handbook.* Elmsford, NY: Pergamon Press.

Dorsey, M. F., Iwata, B. A., Ong, P., & McSween, T. E. (1980). Treatment of self-injurious behavior using a water mist: Initial response suppression and generalization. *Journal of Applied Behavior Analysis, 13,* 343–353.

Drash, P. W., Caldwell, L. R., & Leibowitz, J. M. (1970). Correct and incorrect response rates as basic dependent variables in the operant conditioning of speech in non-verbal subjects. *Psychological Aspects of Disability, 17,* 16–23.

Dunlap, G., & Egel, A. L. (1982). Motivation techniques. In R. L. Koegel, A. Rincover, & A. L. Egel (Eds.), *Educating and understanding autistic children.* San Diego: College Hill Press.

Dunlap, G., & Koegel, R. L. (1980). Motivating autistic children through stimulus variation. *Journal of Applied Behavior Analysis, 13,* 619–627.

Egel, A. L. (1980). The effects of constant vs. varied reinforcer variation on responding by autistic children. *Journal of Experimental Child Psychology, 30,* 455–463.

Egel, A. L. (1981). Reinforcer variation: Implications for motivating developmentally disabled children. *Journal of Applied Behavior Analysis, 14,* 345–350.

Evans, I. M., & Nelson, R. O. (1977). Assessment of child behavior problems. In A. R. Ciminero, K. S. Calhoun, & H. E. Adams (Eds.), *Handbook of behavioral assessment,* New York: Wiley.

Fabry, P. L., & Reid, D. H. (1978). Teaching foster grandparents to train severely handicapped persons. *Journal of Applied Behavior Analysis, 11,* 111–123.

Ferster, C. B. (1961). Positive reinforcement and behavioral change in autistic children. *Child Development, 32,* 437–456.

Ferster, C. B., & DeMyer, M. K. (1961). The development of performances in autistic children in an automatically controlled environment. *Journal of Chronic Diseases, 13,* 312–345.

Ferster, C. B., & DeMyer, M. K. (1962). A method for the experimental analysis of the behavior of autistic children. *American Journal of Orthopsychiatry, 32,* 89–98.

Ferster, C. B., & Skinner, B. F. (1957). *Schedules of reinforcement.* New York: Appleton-Century-Crofts.

Franzini, L. R. (1970). Neglected variables in behavioral case assessment. *Behavior Therapy, 1,* 354–358.

Goldfried, M. R., & Kent, R. N. (1972). Traditional versus behavioral assessment: A comparison of methodological and theoretical assumptions. *Psychological Bulletin, 77,* 409–420.

Goldfried, M. R., & Sprafkin, J. N. (1974). Behavioral personality assessment. In J. T. Spence, R. C. Carson, & J. W. Thibaut (Eds.), *Behavioral approaches to therapy*. Morristown, NJ: General Learning Press.

Goldiamond, I. (1974). Toward a constructional approach to social problems: Ethical and constitutional issues raised by applied behavior analysis. *Behaviorism, 2*, 1–85.

Handleman, J. S. (1979). Generalization by autistic-type children of verbal responses across settings. *Journal of Applied Behavior Analysis, 12*, 273–282.

Handleman, J. S., Arnold, M., Veniar, F., Kristoff, B., & Harris, S. L. (1982). Assessment and remediation of hearing loss in an autistic child. *Hearing Instruments, 33*, 10–12.

Harris, S. L. (1975). Teaching language to nonverbal children—with emphasis on problems of generalization. *Psychological Bulletin, 82*, 565–580.

Harris, S. L., & Milch, R. E. (1981). Training parents as behavior therapists for their autistic children. *Clinical Psychology Review, 1*, 49–63.

Hawkins, R. P. (1979). The functions of assessment: Implications for selection and development of devices for assessing repertoires in clinical, educational, and other settings. *Journal of Applied Behavior Analysis, 12*, 501–516.

Hawkins, R. P., & Dobes, R. W. (1975). Behavioral definitions in applied behavior analysis: Explicit or implicit. In B. C. Etzel, J. M. LeBlanc, & D. M. Baer (Eds.), *New developments in behavioral research: Theory, methods, and applications*. New York: Wiley.

Hay, W. M., Hay, L. R., & Nelson, R. O. (1977). Direct and collateral changes in on-task and academic behavior resulting from on-task versus academic contingencies. *Behavior Therapy, 8*, 431–441.

Hersen, M., & Barlow, D. H. (1976). *Single case experimental designs*. Elmsford, NY: Pergamon Press.

Jones, R. R. (1979). Program evaluation design issues. *Behavioral Assessment, 1*, 51–59.

Kanfer, F. H., & Saslow, G. (1969). Behavioral diagnosis. In C. M. Franks (Ed.), *Behavior therapy: Appraisal and status*. New York: McGraw-Hill.

Kazdin, A. E. (1980). *Behavior modification in applied settings* (rev. ed.). Homewood, IL: Dorsey Press.

Koegel, R. L., Dunlap, G., & Dyer, K. (1980). Intertrial interval duration and learning in autistic children. *Journal of Applied Behavior Analysis, 13*, 91–99.

Koegel, R. L., & Rincover, A. (1974). Treatment of psychotic children in a classroom environment: I. Learning in a large group. *Journal of Applied Behavior Analysis, 7*, 45–59.

Koegel, R. L., & Rincover, A. (1977). Research on the difference between generalization and maintenance in extra-therapy responding. *Journal of Applied Behavior Analysis, 10*, 1–12.

Koegel, R. L., Schreibman, L., Britten, K., & Laitinen, R. (1979). The effects of schedule of reinforcement on stimulus overselectivity in autistic children. *Journal of Autism and Developmental Disorders, 9*, 383–397.

Koegel, R. L., & Williams, J. A. (1980). Direct vs. indirect response-reinforcer relationships in teaching autistic children. *Journal of Abnormal Child Psychology, 8*, 537–547.

Lang, P. J. (1968). Fear reduction and fear behavior: Problems in treating a construct. In J. M. Schlien (Ed.), *Research in psychotherapy* (Vol. 3). Washington, DC: American Psychological Association.

Lindsley, O. R. (1964). Direct measurement and prothesis of retarded behavior. *Journal of Education, 147*, 62–81.

Litt, M. D., & Schreibman, L. (1981). Stimulus-specific reinforcement in the acquisition of receptive labels by autistic children. *Analysis and Intervention in Developmental Disabilities, 1*, 171–186.

Lovaas, O. I., Koegel, R. L., Simmons, J. Q., & Long, J. S. (1973). Some generalization and follow-up measures on autistic children in behavior therapy. *Journal of Applied Behavior Analysis, 6*, 1–36.

Lovaas, O. I., Koegel, R. L., & Schreibman, L. (1979). Stimulus overselectivity in autism: A review of research. *Psychological Bulletin, 86*, 1236–1254.

Lovaas, O. I., Schreibman, L., Koegel, R. L., & Rehm, R. (1971). Selective responding by autistic children to multiple sensory input. *Journal of Abnormal Psychology, 77*, 211–222.

Mash, E. J., & Terdal, L. G. (1976). *Behavior therapy assessment: Diagnosis, design, and evaluation.* New York: Springer.

Mash, E. J., & Terdal, L. G. (1981). Behavioral assessment of childhood disturbance. In E. J. Mash & L. G. Terdal (Eds.), *Behavioral assessment of childhood disorders.* New York: Guilford.

McLaughlin, T. F., & Malaby, J. E. (1975). Elementary school children as behavioral engineers. In E. Ramp & G. Semp (Eds.), *Behavior analysis: Areas of research and application.* Englewood Cliffs, NJ: Prentice-Hall.

McReynolds, L. V. (1970). Reinforcement procedures for establishing and maintaining echoic speech by a nonverbal child. Applications of a functional approach to speech and hearing. In F. Giradeau & J. Spradlin (Eds.), *ASHA Monographs, 14*, 60–66.

Melamed, B. G., & Johnson, S. B. (1981). Chronic illness: Asthma and juvenile diabetes. In E. J. Mash & L. G. Terdal (Eds.), *Behavioral assessment of childhood disorders.* New York: Guilford.

Myerson, W. A., & Hayes, S. C. (1978). Controlling the clinician for the client's benefit. In J. E. Krapfl & E. A. Vargas (Eds.), *Behaviorism and ethics.* Kalamazoo, MI: Behaviordelia.

Nelson, R. O., & Barlow, D. H. (1981). Behavioral assessment: Basic strategies and initial procedures. In D. H. Barlow (Ed.), *Behavioral assessment of adult disorders.* New York: Guilford.

Nelson, R. O., & Hayes, S. C. (1979). Some current dimensions of behavioral assessment. *Behavioral Assessment, 1*, 1–16.

Nelson, R. O., & Hayes, S. C. (1981). An overview of behavioral assessment. In M. Hersen & A. S. Bellack (Eds.), *Behavioral assessment: A practical handbook* (2nd ed.). New York: Pergamon Press.

O'Leary, K. D. (1972). The assessment of psychopathology in children. In H. C. Quay & J. S. Werry (Eds.), *Psychopathological disorders of childhood.* New York.

Orlando, R., & Bijou, S. W. (1960). Single and multiple schedules of reinforcement in developmentally retarded children. *Journal of the Experimental Analysis of Behavior, 3*, 339–348.

Peterson, D. R. (1968). *The clinical study of social behavior.* New York: Appleton-Century-Crofts.

Posavac, E. J., & Carey, R. G. (1980). *Program evaluation: Methods and case studies.* Englewood Cliffs, NJ: Prentice-Hall.

Realmuto, G. M., & Main, B. (1981). Coincidence of Gilles de la Tourette syndrome and infantile autism. *Journal of Autism and Developmental Disorders.*

Sajwaj, T., Libet, J., & Agras, S. (1974). Lemon juice therapy: The control of life-threatening rumination in a six-month old infant. *Journal of Applied Behavior Analysis, 7*, 557–563.

Saunders, R., & Sailor, W. (1979). A comparison of three strategies of reinforcement on two-choice learning problems with severely retarded children. *AAESPH Review, 4*, 323–333.

Schreibman, L., Koegel, R. L., Mills, J. I., & Burke, J. C. (1981). Social validation of behavior therapy with autistic children. *Behavior Therapy, 12*, 610–624.

Shafer, M. S., & Egel, A. L. (1981, November). Response-reinforcer relationships and generalization of responding by autistic children. Paper presented at the 15th annual meeting of the Association for Advancement of Behavior Therapy, Toronto.

Stokes, T. F., & Baer, D. M. (1977). An implicit technology of generalization. *Journal of Applied Behavior Analysis, 10*, 349–367.

Tharp, R. G., & Wetzel, R. J. (1969). *Behavior modification in the natural environment*. New York: Academic Press.

Ullman, L. P., & Krasner, L. (Eds.). (1965). *Case studies in behavior modification*. New York: Holt, Rinehart, & Winston.

Ullman, L. P., & Krasner, L. (1969). *A psychological approach to abnormal behavior*. Englewood Cliffs, NJ: Prentice-Hall.

Van Houten, R. (1979). Social validation: The evolution of standards of competency for target behaviors. *Journal of Applied Behavior Analysis, 12*, 581–591.

Williams, J. A., Koegel, R. L., & Egel, A. L. (1981). Response-reinforcer relationships and improved learning in autistic children. *Journal of Applied Behavior Analysis, 14*, 53–60.

Wolf, M. M. (1978). Social validity: The case for subjective measurement or how applied behavior analysis is finding its heart. *Journal of Applied Behavior Analysis, 11*, 203–214.

Techniques for the Behavioral Assessment of Severe Developmental Disabilities

INTRODUCTION

The activities of behavioral assessment can be organized into three broad domains: (1) clarification of the behavior; (2) data collection; and (3) data evaluation. Chapter 3 provides clinicians with practical techniques designed to address each domain, facilitating comprehensive multidimensional behavioral assessment.

CLARIFICATION OF THE BEHAVIOR

In order to begin a behavioral assessment, the presenting problem must be clarified. This process necessitates a multidimensional interview, resulting in an operationally defined target behavior. Specific activities that aid in the formation of operational definitions are behavioral objectives and task analysis. Each clarification activity will be presented in detail.

Interviewing the Client Behaviorally

The initial interview with severely developmentally disabled clients and their families has two goals. The clinician must first gather detailed information about the target behavior and its determinants so that a multidimensional clinical picture emerges. This clinical description will include information about its unity, duration, interresponse time, latency, and topography (see Chapter 2). In addition, the relevant context in which the target behavior resides must be assessed in order to provide an understanding of operative environmental variables.

Several authors (Evans & Nelson, 1977; Ollendick & Cerney, 1981) have described procedures for conducting behavioral interviews with children and their parents, as well as important objectives for such interviews. When working with the severely developmentally disabled, the authors have found six objectives to be of primary importance. Taken together, they are designed to meet the goals of the initial interview. They are: (1) to establish rapport, (2) to clarify the reason for referral/presenting problem, (3) to assess the family's interactional style, especially as it relates to the reason for referral, (4) to obtain a social history, (5) to obtain a developmental history, and (6) to determine the family's readiness for change.

While the conventional use of the word "initial" refers to "the first," the probability is that one interview rarely will be enough time for clinicians to meet all six objectives. Thus, the "initial interview" is most accurately construed as the period of assessment commencing with the *first* visit for the *first* target behavior for which the client was referred. The initial interview is a time to collect information—stay descriptive. Later interviews will be conducted, and future assessments will doubtless take place. However, all will build upon the informational base established in these first few sessions.

Establishing Rapport

The development of a working relationship with the adults responsible for the client's welfare (parents, teachers, and child-care workers) is an essential first step to assessment and intervention. Without it, benign indifference or active sabotage well may hinder any kind of progress. Most people who work with severely developmentally disabled clients do so out of concern and interest. As such, their feelings of frustration about the presenting problem may need to be aired and acknowledged before moving too far into a description of the problem. Providing them this outlet will not only validate their experience, but it also will communicate to them that the consulting clinician is aware and respectful of the human factors in this difficult job.

In establishing rapport, clinicians must be sensitive to issues of loss and denial. If the client resides at home, have the parents accepted their child as one with a handicap? Have they come to terms with lost expectations of having a healthy child, and replaced these expectations with realistic ones for their child? Parents who are in a stage of denial about the severe condition of their child often "shop around" for an expert opinion that is more palatable—an opinion that says their child is less severely handicapped (Waterman, 1982). For such parents, a clinician's premature conclusion that their child has a serious problem may lead to their resistance in cooperating or early termination.

Finally, and as a note of caution, the quickest way to doom an assessment and/or intervention from the start is to imply that the parents/teacher/child-care worker *caused* the problem. Careful analysis of the presenting problem may in fact functionally relate the behavior of these persons to client behavior. However, a premature description of this relationship does little for the parent's/teacher's/child-care worker's feelings of self-efficacy to change the situation. These feelings are integral to the process of change and should be developed and protected.

Clarifying the Reason for Referral

The following list of questions is not intended to be inclusive, but rather descriptive of some of the important areas to assess.

- What are parental/adult concerns, and how do they label the problem? Why have they come in for assistance? Who was the referral source?
- When did the problem begin? Has it ever been better? Has it ever been worse? Why have they come in *now*?
- Is the problem specific to any one setting (school, home, and so on)?
- Does anyone with whom the client resides have similar problems?
- Ask all the members of the family for their perception of the problem, or how it affects them. Who is most affected by the problem?
- In what situations does this behavior occur (with whom, when, where)?
- When the problem behavior occurs how do family, teachers, and child-care workers respond? Does anyone respond differently?
- Describe the last time the behavior occurred.
- What remedies have they tried in the past?
- Is the client on any medications; which ones; for how long? Have medications been changed recently?
- Parent/adult perceptions:
  - What do *they* think is the reason the client has this problem?
  - What would be an acceptable level of the client's behavior?
- School personnel perceptions:
  - Are teachers aware of the problem?
  - If so, what has the school administration done to remedy the problem?
  - Are the parents satisfied or dissatisfied with the school's attempts to remedy the problem?

While it is important to be aware of the low validity and reliability of parental reports in situations such as these, the data so obtained *do* represent a clinically useful sample of behavior (Ollendick & Cerney, 1981).

Assessing the Family's Interactional Style

It is most useful to have the entire family present for the initial interview, including grandparents and other extended family members if they reside with the client. This objective is based upon the assumption that all who interact with the client affect the client's behavior in some way. Thus, their perceptions of the problem are integral. Moreover, they will doubtless be able to contribute to the solution of the presenting problem, enhancing generalization and maintenance.

When assessing a family's interactional style, it is important for clinicians to focus upon the ways that each member responds to the presenting problem. Patterns of over- or underinvolvement frequently occur, as do those of strictness and leniency. For example, a parent's guilt at having produced a handicapped child may lead to a more lenient approach in parenting that child. In some cases, older siblings may take responsibility for parenting their severely developmentally disabled brother or sister (Harris, 1982). In other cases, siblings may manifest regressive behavior (e.g., bedwetting, tantrumming) in order to shift the attention toward themselves and away from their handicapped brother or sister.

Finally, it is not uncommon to find one parent feeling pessimistic about the severely handicapped child's capabilities, while the other parent overcompensates with unrealistic optimism. Spouses may blame each other for failures in managing the child's behavior, or may displace the anger or frustration arising from their child's shortcomings onto each other or other children in the family. This latter point warrants elaboration. The anger exhibited by parents toward others (including teachers and clinicians) is frequently born of the pain of loss, added responsibility, and perceived future failures. Because of this, their anger will require careful handling with special effort toward validating its existence and appropriately labeling its source. Far from irrational, the natural parental response of anger in the face of raising a severely handicapped child requires acceptance and understanding from clinicians working with these families. Failure to "normalize" this anger often leads parents to feel guilty. This guilt then often leads to inconsistency in dealing with the child.

Obtaining a Social and Developmental History

As this can be a lengthy task, it is most expedient to provide the parents/caretakers with a social and developmental history form to fill out approximately one month before the initial interview. They are instructed to complete the form and return it by mail no later than one week prior to the interview. With the completed document in hand, clinicians can highlight areas to be assessed further during the interviews. The authors have found (the hard way) that providing a self-addressed, stamped envelope and stipulating that the interview cannot take place without the completed form have greatly facilitated parental compliance. Exhibit 3–1 notes some of the topics to be covered. A sample form for collecting a social and developmental history is provided in Appendix A.

Determining the Family's Readiness for Change

Change is almost always difficult. Except where unusually serious behaviors bring the family to the point of a crisis (e.g., severe self-injury, chronic rumina-

Exhibit 3–1 Social and Developmental Areas to be Screened

1. Demographics of the family
2. Problem clarification questions about the target client
3. Birth history of the target client
4. Early development of the target client
5. Recent development of the target client
6. Developmental milestones
7. Educational history of the target client
8. Current status of the target client
   8.1 Self-help
   8.2 Gross-motor
   8.3 Fine-motor
   8.4 Social
   8.5 Language
   8.6 Reading
   8.7 Writing
   8.8 Current activities
9. Behavioral checklist
10. Release of records form

tion), the natural homeostatic function of a family will allow it to "grow accustomed" to minor deviations in behavior by their severely developmentally disabled child. While perceived as "minor" and tolerated by family members, the behavior sometimes has major habilitative ramifications, as in the case of a 21-year-old autistic person who has not yet been taught to stay alone in the house while the parents run a brief errand. Families sometimes grow accustomed to and tolerate such behavior, but then seek professional assistance when the behavior precipitates a crisis. For this reason, an assessment of their readiness to change is needed.

A protocol for the assessment of a family's readiness for change has been developed by Davis and Salasin (1975). While originally created to assess an organization's readiness for change, this protocol—termed the AVICTORY model—provides a useful framework for assessing a family's readiness for change. Each letter in AVICTORY represents a dimension of readiness for change (Ability, Values, Idea, Circumstances, Timing, Obligation, Resistance, Yield). This model is intended to provide a heuristic framework for conceptualizing readiness for change and, as such, should not be followed slavishly. Rather, some of the eight dimensions may be more appropriate for a particular problem than others. Each dimension, and its relevance to the assessment of families of severely developmentally disabled clients, will be described.

Ability (A)

Ability refers to the availability of resources, and the ability or willingness to commit those resources to the change process. There are five resource groups, including human, technological, informational, financial, and physical resources. Each has an impact upon the change process and, depending upon availability, can hinder or promote the family's success with their severely developmentally disabled child.

Human resources are those persons in the family who are available and able to contribute to the change process. It is conceivable that a father's time with his autistic child might be compromised if he must work at two jobs in order to support the family. The responsibility for intervention frequently will fall on the mother, and perhaps some of the siblings. By assessing human resources in this family, the clinician will become aware of the mother's burnout risk and the need for flexibility in programming and/or emergency assistance from the father (Powers, 1984).

Technological resources refer to those specific programs to be implemented by the family. The clinician should determine the skill/knowledge base of the family with regard to behavioral change principles and procedures. For example, a family already trained in the use of behavior modification principles with their severely developmentally disabled child has more information and skill, and therefore a better base from which to learn new programs than does a family never before trained. Families new to the behavioral techniques of assessment and intervention will require an assessment of their entry-level skills. A training program to further develop those skills and teach new ones will then follow assessment. Prior knowledge of behavior modification principles is not a prerequisite to future success. With careful teaching, families with whom the authors have worked have been able to acquire the necessary skills for basic child management in a relatively brief time. An excellent training program for this purpose has been developed by Baker, Brightman, Heifetz, and Murphy (1976).

In short, technological resource assessment addresses the family's prior training experience, their specific skills, and the generalizability of those skills (Powers, 1984).

Informational resources refer to the policies and procedures to which family members adhere as they relate to the affected child's behavior. Of special importance are those policies and procedures that guide the behavior of the family or of individual members. Powers (1984) notes several of these policies, including "philosophical constraints on the use of punishment procedures; religious values; 'family rules'; issues of leniency, strictness, and overprotection; and the agreement or disagreement of the parents on these policies" (p. 4). For example, it is not uncommon to find parents who disagree as to the nature of punishment, sometimes resulting in one parent punishing more contingently than the other. This discrepancy may result in confusion and a less than desired reduction of the target behavior in the child. By becoming aware of this discrepancy prior to intervention, the clinician can solve and resolve the matter with the parents in order to benefit the child.

Financial resources are the funds available (or potentially available) for fees for service, insurance, needed equipment, and the like. By assessing this domain, the clinician can determine prior to intervention whether alternative funding sources are necessary to facilitate the intervention-related activities.

Physical resources are the facilities in which the activities of the intervention will take place. For example, if family counseling is warranted, will it occur in the clinic or in the home of the parents? Similarly, if intervention is to begin, will it take place only at home or at school as well? If time-out is part of the intervention package, the question might well be asked: Do school and home settings both have the necessary physical space for such an arrangement? If not, the intervention will require adjustment in order to accommodate the physical constraints imposed.

To summarize, Powers (1984) notes that the task of addressing a lack of family readiness from the perspective of ability may require a reallocation of the roles and responsibilities of individual family members, or additional funds and physical space. A consulting clinician may be required to remediate skill-deficit areas in the family. This clinician's role also may include assisting the family in adjusting to the many changes in family functioning frequently brought about by the reallocation of family roles and responsibilities.

Values (*V*)

Values refer to the compatibility of the proposed change (the proposed assessment and intervention plans) with the norms and philosophy of the family. The family values must be made explicit and accounted for before proceeding with either assessment or intervention efforts. For example, some families tolerate a good deal of chaotic behavior on the part of their members. For them, the imposition of a rigid structure for data collection may present too great a contrast to the prevailing family style. Because of this structure, the assessment and intervention effort may be doomed for lack of valid and reliable data. The assessment of values with such a family may lead to the development of intermediate goals for data collection, or to the brainstorming of alternative intervention strategies that more closely fit the family's values (Powers, 1984).

In order to address lack of readiness for change related to values, the clinician must spend time and effort in promoting positive attitudes toward the proposed changes. The family may require additional education about the rationale and implications of the proposed intervention, or may benefit from exposure to other families that have successfully intervened in a similar manner with their developmentally disabled child. Encouraging participation of the entire family when actually developing the assessment and intervention strategies may well promote family "ownership" of the change process itself, facilitating compliance, maintenance, and generalization (Powers, 1984).

Idea (*I*)

Powers (1984) notes that idea refers to the clarity of the need for intervention, as well as to the clarity of the proposed intervention itself. Hence, the assessment and intervention programs must be defined clearly before and during the presentation to the family. Moreover, aspects of change must be credible. The family should be convinced of the need for a programmatic response to the target behavior and of the usefulness of the particular assessment or intervention program being offered.

Clinicians can address deficiencies in this domain by clarifying the rationale, by citing prior research, and by anticipating the range of outcomes relating to the intervention, or by better describing the specific procedures to be used. Misunderstandings of the actual assessment or intervention method have been one of the most frequent reasons why families have difficulty with their roles as change agents. This important area of family assessment should not be minimized.

Other techniques for addressing problems within this domain include reviewing the efficacy of alternative approaches with the family or utilizing influential family members or those with close ties to the family to promote the idea. For example, a friend with a similarly afflicted child could be a valuable support to the family.

Circumstances (*C*)

Circumstances refer to those stable characteristics of the family that may support or impede change. For example, the marital relationship, the presence of another immediate family member with either a physical or mental disorder (e.g., alcoholism or depression), the relationships between parents and their other children, and the insularity of the mother (Wahler, 1980) all have an impact on family functioning. Harris and Powers (1984) have noted that the presence of a severely handicapped child may bring about stress-related dysfunctional behavior in an otherwise healthy family. Beyond these stressors, however, concurrent problems such as those mentioned above have been observed. In some cases, these problems may have existed before the birth of the severely handicapped child and were exacerbated by the additional stress (as in the case of an abusive parent). In others, the birth of the disabled child and the pressures of rearing such a child may lead to a more disabling mental disorder, such as depression. In either case, an awareness of relevant circumstances is necessary for planning assessment and intervention strategies (Powers, 1984).

The "tradition of flexibility" within the family is another important area to assess. The imposition of an assessment protocol will represent a change in family functioning, so an assessment of the family's historical ability to respond to new challenges will be crucial. In addition, information related to individual family member's flexibility in response to challenges, the process of conflict resolution (e.g., the father decides what the family will do), and the patterns of success and failure with regard to various types of problems will help the clinician tailor the change process to the special needs of the family.

Powers (1984) describes several remediation steps for problems in this area. Where mental illness is present or suspected, referral to an appropriate service provider may be appropriate. Marital discord may necessitate concurrent marital therapy. Dysfunctional family patterns may require therapeutic intervention with the entire family. In short, possible interventions for relationship problems extend from brief counseling to therapy to hospitalization. Clinicians not qualified to make such decisions must provide a referral to one so qualified.

Timing (*T*)

Timing refers to current or recent events in the family that may influence the acceptance of change. For example, the recent adoption of a new sibling would make a new and time-consuming assessment/intervention program extremely burdensome for a family, despite this family's level of motivation under less stressful circumstances. Other examples of timing variables that are likely to influence the family's readiness for change include a recent separation or divorce between the husband and wife, a death in the family, or a move to a new home or job.

Early implementation of the change process (assessment and/or intervention) or temporary postponement can remedy many problems related to timing. Where these options are not possible, the assessment or intervention can proceed with provision made for additional supports.

Obligation (*O*)

Obligation refers to the pressure or "felt need" to bring about change and thereby solve a problem. It is conceivable, for example, that a mother with maximum child-care responsibilities will perceive a greater need to reduce the daytime toileting accidents of the family's autistic child than her minimally involved husband will. The assessment and intervention plan, however, may require both parents to contribute time and effort. In such a family, the father's perception of the importance of change is essential information that has an impact on the potential ability of the family to implement a toilet-training program.

Deficiencies in this area require the clinician to enhance the discrepant family member's commitment to change. Discussion, clarification, and resolution of the differences in commitment of both parents, or the development of the contingencies relative to compliance with the assessment or intervention program, assist in achieving this goal (Powers, 1984).

Resistance (R)

The single greatest impediment to family change is resistance. Other AVICTORY variables all contain elements of resistant behavior; however, here the emphasis is on the family's expected or feared consequences of change.

Fear of expected consequences of change can follow from the prospect of the change process. It also can be due to the specific intervention program itself, or from a combination of the two. In addition, expectations of both overt and covert changes can lead to fear and resistance. For example, the parents of a severely developmentally disabled child may fear the escalation in face slapping that will result when they begin to systematically ignore that behavior in their child. They may elect not to carry out the assessment or intervention program consistently. The feared consequence in this case can lead to an overt change in the parent's behavior. Despite her diligent adherence to the intervention, however, the mother also may anticipate the negative reactions of strangers and their perceptions of her mothering abilities when she ignores her child's face slapping in public places. This resistance is based upon fear of the perceptions of others and represents a fear of covert change (Powers, 1984).

An assessment for resistance across subsystems that has an impact upon the family must be conducted by the clinician. For example, older siblings may not be invested in changing the tantrumming behavior of their severely retarded brother because they disagree with the use of ignoring techniques. Instead, they may prefer to attend to their brother quickly, plaintively asking him to stop. Grandparents, if involved closely with the family, may exert pressure to alter or deter an intervention to which they are opposed. In these cases, individuals with genuine concern for the well-being of the client may become "benevolent saboteurs" by greatly undermining the consistency needed for a successful behavioral intervention. The clinician's awareness of the propensity of individuals to act in this way facilitates intervention *before* assessment and intervention take place.

Several interventions for resistance exist. The clinician can explain anticipated treatment outcomes to the family in greater detail. A conversation with a parent who has used the intervention successfully can be provided as a "stop-gap" intervention to preclude the feared outcome. The change process also can be broken down into successive approximations of the original goal, allowing the family to pursue change and experience success in small, graduated steps (Powers, 1984).

Yield (*Y*)

The expected benefits or positive consequences of change that will accrue to family members, including the client, are referred to as yield. This dimension can be measured in concrete terms (e.g., a reduction in the number of eye pokes in school) or in more abstract terms (e.g., the likelihood of a more normalized existence for severely handicapped children who can toilet themselves).

We have found that, for many parents, a perceived sense of control over their own lives represents an important yield. Their lives have been controlled by the behavior of their severely handicapped child for a long time, and they wish to regain parental prerogatives through success with behavior management programs.

The clinician can address problems in this domain by promoting a realistic expectation of the positive consequences of change in the target behavior. In addition, a system of reinforcement (e.g., financial reward, additional training, and so on) can be developed and offered contingently to the parents as a part of the intervention itself. For example, a $100 retainer fee can be held in escrow and returned (in whole or in part) to the parents if they meet a previously agreed upon assessment or intervention goal. The goal could involve their completion of a 10-week parent training course with perfect attendance, or their successful collection of data for the week. In all cases, the yield must be reinforcing and attainable by family members.

Defining Behavior

Defining a behavior carefully and specifically can assist clinicians with many aspects of assessment and treatment (Dancer, Braukmann, Schumaker, Kirigin, Willner, & Wolf, 1978; Gelfand & Hartmann, 1980; Swanson & Watson, 1982). An attempt to specify exactly what a client does not only enhances communication between those involved in behavior change, but serves as a basis for continued evaluation of treatment (Baker et al., 1976; Gelfand & Hartmann, 1980). A behavioral description that facilitates systematic observation and measurement avoids the confusion that surrounds such terms as "laziness" or "aggressiveness." For example, by noting that a child does not respond to directions within 10 seconds of the request communicates the parameters of the behavior more effectively than by describing the child as lazy. Such a definition allows all individuals to agree about a particular behavior.

Guidelines for Defining Behavior

Examination of some of the current views on behavioral assessment reveals the following seven guidelines for defining behavior.

1. *A targeted behavior should be a priority in the behavioral repertoire of the client*. Comprehensive and systematic analysis can assist in the identification of those behaviors where further assessment or treatment is necessary (Walker & Shea, 1980). Simply stated, the need for assessment should be apparent prior to defining the behavior. For example, concern for a client's self-injury would probably precede a focus on self-help training.

2. *Definitions typically analyze behavior deficits, behavioral excesses, or stimulus control*. While professional concerns vary, behavioral definitions typically are focused on the goals of either increasing or eliminating certain behaviors or on the durability, generalization, or maintenance of a client's performance (Ellis, 1980; Gelfand & Hartmann, 1980).

3. *Definitions should be initially narrow in scope to focus on a limited range of behavior*. Usually, the more specific the definition, the more informative the measure can be (Walker & Shea, 1980). Often the process of redefining a behavior is necessary to narrow down a more complex behavior, such as certain forms of self-stimulation, in order to focus on more salient features. Initially, a client's self-stimulatory behavior can be defined to include all repetitive movements of a particular limb. As the frequency of the behavior decreases, a finer definition can be created to reflect more subtle movements.

4. *Definitions typically are concerned with the topography and/or the function of the behavior*. It often is useful to include in the definition any salient characteristics of the behavior or apparent function (Gelfand & Hartmann, 1980). For example, when defining a self-injurious act, it would be important to include the part of the body involved.

5. *Definitions should be valid and consistent with the concerns of caretakers and service providers*. Targeted behaviors should define the interest of significant persons in the life of the client (Johnson & Bolstad, 1973). Parents and guardians are important partners in the assessment process as are all professionals involved with the client.

6. *Definitions should include the characteristics of observability*. The behavioral definition is most useful when it facilitates systematic observation (Axelrod, 1977; Swanson & Watson, 1982). Terms that identify the specifics of the behavior or quantity of responses enhance the objectivity of the definition. For example, the following definition of a client's self-stimulatory behavior clarifies the body part, point of contact, and other salient features: two or more repetitive contacts of the hand(s) with an object or body part; a pause of two or more seconds constitutes the end of an episode.

7. *Definitions should be suitable for measurement and aid in the collection of reliable data*. The behavioral definition should set the stage for accurate measurement and consensus of occurrence (Allyon & Azrin, 1968; Gelfand & Hartmann, 1980). Considerations for the type of information required

(e.g., frequency or duration) will make data collection more precise. The preceding example makes provision for both the duration and frequency of the client's particular self-stimulation. Including the notion of a pause assists clinicians in determining when one instance of the behavior ends and another begins.

Behavioral Objectives

The behavioral or operational definition typically includes an objective definition of the behavior that emphasizes the conditions under which the behavior occurs (Walker & Shea, 1980). The addition of a mastery criterion establishes a behavioral objective from which to plan and evaluate learning (Swanson & Watson, 1982).

Mager's (1962) original description of the behavioral objective remains virtually unchanged. The behavioral objective describes a plan of action with an outcome in relation to a terminal behavior. The formulation of the objective is simplified by answers to the following questions:

- What observable behavior is desired?
- What are the conditions under which the behavior is to occur?
- Has a criterion been established?
- Is the measure reliable?

Answers to these questions will meet the three components of a behavioral objective: behavior, conditions, and criterion are described.

When constructing a behavioral objective, the desired or target behavior needs to be described. Clinicians thus indicate what clients will do (e.g., walk, write, eat, and so on). To add objectivity to the description, the condition(s) under which the behavior will occur or be performed must be included. For example, "reading from a book" or "using a clenched fist to hit a piece of furniture" are statements regarding the conditions of the behavior. Finally, mastery or performance criteria are established to indicate completion of the objective (e.g., 90% accuracy, 75% elimination). In the case of a shaping procedure where approximations of a target behavior are considered, relative mastery becomes an important concept. Exhibit 3–2 includes examples of behavioral objectives for various curricular areas.

A performance criterion sets the stage for evaluation of the program. A mastery criterion establishes a reference point from which to monitor the implementation of an objective. For example, if a client's behavior remains stable relative to baseline rates, an assessment of the program should be considered. The following

Exhibit 3–2 Examples of Behavioral Objectives

Management: The frequency of Sally's walking out of the classroom door during group work sessions will be decreased by 25% and will be maintained for 3 consecutive days.

Prespeech: Bill will establish eye contact with his teacher within 10 seconds of the verbal instruction, "Look at me," in 9 out of 10 daily trials, 2 days in a row.

Speech: Joe will imitate the words ball, fork, spoon, and hat within 10 seconds of the verbal instruction, "Joe, say _____," 100% of the time for 2 consecutive training sessions of 20 trials each.

Academic: Lisa will read the safety signs "stop" and "go" presented on the chalk board during morning group within 10 seconds of the instruction, "What is this word?" each day for 4 consecutive days with 100% accuracy.

Self-Help: After being instructed by his dad to "clear the table," Mike will place all dishes and utensils in the sink without prompts, within 10 minutes of the request each night for 1 week.

Prevocational: When presented with 10 cups and 10 spoons, Greg will sort correctly the items into two separate containers without reminders, within 5 minutes of the command, "Sort," for 2 trials in a row.

guidelines can be useful when attempting to identify problem areas in programming.

- Is the reward reinforcing?
- Is the reinforcement schedule too much or too little?
- Is the reward immediate?
- Are clients receiving rewards noncontingently during the day?
- Check measurement procedures; miscalculations or errors in charting may have been made.
- Make sure the measurement reflects the definition.
- Do clients have the prerequisite behaviors to the skill on which they are working?
- Is the program progressing in steps that are too large?
- Are the punishers effective?
- Make sure directions are given when clients are attending.
- Directions given repeatedly may confuse clients.
- Prompting may be ineffective.
- Have the prompts been faded successfully? If not, clients may have become dependent on prompts.

Task Analysis

Task analysis plays an important role in the assessment and education of severely developmentally disabled clients (Van Etten, Arkell, & Van Etten, 1980). The technique refers to the breaking down of complex instructional skills or behavior into component parts (Bijou, 1973; Gold, 1976). The resultant components provide a framework for precise skill analysis after which teaching can proceed according to systematic steps designed to facilitate task success (Gold, 1976).

The notion of task analysis grew from the assumption that a student's failure with a particular task is related, at least in part, to an inability to perform some prerequisite skill (Biggs, 1982). This emphasis on skill assessment provides a process for breaking learning tasks into subskills and sequencing them into an appropriate learning hierarchy. Task analysis facilitates a finer tuning of educational programming by analyzing goals or behaviors for their component parts and identifying more specific teaching objectives.

Williams (1975) suggests two methods for identifying the steps of a task analysis. One approach is to observe a student performing a task and to record each component behavior. Through observation, specific skills can be assessed to determine weaknesses in skill development (Resnick, Wang, & Kaplan, 1973). For a more precise analysis, Williams (1975) describes a "question-recording" technique where the clinician approaches each component behavior in terms of identifying the prerequisite skills. Then, each prerequisite skill is assessed in terms of subtasks. If, for example, dressing is the skill to be task analyzed, the first breakdown probably would include each item of clothing. The next level then would include an analysis of how to handle each item separately, such as putting shirt over head, placing arms through sleeves, and so on. A comprehensive task analysis would further break down each second-level component into necessary skills, such as grasping and pulling.

Two task analysis formats usually are discussed: vertical listing and lattice listing (Smith, Smith, & Edgar, 1976). In vertical listing, component behaviors are included in a single list. Lattice listing presents a breakdown according to analysis level. Using the dressing example, a lattice listing would first identify each item of clothing and then analyze each item according to prerequisite skills. Exhibit 3–3 compares vertical and lattice listing for the task analysis of dressing. Regardless of approach, it is important for clinicians to eliminate nonessential or redundant components in order to facilitate the most appropriate sequencing. With regard to sequencing, Haring (1982) distinguishes between a "natural" sequence and a "teaching" sequence and suggests that for many severely developmentally disabled clients, the developmental or natural progression is not always the most beneficial. Often more progress is facilitated by creating a skill sequence based on the individual needs of these clients.

Exhibit 3–3 Example of Vertical and Lattice Listing

Task Analysis: Dressing

I. Vertical
   A. Put on undergarments.
   B. Put on socks.
   C. Put on pants.
   D. Put on shirt.

II. Lattice
   A. Put on undergarments.
      1. Put on underpants.
         a) Grasp pants.
         b) Place each leg through pant holes.
         c) Pull up pants.
      2. Put on undershirt.
         a) Grasp shirt.
         b) Place arms through sleeve holes.
         c) Place over head.
         d) Pull down.
   B. Put on socks.
      1. Put on right sock.

DATA COLLECTION

Once a behavior is defined operationally, clinicians must collect data to determine its rate, frequency, or duration. Two activities must be undertaken in this regard. The behavior must be measured, and once collected, those data must be presented in such a way as to facilitate integration for treatment planning purposes. Each of these activities will be described. In addition, a popular method of collecting preliminary data for diagnostic or screening purposes—behavioral checklists—will be described and examples provided.

Measurement

Johnson and Bolstad (1973) suggest that empirical orientation is the behavior therapist's most important contribution to the field of human services. The behavioral approach is based on precise measurement and systematic observation and is dependent on accurate collection and interpretation of various forms of data (Dancer et al., 1978). Once a behavior or problem is defined, then consideration is given to accurate measurement. The following guidelines represent important issues to consider when planning strategies for measuring behavior.

Define the measurement environment. An important aspect of measurement concerns the situational characteristics of the behavior (Kazdin, 1979). Considerations might include the setting in which the behavior is observed, or the specific time of day a client engages in a particular act. It is useful to determine during what portion of the day the measurement will occur.

Select the measurement/observation technique. With the escalating demand for accountability within the behavioral sciences, observation techniques become increasingly important. Their use facilitates program evaluation by clinicians and consumers alike, and helps to pinpoint components of the intervention strategy that are in need of change. Three general observation techniques are available: automatic recording, permanent product recording, and observational recording.

Automatic Recording

Automatic recording is used when the behavior being measured occurs over an extended period of time, or when its occurrence is so minute that only continuous attention will reliably note its presence or absence. Automatic recording devices are activated by the behavior being measured and generate a frequency count and/ or duration measure of the target behavior. While more precise and requiring far less supervision than other recording techniques, automatic recording equipment is expensive and lacks the flexibility to measure many less discrete behaviors. Examples of automatic recording devices include the cumulative recorder (for recording response rate) and the event recorder (for recording both rate and duration of response).

Permanent Product Recording

Permanent product recording traditionally has referred to the compilation of records, such as scores on spelling or math tests, where the results (correct responses) are easily translatable into a numerical description for future reference and comparison. Because of such a traditional conceptualization, the use of permanent product recording with the severely developmentally disabled was restricted to a relatively small range of behaviors, particularly graphomotor responses. The recent advent of relatively inexpensive and highly portable video-taping equipment, however, has vastly expanded the use of permanent product recording with this population. It is now possible to make video recordings of chained sequences of behavior terminating in a specific action. Not only does this view present a "whole picture" perspective, but it also facilitates ongoing assessment of more complex behaviors, ones that would otherwise have to be broken down into component parts for the purposes of collecting reliable data. In addition, the use of audiotape and videotape facilitates the reanalysis of data and the measurement of interobserver reliability (Handleman & Harris, 1981), and provides for a multidimensional pre- and postanalysis of the client's behavior.

Checklists, such as the TARC assessment system (Sailor & Mix, 1975), the AAMD Adaptive Behavior Scales (American Association for Mental Deficiency, 1975), and the Behavior Rating Instrument for Autistic and other Atypical Children (BRIAAC) (Ruttenberg, Kalish, Wenar, & Wolf, 1977) also fall within the province of permanent product recording devices. While some of these instruments (e.g., TARC and BRIAAC) have established norms—albeit with small norming samples—they can be used ipsatively with a particular client. That is, those items passed or failed can be used to describe the individual being observed, without regard for the performance of other similarly handicapped persons. Such a use of these instruments greatly facilitates treatment planning.

Observational Recording

While both automatic and permanent product recording techniques allow post hoc scrutiny of a record of previously emitted behavior, observational recording involves the systematic observation of an individual's behavior by another person. While the use of video recording technically provides a permanent product, the efficacious use of such a recording usually involves one or more of the observational recording techniques described.

Continuous Recording. Continuous recording can take the form of continuous anecdotal or continuous event recording. As the name implies, continuous anecdotal recording requires observers to describe everything they observe during recording intervals. Because observers are able to describe numerous classes of behavior, this form is useful during the preliminary phases of assessment. The major disadvantage of this technique is the sheer magnitude of the task; it is nearly impossible to write down everything. Hence, reliability suffers because the data are often inaccurate.

Continuous event recording is somewhat more manageable, in that only one class of behavior is observed. Here, observers count each occurrence of the target behavior for the duration of their interactions with clients. Continuous event recording is particularly useful when generating a SORKC analysis during the assessment phase. The disadvantages for this technique parallel those for continuous anecdotal recording. For example, counting the number of eye pokes over the course of the entire school day will generate a frequency measure. Nelson (1982) and Zlutnick, Mayville, and Moffat (1975) provide examples of continuous event recording. When continuous event recording is warranted, it is most helpful to divide the entire day into 30-minute segments. By so doing, clinicians can identify periods during which high levels of the target behavior are emitted, thereby further narrowing the focus of assessments. Exhibit 3–4 provides an example of a data sheet for use with continuous event recording.

Event Recording. Observers using an event recording technique make a frequency count of the discrete occurrences of a target behavior within a pre-specified time period. A simple tally on a piece of paper or the use of a golf stroke counter worn on the wrist facilitate the use of this procedure. The major disadvantage is the absence of related information (when, where, for how long, what function did the behavior serve) for each occurrence of the target behavior.

Exhibit 3–4 Data Sheet for Continuous Event Recording

| Client _____ Date _____ |
| Clinician _____ |
| Target behavior　"Spitting at others" |

Time	Frequency	Totals
9:00– 9:30	///	3
9:30–10:00	//	2
10:00–10:30	/	1
10:30–11:00	/ / /	3
11:00–11:30	TTTT ////	9
11:30–12:00	TTTT TTTT //	12
12:00–12:30	TTTT //	7
12:30– 1:00	/	1
1:00– 1:30	//	2
1:30– 2:00		0
2:00– 2:30		0
2:30– 3:00	/	1
3:00– 3:30	/	1
3:30– 4:00	TTTT //	7

DAILY TOTAL:　49

Exhibit 3–5 provides a sample data sheet for event recording. Siegel (1982) provides an example of event recording.

Duration Recording. Whenever the amount of time spent emitting a particular behavior is important, duration recording is the appropriate procedure. While second hands on clocks and wrist watches may be used, a stopwatch provides far greater precision, facilitates reliability, and is preferable. An example may be useful here. A client who has tantrums warrants duration recording. The stopwatch would be started at the beginning of the tantrum, and stopped when the tantrumming has terminated. The duration measure, then, is the amount of time (in seconds) that the tantrumming lasts on one occasion. By totaling the duration measures for the entire day, the clinician can generate a measure of time spent each day in tantrumming. When using duration recording, it is helpful to establish an

Exhibit 3–5 Data Sheet for Event Recording

Client _____

Date _____ Clinician _____

Target behavior   "Spitting at others during lunchtime" _____

Time	Frequency
11:00–11:10	
11:11–11:20	
11:21–11:30	
11:31–11:40	
11:41–11:50	
11:51–12:00	
12:01–12:10	
12:11–12:20	
12:21–12:30	

Lunchtime TOTAL _____

interbehavioral interval (say, 3 seconds) to signal the offset of Episode 1 and the onset of Episode 2. Exhibit 3–6 provides an example of a client's episodes of screaming, where instances of screaming must be separated by a 3-second inter-behavior interval. The presence of a predetermined interbehavior interval helps the clinician to identify naturally occurring response phases, providing data on the intensity/severity of the behavior. Extending the example above, a tantrum lasting for 180 seconds may have different controlling variables than six episodes of tantrumming, each lasting 40 seconds or less. Whitman, Mercurio, and Caponigri (1970) provide an example of duration recording. A sample data sheet is shown in Exhibit 3–7.

Interval Recording. With this procedure, clinicians divide a predetermined period of time into equal, continuous intervals of a convenient length (e.g., 10 seconds) and note whether the target behavior was observed in all or part of each episode. For example, a 10-minute observation session can be divided into sixty 10-second intervals. The observer then continuously observes the client and notes, beginning with Interval 1 and ending with Interval 60, whether or not the target behavior was present. The total number of occurrences of the target behavior is then divided by the total number of intervals to yield a ratio representing the percent occurrence. Interval recording is especially useful with long, ongoing

Exhibit 3–6 Duration Recording to Measure Tantrumming

Client _____

Date _____   Clinician _____

Target behavior "Tantrumming during morning group lesson (8:30–9:00);
                 each occurrence is separated by 3 seconds of nontantrumming."

1.   4 seconds
2. 180 seconds
3. 30 seconds
4. 10 seconds
5. 17 seconds
6. 13 seconds
7. 20 seconds
8.   8 seconds

TOTAL duration of screaming: 4 minutes, 42 seconds (282 seconds)

classes of behavior lacking discrete endpoints. It will not, however, generate a frequency or duration measure. Murphy, Hutchinson, and Bailey (1983) and Schreibman, O'Neill, and Koegel (1983) provide examples of interval recording. An example of a data sheet for use with interval recording is provided in Figure 3–1.

Time Sampling: Variation I. Time sampling differs from interval recording in one respect: time sampling intervals are not continuous. Thus, the clinician who chooses to observe a client for 15 seconds, then looks away and records for 5 seconds (and does not attempt to score for any occurrence of the target behavior during the 5-second "record" phase) is engaging in time sampling. As with interval recording, the number of intervals scored divided by the total number of intervals yields a percentage of occurrence ratio. The advantage of this method over interval recording is in the allowance of "writing time" for the observer. The major disadvantage concerns the need for exclusive attention to the client being observed for the duration of the sample. The use of an audiotape, prerecorded to signal the "observe" intervals (e.g., Observe Interval 3) and the "record" intervals (e.g., Record Interval 3) facilitates the use of this procedure. In addition, numbering the intervals on the tape facilitates reliability by reorienting the observer or reliability checker in the event they are confused as to which interval should come next.

Time Sampling: Variation II. A somewhat more practical variation of the time sampling procedure allows the clinician to observe intensively for a small

Exhibit 3–7 Data Sheet for Duration Recording

Client _____ Date _____

Clinician _____

Target behavior _____

Duration of intertrial interval _____

	Duration of Behavior
1.	
2.	
3.	
4.	
5.	
6.	
7.	
8.	
9.	
10.	
•	
•	
x	

TOTAL duration of behavior _____

segment of the total observation period. For example, the clinician could spend 1 minute observing and 4 minutes not observing instances of self-injury (that is, 5-minute intervals) over a longer period of time, say 30 minutes. The number of occurrences of self-injury is then divided by 6 minutes (or the number of 1-minute intervals of observation during the 30-minute period) to generate a self-injury/minute ratio. Alternatively, the clinician could observe for 20 minutes twice a day.

Time Sampling: Variation III. For clinicians who are unable to devote a continuous block of time (10 seconds to 1 minute) to any one client, a "spot-check" procedure may prove to be more realistic. Here, the total observation period is again divided into equal intervals. Instead of observing for the entire interval, however, clinicians need only observe at the *end* of each interval for the target behavior in order to score an occurrence within that interval. Again, an

Figure 3–1 Data Sheet for Interval Recording

10-Second Intervals × 5 Minutes

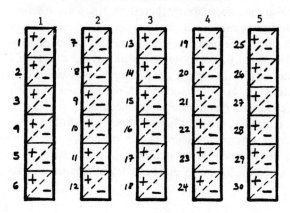

Instructions:

- Circle "+" if the behavior occurs during the interval.
- Circle "−" if the behavior does not occur within the interval.

---

audiotape prerecorded at the appropriate times with the word "observe" frees clinicians from the constraints of watching the clock or resetting a kitchen timer. As for interval recording, it is preferable to state the number of the observation interval with the cue word (e.g., "Observe 2") in order to prevent confusion resulting from a missed interval. Variations on this theme include a scanning procedure whereby several clients are observed at the cue for the occurrence or absence of the target behavior. Doke and Risley (1972) and Quilitch and Risley (1973) provide examples of the "spot-check" procedure.

Issues to Consider with Observation Methods

There are several issues that relate to and can affect client observation. Reactivity, observer bias, and observer drift can interfere with observation methods, sometimes influencing results obtained. While these issues may be more relevant to research efforts than to clinical concerns, awareness of their nature and effects may enhance understanding of observational techniques.

Originally conceptualized by Rosenthal (1969), observer bias refers to certain expectations or hypotheses individuals bring to the assessment situation that ultimately can affect results. This issue has been studied and cautions have been suggested regarding the information given to observers that could potentially bias the outcome of their observations (Azrin, Holz, Ulrich, & Goldiamond, 1961; Ciminero & Drabman, 1977; Haynes, 1978; House, 1980; O'Leary, Kent, & Kanowitz, 1975; Romanczyk, Kent, Diament, & O'Leary, 1973). The presence of an observer also can affect assessment results. Known as reactivity to observation, this phenomenon can cause clients to act or react in unusual ways that are not consistent with current performance (Haynes, 1978; Nelson, Kapust, & Dorsey, 1978). In addition, when pairs of observers work together over time, observer drift can result in a decrease in the accuracy of measurement (Johnson & Bolstad, 1973; Lipinski & Nelson, 1974). For the observer working alone, drift can occur when observation is conducted on an infrequent schedule.

Concern for reactivity, observer bias, and observer drift heightens the importance of observer training. Ensuring that observers are trained well, are accustomed to the observation environment, and are naive regarding specific predictions can increase the purity and accuracy of assessment results.

Reliability

In behavioral assessment, it is not sufficient to make frequent observations of a target behavior; the target behavior must be consistently observed and scored. Reliability is the term used to describe agreement between two or more observers that a behavior has or has not occurred. In order to determine the degree of consistency, procedures for estimating reliability have been developed. Kazdin (1980) describes such procedures for use with frequency, duration, and interval data in detail. These procedures will be described briefly.

The calculation of interobserver reliability with frequency measurement requires that both coder and reliability checker observe the target behavior simultaneously. In addition, each observer must be unaware of the other's responses. At the conclusion of the observation session, the smaller frequency is divided by the larger frequency and the result is multiplied by 100 in order to determine a reliability coefficient. For example, while observing instances of a client ear jabbing over a 30-minute observation period, Observer 1 records 11 instances of the behavior, and Observer 2 records 12. Dividing the smaller frequency by the larger one ($11 \div 12 = 0.92$) and multiplying it by 100 yields a reliability coefficient of 92%.

For duration data, both observers view the same session, each recording the duration of the target behavior. As with frequency measures noted above, reliability is determined by dividing the smaller duration by the larger duration and multiplying by 100. Thus, in a 10-minute observation session, Observer 1 might observe a client exhibiting a 4-minute tantrum, while Observer 2 notes 3.5 minutes of this behavior. These durations of tantrumming can be transformed into seconds to make the determination of interrater reliability easier. In this way, 210 seconds is divided by 240 seconds, and multiplied by 100 for a reliability measure of 81%.

Interval methods of assessment require a somewhat different procedure, termed the agreement/disagreement method of calculating interobserver reliability. Using this method, clinicians divide the total number of intervals in which *both* observers agreed that the behavior was occurring by the number of agreements plus the number of disagreements. This ratio is then multiplied by 100 to yield a reliability coefficient. For example, in Figure 3–2 both observers agree that the target behavior occurred six times. The observers disagreed once. Therefore, agreements divided by agreements plus disagreements times 100 equals 85.7%. It is important to note that intervals during which neither observer recorded the occurrence of the target behavior are not included when calculating reliability using this method (Kazdin, 1980).

Figure 3–2 Method for Calculating Interrater Reliability for Interval Data

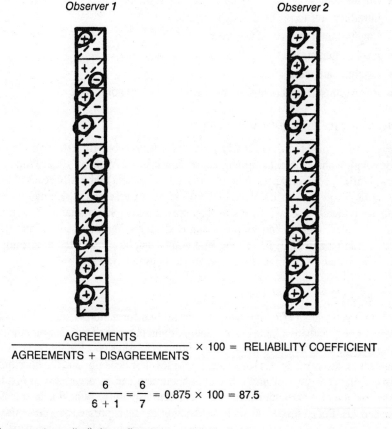

Observer 1   *Observer 2*

$$\frac{\text{AGREEMENTS}}{\text{AGREEMENTS} + \text{DISAGREEMENTS}} \times 100 = \text{RELIABILITY COEFFICIENT}$$

$$\frac{6}{6 + 1} = \frac{6}{7} = 0.875 \times 100 = 87.5$$

Agreements are " + " signs; disagreements are " – " signs.

The agreement/disagreement method of calculating interobserver reliability also can be used with time sampling, Variation I. Variation II would require a different method, however. For Variation II, the clinician would obtain the ratios generated by the observer and the reliability rater, and divide the smaller ratio by the larger ratio to determine a rough measure of reliability. Variation III, the spot check, warrants a point-by-point comparison with the ensuing agreements and disagreements made subject to the agree/disagree method utilized with Variation I.

Training Observers. The measure that is selected will determine both the number of observers required and the amount of prior experience needed by the observers. In addition, the amount of observer training needed before assessment can begin will depend on the complexity of the task. Gelfand and Hartmann (1980) suggest the following guidelines for observation:

- Obtain consent.
- Introduce self to professionals in charge.
- Conduct unobtrusive observations.
- Avoid interactions.
- Disguise interests.
- Accustom self to the environment prior to observation.

Determining the Type of Data Presentation

Presenting collected data clearly provides a framework for effective clinical interpretation and efficient communication (Swanson & Watson, 1982; Walker & Shea, 1980). Accurately presented records are permanent and easily accessible to the various professionals involved in interdisciplinary assessment. Human service agencies typically use two forms of data presentation. Summarizing data in the form of tables, charts, and graphs visually displays important information for quick scanning and analysis. Tables and graphs can be constructed according to particular variables or dimensions specific to interpretation.

Presenting Observational Measures

Graphs provide an effective way of presenting information visually. By using either commercially available graph paper or clinician-made forms, clinicians can construct graphs to display the data in a multitude of ways (see Figure 3–3). After establishing the vertical axis (ordinate) as the level of behavior and the horizontal axis (abscissa) as time or any other unit, the graph can be organized to display varied ranges of a particular behavior, or it can display the behavior in selected time periods. For example, the level of behavior can be expressed as a percentage, or it can be reflective of relative frequency or duration. In addition, more than one behavior can be presented on a single graph to assist in comparing complex data. For example, the upper graph in Figure 3–3 displays two behaviors along the same ordinate and abscissa, whereas the lower graph in Figure 3–3 utilizes only the same abscissa as in the case of a multiple baseline. Changing a criterion or a particular step in programming also can be indicated by a broken vertical line drawn through the data where the change occurred.

Tables and charts provide additional ways to organize and present various types of data. Whether a listing of means (averages) or a ranking of scores, these techniques can summarize data efficiently in situations where clear relationships between data points are not necessary. Tables and charts also can be useful in the initial stages of interpretation where the data can be presented quickly for analysis and eventual organization into a graph.

Behavioral Checklists

Diagnostic checklists serve a useful function in the behavioral assessment of severe developmental disabilities. They help to focus both parents and teachers on specific behavioral excesses and deficits, thereby assisting in the determination of target behaviors (Novick, Rosenfeld, Bloch, & Dawson, 1966). In addition, checklists provide potentially useful information about response clusters, helping clinicians to identify behaviors that co-vary with the target behavior (Ollendick & Cerney, 1981).

When considering a particular diagnostic checklist for use as an assessment method, several criteria should be addressed. For example, reliability data, or the extent to which raters administering the scale at different times agree on the measures obtained from the checklist, can be misleading at times. Reliability computed on the basis of total scores invariably will be greater than point-by-point reliability measures. As a result, a reliable estimate of *total* deviance may be obtained from a checklist, while the reliable identification of *specific* target behaviors is lacking (Ciminero & Drabman, 1977).

The validity of the checklist also must be considered. Validity refers to the ability of a checklist to measure what it purports to measure. For example, a checklist designed to measure degree of autistic behavior must successfully discriminate between autistic and nonautistic subjects. The validity of many rating scales has been established by comparing their results in use with deviant clinical populations with results in use with normal populations, rather than by demonstrating predictive validity (Ciminero & Drabman, 1977). This latter form of validity is of importance because it allows the clinician to predict response to treatment (Kent & O'Leary, 1976; Ollendick & Cerney, 1981). More work in the area of predictive validity of checklists is needed if this assessment method is to realize its potential with severely developmentally disabled clients.

The provision of normative data is an important criterion for a checklist (Ciminero & Drabman, 1977). The sample population should include norms for both

Figure 3–3 Examples of Graphs

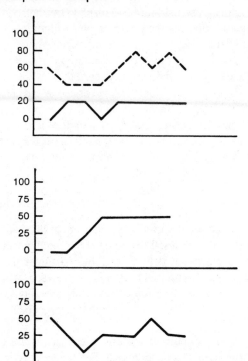

sexes across several age groups. While many scales have established norms (e.g., the TARC Assessment System; Sailor & Mix, 1975), others do not. For this latter group, all data obtained must be interpreted ipsatively. That is, once the presence or absence of a behavior is noted, clients can only be compared to themselves. Decisions regarding which behaviors to increase or decrease would then be based upon the values and philosophical position of the clinician and/or agency, in combination with the functional needs of their clients.

Finally, checklists should provide data on a continuum of behavior, from appropriate to inappropriate. In so doing, behavioral excesses, deficits, and skills will be identified, providing a more comprehensive view of client functioning (Ross, 1963; Ciminero & Drabman, 1977).

There are presently a number of checklists available for use with severely developmentally disabled clients. Exhibit 3–8 lists some of these checklists. These checklists sample from a broad array of behavioral excesses, deficits, and skills in severely developmentally disabled children, and as such, they are a

Exhibit 3–8 Behavioral Checklists

---

1. *Behavior Observation Scale* (Freeman, Ritvo, Guthrie, Schroth, & Ball, 1978)
2. *AAMD Adaptive Behavior Scale* (Nihira, Foster, Shellhaas, & Leland, 1974)
3. *TARC Assessment System* (Sailor & Mix, 1975)
4. *Behavior Rating Scale for Autistic and other Atypical Children* (Ruttenberg, Kalish, Wenar, & Wolf, 1977)
5. *Children's Handicaps, Behavior, and Skills Structured Interview Schedule* (Wing & Gould, 1978)
6. *Childhood Autism Rating Scale* (Schopler, Reichler, DeVellis, & Daly, 1980)
7. *Autism Screening Instrument for Educational Planning* (Krug, Arick, & Almond, 1980)
8. *Psychoeducational Profile of the Individualized Assessment and Treatment for Autistic and Developmentally Disabled Children program* (Schopler & Reichler, 1979)
9. *Vineland Adaptive Behavior Scales* (Sparrow, Balla, & Cicchetti, 1984)

---

welcome addition to the behavioral assessment enterprise. Two of these measures will be presented in detail. Both incorporate numerous important dimensions presented in this chapter.

Childhood Autism Rating Scale. The Childhood Autism Rating Scale (CARS) (Schopler et al., 1980) is the product of more than 10 years of research by Eric Schopler and his colleagues at the University of North Carolina's statewide division for the Treatment and Education of Autistic and Related Communication Handicapped Children (TEACCH project). Formerly referred to as the Childhood Psychosis Rating Scale, the CARS is designed to discriminate two groups of autistic children (mild to moderately autistic and severely autistic) from other developmentally disabled children.

Administration and scoring: The CARS is administered by a rater observing a testing session conducted by a colleague. At the conclusion of the testing session, the rater scores the child based on the observations of the child during the session. Thus, the CARS does not require interval or time-sampling methods of data collection.

Each of the 15 scales is scored on a continuum extending from normal behavior to severely abnormal behavior. Moreover, the clinician considers the child's age when arriving at a rating, acknowledging age-appropriate developmental differences. Behavior within normal limits (adjusting for age) receives a score of 1. Mildly abnormal behavior is scored 2, while moderately abnormal behavior receives a score of 3. Severely abnormal behavior receives a score of 4. Midpoint ratings (1.5, 2.5, 3.5) are acceptable for questionable situations. The score for a client who is administered the CARS will range from 15 to 60.

Areas assessed: There are 15 scales (Schopler et al., 1980) on the CARS including:

1. Impairment in human relationships
2. Imitation
3. Inappropriate affect
4. Bizarre use of body movement and persistence of stereotypes
5. Peculiarities in relating to nonhuman objects
6. Resistance to environmental change
7. Peculiarities of visual responsiveness
8. Peculiarities of auditory responsiveness
9. Near-receptor responsiveness
10. Anxiety reaction
11. Verbal communication
12. Nonverbal communication
13. Activity level
14. Intellectual functioning
15. General impressions

Normative sample: Five hundred and thirty-seven children referred to the University of North Carolina's TEACCH programs over a 10-year period served as the sample. As in the developmentally disabled population in general, males in the sample outnumbered females three to one. Eleven percent of the children in the sample were 10 years of age or older; 34% were aged 6 through 10.9 years; and 55% were less than 6 years of age (Schopler et al., 1980). Because the vast majority of these subjects were under 11 years of age, the utility of this scale is limited to younger developmentally disabled children.

Reliability: Measures of both total score and interrater reliability were reported. A reliability coefficient alpha of .94 was obtained, indicating a degree of internal consistency that is quite high. In addition, interrater reliability was reported for 280 children, ranging from .55 (for intellectual functioning) to .93 (for human relatedness). The average interrater reliability across all scales was .71. In all cases, interrater reliability coefficients were significant at the .0001 level (Schopler et al., 1980).

Validity: Two measures of validity were reported. Total CARS scores were compared with clinicians' ratings of psychosis obtained independently at the same evaluation session. A correlation of .84 ($p < .001$) was obtained, indicating a highly significant relationship between these two independent measures. In addition, the total CARS scores correlated highly significantly ($r = .80, p < .001$) with independent clinical assessments made by a child psychiatrist and child psychologist (Schopler et al., 1980).

Summary: The CARS is an instrument based on direct behavioral observations of the client; thus, prior competence in its use is necessary. It is useful for obtaining a descriptive summary of a client's behavior, but is restricted in terms of the age of the client. Reliability and validity of the CARS are quite good for those ages, but extrapolations upward warrant caution. Particular strengths of this checklist include the attention given to developmental factors and the applicability of the CARS to research, as well as the empirical basis for the inclusion of many of the individual scales.

TARC Assessment System. The TARC Assessment System (Sailor & Mix, 1975) is a short behavioral assessment checklist designed for use with severely handicapped clients. In stressing observable behavioral characteristics, this rating scale provides an index of the current level of functioning across several domains. The TARC Assessment System can be used to provide an educational assessment on which to base general instructional goals and precise instructional objectives, to assess the effect of a particular intervention on client behavior, or to demonstrate progress over time through the use of repeated testings. Because it is based upon the assessment of a narrow sample of behavior, the TARC Assessment System is not a substitute for comprehensive assessment where such an assessment is warranted (Sailor & Mix, 1975).

Administration and Scoring: The TARC is administered by a rater who knows the client, meaning that the rater has observed the client for at least three weeks in a group or class setting. The rater is instructed to make no assumptions or inferences; behaviors not observed should be programmed for by means of a task designed to elicit the behavior in question.

Scoring is accomplished by choosing from one of several scaled scores for each item or by identifying subskills that apply in a given category. For example, 1.1 under Self-Help Skills addresses toileting behavior, specifically soiling. There are five scaled scores ranging from soils pants more than two times per day to never soils pants. In contrast, large muscle coordination (Motor Skills, 2.2) is a categorical item. Here the assessor must identify all large muscle skills that the client demonstrates (e.g., walking, climbing, splashing in the pool safely, and so on).

Scores obtained include item scores, subsection totals, and section totals. A maximum raw score of 194 is possible. Once calculated, these scores are entered onto the profile sheet, designed to provide a graphic representation of the client's strengths and weaknesses.

Areas assessed: There are four major skill areas assessed, with several subskills subsumed under each (Sailor & Mix, 1975).

1. Self-Help Skills
    1.1 Toileting
    1.2 Washing

    1.3 Eating

    1.4 Clothing management

2. Motor Skills

    2.1 Small muscle coordination

    2.2 Large muscle coordination

    2.3 Preacademic skills

3. Communication Skills

    3.1 Receptive speech

    3.2 Expressive speech

    3.3 Preacademic communication skills

4. Social Skills

    4.1 Observed behavior

        4.11 In a group

        4.12 Individual

        4.13 Following directions

        4.14 Interactions with adults

        4.15 Interactions with peers

        4.16 Cooperation in a group

        4.17 Emotional controls

    4.2 Preacademic skills

Normative sample: Two hundred and eighty-three severely handicapped clients were included in the sample. All were associated with the Topeka (Kansas) Association for Retarded Citizens (hence the acronym TARC). Clients ranged in age from 3 to 16 years; both males and females were represented. Neither age groupings of clients nor the proportion of males to females was reported. The primary diagnosis of children in the sample was mental retardation, although there were subgroups of autistic, perceptually handicapped, learning disabled, and cerebral palsied children. All children were functionally retarded in the moderate to profound range. Data related to living arrangements of the clients in the sample (e.g., institutions, group homes, residing with natural family) were not provided.

Reliability: Interrater reliability measures were obtained on 50 severely retarded institutionalized clients and 16 severely retarded clients attending day-care facilities. While the total reliability score was quite high ($.85, p < .01$), the reliability scores for individual subsections were lower, but still adequate (Social: $.78, p < .01$; Communication: $.77, p < .01$; Motor: $.63, p < .01$; Self-Help: $.59, p < .01$). Test-retest reliability with the same sample yielded a reliability coefficient of .80 (Sailor & Mix, 1975).

Validity: Validity data for the TARC Assessment System were not reported in the manual.

Summary: The TARC Assessment System represents an attempt to provide a statement of the behavior of severely handicapped clients across four functional domains. It is based on direct behavioral observation and provides operational definitions of the behaviors to be assessed within each area. While somewhat limited by a restricted range of clients and a lack of reported validity data, the TARC Assessment System nonetheless represents an important addition to the repertoire of the clinician assessing severely developmentally disabled clients behaviorally.

DATA EVALUATION

Ongoing evaluation of program data is one of the hallmarks of behavioral assessment. As noted in Chapter 2, the single-subject design is the evaluation method of choice in behavioral assessment (Hersen & Barlow, 1976). The advantages and liabilities of these designs are described.

Single-Subject Designs for Data Evaluation

One of the most commonly used single-case designs is the *AB design*. Using this design, clinicians obtain repeated measures of target behaviors during the baseline (A) phase, and continue to measure those same target behaviors during the treatment (B) phase. The change between baseline and treatment is then assessed. Figure 3–4 provides an example of an AB design. As can be seen in Figure 3–4, tantrumming behavior occurred at high rates during the baseline phase (A), but decreased over the course of the treatment phase (B) to zero.

The AB design is among the easiest of the evaluation designs to carry out and offers more objectivity than uncontrolled case studies. It has the most utility for classroom teachers and clinicians for whom circumstances (large class size, too few aides, and so on) prevent an investment of time and effort in evaluation. It is not without its limitations, however. Because it does not control well for internal validity, the treatment results obtained may be due to maturation of the client, other incidental learning, or the mere passage of time (see Hersen & Barlow, 1976, or Campbell & Stanley, 1966, for explanation of additional threats to internal validity). For many teachers and clinicians, these limitations present few problems; they are concerned with increasing or decreasing a given behavior and will take the results from wherever they come. Such a stance is less problematic for the single client. The utilization of this same treatment with another client, however, implies an expectation of future success that is based upon a past success. With the AB design, such predictions may not be warranted, and caution is urged. Refer to Eisler and Hersen (1973), Harbert, Barlow, Hersen, and Austin (1974) and Powers and Thorwarth (1983) for examples of AB designs.

A more sophisticated single-case design with greater internal validity is the *reversal or withdrawal design*, represented as ABAB. With this design, clinicians

Figure 3–4 AB Design

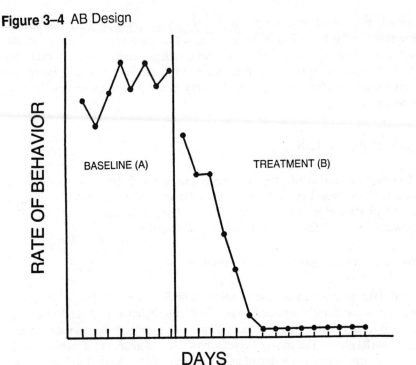

first measure the baseline rate (A) of the target behavior. The baseline then must be allowed time either to stabilize or to demonstrate consistent variability. This generally does not occur in less than five observation days. Stabilization of the baseline is important because it might be unnecessary (and unethical) to intervene to decrease a behavior that is already on a downward trend without treatment.

Once the baseline has stabilized, treatment (B) is introduced. Measurement of the target behavior continues. When change occurs and continues for several days, there is a withdrawal of treatment and a reversal to baseline (A) again. At the completion of this baseline phase, the treatment (B) is reintroduced. To summarize: (1) obtain a baseline, (2) institute treatment, (3) withdraw treatment and revert to baseline, and (4) reinstitute treatment. Figure 3–5 provides an example of a reversal design. In this illustration, a high rate of self-stimulation was observed in the first baseline phase (A_1). Treatment (B_1) quickly reduced the target behavior, only to have it increase to near-pretreatment levels when the second baseline was instituted (A_2). A return to treatment (B_2) decreased self-stimulation again.

The advantages of the ABAB design center around substantially reduced threats to internal validity, with resulting greater and more generalizable statements of effect. However, many clinicians have practical concerns about reversing an

Figure 3–5 Reversal or Withdrawal Design

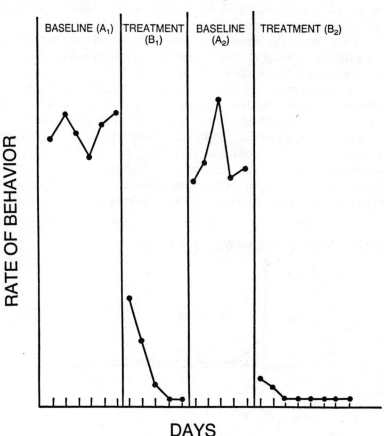

effective treatment, as well as questions about the ethics of such a decision. Reversal designs have important use in certain research situations. Because these designs remove an intervention of demonstrated effectiveness, however, little use can be seen for a reversal design in a clinical treatment situation where a research protocol is not in operation. Multiple baseline designs provide an adequate degree of experimental control and are more appropriate in cases where a formal research program is not in effect. In all cases, use of a reversal design must be based upon an assessment of the risk/benefit ratio for each client and should not be undertaken blindly or as a matter of course.

The *multiple baseline design* addresses many of the pragmatic and ethical concerns of the reversal design. Here, clinicians implement the same treatment at different points in time (1) with different clients, (2) with different behaviors, or

(3) in different settings. The multiple baseline design resembles several AB designs implemented consecutively. In each case, internal validity is not threatened provided that change from baseline (A) occurs when treatment (B) is begun, and not before. When this occurs, clinicians can state with some certainty that improvement was the result of the treatment. Each of the three variations of the multiple baseline will be discussed in detail.

Clinicians may attempt to verify the effectiveness of a particular intervention on the behavior of two or more clients. For such a case, a *multiple baseline across subjects* would be warranted. Here, the baseline rate (A) of the target behavior is measured for all clients under consideration. Once a stable baseline is obtained, the treatment (B) is implemented for *one* client only, and the effects are measured. Measurement of the baseline rate is continued for all other clients. After a period of time (generally four to six days), the treatment program is initiated with the second client, then the third, and so on. Figure 3–6 provides an example of this design. In

Figure 3–6 Multiple Baseline Across Subjects

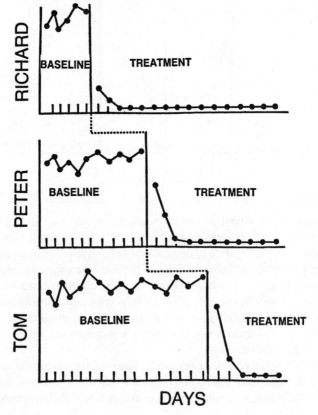

this example, out-of-seat behavior decreased for each client as soon as the treatment was begun for that client. The effectiveness of the intervention in reducing out-of-seat behavior was thus established.

Advantages of this variation include cost effectiveness and the increased ability of clinicians to pinpoint effective intervention techniques. Disadvantages center on the effects of vicarious learning and modeling, whereby clients still in the baseline phase alter their behavior as a function of their peers' change in responding. These effects, while not necessarily undesirable, contaminate the data and make causal statements more tentative. In cases where the focus is solely clinical (and not research), this disadvantage is of relatively little concern.

When a particular client interacts in several settings (e.g., school, home, practical arts, and woodworking areas of an adult activities center), clinicians might be interested in measuring the effect of an intervention in one setting on the client's behavior in other settings. For this purpose, a *multiple baseline across settings* is used. Here, clinicians obtain baseline measures of the target behavior in two or more discrete settings. Then, as in the multiple baseline across subjects, treatment is begun in one setting while baseline continues in the others. Measurement, of course, is ongoing. The treatment program then can be initiated successively in the other settings and the behavioral effects observed. While this variation increases clinicians' abilities to specify causes of behavior change, there are limitations due to generalization effects. For example, clients may alter their behavior in the other nontreatment settings as soon as treatment is begun in one setting. This occasionally happens even after the presence of a stable baseline. Clinically speaking, such generalization is hoped for, even though it makes precise specification difficult. Figure 3–7 illustrates a multiple baseline design across settings.

The last variation to be discussed is the *multiple baseline across behaviors*. With this design, it is possible to assess systematically the effect of an intervention upon several target behaviors in one client. With slight variation, clinicians can observe the changes in several targets across several clients as well. In the case with one client and several target behaviors, clinicians would employ a multiple baseline across behaviors. Clinicians must first operationally define each target behavior. Once the behaviors have been defined, baseline measures are obtained for each one. Treatment is then begun on one of the target behaviors while baseline continues across the others. Eventually, the treatment is introduced for each behavior in succession and the effects noted. Figure 3–8 provides an example of the use of a multiple baseline across behaviors. As can be seen, a program that successfully increased object identification had no effect on rate of eye contact. When an intervention to train eye contact was begun, eye contact increased.

It is particularly important to pay attention to response classes when using a multiple baseline design across behaviors. Response classes refer to two or more behaviors that clients may emit in response to particular stimulus conditions. The

Figure 3–7 Multiple Baseline Across Settings

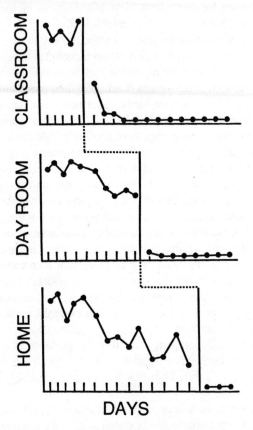

behaviors are said to be members of the same response class. For example, rocking and finger flicking may be part of the same response class, indicating their co-varying relationship to each other. A treatment program designed to reduce one of them would be likely to affect the other as well in a systematic manner. The nature of the effect could be either an increase or a decrease. For clinicians attempting to use rocking as a baseline against which to compare finger flicking, the resulting covariance hopelessly confounds the results. As a result, it would be very difficult to interpret the effects of the treatment per se. The selection of target behaviors that are at the least topographically dissimilar as well as situationally unrelated represents an appropriate first step to prevent against the unwanted effects of response covariation. However, knowing that particular behaviors are members of the same response class (and thus co-vary) is important information for later treatment efforts and should not be discarded.

Figure 3–8 Multiple Baseline Across Behaviors

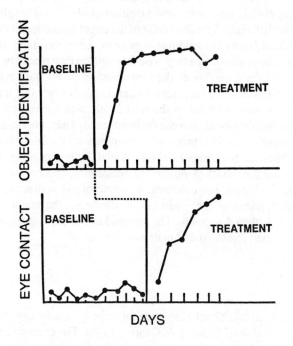

DAYS

The advantages of this design are similar to those noted for other multiple baseline variations. Disadvantages center on the issue of response covariation mentioned above. One solution to this problem has been proposed by Hersen and Barlow (1976). These authors suggest that clinicians should systematically monitor concurrent, nonproblematic behaviors in order to assess response generalization. These data would be useful for future program planning. Sajwaj, Twardosz, and Burke (1972) add that such an assessment is particularly important if negative side effects of treatment are anticipated. For example, Evans (1982) described the effects of a program designed to decrease walking on all fours by a severely developmentally disabled girl. Unbeknownst to the clinicians, walking on all fours and vocalization were part of the same response class. That is, this child would only vocalize when she was also walking on all fours. When the walking behavior was reduced, her vocalizations disappeared. As increasing the rate of spontaneous vocalizations is often a valued goal for many developmentally disabled clients, anticipation and prevention of this negative outcome would be important. Evans' (1982) careful assessment of concurrent behaviors made this issue explicit and opened the way for more sophisticated assessment.

The *changing criterion design* is useful when assessing client responses to tasks that increase in difficulty over time. As a result, this design has particular value when assessing social, academic, and language skills. The changing criterion design begins with the initial measurement of the target behavior and the establishment of an ultimate level of functioning to be achieved by the client. Intermediate criteria (levels to be achieved in a step-wise fashion) are then placed between these two extremes. Training begins at the first criterion level, with reinforcement provided to clients whenever they achieve the criterion. Once this initial level is mastered, the criterion is raised to the next level, with subsequent reinforcers provided only when the *new* criterion level is achieved. Thus, previously mastered criteria are not reinforced. This procedure continues until the final, target response (the ultimate criterion) is mastered and maintained. Failure at any given criterion necessitates "dropping back a notch" to reestablish mastery before moving forward again. As Figure 3–9 indicates, 1 second of eye contact was the initial criterion level required of the client. Once mastered, the client advanced to 2 seconds, then 3, then 4 seconds. The terminal target behavior of 5 seconds of eye contact was then mastered and maintained.

Probes

Probes provide an additional evaluative measure by briefly sampling behavior under selected conditions (Haring & Gentry, 1976). For example, in assessing whether a particular behavior has generalized or has been maintained, a probe can offer a quick test of these and other variables.

A carefully constructed probe can yield accurate information. One important consideration in constructing probes concerns the relationship between instructional and probe materials. Carefully noting similarities and differences between stimuli can facilitate measurement. Also, the fewer confounds present in probe materials, the more easily the results can be interpreted. For example, if both the graphic style and medium of a picture varied from the teaching stimuli, it could be difficult to assess generalization.

Other considerations for designing effective probes include the amount of exposure to probe materials and the schedule and type of reinforcement. Probes should provide a sufficient quantity of information to evaluate the consistency of responding. If stimuli were only presented one time, it would be hard to determine the stability of a particular response. Also, probe results obtained one day could vary from the next day's performance. Provision should be made to assess the durability of responding. Guess and Baer (1973) suggest that probes conducted in the complete absence of contingent reinforcement might result in an extinction condition as evidenced by inconsistent and diminishing performance. While the

Figure 3–9 Changing Criterion Design

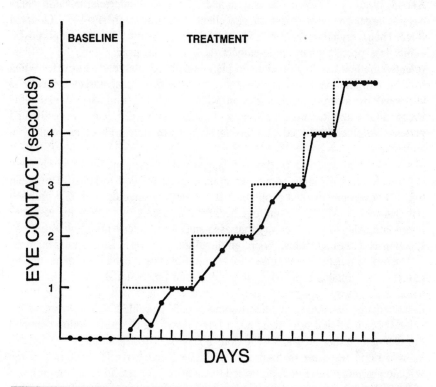

choice of appropriate schedule is not clear (Handleman, Powers, & Harris, 1984), this issue is important to consider when interpreting probe results.

Problem Oriented Record

The single-subject designs attempt to establish a cause-effect relationship between the target behavior and the intervention technique. Some of these designs (e.g., the multiple baseline design) are capable of describing the relationships between an intervention and several target behaviors at once. Keeping track of response interrelationships becomes an unwieldy task, however, when four or more target behaviors exist for a single client. In such cases, it is sometimes necessary for clinicians to sacrifice precision in order to organize data that will help them gain more understanding of the effects of a change in one target behavior on other targets.

The Problem Oriented Record (Hayes-Roth, Longabaugh, & Ryback, 1972; Katz & Woolley, 1975) is one way to address response interrelationships where several target behaviors exist for one client. In addition, the Problem Oriented Record helps organize client data for ongoing assessment and treatment purposes. While less precise than single-subject designs when used alone, the problem oriented method assists clinicians in planning future intervention efforts. When used in conjunction with single-subject designs (i.e., each target behavior is evaluated by a single-subject design with the results summarized using the Problem Oriented Record), it provides clinicians with a degree of evaluation and perspective on response covariation that is not available with either method in isolation.

The problem oriented method of behavioral assessment with the severely developmentally disabled comprises three phases: (1) generation of a problem list, (2) development of a problem matrix, and (3) ongoing use of a problem oriented record (POR). Taken together, these phases seek to describe response interrelationships in such a way that assessment and intervention outcomes can function as part of a feedback loop, guiding future efforts in a more fluid manner.

The problem list is a rank ordered set of multiple target behaviors, generated by clinicians in collaboration with other significant professionals on the treatment team (e.g., nurse, specialist, pediatrician). It is assumed that the problems described are related to each other in some way. The problem behaviors on the list can be organized and prioritized according to any one of several value systems. For example, either the most obnoxious behavior or the behavior most likely to show a rapid response to treatment could be listed first. The criteria for the selection of target behaviors described in Chapter 2 are useful in developing this ranking. Exhibit 3–9 provides an example of a problem list generated for a client.

While response interrelationships are assumed for those target behaviors identified in the problem list, the extent of these relationships must be made clearer to

---

Exhibit 3–9 Problem List

Client's name _____

Clinician _____Date _____

1. Noncompliance with academic tasks _____

2. Self-stimulation (finger gazing) _____

3. Nightime enuresis _____

4. Lack of independent eating skills _____

5. _____

facilitate generalization and maintenance. In order to relate these problem areas more explicitly, a problem matrix (Hay, 1982) is then constructed. A sample problem matrix is presented in Exhibit 3–10.

The problem matrix allows clinicians to gather information on the functional relationship hypothesized between the target behavior drawn from the problem list and other problems on the list. In addition, clinicians can identify how many problem behaviors contribute to any one given target behavior. This information can be used to generate assessment hypotheses to be tested and ultimately aids in the selection of treatment hypotheses, which are themselves tested. Thus, the principal utility of the problem matrix is in its ability to organize data (Hay, 1982). As noted in Chapter 2, however, other factors must be considered before selecting an initial target behavior for intervention.

To construct a problem matrix, the problem list is written down the left side and across the top of a page, as shown in Exhibit 3–10. Clinicians then ask, "Does Problem 1 contribute to Problem 3?" and so forth, until all cells in the matrix have been addressed. The vertical columns are then totaled, providing an index of those problems that contribute to a given target behavior. Totaling the horizontal columns provides an index of how many problems are related functionally to a given target behavior.

Using the data from Exhibit 3–10, noncompliance to academic tasks is hypothesized to be related functionally both to self-stimulatory behavior and to enuresis.

Exhibit 3–10 Problem Matrix

Client's name _____

Clinician _____ Date _____

	(1)	(2)	(3)	(4)	TOTALS
1. Noncompliance with academic tasks	—	YES	YES	NO	2
2. Self-stimulation	YES	—	NO	YES	2
3. Enuresis	NO	NO	—	NO	0
4. Lack of independent eating skills	NO	YES	NO	—	1
TOTALS:	1	2	1	1	

Thus, when further assessing noncompliance, clinicians would attempt to determine how and under what conditions this functional relationship exists. The totals from the vertical columns indicate that self-stimulatory behavior contributes to the most problems. This suggests that an intervention designed to reduce self-stimulatory behavior will have an effect on both noncompliance to academic tasks and lack of independent eating skills.

The POR is a framework for organizing assessment data gathered during baseline and treatment phases (Hayes-Roth et al., 1972). In addition, the POR helps to make explicit those response interrelationships that were hypothesized in the problem matrix. This latter function is achieved by juxtaposing the raw data, data analysis, and planned intervention for each problem with all other problems in the matrix. This point warrants elaboration. When assessing a client in one of the behaviors on the problem list, clinicians utilize one or more assessment techniques (e.g., time sampling, event recording) in order to generate data. When developing a problem oriented record, it is helpful to organize the data according to a Data-Analysis-Plan (DAP) format. This format provides an anecdotal record of data analysis concerns and hypothesized assessment and/or treatment plans. Exhibit 3–11 provides an example of the DAP format used with finger gazing behavior.

Exhibit 3–11 DAP Format

Client _____Date _____
Clinician _____
Target behavior "Self-stimulation (finger gazing)" _____

Problem Oriented Record

D (data): Finger gazing occurs for an average duration of 9 minutes each hour. Frequency of finger gazing ranges from 30–113 per hour, with an average of 52.

A (analysis): Highest rates and duration of finger gazing appear to occur during work sessions, particularly when those sessions are demanding (i.e., new, harder material is being taught). It is hypothesized that finger gazing serves as an escape or avoidance function with respect to academic tasks.

P (plan): In order to test the hypothesis noted above, the frequency and rate of finger gazing will continue to be assessed, and a videotape of four 15-minute samples of teaching sessions will be made. These data will be analyzed and compared to nonteaching samples. In addition, the type of task, teacher, and rate of prior success with the task will be recorded and analyzed.

With the DAP format, the raw data generated by the assessment techniques are recorded anecdotally under the (Data) D section for problem X. In addition, the raw data are presented graphically on a separate sheet. Clinicians' analyses of the raw data and resultant hypotheses form the basis for the (Analysis) A section and are again recorded anecdotally. Finally, data analysis will generate new and more detailed areas for assessment and/or treatment based upon the hypotheses in the preceding (Analysis) section. Tests for these hypotheses are described in the (Plan) P section, with the outcomes of these tests being described in the next Data section. Analysis, Planning, and so forth follows until all of the problems on the list have been addressed.

The DAP data should be updated weekly—more frequently if warranted—preferably at a staff meeting where numerous clinicians are present to provide input. Graphed representations of the data also are presented at these meetings, and prior progress and future directions are discussed and noted.

When the goal of the intervention has been achieved, the problem matrix is again consulted and redrawn to determine where to assess and intervene next. Any changes in the number of functionally related or contributing problems vis-a-vis a given target behavior could be the result of generalization, maturation effects, or the passage of time. While precise specification of treatment effects is a worthy goal, it is sometimes not expedient clinically. Thus, lack of a clear causal relationship between an improved target behavior and other problems on the list may be the best data available under the circumstances. Far from worthless, these data, and their limitations, should be acknowledged and utilized.

Using a new problem matrix to determine future target behavior priorities allows clinicians to account for change over time in those problems that made up the original list. Some may have abated, others may have become worse. New problems may be added and functional/contributing relationships may have shifted. In short, redevelopment of the problem matrix keeps the assessment process fluid, acknowledging the systemic effects of any assessment or intervention procedure.

If clinicians were to intervene simultaneously with two or more behaviors on the problem list, the POR would take on characteristics of an anecdotal multiple baseline. The graphed data and DAP information can still be used to generate treatment and assessment hypotheses, and subsequent matrices will continue to reflect the fluidity of the assessment process.

SUMMARY

Chapter 3 provides the technical base for the behavioral assessment of clients with severe developmental disabilities. These techniques can be used to frame a wide variety of assessment questions. A six-step process for interviewing the client behaviorally has been described, with special emphasis placed on the assessment of readiness to change in the client's family. Guidelines for defining behaviors and methods of data collection then were presented. In order to be useful for decision-making purposes, data must be communicated. To this end, several methods of data presentation are described. The advantages and disadvantages of various single-case experimental designs were noted. Finally, the Problem Oriented Record for organizing ongoing assessment and intervention data was described.

REFERENCES

Allyon, T., & Azrin, N. H. (1968). *The token economy: A motivational system for therapy and rehabilitation.* New York: Appleton-Century-Crofts.

American Association of Mental Deficiency (1975). *Adaptive Behavior Scales.* Washington, D.C.: Author.

Axelrod, S. (1977). *Behavior modification for the classroom teacher.* New York: McGraw-Hill.

Azrin, N. H., Holz, W., Ulrich, R., & Goldiamond, I. (1961). The control of the content of conversation through reinforcement. *Journal of the Experimental Analysis of Behavior, 4,* 25–30.

Baker, B. L., Brightman, A. J., Heifetz, L. J., & Murphy, D. M. (1976). *Behavior problems.* Champaign, IL: Research Press.

Biggs, J. L. (1982). *Teaching individuals with physical and multiple disabilities.* Columbus, OH: Charles E. Merrill.

Bijou, S. J. (1973). Behavior modification in teaching the retarded child. In C. Thorensen (Ed.), *Behavior modification in education.* Chicago: University of Chicago Press.

Campbell, D. T., & Stanley, J. C. (1966). *Experimental and quasi-experimental designs for research.* Chicago: Rand-McNally.

Ciminero, A. R., & Drabman, R. S. (1977). Current developments in the behavioral assessment of children. In B. B. Lahey & A. E. Kazdin (Eds.), *Advances in clinical child psychology* (Vol. 1). New York: Plenum Press.

Dancer, D. D., Brauckmann, C. J., Schumaker, J. B., Kirigin, K. A., Willner, A. G., & Wolf, M. M. (1978). The training and validation of behavior observation and description skills. *Behavior Modification, 2,* 113–134.

Davis, H. R., & Salasin, S. E. (1975). The utilization of evaluation research. In E. L. Struening & M. Guttentag (Eds.), *Handbook of evaluation research* (Vol. 1). Beverly Hills, CA: Sage Publications.

Doke, L. A., & Risley, T. R. (1972). The organization of day-care environments: Required vs. optional activities. *Journal of Applied Behavior Analysis, 5,* 405–420.

Eisler, R. M., & Hersen, M. (1973, August). The A-B design: Effects of a token economy on behavioral and subjective measures of neurotic depression. Paper presented at the 81st annual convention of the American Psychological Association, Montreal.

Ellis, P. (1980). Analysis of social skills: The behavior analysis approach. In W. Singleton, P. Spurgeon, & R. Stamers (Eds.), *The analysis of social skill.* New York: Plenum Press.

Evans, I. M., & Nelson, R. O. (1977). Assessment of childhood behavior problems. In A. R. Ciminero, K. S. Calhoun, & H. E. Adams (Eds.), *Handbook of behavioral assessment.* New York: Wiley.

Evans, I. M. (1982, October). Response covariation in child behavioral assessment. Colloquium presented at Rutgers University, New Brunswick, N.J.

Freeman, B. J., Ritvo, E. R., Guthrie, D., Schroth, P., & Ball, J. (1978). The Behavior Observation Scale for autism. *Journal of the American Academy of Child Psychiatry, 17,* 576–588.

Gelfand, D. M., & Hartmann, D. P. (1980). *Child behavior analysis and therapy.* Elmsford, NY: Pergamon Press.

Gold, M. W. (1976). Task analysis of a complex assembly task by the retarded child. *Exceptional Children, 43,* 78–84.

Guess, D., & Baer, D. M. (1973). An analysis of individual differences in generalization between receptive and productive language in retarded children. *Journal of Applied Behavior Analysis, 6,* 311–329.

Handleman, J. S., & Harris, S. L. (1981, November). Live vs. audio recorder agreement measures of autistic children's verbal responses. Paper presented at the 15th annual meeting of the Association for Advancement of Behavior Therapy, Toronto.

Handleman, J. S., Powers, M. D., & Harris, S. L. (1984). The teaching of labels: An analysis of concrete and pictorial representations. *American Journal of Mental Deficiency, 88,* 625–629.

Harbert, T. L., Barlow, D. H., Hersen, M., & Austin, J. B. (1974). Measurement and modification of incestuous behavior: A case study. *Psychological Reports, 34,* 70–86.

Haring, N. G. (1982). *Exceptional children and youth.* Columbus, OH: Charles E. Merrill.

Haring, N. G., & Gentry, N. (1976). Direct and individualized instructional procedures. In N. Haring & R. Schiefelbush (Eds.), *Teaching special children.* New York: McGraw-Hill.

Harris, S. L. (1982). A family systems approach to behavioral training with parents of autistic children. *Child and Family Behavior Therapy, 4,* 21–35.

Harris, S. L., & Powers, M. D. (1984). Behavior therapists look at the impact of an autistic child on the family system. In E. Schopler & G. Mesibov (Eds.), *The effects of autism on the family.* New York: Plenum Press.

Hay, L. R. (1982). Teaching behavioral assessment to clinical psychology students. *Behavioral Assessment, 4,* 35–40.

Hayes-Roth, F., Longabaugh, R., & Ryback, R. (1972). The problem-oriented medical record and psychiatry. *British Journal of Psychiatry, 121,* 27–34.

Haynes, S. N. (1978). *Principles of behavioral assessment.* New York: Gardner Press.

Hersen, M., & Barlow, D. H. (1976). *Single case experimental designs.* New York: Pergamon.

House, A. E. (1980). Detecting bias in observational data. *Behavioral Assessment, 2,* 29–31.

Johnson, S. M., & Bolstad, O. D. (1973). Methodological issues in naturalistic observations: Some problems and solutions for field research. In L. A. Hamerlynck, L. C. Handy, & E. J. Mash (Eds.), *Behavior change: Methodology, concepts, and practice.* Champaign, IL: Research Press.

Katz, R. C., & Woolley, F. R. (1975). Improving patient records through problem orientation. *Behavior Therapy, 6,* 119–124.

Kazdin, A. E. (1979). Unobtrusive measures in behavioral assessment. *Journal of Applied Behavior Analysis, 12,* 713–724.

Kazdin, A. E. (1980). *Behavior modification in applied settings.* Homewood, IL: Dorsey Press.

Kent, R. N., & O'Leary, K. D. (1976). A controlled evaluation of behavior modification with conduct problem children. *Journal of Consulting and Clinical Psychology, 44,* 586–596.

Krug, D. A., Arick, J. R., & Almond, P. J. (1980). *Autism Screening Instrument for Educational Planning.* Portland, OR: ASIEP Education Co.

Lipinski, D., & Nelson, R. O. (1974). The reactivity and unreliability of self-recording. *Journal of Consulting and Clinical Psychology, 3*, 353–373.

Mager, R. F. (1962). *Preparing instructional objectives.* Palo Alto, CA: Fearon.

Murphy, H. A., Hutchinson, J. M., & Bailey, J. S. (1983). Behavioral school psychology goes outdoors: The effect of organized games on playground aggression. *Journal of Applied Behavior Analysis, 16,* 29–36.

Nelson, R. O., Kapust, J. A., & Dorsey, B. L. (1978). Minimal reactivity of overt classroom observations on student and teacher behaviors. *Behavior Therapy, 9,* 695–702.

Nelson, W. M., III. (1982). Behavioral treatment of childhood trichotillomania: A case study. *Journal of Clinical Child Psychology, 11,* 227–230.

Nihira, K., Foster, R., Shellhaas, M., & Leland, H. (1974). *AAMD Adaptive Behavior Scale* (rev. ed.). Washington, DC: American Association on Mental Deficiency.

Novick, J., Rosenfeld, E., Bloch, D.A., & Dawson, D. (1966). Ascertaining deviant behavior in children. *Journal of Consulting Psychology, 30,* 230–238.

O'Leary, K. D., Kent, R. N., & Kanowitz, J. (1975). Shaping data collection congruent with experimental hypotheses. *Journal of Applied Behavior Analysis, 8,* 92–100.

Ollendick, T. H., & Cerney, J. A. (1981). *Clinical behavior therapy with children.* New York: Plenum Press.

Powers, M. D. (1984). *Assessing readiness for change in families with severely developmentally disabled children.* Manuscript submitted for publication.

Powers, M. D., & Thorwarth, C. A. (1983). *The effect of negative reinforcement on intolerance of physical contact in a preschool autistic child.* Manuscript submitted for publication.

Quilitch, H. R., & Risley, T. R. (1973). The effects of play materials on social play. *Journal of Applied Behavior Analysis, 6,* 573–578.

Resnick, L. B., Wang, M. C., & Kaplan, J. (1973). Task analysis in curriculum design: A hierarchically sequenced introductory mathematics curriculum. *Journal of Applied Behavior Analysis, 6,* 679–710.

Romanczyk, R. G., Kent, R. N., Diament, C., & O'Leary, K. D. (1973). Measuring the reliability of observational data: A reactive process. *Journal of Applied Behavior Analysis, 6,* 173–184.

Rosenthal, R. (1969). Interperson expectations: Effects of the experimenter's hypothesis. In R. Rosenthal & P. L. Rosnow (Eds.), *Artifact in behavioral research.* New York: Academic Press.

Ross, A. O. (1963). The issue of normality in clinical child psychology. *Mental Hygiene, 47,* 267–272.

Ruttenberg, B. A., Kalish, B. I., Wenar, C., & Wolf, E. G. (1977). *The Behavior Rating Scale for Autistic and other Atypical Children (BRIAAC)* (rev. ed.). Philadelphia: Developmental Center for Autistic Children.

Sailor, W., & Mix, B. J. (1975). *The TARC Assessment System.* Lawrence, KS: H & H Enterprises.

Sajwaj, T., Twardosz, S., & Burke, M. (1972). Side effects of extinction procedures in a remedial preschool. *Journal of Applied Behavior Analysis, 5,* 163–175.

Schopler, E., & Reichler, R. J. (1979). *Psychoeducational profile: Individualized assessment for autistic and developmentally disabled children* (Vol. 1). Baltimore: University Park Press.

Schopler, E., Reichler, R. J., DeVellis, R. F., & Daly, K. (1980). Toward objective classification of childhood autism: Childhood Autism Rating Scale (CARS). *Journal of Autism and Developmental Disorders, 10,* 91–103.

Schreibman, L., O'Neill, R. E., & Koegel, R. L. (1983). Behavioral training for siblings of autistic children. *Journal of Applied Behavior Analysis, 16,* 129–138.

Siegel, L. J. (1982). Classical and operant procedures in the treatment of a case of food aversion in a young child. *Journal of Clinical Child Psychology, 11,* 167–172.

Smith, D., Smith, J., & Edgar, E. (1976). Prototypic model for the development of instructional materials. In N. G. Haring & L. J. Brown (Eds.), *Teaching the severely handicapped.* New York: Grune & Stratton.

Sparrow, S. S., Balla, D. A., & Cicchetti, D. V. (1984). *Vineland Adaptive Behavior Scales.* Circle Pines, MN: American Guidance Service.

Swanson, H. L., & Watson, B. L. (1982). *Educational and psychological assessment of exceptional children.* St. Louis: C. V. Mosby.

Van Etten, G., Arkell, C., & Van Etten, C. (1980). *The severely and profoundly handicapped: Programs, methods, and materials.* St. Louis: C. V. Mosby.

Wahler, R. G. (1980). The insular mother: Her problems in parent-child treatment. *Journal of Applied Behavior Analysis, 13,* 207–219.

Walker, J. E., & Shea, T. M. (1980). *Behavior modification: A practical approach for educators.* St. Louis: C. V. Mosby.

Waterman, J. (1982). Assessment of the family system. In G. Ulrey & S. J. Rogers (Eds.), *Psychological assessment of handicapped infants and young children.* New York: Thieme-Stratton.

Whitman, T. L., Mercurio, J. R., & Caponigri, V. (1970). Development of social responses in two severely retarded children. *Journal of Applied Behavior Analysis, 3,* 133–138.

Williams, W. (1975). Procedures of task analysis as related to developing instructional programs for the severely retarded. In L. Brown, T. Crowner, W. Williams, & R. York (Eds), *Madison's alternative for zero exclusion: A book of readings* (Vol. 5). Madison, WI: Madison Public Schools.

Wing, L., & Gould, J. (1978). Systematic recording of behaviors and skills of retarded and psychotic children. *Journal of Autism and Childhood Schizophrenia, 8,* 79–97.

Zlutnick, S., Mayville, W. J., & Moffat, S. (1975). The modification of seizure disorders: Interruption of behavioral chains. *Journal of Applied Behavior Analysis, 8,* 1–12.

Chapter 4

Issues in the Assessment of Social Skills and Interpersonal Responsiveness

INTRODUCTION

Deficits in social skills are endemic in severely developmentally disabled people. Current diagnostic schemata for the severely and profoundly mentally retarded (American Psychiatric Association, 1980; Grossman, 1983) and for children with infantile autism or childhood onset pervasive developmental disorder (American Psychiatric Association, 1980; Schopler, 1978) emphasize impairments in social responsiveness and adaptive behavior. The type and severity of social skill deficits, however, may vary across the population of severely developmentally disabled clients due to the heterogeneity of disorders contained therein. For example, Kanner's original (1943) definition of the syndrome of autism stressed that autistic children exhibited deficits in interpersonal relatedness, especially in avoidance of eye contact and the absence of an anticipatory response when they were picked up by an adult. Grossman (1983), in contrast, emphasized deficits in adaptive behavior, including toileting, self-feeding, and playing skills (coupled with significant cognitive impairment), when identifying mental retardation in clients.

While the advantages to grouping clients together by diagnostic category are clear, such a restricted view poses problems in the assessment of social skills in the severely developmentally disabled. Thus, our approach to the behavioral assessment of social skills with this population takes a functional approach. In a manner of speaking, diagnosis is relatively unimportant for treatment purposes. What matters most in the final assessment analysis is: What necessary social/adaptive behaviors are absent or underused? What situational determinants control these behaviors? How can environmental and organismic contingencies be arranged to facilitate performance of these behaviors? In this way, social skill deficits across the entire heterogeneous population of severely developmentally disabled clients can be considered.

In addition to a focus on the social skill deficit itself, other organismic and systemic factors must be considered. For example, before generalized statements about the social skills of the severely developmentally disabled can be made, age, nonverbal intelligence, and language impairment must be taken into account (Howlin, 1978). Bartack and Rutter (1976) and DeMyer, Barton, DeMyer, Nort, Allan, and Steele (1973) report evidence that severity of social skill deficits is influenced by the client's language and cognitive skills. These findings suggest that the social skill deficits of severely developmentally disabled clients may be more a result of an inability to *understand* social situations than a desire to *avoid* such situations (Howlin, 1978).

It is also important to consider systemic factors. When assessing social skills, it is important to observe and note the interactions between many different behaviors (Bellack, 1979; Howlin, 1978; Hutt & Hutt, 1970) within particular interpersonal contexts (Eisler, 1976). Sole reliance upon frequency counts from a small sample of behavior is of limited utility, as generalizations from the sample to other settings may well lead to incorrect conclusions (Howlin, 1978). For example, performance of appropriate eating and drinking behaviors may be demonstrated in the classroom or even on a field trip to MacDonalds. Concluding, without further assessment, that these behaviors are established and will be performed reliably when grandma and grandpa take their grandchild to a restaurant may be unwarranted. The point here is that multiple stimuli control behavior and numerous contingencies facilitate generalization and maintenance. To fail to consider grandma's easygoing, noncontingent, low-demand style or the particular stresses of a restaurant versus those of MacDonalds, could lead to nonperformance of "learned" adaptive behaviors. Thus, the sequence and pattern of behavior over time is at least as important as the frequency or duration of that behavior.

Finally, the acquisition of social, adaptive behaviors by the severely developmentally disabled will depend upon how well the clinician identifies the ways in which *others* respond to the client's behavior, and on how successful the clinician is in modifying others' interactions with the client to facilitate production of desired behavior. Thus, a critical area for assessment of social, adaptive behavior is the interaction that occurs between the client and others around social skill situations. Knowledge of these interactions, when coupled with information on a client's cognitive functioning, age, language skills, and developmental level, allows the clinician to place the social skill into a relevant context. When used appropriately, knowledge of relevant context can serve to guide treatment planning.

Thus far, social skill and adaptive behavior assessments have been combined to develop the concept of "behavioral heterogeneity." It will be useful now to discuss separately the two interrelated components of social functioning: (1) assessment of social perception (Bellack, 1979) and (2) assessment of motor behavior.

Bellack (1979) describes an aspect of social skill behavior known as "social or interpersonal perception" (p. 171). In distinguishing this dimension from motor responses, Bellack (1979) describes five components of social perception: "(1) knowledge of social mores; (2) knowledge of the significance or meaning of various response cues; (3) attention to relevant aspects of the interaction, including the context and responses emitted by others; (4) information processing capability; and (5) the ability to predict and evaluate interpersonal consequences" (p. 171). Each of these dimensions has relevance to acquisition, generalization, and maintenance of social and adaptive behaviors and should be considered as part of a comprehensive behavioral assessment.

The assessment of motor behavior takes a decidedly different approach than social perception. In this component, the clinician assesses the motor components of the adaptive behavior based upon a task analysis of that behavior (Greer, Powers, & Shanley, 1980; Powers, Shanley, & Greer, 1980). In so doing, the clinician can identify those preparatory skills necessary to the performance of the terminal adaptive response, assess client performance on the skill hierarchy, and determine the starting point for training the motor components of the social adaptive response (Powers et al., 1980).

Combining data from an assessment of social perception with an assessment of motor components will permit a more comprehensive training package, facilitating response acquisition, generalization, and maintenance.

There are several other issues to consider when assessing social skills with severely developmentally disabled clients. These include performance versus skill deficits; molar versus molecular levels of behavior; response covariation; stimulus overselectivity; and situational specificity.

PERFORMANCE VERSUS SKILL DEFICIT

There are two possible explanations for the absence of observed social skill behavior (Eisler, 1976). Severely developmentally disabled clients may fail to emit a particular social response because the antecedent and stimulus conditions (informational cues and expectations of reward or punishment) are not facilitating the *performance* of the behavior. In such a case, a behavior already established in other situations does not occur in the target setting. An example would be a client who has learned to respond nonaggressively at home, but hits and bites his teacher in school. In contrast, a *skill* deficit refers to a lack of prior learning about how to behave in particular social situations. Determination of the "cause" of the observed social skill deficit has important treatment implications.

There are many methods for assessing performance versus skill deficits with the social skill behavior of severely developmentally disabled children. Perhaps the simplest way would be to ask various individuals who have frequent contact with the client (parents, teachers, cottage staff) whether they have observed the target behavior. Agreement as to the target behavior's absence will preclude the need for further molar levels of assessment, and will lead to the completion of the four-step behavioral assessment process described in Chapter 2. In such a case, the "cause" of the observed lack of social skill behavior is a skill deficit. Other methods to assess for a skill deficit would be to observe client behavior in a variety of naturalistic settings or to assess social skill behavior in enactment analogues.

Should observers differ in their judgment of the absence or presence of the social skill, a performance deficit may be implicated. In such cases, more detailed data must be collected during those situations where the social skill does or does not occur. This more molecular level of analysis will determine several factors. First, the motivation for the absence or presence of the behavior must be assessed. For example, after soiling his pants, Jacob receives great quantities of physical and verbal attention while his clothes are changed. At home, the opposite is true. One might hypothesize that his performance deficit in school is maintained by its reinforcing consequences. Durand and Carr (1982) found that disruptive behavior in developmentally disabled children was sometimes a function of teacher demands or difficult tasks. Their results support the notion that a social skill performance deficit also can be due to a client's desire to escape or avoid demanding social situations.

Second, when an assessment is done, those stimuli controlling a client's response must be elucidated (Kazdin, 1979b). The goal is to identify which stimuli lead to performance and under what conditions. For example, one child with whom the authors worked gave an appropriate greeting response (e.g., "Hi Mike" or "Hi Jan") contingent upon the discriminative stimulus (S^D), "Hi Carl." Whenever Carl was greeted with a different form of verbal greeting (e.g., "How are you doing today, Carl?"), he would either become echolalic or not respond at all. Thus, an assessment of his greeting behavior identified the particular verbal stimulus that was controlling Carl's responding.

Skill deficits may be due to a variety of factors. The severely developmentally disabled client may never have learned social skill behaviors, due to impaired language and cognitive skills (Howlin, 1978), age and developmental factors (Harris & Ferrari, 1983), overselective responding during teaching situations (Lovaas, Koegel, & Schreibman, 1979), or poor educational planning. Once a social skill deficit is identified, the skill is taught like any other behavior. One particular point of emphasis, however, is to teach the social skill within a functional context. That is, opportunities for clients to practice greeting responses should become part and parcel of the treatment plan, and will facilitate clinicians' ongoing naturalistic or analogue assessment (as opposed to clinicians presenting the client with 10 trials twice a day and asking, "What do you say when someone says hello to you?" then expecting the response, "Hi").

MOLAR VERSUS MOLECULAR LEVELS OF BEHAVIOR

Recent work in the behavioral assessment of social skills has distinguished the assessment of molar levels of behavior from molecular levels (Bellack, 1979; Hersen & Bellack, 1976). Molar skills refer to broader, more global social skills such as "toileting," while molecular skills refer to subskills that constitute the molar skill. Thus, "eating skills" (a molar social skill) may comprise several molecular behaviors, including the ability to

- use a fork, spoon, and knife;
- sit at the table without behaving disruptively;
- pour liquid from a container into a glass;
- drink from a glass or cup;
- request assistance with food or drink as necessary.

Clearly, molecular skills will vary widely across particular clients, depending on individual behavioral strengths and deficits. It is useful, however, to use task analysis (see Chapter 3) to develop behavioral taxonomies for molar social skills (Powers et al., 1980). These taxonomies are most appropriately drawn from the developmental sequences of normal children for the social skill under consideration. By using typical developmental sequences as benchmarks, clinicians may avoid treatment suggestions that are based upon preparatory behaviors that were absent and not assessed (Paronson & Baer, 1978).

For example, the literature on the development of toileting behavior in non-handicapped children notes that such children typically demonstrate bowel continence prior to bladder continence and daytime bladder control prior to nighttime bladder control. Ignorance of this developmental sequence may lead clinicians to inappropriate treatment suggestions. Hence, when assessing social skills in severely developmentally disabled clients, it is critical to assess their developmental status for that social skill and to proceed accordingly. The absence of published or well-defined taxonomies of behavior necessitates a task analysis of the social skill.

The distinctions between molar and molecular levels of behavior lead to three guidelines for the behavioral assessment of social skills with severely developmentally disabled clients:

1. Assess the social skill in the context of a client's general developmental level. This may require assessments of age, nonverbal intelligence, or language impairment (Howlin, 1978) prior to assessment of the social skill itself.
2. Assess molar skills first. This can be done through an informal survey of caretakers, teachers, parents, and so on, with the goal of identifying all areas

of perceived social skill deficits in a client. These areas then can be evaluated and prioritized through social validation (Kazdin, 1977; Wolf, 1978).
3. Once a molar social skill has been identified as a high priority, its molecular components must be identified and assessed individually. In this regard, it is most useful to develop a taxonomy of the molar social skill to guide assessment efforts.

Taken together, these guidelines will help guard against social skill treatment programs doomed to failure because of incomplete assessments.

RESPONSE COVARIATION

Professionals working with severely developmentally disabled clients sometimes are confronted with unplanned change occurring concurrently with a planned intervention for a specific target behavior. This phenomenon, termed response covariation or response interrelationship, has been the subject of recent work (Kara & Wahler, 1977; Voeltz & Evans, 1982; Wahler, 1975), and has important implications for the behavioral assessment of these clients.

Bijou and Baer (1978) and Lovaas (1961) have proposed the existence of response classes to explain observations of quasi-orderly change in nontarget behaviors. This notion suggests that certain behaviors in a client's repertoire are under the control of similar controlling variables. These controlling variables could be either antecedent or consequent stimuli. Thus, the alteration of the controlling variables for one behavior (the target behavior) may bring about unplanned change in other, nontarget behaviors. These changes are often of a positive nature. For example, Koegel & Covert (1972) reported increased rates of learning in clients when self-stimulation was suppressed. However, some negative effects have been reported with the use of electric shock on autistic children (Lichstein & Schreibman, 1976).

Extending the investigation of collateral change, Wahler (1975) found that several responses co-varied predictably in one child. Moreover, the covariations were situation specific. That is, the child's responses that reliably co-varied at home did not co-vary in school. This latter point is particularly important to the initial assessment of controlling variables prior to intervention.

Wahler's (1975) findings led to the coining of a new term—keystone behaviors—referring to those members of a response class that can be thought of as holding other behavioral elements in place. Hence, alteration of a keystone behavior will have an effect on many or most other behaviors in that same response class. Voeltz and Evans (1982) note that a response may function as a keystone for two reasons. The response may expose the client to a natural community of reinforcers, bringing about a cumulative effect in the density of available reinforcers. In other cases, the response may be an essential, "preparatory" response upon which other appropriate behaviors build. An example of this latter case would be the response of maintaining eye contact with an adult. Once established, this behavior forms the basis for speech and language development (see Harris, 1975).

It has been suggested that the equivocal results of many behavioral interventions with severely handicapped clients may be due to clinicians' failure to assess response covariation prior to intervention (Voeltz & Evans, 1982). Accordingly, Voeltz and Evans (1982) provide several guidelines for the behavioral assessment of response covariation in severely developmentally disabled clients.

- Assess whether the undesirable target behavior is part of a naturally occurring chain. That is, does it co-vary reliably with a sequence of other behaviors? The implications for treatment are that clinicians may be able to intervene indirectly, modifying a less difficult response earlier in the response chain.

- Assess those preparatory responses that are necessary for the commission of the (appropriate) target behavior. A client's emission of a particular onset response will depend upon the availability of prerequisite responses. For example, the behaviors eye contact, sitting still in a chair, and forward body orientation co-vary reliably when a severely developmentally disabled child has learned how to succeed in school. When clinicians are presented with clients who are having difficulty attending in school, assessments of these behaviors may help them determine where to intervene first. Thus, in dealing with the client, clinicians might follow Harris' (1976) suggested sequence of (1) sitting still, (2) body oriented forward, and (3) eye contact, beginning treatment at the point in the sequence where the response breaks down.

- Assess to determine whether the behaviors hypothesized to be interrelated are functionally similar. This is important because if they are, reductions or increases in *one* behavior will lead to change in another.

- When assessing behavioral excesses, conduct a functional analysis of the target behavior to determine whether a more appropriate behavior can be taught the client that will serve a function similar to the unwanted behavioral excess. Carr (1983) has suggested, for example, that self-injurious behavior may function as a means of communication, effectively signaling clients' desires for interaction with their caretakers. When taught a verbal or signed communication to fulfill the same function, these clients significantly decrease their rate of self-injury (Durand & Carr, 1982).

- Paronson & Baer (1978) note that clinicians' failure to acknowledge normal developmental sequelae often leads to failures with the generalization and maintenance of learned behavior. Thus, when assessing response interrelationships, be mindful of the normal developmental sequences of children. Failure at a particular skill may well be due to the absence of necessary preparatory behaviors. As uneven developmental rates are endemic to severely developmentally disabled clients, assessment of those behaviors needed for the occurrence of the target behavior is critical.

There are several problems encountered when attempting to gather data on responses that are presumed to co-vary. Voeltz and Evans (1982) note that typical within-subjects single-case designs (multiple baselines and alternating treatment designs in particular) obfuscate the interpretation of response interrelationships. Moreover, changes in nontarget behaviors may be due to response generalization, adventitious reinforcement, or modification of an organizing keystone behavior. As an alternative, Voeltz and Evans (1982) suggest the use of multiple response monitoring for the collection of simultaneous data. Romanczyk's (1983) work using real-time analysis of self-injury and self-stimulation represents the forefront of this work. Presently, however, such analyses require computer technology beyond the budgets of many treatment centers.

Voeltz and Evans (1982) suggest an alternative means of collecting data useful for hypothesis testing for response covariation. They suggest asking caretakers (staff, parents) about the status of nontarget behaviors of concern before and after intervention with the target behavior. While not obtained through rigorous experimental efforts, these data will begin to broaden the scope of understanding of the client's behavior, effectively contextualizing it into a larger system.

The expansion to larger systems complicates the assessment of the behavior of severely developmentally disabled clients. It is nonetheless important for two reasons. First, the multiple treatment needs of so many of these clients require an investigation of the larger system in order to determine which behaviors take priority for intervention. Second, behavioral assessment techniques frequently impose an artificiality on the behavior of severely developmentally disabled clients by arbitrarily "chunking" behavior into discrete units for purposes of observation. While this may assist in assessment, the practice is a two-edged sword. Chunking obfuscates natural patterns of behavior, often leading clinicians to incorrect assumptions about the function of a given behavior. An awareness of response interrelationships helps guard against this artificiality.

STIMULUS OVERSELECTIVITY

Research efforts in behavior modification with severely developmentally disabled children have frequently focused on the relationship between reinforcement variables and learning. In recent years, however, interest in the role of stimulus variables in the acquisition of new behaviors in these children has led to important advances. The transfer of stimulus control once was thought to occur naturally in children with severe developmental disabilities. However, Lovaas and his colleagues (Lovaas, et al., 1979; Koegel and Wilhelm, 1973; Lovaas, Schreibman, Koegel, and Rehm, 1971; Schover and Newsom, 1976; Schreibman & Lovaas, 1973) have identified an attentional deficit in severely developmentally disabled children that inhibits stimulus transfer. Termed "stimulus overselectivity" (Lovaas et al., 1971), this phenomenon results in the handicapped client selectively attending to only a small part of the stimulus array. Stimulus overselectivity has been implicated with numerous sensory deficits in developmentally disabled children (Lovaas et al., 1979), as well as with their deficiencies in responding to social stimuli (Schreibman & Lovaas, 1973).

An example may help to explain this deficiency in these children's learning and underscore its implications for their assessment and treatment. Schreibman and Lovaas (1973) sought to investigate the relationship between stimulus overselectivity and responses by autistic children to social cues. They trained autistic and normal subjects to discriminate between boy and girl figures (Barbie and Ken dolls). When the discrimination was established, component stimuli, such as heads, shoes, pants, skirt, and socks, were interchanged systematically in an attempt to determine which stimuli were controlling a child's initial discrimination.

Results indicated that while all subjects learned the initial boy-girl discrimination, normal children learned it significantly faster. In addition, six of seven autistic subjects exhibited stimulus overselectivity, responding to only a small number of cues within the stimulus. For example, after acquiring the initial discrimination, some autistic subjects switched their response when the boy's and girl's shoes were interchanged. In contrast, normal children responded to the heads of the figures. To ensure that the normal group was not simply attending selectively to one relevant cue, the heads were removed and stimulus control was again assessed. Results obtained show that the normal children were able to discriminate between the figures on the basis of other component parts, indicating that their responding was not overselective.

In their discussion of these results, Schreibman and Lovaas (1973) suggest that overselective responding to social stimuli may help explain the variable nature of social responding exhibited by many autistic clients. By selectively attending to an irrelevant stimulus (e.g., shoes or shirt), clients may become locked into a restrictive pattern of responding such that they would be unable to respond in a socially appropriate way when the controlling stimuli were altered or absent. Moreover, the more severe the behavioral deficits, the greater the degree of stimulus overselectivity observed. Thus, it is possible that the overselective responding may reduce a client's number of potentially salient cues from which to learn, contributing to a generalized deficit in social skills.

The tendency toward overselective responding has two important implications for the behavioral assessment of social skills in clients with severe developmental disabilities. First, when conducting an assessment of previously trained social skills, professionals must be aware that performance may be influenced by the presence or absence of particular cues in the environment. Consider, for example, a client taught the verbal greeting response, "Hi," through a training program that had the therapist approach the client, give a handwave, and say, "Hi," thereby eliciting the greeting response from the client. When greeted by a novel person who says, "Hi," but who omits the motor behavior (handwave), the previously trained client fails to respond. Another novel person who greets the client with a handwave but gives no verbal greeting elicits the previously trained verbal "Hi," from the client. In this case, the client has selectively attended to the handwave during training, effectively ignoring the verbal component of the stimulus array. This example underscores the necessity for assessing multiple cues that may be controlling the performance of a social skill. In addition, once identified, systematic generalization training (see Stokes & Baer, 1977) may be required to broaden those stimuli associated with behavioral control.

Second, the research on stimulus overselectivity has made explicit the relationship between severity of handicap and selective attention. Thus, the more severely developmentally disabled a person is, the more restricted the range of cues controlling the performance of that person's behavior. When assessing social skills with more cognitively impaired members of this population, clinicians should be sensitive to the potential for performance and skill deficits that are a function of low levels of cognitive functioning.

SITUATIONAL SPECIFICITY

A central theme in behavioral assessment that distinguishes it from more traditional forms of assessment is that behavior is situationally specific. Thus, a severely developmentally disabled client may exhibit a desirable social skill in school, where the conditions for performance are optimal, but not at home or in public. The presence of situational specificity in client responding has a considerable influence on the behavioral assessment of severely developmentally disabled clients.

Kazdin (1979b) identifies three conditions that influence specificity of performance: (1) information, (2) context or setting, and (3) obtrusive measures. Information refers to instructions, demands, and performance expectations provided the client during assessment. For example, Borkovec (1973) found that fearful subjects who were given "high" demands to approach snakes were more likely to comply than their counterparts who were given "low" demands. Clearly, training settings where performance demands are high will be likely to lead to demonstration of the social skill, providing that the behavior has been established (i.e., a *performance* deficit rather than a *skill* deficit is the problem).

Performance may vary across contexts. In particular, specific settings (e.g., home, school) or persons (e.g., teacher, parent, researcher) (Kazdin, 1979a) can influence client behavior. These changes can be due to an alteration of consequences in one setting versus another (Marholin, Siegel, & Phillips, 1976), to changes in specific antecedent stimuli used previously to elicit the target behavior (Kazdin, 1979b), or to changes in the setting events (Steinman, 1977) that "set the stage" for the performance of the behavior. Antecedent stimuli are those discriminative stimuli (S^Ds) that have come to signal the potential for reinforcement or punishment. In contrast, setting events (Steinman, 1977) are those global conditions (e.g., presence in the classroom) that in the past have been associated with performance of the target behavior. The client's awareness that assessment data are being collected is the third condition that may influence performance (Kazdin, 1979a). Here the concern is with client reactivity to the obtrusiveness of the measures being used.

In general, the first and second conditions—information and context—have been found to be the most relevant to severely developmentally disabled clients. While client reactivity is sometimes observed, the severe nature of the handicapping conditions of these clients restricts the impact of obtrusive measures to those that are highly intrusive. For example, the presence of a video camera and wires around the classroom often will be more intrusive than the presence of a paraprofessional taking behavioral ratings. Likewise, the use of a one-way mirror and hidden microphones will be less conspicuous than the presence of another person in the room. Overall, two rules of thumb apply here: (1) create assessment measures that are as unobtrusive as possible given the type of data to be collected, and (2) if a more obtrusive method is necessary, allow a period of time (one or two weeks) for the client to grow accustomed to the device in an effort to reduce reactivity. An example of this latter "rule" is described by Powers and Crowel (1983). Their assessment methodology required a client to wear a small remote control microphone in order for them to gain random measures of the client's verbal behavior. To forestall reactivity, the client wore the microphone for two weeks prior to the first day of data collection.

Armed with this information, clinicians must be prepared to assess the target behavior in a variety of settings where it might be emitted appropriately. For example, a client may have achieved urinating in the toilet in school, but not at home. An assessment of toileting skills in only one of these settings would lead to inappropriate conclusions and errors in treatment planning.

In addition to multisituational assessment, the presence of situational specificity requires an assessment of those variables controlling the performance of the behavior (Kazdin, 1979b). To extend the example above, if Paul urinates in the toilet at school but not at home, the clinician must ascertain which antecedent and consequent conditions maintain the behavior in school. Then, the presence or absence of these antecedent or consequent conditions must be assessed at home.

Treatment planning will focus on incorporating into the home those conditions that facilitate appropriate urination at school.

Finally, clinicians should assess behavior in the natural environment wherever possible (Kazdin, 1979b). In the event that situational constraints prevent naturalistic assessment, analogue assessments can be utilized and interpreted with caution.

The section that follows presents the *most desirable* state of affairs. This may not be possible to achieve in many service delivery settings. The issues are pertinent, however, for program planning, for research, or for troubleshooting purposes.

Naturalistic Assessment

The assessment of behavior in the client's natural environment provides the clinician with data that are more likely to reflect actual performance than data gathered with analogue measures. This added accessibility, however, brings with it the increased potential for client reactivity to the assessment devices or methods. Thus, when using naturalistic assessment, minimizing the obtrusiveness of the assessment method becomes critically important.

Kazdin (1979a) describes several unobtrusive assessment techniques for collecting data from naturalistic settings. These include (1) direct observation utilizing one-way mirrors, videotaping teacher observations, and trained confederates; (2) archival data, including nursing reports, accident reports, and incident reports; and (3) physical traces (material deposited in or removed from the setting), including job tasks completed, litter, items stolen, and soiled diapers. While underutilized in behavioral research, these methods represent an important area for future outcome evaluation research.

These measures are not without limitation. Acceptable levels of interrater reliability can be difficult to obtain due to observer drift (see Chapter 3). In addition, methods assumed by clinicians to be unobtrusive may be perceived as obtrusive by clients. Finally, the ethics of operating without clients' informed consents must be considered from a risk/benefit standpoint prior to the implementation of unobtrusive measures (Kazdin, 1979a).

There are numerous sources of measurement error when using direct observation in naturalistic settings. These sources will contribute to the unreliability of the data to varying degrees, ranging from minor errors quickly and easily corrected (e.g., observer drift) to more serious errors that render the data invalid (e.g., cheating among the observers). Kent and Foster (1977) describe many of these methodological concerns in detail, including expectation biases, reactivity, biasing factors influencing reliability, consensual drift among observers, and concomitant multiple sources of bias. They extensively discuss these factors and the methods to remedy error (Kent & Foster, 1977).

Analogue Assessment

Analogue assessment is the process of presenting, in a controlled clinical setting, stimuli that normally occur in the natural environment (Epstein, 1976). The use of this assessment method has the advantage of allowing clinicians control over important variables relevant to the social skill being assessed. However, analogue assessment methods have the disadvantage of being contrived. This state of affairs requires a priori weighing of two competing factors prior to the selection of an analogue measure: control of the assessment setting versus representativeness of the assessment stimuli. For example, when assessing the ability of a severely developmentally disabled child to sit in a chair in a group, the clinician may choose to gather four other children together who *can* sit in a group, add the target child, and assess the target behavior. Unfortunately, this contrived situation may yield data that are not valid. For our target child, "sitting in a group" may be under the control of variables in the analogue setting that are absent from the naturalistic (classroom) setting. Hence, the target behavior has been pulled from its relevant context and important data lost.

Stimulus situations in analogue assessment can be presented in several ways, including paper and pencil tasks, audiotape and videotape recordings, role plays, and actual enactments (Nay, 1977). Due to the extreme skill and performance deficits encountered in clients with severe developmental disabilities, it is most practical and relevant to focus on enactments for the assessment of social skills in this population.

Enactment analogues can be characterized by bringing relevant stimuli (persons, situations, or objects) that exist in the natural environment into the clinical setting (Nay, 1977). In so doing, the client's responses to those stimuli can be assessed in the present (rather than assessed on reports of past performance). Nay (1977) describes guidelines that should be observed when constructing enactment analogues. First, select an ordinary stimulus situation (person, event, activity, and so on) that occurs in the natural environment. Second, select the clinical setting where the contrived stimulus situation will be presented. Next, modify the clinical setting in whatever ways feasible to approximate as naturalistic a setting as possible. Fourth, build in ways for the client to respond both verbally and physically whenever possible (nonvocal clients may be requested to gesture). Fifth, wherever possible gather data on component responses as well as on terminal responses. Thus, when a videotape recording of the client answering the telephone is made, molecular responses (i.e., orienting to the phone when ringing, picking it up, putting it to the ear, saying "Hello") as well as molar, terminal ones (i.e., the completed social skill of answering a telephone) can be assessed using techniques such as time sampling and interval recording described in Chapter 3. Moreover, permanent product data will facilitate the identification of those variables that control responding. Sixth, consider using enactment analogues as one dependent measure. This can be done in a pre-posttest format or by periodic probing. In cases where skill deficits are in the process of being remediated, the enactment analogue can be used as an ongoing behavioral assessment technique.

An example of an enactment analogue may be useful to illustrate these guidelines. One of the authors (MDP) once worked in a group home for autistic children that focused on teaching daily living skills to the residents. It was determined that one particular adolescent resident, Billy, would benefit from training in answering the door. Following the determination using task analysis of the component behaviors that were comprised in "appropriate door answering," the staff undertook a behavioral assessment of Billy's current level of functioning on the target behavior. A videotape recorder was placed unobtrusively across the room and switched on. Then one staff member went out the back door, came around the front, and rang the bell. Billy responded to the stimulus (the doorbell) by walking back and forth from the entrance foyer to the dining room in a somewhat agitated manner. This pattern of responding maintained over several "trials" of answering the doorbell.

The consistency of Billy's responding suggested a skill (as opposed to a performance) deficit. The videotapes subsequently were analyzed for their component subskills, including (1) orienting to the door; (2) saying, "Someone's at the door;" (3) walking toward the door; (4) unlocking the door; (5) grasping and turning the handle, and opening the door; (6) saying to the caller, "Hello, can I help you?" These analyses identified the presence of an orienting response (1), but an absence of behaviors 2 through 6. Training then proceeded along the lines of this task analysis of doorbell answering, from behavior 2 through 6. Periodically, performance of the terminal response and component behaviors was assessed using a written checklist of behaviors 1 through 6 in enactment analogue situations. In this particular case, slight modifications of the training program were initiated as a result of ongoing assessment data.

The foregoing discussion of naturalistic and analogue assessment has stressed the interaction of each of these methods with the concept of situational specificity. Issues such as obtrusiveness of the observation technique and reactivity also are operative to varying degrees in both naturalistic and analogue settings. Some of these suggestions may be difficult (and in some cases impossible) to implement. In some work environments, chronic understaffing renders anything but periodic behavior checks unworkable. In situations such as these, do the best that can be done. With that caveat, discussions of reactivity, analogue assessment, natural assessment, and so forth are offered for those who *are* able to change, or for those clinicians who would like to consider these issues during assessment. The authors have stated a preference for multidimensional assessment in the natural environment, but recognize the practical limitations such assessment imposes. When naturalistic assessment is not feasible, enactment analogues are the methods of choice for assessing social skills in severely developmentally disabled clients.

SUMMARY

Several factors can affect the assessment and acquisition of social skills in clients with severe developmental disabilities. A functional approach to social skill assessment appears to be most useful for this population. Issue was taken with earlier "avoidance" paradigms, and it was suggested that social skill deficits may well be due to deficits in interpersonal perception. When assessing social skills, clinicians must consider molar and molecular aspects of the target behavior. It should be determined whether the absence of the social behavior is due to a performance deficit or a skill deficit. Response covariation—the degree to which a change in the target behavior influences other, nontarget behaviors—is important to consider. Overselective responding may interfere with the acquisition of social behaviors in severely developmentally disabled clients, and should be considered. Finally, the impact of situational specificity on the assessment of social skills was discussed, with a special emphasis on naturalistic and analogue methods of assessment.

REFERENCES

American Psychiatric Association. (1980). *Diagnostic and statistical manual of mental disorders* (3rd ed.). Washington, DC: Author.

Bartack, L., & Rutter, M. (1976). Differences between mentally retarded and normally intelligent autistic children. *Journal of Autism and Childhood Schizophrenia, 6,* 109–120.

Bellack, A. S. (1979). A critical appraisal of strategies for assessing social skill. *Behavioral Assessment, 1,* 157–176.

Bijou, S. J., & Baer, D. M. (1978). *Behavior analysis of child development.* Englewood Cliffs, NJ: Prentice-Hall.

Borkovec, T. D. (1973). The effects of instructional suggestion and physiological cues on analogue fear. *Behavior Therapy, 4,* 185–192.

Carr, E. G. (1983, May). The social motivation of self-injurious behavior. Address presented at the National Conference on Self-Injurious Behavior, Valley Forge, PA.

DeMyer, M. K., Barton, S., DeMyer, W. E., Nort, J. A., Allan, J., & Steele, R. (1973). Prognosis in autism: A follow-up study. *Journal of Autism and Childhood Schizophrenia, 3,* 199–246.

Durand, V. M., & Carr, E. G. (1982, August). Differential reinforcement of communicative behavior (DRC): An intervention for the disruptive behaviors of developmentally disabled children. In R. L. Koegel (Chair), *Research on Clinical Intervention with Autistic and Psychotic Children.* Symposium conducted at the 90th Annual Convention, American Psychological Association, Washington, DC.

Eisler, R. M. (1976). The behavioral assessment of social skills. In M. Hersen & A. S. Bellack (Eds.), *Behavioral assessment: A practical handbook.* Elmsford, NY: Pergamon Press.

Epstein, L. H. (1976). Psychophysiological measurement in assessment. In M. Hersen & A. S. Bellack (Eds.), *Behavioral assessment: A practical handbook.* Elmsford, NY: Pergamon Press.

Greer, R. D., Powers, M. D., & Shanley, D. (1980, April). Defining the social components of an IEP via task-analysis of non-academic school behavior. Workshop presented at the 58th Annual Convention, Council for Exceptional Children, Philadelphia.

Grossman, H. (Ed.). (1983). *Classification in mental retardation* (rev. ed.). Washington, DC: American Association on Mental Deficiency.

Harris, S. L. (1975). Teaching language to nonverbal children—with emphasis on problems of generalization. *Psychological Bulletin, 82,* 565–580.

Harris, S. L. (1976). *Teaching speech to a nonverbal child.* Lawrence, KS: H & H Enterprises.

Harris, S. L., and Ferrari, M. (1983). Developmental factors in child behavior therapy. *Behavior Therapy, 14,* 54–72.

Hersen, M., & Bellack, A. S. (1976). *Behavioral assessment: A practical approach.* Elmsford, NY: Pergamon Press.

Howlin, P. (1978). The assessment of social behavior. In M. Rutter & E. Schopler (Eds.), *Autism: A reappraisal of concepts and treatment.* New York: Plenum Press.

Hutt, S. J., & Hutt, C. (1970). *Behaviour studies in psychiatry.* Elmsford, NY: Pergamon Press.

Kanner, L. (1943). Autistic disturbances of affective contact. *Nervous Child, 2,* 181–197.

Kara, A., & Wahler, R. G. (1977). Organizational features of a young child's behaviors. *Journal of Experimental Child Psychology, 24,* 24–39.

Kazdin, A. E. (1977). Assessing the clinical or applied importance of behavior change through social validation. *Behavior Modification, 1,* 427–452.

Kazdin, A. E. (1979a). Unobtrusive measures of behavioral assessment. *Journal of Applied Behavior Analysis, 12,* 713–724.

Kazdin, A. E. (1979b). Situational specificity: The two-edged sword of behavioral assessment. *Behavioral Assessment, 1,* 57–75.

Kent, R. N., & Foster, S. L. (1977). Direct observational procedures: Methodological issues in naturalistic settings. In A. R. Ciminero, K. S. Calhoun, & H. E. Adams (Eds.), *Handbook of behavioral assessment.* New York: Wiley.

Koegel, R., & Covert, A. (1972). Relationship of self-stimulation to learning in autistic children. *Journal of Applied Behavior Analysis, 5,* 381–387.

Koegel, R., & Wilhelm, W. (1973). Selective responding to components of multiple visual cues by autistic children. *Journal of Experimental Child Psychology, 15,* 442–452.

Lichstein, K., & Schreibman, L. (1976). Employing electric shock with autistic children: A review. *Journal of Autism and Childhood Schizophrenia, 6,* 163–173.

Lovaas, O. I. (1961). Interaction between verbal and nonverbal behavior. *Child Development, 32,* 329–336.

Lovaas, O. I., Koegel, R. L., & Schreibman, L. (1979). Stimulus overselectivity in autism: A review of research. *Psychological Bulletin, 86,* 1236–1254.

Lovaas, O. I., Schreibman, L., Koegel, R., & Rehm, R. (1971). Selective responding by autistic children to multiple sensory input. *Journal of Abnormal Psychology, 77,* 211–222.

Marholin, D., Siegel, L. J., & Phillips, D. (1976). Treatment and transfer: A search for empirical procedures. In M. Hersen, R. M. Eisler, & P. M. Miller (Eds.), *Progress in Behavior Modification* (Vol. 3). New York: Academic Press.

Nay, W. R. (1977). Analogue measures. In A. R. Ciminero, K. S. Calhoun, & H. E. Adams (Eds.), *Handbook of behavioral assessment.* New York: Wiley.

Paronson, B. S., & Baer, D. M. (1978). Training generalized improvisation of tools by preschool children. *Journal of Applied Behavior Analysis, 11,* 363–380.

Powers, M. D., & Crowel, R. L. (1983, December). The use of positive practice overcorrection to reduce noncontextual vocalizations and teach responses to social questions with an autistic child. Paper presented at the World Congress on Behavior Therapy, 17th Annual Convention of the Association for Advancement of Behavior Therapy, Washington, DC.

Powers, M. D., Shanley, D., & Greer, R. D. (1980, August). Teaching social skills to the autistic child: Strategies for definition and assessment. Workshop presented at the National Conference on the Seriously Emotionally Disturbed, Council for Exceptional Children, Minneapolis.

Romanczyk, R. G. (1983, May). Self-injurious behavior: Models and the myth of a response class. Address presented at the National Conference on Self-Injurious Behavior, Valley Forge, PA.

Schopler, E. (1978). National Society for Autistic Children: Definition of the syndrome of autism. *Journal of Autism and Child Schizophrenia, 8,* 162–166.

Schover, L., & Newsom, C. (1976). Overselectivity, developmental level and overtraining in autistic and normal children. *Journal of Abnormal Child Psychology, 4,* 289–298.

Schreibman, L., & Lovaas, O. I. (1973). Overselective response to social stimuli by autistic children. *Journal of Abnormal Child Psychology, 1*(2), 152–168.

Steinman, W. (1977). Generalized imitation and the setting event concept. In B. Etzel, J. LeBlanc, & D. Baer (Eds.), *New developments in behavioral research.* New York: Wiley.

Stokes, T. F., & Baer, D. M. (1977). An implicit technology of generalization. *Journal of Applied Behavior Analysis, 10,* 349–367.

Voeltz, L. M., & Evans, I. M. (1982). The assessment of behavioral interrelationships in child behavior therapy. *Behavioral Assessment, 4,* 131–165.

Wahler, R. G. (1975). Some structural aspects of deviant child behavior. *Journal of Applied Behavior Analysis, 8,* 27–42.

Wolf, M. M. (1978). Social validity: The case for subjective measurement or how applied behavior analysis is finding its heart. *Journal of Applied Behavior Analysis, 11,* 203–214.

Guidelines for the Behavioral Assessment of Social Skills

INTRODUCTION

Chapter 4 describes several important issues to consider when assessing social skills in clients who are severely developmentally disabled. Chapter 5 presents guidelines for the behavioral assessment of play; social interactions (including social/approach behaviors and social communicative behaviors); vocational skills; mealtime behaviors; and community living skills. These areas have been chosen because they are often-cited priorities for intervention with the severely developmentally disabled. Assessment methods for these behaviors can be generalized to other social skills not included in Chapter 5. In addition, a framework for the assessment of self-injurious behavior (SIB) is described. Because SIB frequently interferes with the acquisition of many adaptive behaviors, including social skills, an assessment methodology leading to specific treatment decisions is an important adjunct to the assessment of social skills.

PLAY AND LEISURE BEHAVIOR

Clients with severe developmental disabilities frequently exhibit deficiencies in play- or leisure-time skills. For professionals concerned with habilitation of autistic and severely or profoundly retarded individuals, it is important to give attention to this deficit. While attention to deficits in social interaction, adaptive self-care behaviors, and behavioral excesses (e.g., self-stimulation) is critical to treatment efforts, the adaptive use of "nontreatment" time remains an area of concern for many severely developmentally disabled clients. Thus, it is useful to consider play-skill assessments when developing intervention programs for this population.

Preparatory Assessment of Play

Prior to any formal assessment of play skills, certain information must be obtained to assist in assessment planning. An assessment of self-stimulatory behavior should be conducted in order to determine whether topography, rate, and frequency potentially will interfere with the assessment of play skills and/or subsequent intervention. Koegel, Firestone, Kramme, and Dunlap (1974) found that high rates of self-stimulation were incompatible with spontaneous play. Reducing self-stimulation led to increases in play behavior. Hence, an assessment of self-stimulatory behavior will lead to the determination of whether this behavior will need to be reduced prior to assessment and intervention with play.

Knowledge of the reinforcement value of various toys and leisure activities will allow clinicians a firmer base from which to begin formal assessment of play skills. For example, knowing that a client prefers objects that provide sensory feedback (e.g., electronic games) over objects that are manipulated or constructed (e.g., blocks or Legos) might lead the clinician to an assessment of the client's ability to use a "see and spell" toy. Thus, the principal determination to be made prior to formal assessment involves which type of leisure activity or toy the client finds attractive. Clinicians armed with this information can increase the likelihood that leisure skills will be maintained and generalized once taught to clients.

The assessment of reinforcer values can be accomplished by surveying parents, teachers, and caretakers for suggestions, arranging these suggestions in a free-choice format, and recording client preferences. The choices also can be included in a reinforcement menu, made available contingent upon task completion or appropriate behavior. Here again client preferences are noted. These preferred activities can then be validated by pairing high-demand activities with low- and medium-demand activities and recording client choices (see Favell & Cannon, 1977; Mithaug & Hanawalt, 1978). Alternatively, social validation techniques can be used (Wolf, 1978) whereby the opinions of family and community members are sought. Finally, it may be necessary to assess communicative skills so clients' optimal mode of responding can be utilized when their preferences are assessed. Reid & Hurlbut (1977) assessed and subsequently trained multi-handicapped retarded clients to use a communication board so leisure activity preferences could be made known. With clients for whom preferred activities have been identified, vocal and nonvocal gestures may suffice in the free-choice format described above. In all cases, it is important to consider client preferences rather than our own. Social convention often dictates what professionals and caretakers would choose as a potentially reinforcing appropriate play activity. Given the often idiosyncratic reinforcement needs of many severely developmentally disabled clients, however, allowing their choice may facilitate generalization, maintenance, and more efficient use of toys.

Assessment of Play

Two general approaches to the assessment of play are described in the literature. One is best characterized as a behavioral task analytic model and the other as a developmental behavioral model. Each model approaches the process of assessment with different assumptions. While not mutually exclusive for practical assessment purposes, each will be described separately.

Behavioral Task Analytic Model

This approach begins with the identification of a specific play/leisure skill to be assessed. The model is behavioral in that it attempts to measure operationally defined behaviors occurring in naturalistic or analogue settings. In addition, each specific skill is broken down into its component subskills through task analysis (see Chapter 3). Exhibit 5-1 presents a generic model for the behavioral task analytic assessment of play/leisure skills with severely developmentally disabled clients.

The utility of task analysis for training leisure/play behaviors is well documented (Nietupski & Williams, 1974; Peterson & McIntosh, 1973; Schleien, Wehman, & Kiernan, 1981; Wehman, Renzaglia, Shutz, & Karan, 1976; Wehman, 1978; Williams, Pumpian, McDaniel, Hamre-Nietupski, & Wheeler, 1975). However, its use for assessment purposes prior to treatment has been less well documented (Greer, Powers & Shanley, 1980; Powers, Shanley & Greer, 1980). Such an approach has much to commend it and will be described.

The behavioral task analytic model begins with a task analysis of the terminal behavior in which component subskills are identified (step one). In the second step, *motor* and *attentional* responses necessary for the performance of each subskill are determined (Schleien et al., 1981). Motor responses include hand positioning, physical placement, and so on. Attentional responses include verbal behaviors, listening, following commands, and so on. Following task analysis,

---

Exhibit 5-1 Generic Model for Behavioral Task Analytic Assessment

---

Play and Leisure Skills

1. Task analyze play behavior.
2. Determine motor and attentional responses necessary for performance.
3. Define subskills operationally.
4. Determine levels of prompts.
5. Select assessment method.
6. Implement assessment plan.

each subskill must be defined operationally for purposes of assessment recording (step three). The fourth step involves a determination of prompt levels. Stokes, Baer, and Jackson (1974) describe four prompt levels:

1. Give full prompt (clinician "takes client through" task).
2. Give graduated guidance (help is provided only if a client response breaks down).
3. Shadow physical prompt (clinician's hand shadows, but does not touch, client's hand).
4. Verbalize the desired action (clinician instructs client to perform act).

To these the authors add: model, or perform the action in view of the client; and orient or nonverbally direct the client to the activity by gesturing, pointing, glancing, and so on. For assessment purposes, modeling would be placed before verbalizing (4) in Stokes and colleagues' (1974) scheme, and orienting would precede verbalizing. Thus, a useful prompt level hierarchy might be: (1) orienting, (2) verbalizing, (3) modeling, (4) shadowing physical prompt, (5) giving graduated guidance, (6) giving full prompt. It is important to note that assessing the level of prompt necessary for a client to perform a subskill entails *forward chaining*, that is, beginning at Level 1 and proceeding upward until the subskill is performed. In contrast, training a client to perform a skill typically involves the use of *backward chaining*, or gradually requiring the client to perform more and more of the skill in an independent manner.

The fifth step involves the selection of an assessment method. Wehman (1978) advises the use of videotaping wherever possible, with subsequent continuous recording of the client's responses with the use of a code. This facilitates interrater reliability checks, especially when assessment is conducted with a single client at a time. In contrast, time sampling provides for high rates of interrater reliability but captures fewer aspects of play behavior. Clearly, the choice of assessment methods will be dictated by such factors as staff time, financial resources, and so on, in addition to these and other methodological considerations. When planning or interpreting assessment data, however, it is useful to consider issues that may have an impact on the data collected. It is beyond the scope of the present section to detail methodological issues; refer to Nay (1977) and Kent and Foster (1977) for a thorough discussion.

Step six represents the implementation of the assessment plan. Motor, attentional, and terminal responses necessary for performance are assessed. In addition, level of prompt necessary for each subskill is assessed. All of these assessments are conducted using the assessment method selected in step five. Once completed, this process provides the starting point for training. Finally, the unique features of the behavioral task analytic approach permit the use of changing criterion designs (Hartmann & Hall, 1976) during treatment phases.

Developmental Behavioral Model

This approach is best characterized as a stage model based upon developmental theory (particularly the work of Piaget) that utilizes behavioral assessment methods. A fundamental assumption of this model is that knowledge of the specific stage of play a client engages in will facilitate treatment planning. An assessment of play stage will permit clinicians to choose stage-appropriate activities, and will direct their intervention efforts upward through the play hierarchy.

Several developmental behavioral assessment frameworks have been reported (Clune, Paolella & Foley, 1979; Lowe, 1975; Riguet, Taylor, Benaroya, & Klein, 1981; Ungerer & Sigman, 1981; Whittaker, 1980; Wintre & Webster, 1974). Each assessment framework utilized an observational code containing from 5 to 11 categories of play. Units of observation were coded categorically; time sampling or interval recording methods were used. Interrater reliability was reportedly high in these studies (range = 85.9 to 98.0).

This approach to assessment assumes that a determination of developmental stage is a necessary precursor to intervention. Unfortunately, no research exists comparing behavioral task analytic and developmental behavioral models on the basis of play skill acquisition, generalization, and maintenance. The utility of developmental psychology to child behavioral assessment and therapy with less disabled clients has been noted elsewhere (see Harris & Ferrari, 1983). This research question extends the proposal made by Harris and Ferrari (1983) and remains an important area of future work. In the meantime, developmental behavioral models have much to commend them, particularly in the selection of stage-appropriate play activities.

The assessment of play behaviors should be conducted in both structured and unstructured free-play settings (Ungerer & Sigman, 1981). Structured settings typically employ a standardized set of toys spanning developmental levels and may have a standardized procedure to control adult-client interaction. In contrast, free-play assessment involves direct observation of clients' interactions with those materials available to them in the classroom, home, and dayroom.

Clune and colleagues (1979) and Wintre and Webster (1974) describe assessment scales for use with severely developmentally disabled children. While both scales were used in free-play (unstructured) situations, they easily are adaptable to structured settings. Clune and colleagues (1979) assessed play behavior using a code with 7 categories. These categories extended from minimal manipulation/ examination of the play material while a client is holding it, through unelaborate simple pretending by a client for brief episodes, to highly elaborate appropriate play involving the use and integration of several materials by a client engaged in fantasy activities. Each unit of play was scored for one of the 7 categories. Interrater reliability was greater than .90.

A different scale was reported by Wintre and Webster (1974), based upon earlier work by Parten (1932), on the social play of psychotic and autistic children using a 7 category scale of:

1. unoccupied behavior
2. solitary independent play
3. onlooker
4. parallel activity
5. associative play
6. cooperative or organized supplementary play
7. adult-directed nonplay behavior

Reliability of 85.9 was reported over the five-week investigation. Moreover, all coders were inexperienced, suggesting the utility of this code for paraprofessionals and cottage staff.

A sophisticated assessment method was described by Ungerer and Sigman (1981) who developed an assessment scale comprising four areas (simple manipulation, relational play, functional play, symbolic play) with a total of 11 categories. Play was assessed in both structured and free-play settings with 16 autistic children (mean age = 51.7 months). Play behavior was videotaped and subsequently coded using an interval recording method (10-second intervals). Duration of play was measured by totaling the number of intervals in which each category occurred, and diversity of play behavior was determined by comparing a frequency measure of relational versus manipulation versus functional versus symbolic play intervals. Reliability for all but 2 categories was .90 or greater.

This assessment method is noteworthy for its use of interval recording, a complex code, and well-defined behavioral categories. Its use may facilitate treatment planning better than other assessment scales reported. While Ungerer and Sigman (1981) used descriptive methods to report correlations between levels of language and play in their subjects, the treatment planning capacities of this assessment scale represent an important area for future research.

Taken as a group, the developmental behavioral assessment models presented have certain limitations. Because they are based upon developmental play sequences of young children, they may have little generalizability to older adolescent or adult severely developmentally disabled clients. For such clients, assessment and programming for leisure activities (e.g., games) may be a more fruitful enterprise. In addition, Wehman (1978) notes that the use of time sampling and interval recording methods may obfuscate naturally occurring chains or sequences of behavior. These chains frequently provide important data for treatment planning, often saving considerable programming time. Thus, while developmental behavioral approaches show promise, final judgment as to their utility and cost-effectiveness must be reserved until comparative research is done. For the present, they most appropriately are regarded for their heuristic value.

SOCIAL INTERACTIONS

The assessment of social interactions with severely developmentally disabled clients encompasses behaviors ranging from eye contact to the ability to use a telephone. Moreover, special consideration must be given to interpersonal skills. These molecular behaviors include voice loudness and tone, intonation, smiling, posture, and so on. While these skills are frequently ignored as areas for intervention, their development facilitates habilitation by increasing social appropriateness and reducing dissonance with nonhandicapped members of society (Powers et al., 1980).

The assessment of social interactions can be divided into assessment of social communicative behaviors and assessment of social or approach behaviors. Each is discussed separately, although in practice considerable overlap exists. Prior to the formal assessment of these domains, however, preparatory behaviors must be assessed.

Preparatory Assessment

As in the assessment of play behaviors, clinicians will need certain information before proceeding with an assessment of interpersonal or social/approach behaviors. Foxx (1977) notes that an assessment of salient reinforcers is an important prerequisite to helping severely developmentally disabled clients acquire social skills. In addition, eye contact must be assessed (Foxx, 1977; Harris, 1976). Eye contact is a prerequisite to teaching numerous behaviors to severely developmentally disabled clients, particularly where modeling is involved. When assessing eye contact, clinicians must determine (1) compliance to the verbal command, "Look at me," (2) duration of sustained eye contact after command compliance; and (3) degree of prompting required to establish eye contact if clients do not comply with commands. Exhibit 5-2 describes prompt levels to be assessed for eye contact.

Imitative ability may need to be assessed, depending upon the terminal social skill to be taught. Both nonverbal and verbal imitation should be assessed (see Harris, 1976). Nonverbal imitation is defined as the imitation of motor acts after the clinician models them and says, "Do this." Verbal imitation is defined as the client repeating the clinician's modeled verbal behavior. The need to assess these skills varies. For example, if an instructional goal of independent telephone use were contemplated, both verbal and nonverbal imitative abilities would enhance training and thus would be assessed.

Exhibit 5-2 Prompt Levels to Consider when Assessing Eye Contact

In order to establish eye contact for at least one second, do clients require:
1. food held at the bridge of the clinicians' noses;
2. their faces "shadowed" by the clinicians' hands as they turn in the direction of the clinicians' eyes;
3. their faces guided gently by the clinicians' fingers until eye contact is established;
4. a full physical prompt (i.e., the clinicians hold clients' faces in their hands while gazing into their clients' eyes)?

Command compliance is an important preparatory behavior to assess (Greer et al., 1980). The clinician should determine the client's ability to follow directions and to stop on command and should identify the antecedent and consequent conditions that facilitate command compliance.

An assessment of the client's social approach behavior should be conducted prior to the formal assessment of specific social interactive behaviors. Strain and his colleagues (Strain & Timm, 1974; Strain, Shores, & Timm, 1977) have demonstrated that the social initiation and approach behavior of behaviorally disordered children can be increased by reinforcing those behaviors in non-handicapped playmates. These authors also found, however, that those target children who exhibited abusive or disruptive behaviors toward their peers were less likely to be approached by the other children, thereby effectively reducing opportunities for interaction. Clinicians should remember that social interactions are dyadic in nature. That is, interactions occur within a social context where the severely developmentally disabled client is but one member of the dyad. Thus, before teaching social interactive behaviors to severely developmentally disabled clients, clinicians must determine whether any of the clients' behavior may elicit an *avoidance* response in others. Such behaviors include clients standing too close to listeners, clients spitting when talking, or clients engaging in self-stimulatory hand flapping when excited. As disruptive behavior of this type may inhibit the approach behavior of others—effectively reducing opportunities for interaction—the reduction of disruptive or abusive behavior may be an important goal *prior* to teaching social interactions.

Finally, for some programs, an assessment of object identification might be necessary. For example, a client being taught to cross the street should be able to identify a stop sign, stoplight, and walk signal. Similarly, when training clients to use buses or answer telephones, clinicians must assess their abilities to label these objects. Finer discriminations needed for effective use of the object must also be assessed, such as a public bus versus a school bus. Attention to these areas will allow for more comprehensive and individualized training, facilitating maintenance and generalization of learned skills.

Special Considerations

The behavioral assessment of both interpersonal skills and social/approach behaviors is best conducted using a task analysis of the terminal behavior. As with the assessment of play, a determination of the motor and attentional responses necessary for task performance follows task analysis. All subskills then are defined operationally, and prompt levels are determined. An assessment method is then selected, and the assessment plan is implemented. This generic framework allows clinicians to account for situational or methodological constraints that are inherent in the particular social skill being assessed.

Foster and Richey (1979) note that situational parameters (antecedents and consequences and setting events) and behavior of others present are important dimensions to consider in social skill assessment with children. Failure to consider these factors removes the behavior from its relevant context, thereby reducing the social validity of the data.

Foster and Richey (1979) also suggest the use of behavioral observations as the assessment method of choice (instead of, for example, parental or staff report) for five reasons:

1. The focus on well-defined, specific behaviors (as opposed to constructs) limits inferences.
2. Reliability is under the control of clinicians, not clients.
3. Biases that influence observational data (e.g., observer drift, bias, and reactivity) have been investigated, and remedial steps have been proposed.
4. Observational data lead directly to treatment.
5. Observational data facilitate the functional analysis of the target behavior.

Attention to these situational and methodological constraints will forestall several of the major problems that often invalidate social skill assessment data.

Assessment of Social/Approach Behaviors

Telephone Use

Leff (1974, 1975) describes a device and procedure to teach severely developmentally disabled clients to dial the telephone (see Figure 5–1). Her approach, based upon a task analysis of motor responses that her clients needed to learn the procedure, includes the following assessment steps.

- *Preparatory assessment:* assess the client's ability (a) to match-to-sample colors and numbers; (b) to point; (c) to dial a telephone *without* using the device (thereby precluding the need for training); (d) to insert a finger into the appropriate hole on the dial when the device is attached.

Figure 5–1 A Device for Assessing and Teaching Telephone Use

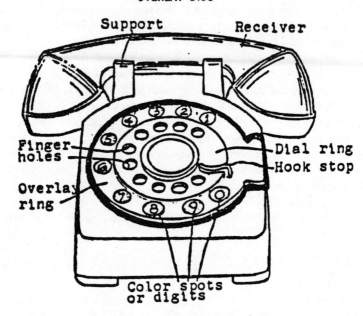

OVERLAY DISC *

FIGURE 2
SLIDE *

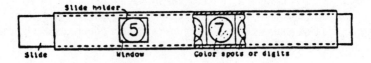

FIGURE 3
SLIDE HOLDER *

Source: Leff, R. B. (1974). Teaching the TMR to dial the telephone. *Mental Retardation, 12,* p. 12.
Copyright 1974 by the American Association on Mental Deficiency. Reprinted by permission.

Figure 5–1 continued

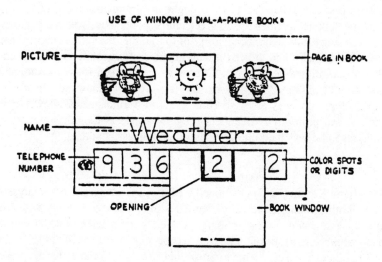

USE OF WINDOW IN DIAL-A-PHONE BOOK•

Source: Leff, R. B. (1975). Teaching TMR children and adults to dial the telephone. *Mental Retardation,* *13,* p. 10. Copyright 1975 by the American Association on Mental Deficiency. Reprinted by permission.

*Patent is pending.

- *Training assessment:* assess client's ability (a) to place discs over the telephone (disc A = 10 numbers; disc B = 10 colors with numbers on them); (b) to push the slide with numbers on it into the slide holder until the first number appears; (c) to point to the color in the window of the slide holder, point to the matching color/number on the disc, put finger into corresponding adjacent hole, and dial; (d) to pull slide one square to the left until the next color appears in the window and repeat step c; (e) to continue step d until the telephone number is dialed.

Each step can be assessed following one demonstration by the clinician, with each step scored (+) or (−). Training then follows assessment, beginning at the first step failed. Leff (1974, 1975) notes that knowledge of mental age is helpful, as clients with a mental age of less than five years performed better with numbered discs. Moreover, clients with visual motor difficulties had more difficulty learning to dial the telephone using this device. Hence, an assessment of mental age and visual motor abilities should be helpful in treatment planning.

Greeting Response

Stokes, Baer, and Jackson (1974) taught institutionalized severely or profoundly mentally retarded clients to greet adults spontaneously with a handwave. When assessing handwaving behavior prior to training, the authors defined handwaving operationally and created a naturalistic assessment setting using unobtrusive observational recordings. Clients were assessed for (a) spontaneous handwaves, (b) prompted handwaves, and (c) incorrect handwaves. In addition, the level of prompt was assessed (full, graduated guidance, shadow physical prompt, verbal prompt). A treatment program aimed at training a generalized greeting response was then initiated based upon assessment data.

Toothbrushing

Horner and Keilitz (1975) developed a careful and elaborate task analysis for teaching toothbrushing to mentally retarded adolescents (see Exhibit 5–3). Their naturalistic assessment prior to training involved bringing clients into a room with a sink, a toothbrush, a tube of toothpaste, a paper cup, and a box of tissues near the sink. The clinician asked clients to brush their teeth using the materials present. The presence or absence of each step in the task analysis was recorded on a data sheet. After finishing the baseline assessment (with no clinician assistance), each client was assessed a second time and the level of prompt required for performance of each step was recorded (e.g., no help; verbal instruction; demonstration by

---

Exhibit 5–3 Task Analysis of Toothbrushing

1. Pick up and hold toothbrush.
2. Wet toothbrush.
3. Remove cap from toothpaste.
4. Put toothpaste on brush.
5. Replace cap on toothpaste.
6. Brush *outside* surfaces of teeth.
7. Brush *biting* surfaces of teeth.
8. Brush *inside* surfaces of teeth.
9. Fill a cup with water.
10. Rinse mouth.
11. Wipe mouth.
12. Rinse toothbrush.
13. Rinse sink.
14. Put all equipment away.
15. Throw away paper cup and used tissues.

Source: Adapted from Horner, R. D., & Keilitz, I. (1975). Training mentally retarded adolescents to brush their teeth. *Journal of Applied Behavior Analysis, 8,* p. 303.

clinician with a verbal instruction; graduated guidance with a verbal instruction). These data then were combined with those from the first baseline in developing an individualized treatment plan.

Behavioral assessment protocols for social/adaptive behaviors are based largely on a comprehensive task analysis. While it is beyond the scope of Chapter 5 to describe other analyses, Kelley (1978) and Anderson, Hodson, and Jones (1975) give detailed task analyses of numerous social/adaptive behaviors.

Assessment of Social Communicative Behaviors

Interpersonal skill deficits are endemic to the severely developmentally disabled population. Clients frequently exhibit pronounced deficits in social communicative behaviors, impeding their ability to interact with the larger environment in socially acceptable ways. Problematic behaviors in this subset include voice loudness; conversational skills; negative behaviors, such as interrupting or cursing; speech latency; rate of speech; intonation; posture; requesting things; self-introduction; and smiling (Bornstein, Bach, McFall, Friman, & Lyons, 1980; Jackson & Wallace, 1974; Matson & Andrasik, 1982; Matson & Earnhart, 1981; Matson & Zeiss, 1979; Nelson, Gibson, & Cutting, 1973; Ross, 1969; Wheeler & Wislocki, 1977).

The proper performance of these behaviors serves both social and habilitative functions (Powers et al., 1980). Their presence in the repertoire of severely developmentally disabled clients means that these people are more likely to be viewed as socially appropriate by others. As a result, nonhandicapped people are likely to increase their social contact with handicapped ones (approach behaviors). In addition, social communicative behaviors are often prerequisites for severely developmentally disabled people to obtain sanctions to be trained in other, more habilitative skills. For both of these reasons, the comprehensive assessment of social communicative behaviors is warranted.

Voice Loudness

Training severely developmentally disabled clients to modulate their voices when speaking has been an area of recent interest (Bornstein et al., 1980; Jackson & Wallace, 1974; Matson & Andrasik, 1982). Jackson and Wallace (1974) note that any assessment of inaudible speech must account for social and/or environmental stimuli that might encourage clients to maintain low-volume speech. The generic behavioral assessment framework described in Chapter 2 is useful in this regard. In addition, these authors suggest assessment techniques sensitive to slight increases in volume (e.g., a decibel meter) so that the behavior can be shaped over the course of treatment. Finally, situational specificity and generalization of training effects should be assessed over time in both naturalistic and analogue settings. (Jackson & Wallace, 1974).

Matson and Earnhart (1981) assessed loud talking in four institutionalized mentally retarded adult women. Each client was first assessed on the ward by independent raters to determine rate of response. Following that, assessment analogues were conducted consisting of scenes representing situations that historically had elicited the target response in the clients. Following collection of rate of response in the analogue settings, training was conducted using the scenes. While the use of problem social situations as analogue assessment settings is novel and deserves future attention, the lack of generalizability of such analogues due to situational specificity or stimulus overselectivity with some severely involved clients must be considered in planning and remains an area for future research.

Bornstein and colleagues (1980) have developed an assessment and treatment protocol for mentally retarded adults' interpersonal skill deficits, including loudness. Their assessment method is noteworthy in several respects. Each client was videotaped three times over a one-week assessment period, and each tape was subsequently analyzed. The use of videotape facilitated unobtrusive assessment (see Kent & Foster, 1977; Kazdin, 1979), and the use of multiple assessment sessions reduced the effects of situational specificity (see Kazdin, 1979). Their assessment method consisted of a five-point, Likert-type scale for rating loudness on an inappropriate-to-appropriate continuum. Interrater reliability was high, indicating that each target behavior was defined clearly. Finally, the use of continua recognizes that "loudness" is a relative behavior; in some situations it is more appropriate than in others.

Conversational Skills

Several authors have assessed and treated deficits in conversational skills. Matson and Andrasik (1982) have broken this construct into a wide variety of subskills for mentally retarded adults. The subskills include introducing oneself; asking questions or favors of others; giving compliments; and talking politely. In their assessment phase, these authors used a naturalistic setting (a leisure hour) and noted the occurrence/nonoccurrence of each target behavior to be increased. Also noted were inappropriate conversational behaviors to be decreased (e.g., complaining, non sequiturs, talking to self or to objects). These ratings then served as baseline data for treatment evaluation. The success of the assessment and treatment program underscores the necessity for carefully designed operational definitions when assessing conversational skills in this population.

Matson and Zeiss (1979) assessed and reduced several inappropriate conversational behaviors in two mentally retarded psychotic adults. Target behavior included insulting or unreasonable statements; interrupting; arguing; and tantrumming. In an effort to assess the pervasiveness of the target behaviors, all clients self-recorded their behavior and a "buddy's" behavior in the clinician's office and on the ward eight hours a day, seven days a week. Independent observers also rated client behavior in both settings. This study is noteworthy for its use of multiple assessment environments, naturalistic and analogue assessment settings in combination, and for its use of a "buddy system" where two clients were paired, facilitating modeling effects during training.

Client self-monitoring can be expected to produce considerable reactivity. In some clinical situations, self-monitoring is used as an intervention. Matson and Zeiss (1979) doubtless were aware of this effect, and reported treatment effects due to the treatment *package* rather than to any one component. In settings where valid and reliable pretreatment data are required, the "buddy system" monitoring is less desirable. However, the vast majority of clinicians working with the severely developmentally disabled must be prepared to take positive behavioral change from wherever it can be obtained. In these situations, the issue of reactivity is of little importance.

Wheeler and Wislocki (1977) assessed and treated peer interactions among four institutionalized severely retarded adult women. Peer conversation was defined on three levels:

1. an utterance connected to/related to an exchange of tokens (given for work completion);
2. an utterance directed toward the attendant or the group in general;
3. a comment or question directed toward one other member of the group.

As in the Matson and Zeiss (1979) study, peer-interactive behavior was assessed in multiple settings (work and snack sessions). Wheeler and Wislocki (1977), however, measured target behaviors using an interval recording method (15-second intervals for 2- to 15-minute periods daily). This latter point is noteworthy, as interval recording provides for more precise data collection.

Interval recording also was used by Nelson, Cone, Gibson, and Cutting (1973) in assessing three social-interactive behaviors in a mentally retarded boy (using grammatically correct forms of speech when answering questions; smiling; and speaking on appropriate topics). In addition, these authors utilized an analogue assessment session with a confederate (an eight-year-old nonhandicapped boy) who was trained to interact with his retarded peer using a standardized script. All observations were conducted from behind a one-way mirror using a behavior code (reliability = .86) with six possible responses scored as present or absent. Training followed assessment, using the nonhandicapped confederate in the analogue setting.

This study has several strengths. The utility of a relatively short baseline session (5 minutes) was offset by nine postbaseline assessment sessions and a three and one-half month follow-up. The use of a confederate and a standardized analogue raises interesting questions for future research. For example, confederates might be employed in naturalistic settings, and client performance with confederates versus nonconfederates assessed. Finally, a well-defined code was used with interval recording methods, contributing to the overall reliability and validity of the data.

Bornstein and colleagues (1980) describe several subskills of speech, including enunciation and speech latency. While so molecular as to appear unimportant, deficits of this type often have a cumulative effect. These subskills frequently warrant attention with severely developmentally disabled clients.

As can be seen in Exhibit 5–4, multimethod assessment greatly facilitates the assessment of subskills subsumed under the construct "conversational skills." Clinicians developing assessment and treatment plans for conversational skills with this population thus would do well to consider the full range of options

---

Exhibit 5–4 Social Interaction Target Behaviors and Assessment Methods

Target Behavior	Assessment Method
1. Number of words spoken	Measurement of total number of words spoken in response to prompts
2. Speech latency	Length of time (in seconds) from end of clinician's prompt to the beginning of client's response
3. Inappropriate hand-to-face gestures	Duration of face touches
4. Overall interpersonal effectiveness	Five-point, Likert-type scale where 1 = poor and 5 = very effective
5. Posture	Score sitting position on a five-point Likert-type scale from inappropriate sitting to highly appropriate sitting
6. Enunciation	Intelligibility of response and crispness of vowel-consonant speech forms were rated on five-point scales
7. Inappropriate speech content	Duration of inappropriate speech divided by corresponding duration of speech
8. Loudness	Five-point scale: appropriate to inappropriate
9. Inappropriate hand movement	Duration measure (in seconds)
10. Intonation	Five-point scale, based on pitch and voice quality
11. Eye contact	Duration measure (in seconds)
12. Rate of speech	Ratio of number of words spoken divided by duration of speech

Source: Adapted from Bornstein, P. H., Bach, P. J., McFall, M. E., Friman, P. C., & Lyons, P. D. (1980). Application of a social skills training program to the modification of interpersonal deficits among retarded adults: A clinical replication. *Journal of Applied Behavior Analysis, 13,* 171–176.

described in Chapter 3 (e.g., duration, event recording, and so on), tailoring their choice to the particular assessment question.

VOCATIONAL SKILLS

As severely developmentally disabled children grow older, the focus of educational programming shifts from academics to prevocational and vocational training (Fredericks, Buckley, Baldwin, Moore, & Stremel-Campbell, 1983). As a result, it becomes important to assess each client for preparatory skills and those behaviors required for completion of a specific work task. However, because vocational training is dependent upon the involvement of the community at large (e.g., soliciting job contracts, using public transportation to get to the work place), ecological assessment is warranted also. Thus, in contrast to other social skill domains, vocational assessment *must* extend to a larger system level to ensure skill acquisition, maintenance, and generalization.

There are three goals of vocational assessment. Revell and Wehman (1978) note that such assessment should provide a predictive statement of the severely developmentally disabled client's vocational capabilities. In addition, descriptive statements of the types of training needed to develop this potential should be provided. Finally, Rusch (1979) notes that maintenance of employment is a critical goal of vocational assessment. Clearly, these goals transcend the individual level of assessment, and often will require use of a wide variety of assessment methods, from community surveys to direct observation in naturalistic settings. Strategies to achieve these goals and relevant assessment methods will be discussed.

Community Assessment

Prior to any assessment of individual client skills, it is important to assess possible job opportunities in the community (Revell & Wehman, 1978; Rusch, 1979; Wehman & Hill, 1981). This assessment will allow clinicians to determine the general requirements of jobs available, as well as particular skills necessary for each. Rusch (1979) distinguishes between *social* survival skills and *vocational* survival skills when assessing community job placements. Social survival skills include such behavioral skills as managing activities independently, meeting minimal requirements for cleanliness, or demonstrating the ability to follow directions to begin or cease an activity. In addition, "looking busy" (attending to task) may be a useful social survival skill (Rusch, 1979). In contrast, vocational survival skills are related more directly to work-related behaviors. These include the ability to make basic needs known, to move around in the work space safely, and to perform particular work behaviors required for the job—for example, social-interactive skills for a restaurant busboy (Rusch, 1979).

Client Assessment

This phase seeks to describe vocational potential and necessary training to reach that potential. It builds upon the assessment data gathered from prospective employers, and focuses on a client-job match that will have a high likelihood of maintenance over time.

Revell and Wehman (1978) have divided client assessment phases into: (a) clinical assessment; (b) work evaluation; (c) work adjustment; and (d) on the job assessment. *Clinical assessment* compiles and interprets medical, social, educational, and psychological data in an effort to determine current level of functioning, as well as strengths and limitations that might affect a client's job performance. These data can be gathered from archival records or formal assessments when past records are unavailable.

The *work evaluation* is concerned with obtaining information about the work habits, attitudes, and particular work skills of the severely developmentally disabled client. Assessment methods include intake interviews with family members or significant others; work and job samples designed to assess both acquisition skills (i.e., learning style) and production skills; and situational assessments of the work site (see Brolin, 1976; Revell & Wehman, 1978).

Revell and Wehman (1978) provide several guidelines for an assessment of work and job samples.

- Task analyze the job to be learned, so each step can be assessed/learned *prior* to an evaluation of total job performance.
- Assess all prerequisite behavior (visual attention, using a wrench, and so on).
- Assess salient reinforcers.
- Assess level of prompt necessary for clients to complete a task.
- Assess functional determinants of all failures to learn (antecedent and consequent events).

These guidelines can be expanded according to the particular constraints of the case.

Work adjustment evaluation seeks to gather and interpret information on the client's overall level of adjustment as it has an impact on performance (Revell & Wehman, 1978). Ratings of client, coworker, and employer satisfaction are useful in this regard. These ratings can be compared to measures of productivity to determine relationships between attitude and productivity. In those cases where more formal ratings of satisfaction are impractical, informal sampling may provide useful information.

Finally, *on-the-job assessments* must be conducted. Wehman and Hill (1981) describe three domains to be assessed in this phase.

1. Proficiency must be assessed (i.e., the client's ability to perform all behaviors identified in the task analysis in the work environment).
2. Assess level of independence over several day's time; independence is defined as the amount of trainer assistance (none, verbal reminders, gestures, physical prompts) clients require in order to complete a job.
3. Assess nontask vocational skills necessary to job performance (e.g., use of telephone, use of public transportation).

The completion of these four phases of client assessment (i.e., clinical, work evaluation, adjustment, on-the-job) leads to placement and ongoing evaluation. The goal of placement evaluation is to help clinicians make judgments about the work program so that it can be modified, expanded, or terminated. Relevant assessment dimensions and methods include: (1) observe on-and-off-task behavior at intervals during the work day; (2) record frequency of trainer assistance needed; (3) assess client's behavior for appearance, productivity, social behavior, absenteeism, and so on at the end of each day; (4) write supervisor evaluations; (5) record weekly wages earned (Wehman & Hill, 1981). These methods represent only a sample of possible ways to collect evaluative data. Others will be developed based on the needs and constraints of the system, and the creativity of the staff.

Assessment of Vocational Skills

Assessment of specific vocational tasks follows the framework outlined earlier in Chapter 5 for other social skill behaviors (e.g., play, social interactions, and so on). The motor and attentional behaviors necessary for job performance first must be task analyzed and defined operationally. Prompt levels then must be determined, and an assessment method selected. Finally, the assessment plan is implemented, with the resultant data used to guide treatment.

The use of task analysis in teaching vocational skills is not a recent development. Crosson (1969), for example, developed a taxonomy for operating a drill press and trained severely and profoundly mentally retarded clients in its use. However, this and other training protocols frequently have eschewed formal behavioral assessment, as training was moved to directly after an initial determination of skill absence. In addition to leaving clinicians with few data against which to evaluate treatment outcome, such an approach neglected all but gross levels of prior skill and ignored important situational events.

As the utility of behavioral assessment for treatment planning became more evident, this narrow use of task analysis began to shift. It is beyond the scope of Chapter 5 to provide an exhaustive description of vocational task analyses. However, a recent example by Cuvo, Leaf, and Borakove (1978) is prototypical and should be instructive.

Cuvo and colleagues (1978) developed a program to teach janitorial skills to mentally retarded adolescents. Janitorial skills were defined as cleaning the bathroom. This was further defined as:

- cleaning the mirror
- cleaning the sink
- cleaning the urinal
- cleaning the toilet
- emptying the wastebasket
- sweeping the floor
- mopping the floor
- returning all equipment

Each of these eight tasks had component subtasks (see Exhibit 5–5). The task analysis of the entire procedure (i.e., all 8 steps, from start to finish) comprised 181 steps. Client performance on cleaning the bathroom was assessed in the natural environment. Each client was led to a bathroom where all materials necessary were present and visible. The clinician then instructed the client to clean the entire bathroom using the materials present. Client performance on each step of the task analysis was noted. Training then followed assessment, with assessment of response generalization occurring after skill acquisition.

It should be noted that only the 8 subskills were assessed (i.e., cleaning mirror, sink, toilet, and so on) prior to training. Subtasks making up each subskill (see Exhibit 5–5) were used only for training and for assessment of response generalization.

This study highlights several important aspects of vocational skill assessment. First, the skill in question must be well defined. Second, "benchmark" tasks can be assessed initially, rather than each component subtask. For example, it is sufficient to note that a client was unable to clean the sink when the client failed to perform any action at all at the sink. An assessment of the 17 steps in Exhibit 5–5 would have been superfluous. Third, the assessment of component subtasks is necessary once treatment has begun and during generalization probes. Fourth, assessment in the natural environment is preferred. While this study did not report attentional behaviors that were assessed, they presumably were sufficient judging by rate of skill acquisition. In other situations, clinicians would do well to identify and assess these behaviors more formally.

Vocational task training is a related area of vocational skill assessment and the principal goal of vocational programs. When several possible tasks exist for a given client, staff frequently make decisions as to which skill to train in the client. Mithaug and Hanawalt (1978) describe a procedure that allowed nonverbal severely retarded clients to choose work tasks; then they validated those choices.

Exhibit 5–5 Task Analysis of Cleaning the Sink

1. Take spray cleaner from container.
2. Shake spray cleaner.
3. Spray entire sink with back-and-forth sweeping motions.
4. Replace cleaner in container.
5. Reach over to towel dispenser.
6. Pick up two paper towels.
7. Put paper towels together.
8. Wipe sink sides and edges with back-and-forth strokes.
9. Wipe between faucets with back-and-forth strokes.
10. Wipe faucets by lightly grasping them with towel and twisting back-and-forth.
11. Wipe sink bowl with circular and back-and-forth motions.
12. Turn on cold water.
13. Swish water around bowl with towel.
14. Turn off cold water.
15. Wipe sink bowl again with towel, using circular and back-and-forth motions.
16. Bend over wastebasket, which is located under sink.
17. Throw dirty towels in wastebasket.

Source: Cuvo, A. J., Leaf, R. B., & Borakove, L. S. (1978). Teaching janitorial skills to the mentally retarded: Acquisition, generalization, and maintenance. *Journal of Applied Behavior Analysis, 11,* p. 347. Copyright 1978 by the Society for the Experimental Analysis of Behavior. Reprinted by permission.

The implications of this research are obvious. By allowing clients to choose tasks, motivation is enhanced. As enhanced motivation increases performance, both client and workshop contractor benefit.

There were two phases to the study by Mithaug and Hanawalt (1980). Phase 1 entailed the repeated random presentation of two tasks selected from a pool of six typical prevocational tasks (e.g., collating, stuffing envelopes, attaching electronic resistors to a circuit board, and so on). The client chose one of the two tasks presented and was allowed to work at it. This procedure occurred daily for 34 days. At the end of this period, "most," "least," and "moderately" preferred tasks were determined for each client based upon frequency of choice.

Phase 2 consisted of forced comparisons, requiring clients to choose from pairings ("most" with "least," "moderate" with "least") designed to validate Phase 1 findings. Of the Phase 1 choices, 75% were completely validated, and an additional 32% were partially validated. Mithaug and Hanawalt's (1980) procedures appear relevant to other vocational settings as well. Further empirical research will be needed to determine whether productivity and client satisfaction do in fact increase when clients are allowed to choose their work tasks.

Time management is a frequent problem for severely developmentally disabled clients in vocational settings. As punctuality is almost always a requirement of community employers, time management assessment and training is an important goal for this population. Sowers, Rusch, Connis, and Cummings (1980) developed an assessment and training program to teach trainable mentally retarded adults to leave for and return from lunch and coffee breaks on time.

Assessment was divided into two phases: (a) time-telling, and (b) time management. In the first phase, each client's ability to tell time was assessed at all hour times and at random 5-minute intervals. A wall clock was used, and all responses were recorded. Assessment in the second phase consisted of telling clients their assigned breaks and lunch times daily, and then recording whether they left or returned in a timely manner (plus or minus 10 minutes). A program designed to train punctuality was then implemented successfully (Sowers et al., 1980).

Transportation to and from vocational job placements is an important area for assessment with severely developmentally disabled clients. Page, Iwata, and Neef (1976) assessed and trained retarded clients to cross city streets. Neef, Iwata, and Page (1978) assessed and taught bus riding to a similar group of clients residing in a city. In both cases, the authors used a detailed task analysis to construct a decision tree for training (see Figure 5–2). In addition, Page and colleagues (1976) and Neef and colleagues (1978) used analogue settings to conduct the initial assessment and training. Generalization and maintenance probes then were conducted in the natural environment. Both studies utilized direct observation methods; each step of the task analysis was scored for presence or absence of the response. Figure 5–2 provides a diagram of the task analysis and resultant decision tree developed for crossing the street by Page and colleagues (1976). This model should serve a heuristic function when developing treatment protocols that clearly link assessment to intervention.

MEALTIME BEHAVIOR

Habilitative skills, such as eating, drinking, or using utensils appropriately, often are poorly developed with severely developmentally disabled clients. These deficits represent important areas for assessment for several reasons. Lack of appropriate mealtime behaviors restricts the range of normalizing experiences to which clients can be productively exposed. In addition, such deficits place extra demands on staff time; without training, these deficits become chronic. Finally, the presence of behaviors that are socially desirable (e.g., independent eating and toileting) give the client access to the natural community of reinforcers (Stokes & Baer, 1977). For these reasons, assessment and training of mealtime behaviors are important goals for this population.

Assessment of Mealtime Behavior

A wide variety of treatment programs for training mealtime skills have been reported. These include training clients in the use of utensils (Barton, Guess,

Figure 5–2 Task Analysis and Decision Tree for Assessing Client's Ability to Cross Street

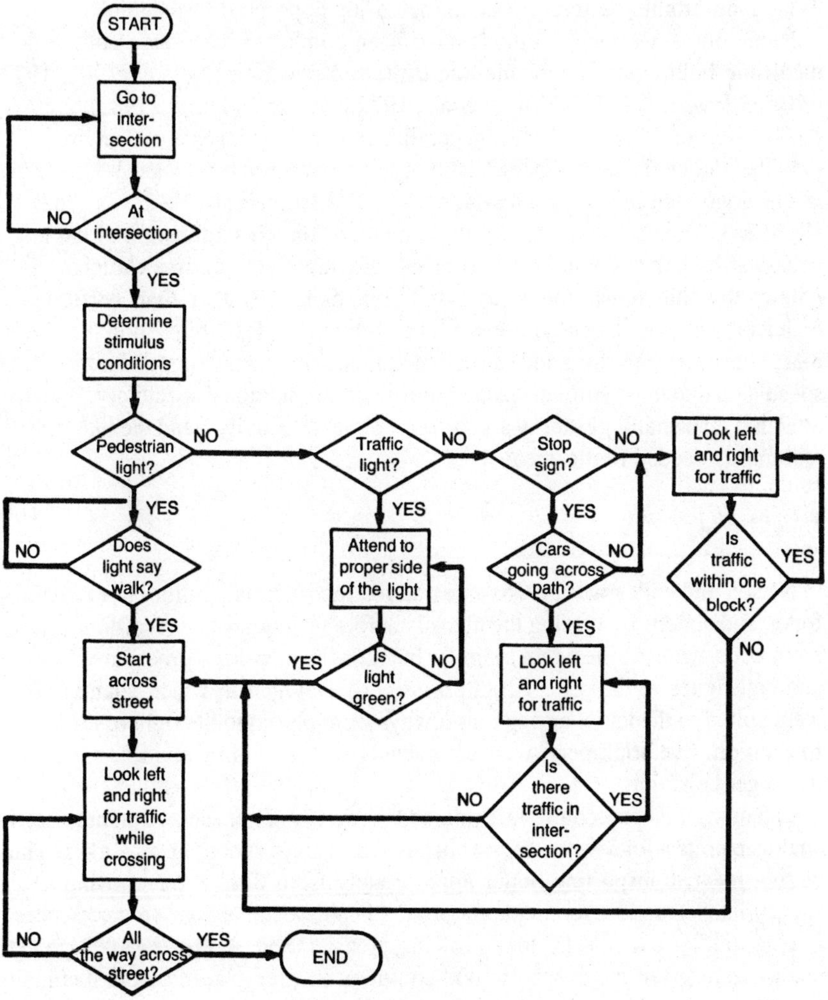

Source: Page, T. J., Iwata, B. A., & Neef, N. A. (1976). Teaching pedestrian skills to retarded persons: Generalization from the classroom to the natural environment. *Journal of Applied Behavior Analysis, 9,* p. 439. Copyright 1976 by the Society for the Experimental Analysis of Behavior. Reprinted by permission.

Garcia, & Baer, 1970; Nelson et al., 1975; O'Brien & Azrin, 1972; O'Brien, Bugle, & Azrin, 1972; Zeiler & Jervey, 1968), the use of napkins (O'Brien & Azrin, 1972), appropriate social behavior in restaurants (van den Pol, Iwata, Ivancic, Page, Neef, & Whitley, 1981), and appropriate verbal behavior when ordering food in restaurants (van den Pol et al., 1981). While some studies have focused on reducing inappropriate mealtime behavior (e.g., Barton et al., 1970), in the main training efforts focus on increasing appropriate behaviors.

Numerous assessment methods have been employed when assessing various mealtime behaviors. These include direct observation (Nelson et al., 1975; O'Brien & Azrin, 1972; O'Brien et al., 1972; van den Pol et al., 1981), archival records (Zeiler & Jervey, 1968), generalization probes to the natural environment (van den Pol et al., 1981), naturalistic observation settings (Nelson et al., 1975), and analogue settings (O'Brien & Azrin, 1972; O'Brien et al., 1972; van den Pol et al., 1981). The use of any one of these methods remains a function of the target behavior in concert with the resources and creativity of the clinician. It is noteworthy that most studies assessed skill deficits (rather than performance deficits) of clients. Hence, little work has been done describing stimulus factors that contribute to performance deficits with mealtime behaviors. While it can be speculated that these stimulus factors may include situational specificity, selective attention (especially gustatory and olfactory overselectivity), and the like, further research is needed in this area.

Utensil Use

Nelson and colleagues (1975) assessed retarded clients' abilities to use knives, forks, and spoons by placing the utensils before the clients and recording correct/incorrect use during meals. In a similar but more standardized procedure, O'Brien and colleagues (1972) created an assessment analogue in which clients' bowls were bolted to the table, and spoons always were placed to the right of the bowls. In addition, five brief meals were conducted daily, providing multiple samples of the target behavior.

Extending this procedure, O'Brien and Azrin (1972) developed an assessment analogue pretest for seven mealtime behaviors (using a spoon, glass, fork, napkin; cutting meat; transporting butter appropriately from dish to plate; using hands appropriately) and several inappropriate mealtime behaviors (e.g., drooling; licking; taking oversized bites; throwing utensils, and so on). For this pretest, clients were given meals where food and utensils were placed before them, and they then were instructed to eat. A one-hour limit (or completion of the meal) was imposed. Each appropriate and inappropriate mealtime behavior was defined operationally, and an observer recorded client responses. Results of this assessment led to training based upon individual client deficits.

Several aspects of this assessment protocol are noteworthy. The use of a standardized assessment package allowed evaluation of treatment effects during and after training. Target behaviors were specified clearly and defined operationally. A descriptive statement of skills needed was developed in lieu of a task analysis. This latter method is more suited to behaviors where process or order are important. In O'Brien and Azrin's case, it mattered little whether clients ate with a fork or spoon first, as long as they did not eat with their hands.

Restaurant Behavior

While task analysis was less appropriate for assessing and training utensil use, it is the method of choice for more complex sequences of behavior, such as ordering a meal from a fast-food restaurant. Independent eating, appropriate social behavior in a restaurant, and appropriate verbal behavior when clients ordered food and used money was task analyzed by van den Pol and colleagues (1981). This analysis formed the basis for assessment and training in an analogue setting and for generalization assessment probes (see Exhibit 5–6). As is evident from Exhibit

---

Exhibit 5–6 Task Analysis of Restaurant Skills

Skill	Appropriate Response
1.1	Does not initiate social interaction. Does not self-stimulate.
1.2	Enters double door within 2 min of start.
1.3	Goes directly to counter. Does not leave line except to go into shorter line.
2.1	Makes ordering response within 10 sec of cue. If written, finishes within 2 min.
2.2	Says "How much for . . .?" when giving order.
2.3	Orders food that he can afford, appropriate item combination (i.e., minimum order—sandwich & drink; maximum—sandwich, drink, side order, & any other item).
2.4	Says "Eat here" when asked.
3.1	Begins to get money within 10 sec of cue. Does not let go of money on counter before cashier cue.
3.2	Hands cashier appropriate combination of bills.
3.3	Displays fingers on at least one hand.
3.4	Inquires "Mistake?" If short billed.
3.5	Puts money in pocket.
3.6	Requests salt, pepper, or catsup.
3.7	Takes a napkin from dispenser.
3.8	Says "Thank you."
4.1	Sits at unoccupied, trashfree table within 1 min of availability.
4.2	Eats food placed only on paper.
4.3	Puts napkin in lap *and* wipes mouth or hands.
4.4	Does not spill food or drink.
4.5	If spills occur, picks up every one, does not eat any spilled item.
4.6	Puts trash in container, tray on top, within 2 min of finishing eating.
4.7	Exits within 1 min of trash or 3 min of finishing eating.

Source: van den Pol, R. A., Iwata, B. A., Ivancic, M. T., Page, T. J., Neef, N. A., & Whitley, F. P. (1981). Teaching the handicapped to eat in public places: Acquisition, generalization, and maintenance of restaurant skills. *Journal of Applied Behavior Analysis, 14*, p. 63. Copyright 1981 by the Society for the Experimental Analysis of Behavior. Reprinted by permission.

5–6, assessment was divided into phases (e.g., preparatory behavior and entering: 1.1 to 1.3; ordering: 2.1 to 2.4, and so on). Thus, each phase could be assessed and client behavior could be trained separately, if necessary.

This study is important in that it utilized analogue *and* naturalistic assessment settings in combination with observational recording. In addition, generalization probes were conducted in multiple settings (MacDonalds and Burger King). Finally, a molar skill—eating at a restaurant—was the terminal behavior in which clients were trained. Thus, not only did these authors assess several molecular behaviors and train their clients accordingly but they also gave these clients an important, socially desirable behavior that will give them access to a wide variety of social (and primary) reinforcers. Kelley (1978) and Anderson, Hodson, and Jones (1975) give numerous examples of mealtime task analyses suitable for assessment and training.

ASSESSMENT OF COMMUNITY LIVING SKILLS

The recent emphasis on deinstitutionalization of many autistic, severely retarded, and profoundly retarded clients has led to an increase in the demand for alternative living situations (Lettick, 1983). For many of these clients, living at home is not a suitable option. It thus becomes necessary to assess clients for placement, often into small, professionally staffed group homes in the community.

In developing assessment models for other social skills, the individual level has largely been the focus. That is, a single client's behavioral strengths and weaknesses are assessed against a standard (e.g., a task analysis of the terminal behavior). Assessment of community living skills requires a similar assessment, plus much more. Here, also, there must be concern for the ecological competence (Sundberg, Snowden, & Reynolds, 1978) of clients within the respective community environment. Thus, client/group home compatibility should be assessed.

Landesman-Dwyer (1981) describes these two assessment domains in considerable detail. She notes that when assessing a client's ability to reside in a group home setting, an ecological assessment is imperative. That is, an assessment of group home characteristics and community characteristics must be conducted. Relevant areas of inquiry include the number and training of staff; the extent of environmental barriers for clients with special needs; the level of functioning and behavioral excesses and deficits of other residents; the staff's competence with behavioral procedures for unusual problems (e.g., self-injury; aggression); the consulting and/or support staff available; the type and extent of home-based training available; the amount of structure available; the theoretical orientation of program (e.g., behavioral, milieu); the integration of group home with community; and the outings and other normalizing experiences available.

Client characteristics (strengths, weaknesses, behavioral excesses, and deficits) also must be assessed (Landesman-Dwyer, 1981). These include special medical- or nursing-care needs; personal hygiene skills; care of clothing (e.g., washing); use of clothing (e.g., independent dressing); home maintenance skills (e.g., vacuuming); meal preparation; social behavior; communication skills; leisure skills; use of community resources (e.g., public transportation, pedestrian skills); and extent and magnitude of self-stimulation, self-injury, and aggression.

Data collection methods will run the gamut from observational recording in naturalistic or analogue (clinic) settings to the use of archival data (incident reports, adaptive behavior notes, accident and medical records). There are no hard and fast rules concerning selection of methods, but several points should be born in mind. Valid and reliable data, preferably corroborated by multiple sources in several settings, are most useful. Practical considerations may compromise aspects of selection, however, In such cases, sources of error should be acknowledged and reviewed when evaluating the initial placement.

Armed with information from both ecological and client assessments, those persons responsible for the client should prioritize the needs of the client and compare this list with the ability of the group home to meet those needs. Maher's (1981) decision analytic model may be useful in this regard. Completion of this comparison then leads to a placement selection. In most cases, placement choices should be considered provisional for a period of two to six months, at which time further assessment will determine continuation or termination.

SELF-INJURIOUS BEHAVIOR

Self-injurious behavior (SIB) is one of the most extreme and pernicious behaviors exhibited by clients manifesting severe developmental disabilities. Fortunately, it is a relatively infrequently observed behavior within this population, with reports ranging from 4%–5% (Frankel & Simmons, 1976) to 8%–17% or more (Rincover & Devany, 1982; Schroeder, Schroeder, Smith, & Dalldorf, 1978). Self-injurious behavior takes many forms, from pica, scratching, and self-biting to eye gouging and head banging resulting in bleeding and/or concussion. Treatment of SIB typically employs operant conditioning procedures and has been comprehensively summarized in recent reviews (Baumeister & Rollings, 1976; Favell, 1983; Frankel & Simmons, 1976; Picker, Poling, & Parker, 1979).

Despite this intensive treatment effort, relatively little work has been reported assessing SIB prior to intervention. Much of the treatment literature describes a quick assessment of topography, frequency, and intensity of SIB with little assessment of motivational factors (however, see Iwata, Dorsey, Slifer, Bauman, and Richman, 1982; and Durand and Carr, 1982 for notable exceptions). While the failure to assess SIB in a comprehensive manner may sometimes be co-opted by the life-threatening nature of the behavior, such situations are fortunately the exception rather than the rule. More often, the failure to assess comprehensively is based upon the (fallacious) assumption that baseline rates of frequency, duration, and intensity are sufficient. Unfortunately, treatment failures, including failure to generalize and maintain the absence of self-injury, exist and serve to point out the faulty logic inherent in such an assumption. This section describes a framework for the assessment of self-injury in severely developmentally disabled clients. In so doing, Carr's (1977) motivational hypotheses and the subsequent work it spawned is relied upon heavily.

Carr (1977) reviewed the literature on SIB and hypothesized four potential motivators. Each serves a different function for the client, and has different assessment and treatment implications. They are as follows:

- Self-injurious behavior may be maintained by positive social reinforcement (e.g., adult attention and approval).
- Self-injurious behavior may have an escape or avoidance function, and thus may be maintained by negative reinforcement (e.g., SIB occurs when demands are high).
- Self-injurious behavior may be an extreme form of self-stimulation, and thus may serve to provide the client with sensory stimulation (e.g., eye poking often produces a retinal flash).
- Self-injurious behavior may be due to organic factors (e.g., Leysch-Nyhan syndrome or otitis media).

It was further suggested that self-injury may serve more than one function in a given client, depending upon environmental conditions (Carr, 1977). This notion has received recent empirical support (Carr, 1983; Carr & McDowell, 1980; Durand & Carr, 1982; Iwata et al., 1982).

Recent research has addressed each of these functions of SIB. For example, Lovaas, Freitag, Gold, and Kassorla (1965) found that the severely developmentally disabled maintained high rates of self-injury when adult attention was given for such behavior. Conversely, a substantial body of literature exists documenting the effects of removal of social approval on decreasing self-injury (see Frankel and Simmons, 1976; and Picker and colleagues, 1979, for extensive reviews).

Academic or other demanding situations sometimes create a level of frustration in severely developmentally disabled children which they seek to escape or avoid altogether. Iwata and colleagues (1982) found that a boy with Rubenstein-Taybi syndrome engaged in higher rates of face slapping, head banging, and hand biting when exposed to academic tasks. This same pattern was observed by Carr, Newsom, and Binkoff (1976) and Durand and Carr (1982) with severely developmentally disabled children.

Self-injurious behavior may be an extreme form of self-stimulatory behavior for some severely developmentally disabled clients (Baumeister & Forehand, 1973; Lewis, 1983). In such cases, SIB may be maintained by the sensory stimulation resulting from the acts. Recent attempts to remove or reduce sensory consequences from SIB have succeeded in decreasing high rates (Dorsey, Iwata, Reed, & Davis, 1982; Rincover & Devany, 1982). In addition, Favell, McGimsey, and Schell (1982) were able to reduce self-injury in a client by substituting responses that produced topographically identical stimulation, but were not harmful to the client (e.g., chewing on toys was substituted for pica). This latter study illustrates the point that self-injury exists on at least two continua simultaneously. It can be placed on the far right of the continuum of self-stimulatory behaviors, and it also exists on a more relative continuum, that of social acceptability. Few would argue that toy chewing is less acceptable than pica, although both are seen as socially and developmentally primitive. Treatment choices such as those made by Favell and colleagues (1982) often represent the least restrictive intervention and deserve further exploration experimentally and through social validation (see Wolf, 1978).

Finally, SIB may be due to organic or biological factors, such as Lesch-Nyhan syndrome, Cornelia de Lange syndrome, or Riley-Day syndrome (insensitivity to pain) (Cataldo & Harris, 1982). However, while the genesis of the self-injurious behavior may have been biologically based, other functions, such as social reinforcement or escape/avoidance, may maintain the behavior once the biological cause is no longer present (Carr & McDowell, 1980).

Assessment of Self-Injurious Behavior

The assessment framework for self-injury relies heavily on the seminal work of Carr (1977) and subsequent experimental investigations of his hypotheses. The generic behavioral assessment framework presented in Chapter 2 applies to self-injury as well. However, particular emphasis is placed on the identification of environmental and organismic controlling variables (at a molecular level) and the development of a treatment plan (at a more molar level). The ensuing model focuses on variables controlling the self-injury. Refer to Chapter 2 for assessment considerations for treatment planning.

Assess for Organic Abnormalities

This may involve genetic screening for Lesch-Nyhan, de Lange, or Riley-Day syndromes, or a medical screening for ear infections (Carr, 1977). In addition, assess for positively or negatively reinforcing consequences that may be maintaining the behavior beyond an organic cause.

Figure 5–3 A Framework for the Behavioral Assessment of Self-Injury

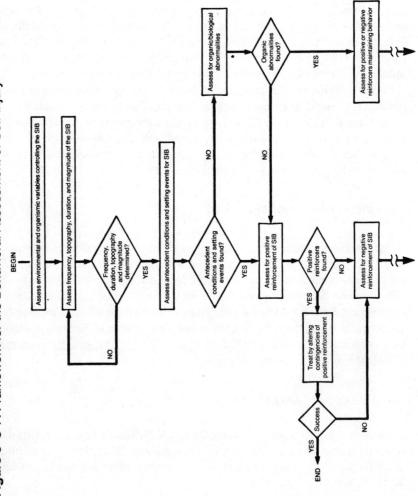

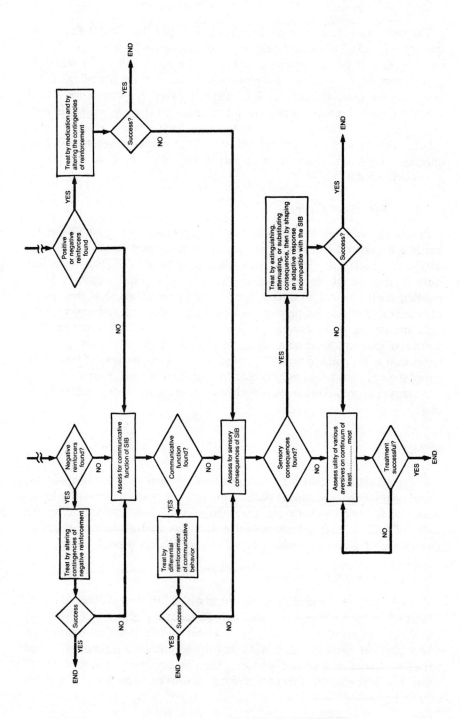

The third assessment to be conducted is based upon the work of Favell and colleagues (1982). The client should be assessed for sensory reinforcers that may take the place of the self-injurious behavior. Wherever possible, the substitute sensory reinforcer should have a functional relationship to the site being injured and providing sensory feedback. For example, Favell and colleagues (1982) substituted chewable toys for pica and prisms and lights for eye poking. In both cases, the new self-stimulatory behavior was related functionally to the self-injury (placing objects in the mouth and creating visual images, respectively). The alternative behaviors, however, were less socially undesirable as well as not physically harmful.

Assess for Behavioral Chains

Frequently, self-injurious behavior exists as part of a complex chain of behavior. It is important to identify these chains, because recent research (Zlutnick, Mayville, & Moffat, 1975; Angle, Hay, Hay, & Ellinwood, 1977) has found that early interruption of the chain often preempts the terminal response. Thus, recalling the example in Chapter 2, hand biting by an autistic child was always preceded by the child's jumping up from the chair, screeching, and waving of the right arm during work sessions. An assessment of behavioral chains made it possible to intervene at the point where the child was jumping up from the chair, rather than at the point of the child's hand biting. An assessment of behavioral chains should be conducted regardless of the function of the self-injury determined previously. Figure 5–3 summarizes each of the above assessment phases in a flow chart.

SUMMARY

Chapter 5 outlined assessment strategies for the behavioral assessment of play, social interactions, vocational skills, mealtime behaviors, community living skills, and self-injurious behavior. Throughout, emphasis has been placed on the utility of multidimensional assessment methods as well as the assessment of preparatory behaviors upon which the various social skills depend.

Assess for Positive Reinforcement

Consider those environmental situations in which SIB is most likely to occur. Assess for positive consequences that may be following emission of SIB. This could take the form of positive or negative verbal attention; physical intervention where physical contact is at a minimum in the client's environment; visual attention (a brief or extended glance); excessive confusion as staff members scramble to intervene with the client; a change in work routines. It is helpful at this point to recall those reinforcers that are known to be salient to the client and to determine whether any of these are available when episodes of SIB occur. Assess antecedent stimuli for events that might "bring about" self-injury (e.g., a particular child screaming, the presence of a certain staff member, a particular time of day or place). Any setting event found to co-occur reliably with self-injury should be included. Assess for a possible communicative function of the self-injury (see Durand & Carr, 1982). Is the client using self-injury as a means of expressing a need or desire? If so, consider alternative ways the client might express that wish (e.g., verbal response, manual sign, gestures).

Assess for Negative Reinforcement

Consider all situations that might be demanding to the client where SIB occurs. Assess these for instances of self-injury occurring (a) when demand is made of the client or (b) when the client enters the room where demands are made. If SIB occurs when the client merely enters the demanding situation, that situation can be negatively reinforcing. In such cases, desensitization or an alternate mode of task presentation may be warranted (Carr et al., 1976). Should self-injury only occur when the verbal demand is made, counterconditioning or pairing the verbal demand with a pleasant reinforcing context may suffice (Carr et al., 1976). Finally, assess for a communicative behavior that might be substituted for the self-injurious behavior as a means of escaping the demanding situation (see Durand & Carr, 1982). The goal here is not to allow the client to avoid demands altogether, but rather to begin teaching a new, complex response chain that can be shaped toward higher levels of frustration tolerance over time once the self-injury has abated.

Assess for Sensory Stimulation

Three distinct but related lines of assessment are required here. The first is to determine whether the sensory consequences of the self-injury are maintaining the behavior. Because sensory reinforcement is an internal, covert phenomenon for each person, this assessment begins with the exclusion of the three above hypotheses. Once this is done, two further assessments must be conducted. An assessment of ways to attenuate the sensory consequences of the self-injury must be undertaken. This is, by definition, functionally dependent upon the topography of the self-injury. Thus, if a client frequently bangs his head on a lunch table, try covering the table with another substance (rug, foam) to determine whether sensory reinforcement maintains the self-injurious behavior. The ability of a prosthetic device to extinguish SIB can be assessed by requiring the head banger to wear a padded helmet (Rincover & Devany, 1982) and by recording changes in the rate and intensity of self-injury.

REFERENCES

Anderson, D. R., Hodson, G. D., & Jones, W. G. (1975). *Instructional programming for the handicapped student.* Springfield, IL: Charles C Thomas.

Angle, H. V., Hay, L. R., Hay, W. M., & Ellinwood, E. H. (1977). Computer assisted behavioral assessment. In J. D. Cone & R. P. Hawkins (Eds.), *Behavioral assessment: New directions in clinical psychology* New York: Brunner/Mazel.

Barton, E. S., Guess, D., Garcia, E., & Baer, D. M. (1970). Improvement of retardate's mealtime behaviors by timeout using multiple baseline techniques. *Journal of Applied Behavior Analysis, 3,* 77–84.

Baumeister, A. A., Forehand, R. (1973). Stereotyped acts. In N. R. Ellis (Ed.), *International review of research in mental retardation* (Vol. 6). New York: Academic Press.

Baumeister, A. A., & Rollings, J. P. (1976). Self-injurious behavior. In N. R. Ellis (Ed.), *International review of research in mental retardation* (Vol. 9). New York: Academic Press.

Bornstein, P. H., Bach, P. J., McFall, M. E., Friman, P. C., & Lyons, P. D. (1980). Application of a social skills training program to the modification of interpersonal deficits among retarded adults: A clinical replication. *Journal of Applied Behavior Analysis, 13,* 171–176.

Brolin, D. E. (1976). *Vocational preparation of retarded citizens.* Colombus, OH: Charles E. Merrill.

Carr, E. G. (1977). The motivation of self-injurious behavior: A review of some hypotheses. *Psychological Bulletin, 84,* 800–816.

Carr, E. G. (1983, May). The social motivation of self-injurious behavior. Address presented at the National Conference on Self-Injurious Behavior, Valley Forge, PA.

Carr, E. G., & McDowell, J. J. (1980). Social control of self-injurious behavior of organic etiology. *Behavior Therapy, 11,* 402–409.

Carr, E. G., Newsom, C. D., & Binkoff, J. A. (1976). Stimulus control of self-destructive behavior in a psychotic child. *Journal of Abnormal Child Psychology, 4,* 139–153.

Cataldo, M. F., & Harris, J. (1982). The biological basis for self-injury in the mentally retarded. *Analysis and Intervention in Developmental Disabilities, 2,* 21–39.

Clune, C., Paolella, J. M., & Foley, J. M. (1979). Free-play behavior of autistic children: An approach to assessment. *Journal of Autism and Developmental Disorders, 9,* 61–72.

Crosson, J. E. (1969). A technique for programming sheltered workshop environments for training severely retarded workers. *American Journal of Mental Deficiency, 73,* 814–818.

Cuvo, A. J., Leaf, R. B., & Borakove, L. S. (1978). Teaching janitorial skills to the mentally retarded: Acquisition, generalization, and maintenance. *Journal of Applied Behavior Analysis, 11,* 345–355.

Dorsey, M. F., Iwata, B. A., Reid, D. H., & Davis, P. A. (1982). Protective equipment: Continuous and contingent application in the treatment of self-injurious behavior. *Journal of Applied Behavior Analysis, 15,* 217–230.

Durand, V. M., & Carr, E. G. (1982, August). Differential reinforcement of communicative behavior (DRC): An intervention for the disruptive behaviors of developmentally disabled children. In R. L. Koegel (Chair), *Research on Clinical Intervention with Autistic and Psychotic Children.* Symposium conducted at the 90th Annual Convention of the American Psychological Association, Washington, DC.

Favell, J. E. (1983). The management of aggressive behavior. In E. Schopler & G. B. Mesibov (Eds.), *Autism in adolescents and adults.* New York: Plenum Press.

Favell, J., & Cannon, P. (1977). Evaluation of entertainment materials for severely retarded persons. *American Journal of Mental Deficiency, 81,* 357–361.

Favell, J. E., McGimsey, J. F., & Schell, R. M. (1982). Treatment of self-injury by providing alternate sensory activities. *Analysis and Intervention in Developmental Disabilities, 2,* 83–104.

Foster, S. L., & Ritchey, W. L. (1979). Issues in the assessment of social competence in children. *Journal of Applied Behavior Analysis, 12,* 625–638.

Foxx, R. M. (1977). Attention training: The use of overcorrection avoidance to increase the eye-contact of autistic and retarded persons. *Journal of Applied Behavior Analysis, 10,* 489–499.

Frankel, F., & Simmons, J. Q. (1976). Self-injurious behavior in schizophrenic children. *American Journal of Mental Deficiency, 80,* 512–522.

Fredericks, H. D., Buckley, J., Baldwin, V. L., Moore, W., & Stremel-Campbell, K. (1983). The education needs of the autistic adolescent. In E. Schopler and G. Mesibov (Eds.), *Autisim in adolescents and adults.* New York: Plenum Press.

Greer, R. D., Powers, M. D., & Shanley, D. (1980, April). Defining the social components of an IEP via task-analysis of non-academic school behavior. Workshop presented at the 58th Annual Convention of the Council for Exceptional Children, Philadelphia.

Harris, S. L. (1976). *Teaching speech to a nonverbal child.* Lawrence, KS: H & H Enterprises.

Harris, S. L., & Ferrari, M. (1983). Developmental factors in child behavior therapy. *Behavior Therapy, 14,* 54–72.

Hartmann, D. P., & Hall, R. V. (1976). The changing criterion design. *Journal of Applied Behavior Analysis, 9,* 527–532.

Horner, R. D., & Keilitz, I. (1975). Training mentally retarded adolescents to brush their teeth. *Journal of Applied Behavior Analysis, 8,* 301–309.

Iwata, B. A., Dorsey, M. F., Slifer, K. J., Bauman, K. E., & Richman, G. S. (1982). Toward a functional analysis of self-injury. *Analysis and Intervention in Developmental Disabilities, 2,* 3–20.

Jackson, D. A., & Wallace, R. F. (1974). The modification and generalization of voice loudness in a 15-year old retarded girl. *Journal of Applied Behavior Analysis, 7,* 461–471.

Kazdin, A. E. (1979). Situational specificity: The two-edged sword of behavioral assessment. *Behavioral Assessment, 1,* 57–75.

Kelley, M. J. (Ed.). (1978). *Yes they can! A primer for educating the severely and profoundly retarded.* Watertown, WI: Bethesda Lutheran Home.

Kent, R. N., & Foster, S. L. (1977). Direct observational procedures: Methodological issues in naturalistic settings. In A. R. Ciminero, K. S. Calhoun, & H. E. Adams (Eds.), *Handbook of behavioral assessment.* New York: Wiley.

Koegel, R. L., Firestone, P. B., Kramme, K. W., & Dunlap, G. (1974). Increasing spontaneous play by suppressing self-stimulation in autistic children. *Journal of Applied Behavior Analysis, 7,* 521–528.

Landesman-Dwyer, S. (1981). Living in the community. *American Journal of Mental Deficiency, 86,* 223–234.

Leff, R. B. (1974). Teaching the TMR to dial the telephone. *Mental Retardation, 12,* 12–13.

Leff, R. B. (1975). Teaching TMR children and adults to dial the telephone. *Mental Retardation, 13,* 9–11.

Lettick, A. L. (1983). Benhaven. In E. Schopler & G. Mesibov (Eds.), *Autism in adolescents and adults.* New York: Plenum Press.

Lewis, M. H. (1983, May). Neurobiological correlates of self-injurious behavior. Address presented at the National Conference of Self-Injurious Behavior, Valley Forge, PA.

Lovaas, O. I., Freitag, G., Gold, V. J., & Kassorla, I. C. (1965). Experimental studies in childhood schizophrenia: I. Analysis of self-destructive behavior. *Journal of Experimental Child Psychology*, *2*, 67–84.

Lowe, M. (1975). Trends in the development of representational play. *Journal of Child Psychology and Psychiatry*, *16*, 33–47.

Maher, C. A. (1981). Decision analysis: An approach for multidisciplinary teams in planning special service programs. *Journal of School Psychology*, *19*, 340–349.

Matson, J. L., & Andrasik, F. (1982). Training leisure-time social-interaction skills to mentally retarded adults. *American Journal of Mental Deficiency*, *86*, 533–542.

Matson, J. L., & Earnhart, T. (1981). Programming treatment effects to the natural environment. *Behavior Modification*, *5*, 27–37.

Matson, J. L., & Zeiss, R. A. (1979). The buddy system: A method for generalized reduction of inappropriate interpersonal behavior of retarded psychiatric patients. *British Journal of Social and Clinical Psychology*, *18*, 401–405.

Mithaug, D. E., & Hanawalt, D. A. (1978). The validation of procedures to assess prevocational task preferences in retarded adults. *Journal of Applied Behavior Analysis*, *11*, 153–162.

Nay, W. R. (1977). Analogue measures. In A. R. Ciminero, K. S. Calhoun, & H. E. Adams (Eds.), *Handbook of behavioral assessment*. New York: Wiley.

Neef, N. A., Iwata, B. A., & Page, T. J. (1978). Public transportation training: In vivo vs. classroom instruction. *Journal of Applied Behavior Analysis*, *11*, 331–344.

Nelson, G. L., Cone, J. D., & Hanson, C. R. (1975). Training correct utensil use in retarded children: Modeling vs. physical guidance. *American Journal of Mental Deficiency*, *80*, 114–122.

Nelson, R. O., Gibson, F., & Cutting, D. S. (1973). Videotaped modeling: The development of three appropriate social responses in a mildly retarded child. *Mental Retardation*, *11*, 24–28.

Nietupski, J., & Williams, W. (1974). Teaching severely handicapped students to use the telephone to initiate selected recreational activities and to respond appropriately to telephone requests to engage in selected recreational activities. In L. Brown, W. Willliams, & R. Crowner (Eds.), *A collection of papers and programs related to public school services for severely handicapped students*. Madison, WI: Madison Public Schools.

O'Brien, F., & Azrin, N. H. (1972). Developing proper mealtime behaviors of the institutionalized retarded. *Journal of Applied Behavior Analysis*, *5*, 389–399.

O'Brien, F., Bugle, C., & Azrin, N. H. (1972). Training and maintaining a retarded child's proper eating. *Journal of Applied Behavior Analysis*, *5*, 67–72.

Page, T. J., Iwata, B. A., & Neef, N. A. (1976). Teaching pedestrian skills to retarded persons: Generalization from the classroom to the natural environment. *Journal of Applied Behavior Analysis*, 433–444.

Parten, M. B. (1932). Social participation among preschool children. *Journal of Abnormal and Social Psychology*, *27*, 243–269.

Peterson, R., & McIntosh, E. (1973). Teaching tricycle riding. *Mental Retardation*, *11*, 32–34.

Picker, M., Poling, A., & Parker, A. (1979). A review of children's self-injurious behavior. *Psychological Record*, *29*, 435–452.

Powers, M. D., Shanley, D., & Greer, R. D. (1980, August). Teaching social skills to the autistic child: Strategies for definition and assessment. Workshop presented at the National Conference on the Seriously Emotionally Disturbed, Council for Exceptional Children, Minneapolis.

Reid, D. H., & Hurlbut, B. (1977). Teaching nonvocal communication skills to multihandicapped retarded adults. *Journal of Applied Behavior Analysis*, *10*, 591–604.

Revell, W. G., & Wehman, P. (1978). Vocational evaluation of severely and profoundly retarded clients. *Rehabilitation Literature, 39*, 226–231.

Riguet, C. B., Taylor, N. D., Benaroya, S., & Klein, L. S. (1981). Symbolic play in autistic, Downs', and normal children of equivalent mental age. *Journal of Autism and Developmental Disorders, 11*, 439–448.

Rincover, A., & Devany, J. (1982). The application of sensory extinction procedures to self-injury. *Analysis and Intervention in Developmental Disabilities, 2*, 67–81.

Ross, S. A. (1969). Effects of intentional training in social behavior on retarded children. *American Journal of Mental Deficiency, 73*, 912–919.

Rusch, F. R. (1979). Toward the validation of social/vocational survival skills. *Mental Retardation, 17*, 143–145.

Schleien, S. J., Wehman, P., & Kiernan, J. (1981). Teaching leisure skills to severely handicapped adults: An age-appropriate darts game. *Journal of Applied Behavior Analysis, 14*, 513–519.

Schroeder, S. R., Schroeder, C. S., Smith, R., & Dalldorf, J. (1978). Prevalence of self-injury in a large state facility for the retarded: A three year follow-up study. *Journal of Autism and Childhood Schizophrenia, 8*, 261–269.

Sowers, J., Rusch, F. R., Connis, R. T., & Cummings, L. E. (1980). Teaching mentally retarded adults to time-manage in a vocational setting. *Journal of Applied Behavior Analysis, 13*, 119–128.

Stokes, T. F., & Baer, D. M. (1977). An implicit technology of generalization. *Journal of Applied Behavior Analysis, 10*, 349–367.

Stokes, T. F., Baer, D. M., & Jackson, R. (1974). Programming the generalization of a greeting response in four retarded children. *Journal of Applied Behavior Analysis, 7*, 599–610.

Strain, P. S., Shores, R. E., & Timm, M. A. (1977). Effects of peer social interactions on the behavior of withdrawn preschool children. *Journal of Applied Behavior Analysis, 10*, 289–298.

Strain, P. S., & Timm, M. A. (1974). An experimental analysis of social interaction between a behaviorally disordered preschool child and her classroom peers. *Journal of Applied Behavior Analysis, 7*, 583–590.

Sundberg, N. D., Snowden, L. R., & Reynolds, W. M. (1978). Toward assessment of personal competence and incompetence in life situations. *Annual Review of Psychology, 29*, 179–221.

Ungerer, J. A., & Sigman, M. (1981). Symbolic play and language comprehension in autistic children. *Journal of the American Academy of Child Psychiatry, 20*, 318–337.

van den Pol, R. A., Iwata, B. A., Ivancic, M. T., Page, T. J., Neef, N. A., & Whitley, F. P. (1981). Teaching the handicapped to eat in public places: Acquisition, generalization, and maintenance of restaurant skills. *Journal of Applied Behavior Analysis, 14*, 61–69.

Wehman, P. (1978). Leisure skills programming for severely and profoundly handicapped persons: State of the art. *British Journal of Social and Clinical Psychology, 17*, 343–353.

Wehman, P., & Hill, J. W. (1981). Competitive employment for moderately and severely handicapped individuals. *Exceptional Children, 47*, 338–345.

Wehman, P., Renzaglia, A., Schulz, R., & Karan, O. (1976). Training leisure time skills in the severely and profoundly handicapped: Three recreation programs. In O. Karan, P. Wehman, A. Renzaglia, & R. Schutz (Eds.), *Habilitation practices with the severely developmentally disabled* (Vol. 1). Madison, WI: University of Wisconsin Rehabilitation Research and Training Center.

Wheeler, A. J., & Wislocki, E. B. (1977). Stimulus factors effecting peer conversation among institutionalized retarded women. *Journal of Applied Behavior Analysis, 10*, 283–288.

Whittaker, C. A. (1980). A note on developmental trends in the symbolic play of hospitalized profoundly retarded children. *Journal of Child Psychology and Psychiatry, 21*, 253–261.

Williams, W., Pumpian, I., McDaniel, J., Hamre-Nietupski, S., & Wheeler, J. (1975). Social interaction. In L. Brown, T. Crowner, W. Williams, & R. York (Eds.), *Madison's Alternative for zero exclusion: A book of readings*. Madison, WI: Madison Public Schools.

Wintre, M. G., & Webster, C. D. (1974). A brief report on using a traditional social behavior scale with autistic children. *Journal of Applied Behavior Analysis, 7*, 345–348.

Wolf, M. M. (1978). Social validity: The case for subjective measurement or how applied behavior analysis is finding its heart. *Journal of Applied Behavior Analysis, 11*, 203–214.

Zeiler, M. D., & Jervey, S. S. (1968). Development of behavior: Self-feeding. *Journal of Consulting and Clinical Psychology, 32*, 164–168.

Zlutnick, S., Mayville, W. J., & Moffat, S. (1975). Modification of seizure disorders: The interruption of behavioral chains. *Journal of Applied Behavior Analysis, 8*, 1–12.

Chapter 6

Behavioral Assessment of Communication

INTRODUCTION

Concern for the development of communication skills by severely developmentally disabled clients has grown in the last 25 years. Since Skinner's (1957) affirmation of the operant nature of language, considerable attention has been directed toward the application of behavioral principles to the instruction and remediation of speech, language, and communication skills of language deficient learners (Harris, 1975; Howlin, 1981; Hollis & Sherman, 1967; Isaac, Thomas, & Goldiamond, 1960; Lovaas, 1981; Sherman, 1965). The work of Ivar Lovaas in the late 1960s (Lovaas, Berberich, Perloff, & Schaefer, 1966) has initiated increased interest in the identification of important assessment and educational strategies for teaching language to nonverbal and verbally deficient children. Comparative examination of the more prominent views on communication programming with severely developmentally disabled clients reveals the following common assessment/remediation components.

ASSESSMENT OF CENTRAL AND PERIPHERAL SYSTEMS

While numerous authors address the importance of assessing the integrity of neurological and sensory systems (Bricker & Bricker, 1970; Handleman, Arnold, Veniar, Kristoff, & Harris, 1982; Newsom & Rincover, 1981; Sailor, Guess, & Baer, 1973; Wetherby & Koegel, 1982), such assessment often is difficult to conduct with severely developmentally disabled clients. Physiological conditions that can influence behavior should be investigated thoroughly prior to programming. For example, the identification of a hearing deficit, visual difficulty, or motor or speech mechanism problem would direct the focus of comprehensive assessment and instruction. Diagnostic information can provide clinicians with useful information for the design of communication programs (Handleman et al., 1982).

Neurological, audiologic, visual, and oral examinations of severely developmentally disabled children often are complicated by their severe language and social deficits (Handleman et al., 1982). The extreme behavioral manifestations, such as tantrums and aggressiveness, that clients usually exhibit in the presence of physicians and other professionals interfere with and often prevent examination. As a consequence, many physicians resort to sedating children to complete their examinations. Many times this assessment process is complicated further by the reluctance of parents to pursue medical examinations for their children. The anticipated reaction of the child and the possibility of sedation are factors that contribute to parental hesitancy. Appointments may be delayed for months or years and sometimes ignored.

Those individuals involved in the education and treatment of the client can assist the initial referral by providing the examiner with critical information. Along with information regarding the client's communication ability and general compliancy, the records of behavioral observations of relevant behaviors and videotapes can be made available to the professional. Often a preexamination consultation is useful to identify important information, such as past experience and responsiveness of clients to professionals and the results and recommendations of other evaluations. Many times it may be necessary for the assessor or clinician to prepare the client for assessment. For example, an audiologic evaluation can be assisted considerably if a client has had prior practice in wearing headsets. Also, the tactile defensive client needs to become more tolerant of touch if an examination is to be successful. These and many other experiences can be provided by those familiar with the client prior to the actual evaluation. The following guidelines describe possible areas to consider when planning prerequisite experiences for the evaluation.

1. *Consider the client's comfort with professional environments.* Many severely developmentally disabled clients are afraid of settings such as doctor's offices and hospitals. Often providing the client with preevaluation visits to the site can serve to lessen these fears.
2. *Consider the client's interaction experience with novel professionals.* The difficulties that severely developmentally disabled clients have with transferring skills from one person to another are well known. Providing the client with various opportunities to respond to different individuals can enhance consistency and generalization of behavior.
3. *Consider the client's history with unusual evaluative procedures.* Most evaluations include either equipment or procedures that the severely developmentally disabled client may find frightening. Any type of physical examination will be difficult with the tactile defensive client, as will be the

wearing of headsets or glasses for the fearful client. Providing the client with prior experiences with the particular piece of equipment or technique can facilitate the success of the evaluation.

The actual assessment can be aided considerably by the presence of the child's teacher or clinician (Handleman et al., 1982). The teacher adds an element of security in unfamiliar surroundings and can provide useful on-the-spot information to the examiner. The client's teacher often can facilitate consistent responding by the client and can report whether a behavior is in response to a particular stimulus or from the client's repertoire irrespective of stimulation. The variable of familiarity introduces common elements to the novel situation, which can enhance generalization of responding.

While the assessment process can be modified and expanded to ensure greater success, parent reluctance is difficult to overcome. It is important for the teacher or clinician to remain sympathetic while trying to convince parents of the usefulness of the referral. It is equally useful to maintain a roster of local physicians who are particularly skillful with the severely developmentally disabled and with whom cooperative relationships have been established.

ASSESSMENT OF STUDENT MOTIVATION

The lack of curiosity and general unresponsiveness of the severely developmentally disabled add to the difficulties in motivating such clients (Dunlap & Egel, 1982; Koegel & Schreibman, 1977). Motivation therefore becomes a pivotal component of behavioral assessment and intervention.

The identification and selection of reinforcers is basic to the motivation of severely developmentally disabled clients (Dunlap & Egel, 1982; Koegel & Egel, 1979; Murphy, 1982; Sailor et al., 1973) and vital to the professionals' attempt to increase their verbal behavior and ability to communicate. Initial treatment often is dependent on the continual use of primary reinforcement in an effort to condition secondary and more naturally occurring reinforcers. A client may be rewarded first with primary reinforcement upon each occurrence of a random vocalization and then for closer approximations of a desired sound. Once sounds and eventually words are mastered, response maintenance often is facilitated by social praise and touch only.

Results of numerous experimental and applied research have identified many characteristics of a useful reinforcer (Gelfand & Hartmann, 1980).

- A reinforcer should be highly preferred.
- A reinforcer should be administered in small units.

- A reinforcer should be administered immediately after the occurrence of the desired behavior.
- A reinforcer should be practical.
- A reinforcer should be compatible with the treatment program.

Other considerations include the naturalness of the reinforcer to enhance normalization (Rincover & Koegel, 1977) and the notion of variety to maintain reward potency (Koegel & Felsenfeld, 1977). These factors, combined with the idiosyncrasies of the person, make determination of the most effective primary and secondary reinforcement systems an individual and often intricate process. Apparent reinforcing events may be ineffective in increasing behavior and less typical rewards, such as escape from a task, are more successful. The following three strategies may be useful for assessing client motivation.

1. *Be familiar with the client's behavioral repertoire.* Familiarity with the client through observation and interaction is a first step in the selection of reinforcers. Determining the client's naturally occurring high-rate behaviors for use as reinforcers for low-rate behaviors is often effective. Conducting a two- or three-day frequency count of the toys a child selects during play time may indicate some of the child's possible preferred items. Also, conducting a probe where activities such as jumping and shaking are delivered noncontingently and client responses are observed could assist the identification of potential rewards.
2. *Interview parents and other invested individuals.* Talking with parents and other caretakers can be informative and useful in identifying a client's preferred items and activities. Asking those individuals to list the client's favorite foods, toys, or activities can provide a core of potential reinforcers. It may be helpful to provide parents with a predetermined checklist of items to assist their recall of idiosyncratic items or events.
3. *Have the client sample various items and events.* Presenting clients with a menu of items can assist in determining potential reinforcers. Allowing clients to select their rewards from a tray of various food or toy items may reveal a pattern of their preferred items. Also, the more verbally able clients can be given a choice of activities contingent on an appropriate response. In both cases, a frequency count over a few sessions or days will identify choice events and items.

Reinforcement is defined with respect to a resultant increase in a targeted behavior. Therefore, the test of a potential reward is the effect that its delivery has on behavior. Monitoring graphed data will quickly indicate the effectiveness of the treatment plan, and modification of reinforcers or reinforcement schedules can be assessed systematically.

ASSESSMENT OF ATTENDING BEHAVIORS AND INSTRUCTIONAL CONTROL

The ability to focus on the environment and begin to respond to the multitude of stimuli is basic to communication instruction for severely developmentally disabled clients. Being able to attend to environmental events is considered by many to be a prerequisite to learning (Cook, Anderson, & Rincover, 1982; Lovaas, 1981; Lovaas et al., 1966; Sailor et al., 1973). In addition, the abilities to sit in an instructional setting, to not engage in behaviors that compete with learning, and to follow directions provide further building blocks for communication training of the severely developmentally disabled.

Establishing eye contact has been suggested as the most fundamental of attending behaviors (Altman & Krupsaw, 1982; Harris, 1975). The assessment and remediation of both interpersonal and environmental attending are basic to communication programming. Determining the frequency and duration of a client's ability to establish eye contact and focus on common objects and actions is facilitated by systematic observation and accurate record keeping. A client's performance with eye contact on command can be assessed by having a variety of significant persons record successes and failures over various trials and days. It is also useful to assess the client's ability to maintain eye contact for increasing lengths of time, such as for one, two, three, four, and five seconds. Of increasing interest is the importance of establishing spontaneous eye contact (Sosne, Handleman, & Harris, 1979). Assessing whether children will attend upon hearing their names or when presented with stimulus materials also can provide useful information for communication programming.

While interpersonal eye contact is important for clients to receive information and model their verbal behavior, the ability to focus on objects and actions is basic to building a receptive repertoire. Gathering baseline data on variables, such as variety of objects and location, also will provide clinicians with needed information to design comprehensive communication programs. For example, will a client attend to information presented on the blackboard, or will a client attend only when the stimulus material is placed on the desk?

Compiling data on a client's ability to maintain sitting in various instructional situations, such as one-to-one and small group settings, in addition to a client's compliance to general environmental instructions, completes an assessment of instructional control behaviors. Variables to include when assessing a client's ability to follow directions are complexity of command and number of commissions to execute. When considering the complexity of a particular command, the presence of a contextual cue, such as a book to close, often becomes an easier task to perform than when no context is provided. The following list presents examples of one-commission commands that can be included in an assessment probe.

- One-commission commands that are given with contextual cue.
  - Close the door.
  - Open the book.
  - Place the peg in the board.
  - Pull the string on the doll.
  - Put the block in the box.
  - Put the paper in the garbage.
  - Put the straw in the cup.
  - Stack the blocks.
  - String the beads.
  - Turn the knob.
- One-commission commands that are given without contextual cue.
  - Clap your hands.
  - Come here.
  - Get your lunch box.
  - Sit down.
  - Stand up.
  - Stamp your feet.
  - Touch your head.
  - Turn off the lights.
  - Walk to the door.
  - Wave bye.

Ensuring that a child is not engaging in competing behaviors, such as self-stimulation, aggressiveness, or tantrumming, is basic for establishing instructional control. Depending on the frequency of the behavior, a continual or time sample method of data collection would be appropriate for baseline data recording. Also, interval recordings may be particularly useful for measuring self-stimulatory behavior. Designing a treatment package to focus on disruptive and competing behaviors initially includes the identification of appropriate consequences for the target behavior. Chapter 2 discusses considerations for the assessment of such consequences.

ASSESSMENT OF NONVERBAL AND VERBAL IMITATION

The importance of imitation as a prerequisite to communication is well documented (Baer, Peterson, & Sherman, 1967; Harris, 1975; Hewett, 1965; Lovaas, 1981). While the relationship between nonverbal and verbal imitation is not certain (Haring, 1982), many clinicians suggest that gross motor imitation should precede vocal imitation (Bricker & Bricker, 1970). Two important issues are presented with regard to nonverbal imitation training. The first is a need to establish generalized imitative repertoires (Peterson, 1968), and the other is to design programming that eventually focuses on the imitation of mouth movements (Lovaas, 1981; Marshall & Hegrenes, 1970; Sloan, Johnston, & Harris, 1968).

Assessment of a client's performance with nonverbal imitation includes an initial screening of gross and fine motor abilities. Observing a client execute activities such as throwing a ball, jumping, or climbing stairs informs the examiner about a client's gross motor ability. Also, observation of a client opening a lunch box or handling small items offers information about fine motor development. Activities observed in unstructured situations then can be targeted for imitation training. A pretest including a combination of gross and fine motor items, as presented in the following list, can be constructed to assess responses to the instruction, "Do this."

- gross motor movements
  - arms in air
  - hand wave
  - hands on head
  - head nod
- fine motor movements (focus on hands)
  - arm wave
  - finger wave
  - fist clap
  - fist making
  - pointing
- fine motor movements (focus on mouth)
  - mouth opened
  - lips pursed
  - teeth touched
  - tongue extended
  - tongue to teeth

Additional variables to assess include response latency and number of prompts needed for successful imitation. A timer or watch can be used to measure the amount of time a client requires to respond after a particular direction is given. Also, the number and type of prompts needed for success can be recorded. Both types of information can be collected over various sessions or days and averaged to provide measures of response latency and prompting.

There are many discussions on establishing verbal imitation with language deficient clients (Koegel & Traphagen, 1982; Lovaas et al., 1966; Risley & Wolf, 1967; Wolf, Risley, & Mees, 1964). Lovaas et al. (1966) presents guidelines for the selection of initial vocal responses. For example, those sounds that can be prompted manually (e.g., *m, w, f, ŏ, ē, p, oo*) should be attempted first. Next, sounds that have visual salience (*p, b, m, w, f, th, ŏ, ē, ō*) or those that a client can use already should follow. Verbal imitation training eventually includes words, phrases, and sentences (Harris, 1975; Koegel & Traphagen, 1982). An assessment probe of verbal imitation in response to the stimulus, "Say————," can therefore include manually prompted and visually salient sounds, in addition to those words that have been reported by parents and other significant persons as part of the client's repertoire, as inconsistent as they may be. This probe also can include single and multiple syllable words describing common environment objects, such as chair, clock, table, puzzle, banana, and telephone. The Goldman Fristoe Test of Articulation provides a thorough sequence of sounds, sound combinations, and words to augment an assessment of verbal imitation.

Observation and recording of the vocalizations that a preverbal client spontaneously emits provide basic information regarding the client's verbal ability. After establishing a baseline of naturally occurring vocalizations, assessing the effects that contingent reinforcement has on the rate of vocalizing can be useful in determining what degree of stimulus control can be established. This can be accomplished by reinforcing spontaneous vocalizations with a preferred reward and by monitoring the effect on the rate of the behavior over the course of a few days. An increase in the frequency of vocalizations indicates that stimulus control is established with regard to the behavior.

ASSESSMENT OF FUNCTIONAL COMMUNICATION

A discussion of functional communication is many faceted. When basic instructional control and rudiments of speech are established, attention is focused on the development of functional language (Harris, 1975; Lovaas, 1981; Sailor et al., 1973). In addition, the literature raises a variety of assessment and programming concerns when planning language instruction. For example, interest in alternatives to speech has grown as well as concern for the problems of generalization and spontaneity displayed by many severely developmentally disabled clients.

Functional Language

Many areas of curriculum relate to the functional use of language. Initially, programming is designed to establish and expand receptive and expressive identification of objects and actions (Harris, 1975; Hewett, 1965; Litt & Schreibman,

1981; Risley & Wolf, 1967; Sailor & Guess, 1983). Next, strategies are suggested to increase the complexity of language to include the use of prepositions (Lovaas, 1981), compound sentences (Lovaas, 1981; Stevens-Long & Rasmussen, 1974), question formations (Sherman, 1965), and other syntactical forms. A number of issues also need to be considered when a language curriculum is being planned. There is repeated confirmation of the effect that reinforcement and modeling have on the formation of generative grammar by severely developmentally disabled students (Bennet & Ling, 1972; Fygetakis & Gray, 1970; Garcia, Guess, & Byrnes, 1973; Hart & Risley, 1968; Sailor, 1971). For example, many clients demonstrate expanded repertoires after receiving training on only a few instances of a grammatical form. Also, while some authors write about adhering to developmental sequences, such as receptive training before expressive instruction, when language experiences are programmed, there is data suggesting that the developmental model may not apply to all clients (Sternberg, 1982).

A probe designed to include a sampling of items from established curricular areas, combined with language concepts targeted for instruction, can provide an initial assessment of functional communication ability and the baseline data from which to compare progress. Maintaining systematic acquisition data then ensures for ongoing evaluation. Functional language concepts that can be included in an assessment probe are:

- labels common objects
- labels body parts
- labels pictorial representations of objects
- labels actions
- labels plural nouns
- forms noun-verb descriptions
- uses pronouns
- forms agent-action-object combinations
- uses negatives
- responds to who, what, where, when, and why questions
- labels adjectives of color, shape, size, and number
- uses color concepts correctly
- uses prepositions
- requests items
- asks questions to seek information
- requests assistance
- describes a picture
- answers social questions

The use of formal assessment measures with severely developmentally disabled clients for normative purposes is difficult and often inappropriate. A few instruments have been used, however, to establish baselines on communication performance from which to evaluate progress. For example, the Peabody Picture Vocabulary Test Revised (PPVT-R) and the One-word Expressive Picture Vocabulary Test (One-word Expressive) provide measures of receptive and expressive language ability. Also, the Bankson Language Screening Test (Bankson) assesses a client's ability with various functional language tasks.

Alternatives to Verbal Communication

There has been growing interest in the consideration of nonspeech forms of communication with severely developmentally disabled clients. Sign language, communication boards, electronic devices, and bliss symbols are commonly used alternatives to oral communication with various clients (Silverman, 1980). The efficacy of the use of sign language, however, with the severely developmentally is well discussed (Alpert, 1980; Banaroya, Wesley, Ogilvie, Klien, & Meaney, 1977; Bonvillian, Nelson & Rhyne, 1981; Carr, 1981; Carr, Binkoff, & Kiernan, 1981; Kiernan, 1977; Walker, Hinerman, Jenson, & Peterson, 1981). Currently, two of the more commonly used sign language systems are American Sign Language and Signing Exact English.

There appears to be agreement that the decision to introduce sign language training should be made only after a client's communication ability, including speech, has been carefully assessed (Carr, 1982). The prerequisites for sign language are similar to those for speech communication. Assessment of central and peripheral systems as well as assessment of motivation are equally important. Also, examination of a client's abilities with gross and fine motor imitation may be necessary to assist the selection of those signs that a client is capable of forming. In addition, critical evaluation of a client's speech mechanisms can be useful in assessing the integrity of speech producing systems. An assessment probe in this area can include these elements:

- ability to hold head erect
- presence of "chest collapse"
- evidence of involuntary head movements
- symmetry of facial features
- evidence of tongue protrusion during mouth breathing
- evidence of rooting, sucking, and bite reflexes
- evidence of normal breathing
- ability to open mouth to receive food
- use of teeth to bite and chew

- evidence of tongue lateralization
- ability to retrieve food from mouth corner using tongue
- presence of tongue thrust during swallowing
- ability to drink from cup without tipping head
- use of straw
- evidence of tongue elevation
- ability to protrude tongue to get food

These behaviors are easily observed and assessment can be conducted in various situations over time to determine consistency of responding.

Generalization and Spontaneity

Regardless of the mode of communication, there exists concern about both the spontaneity and generalization of responding with severely developmentally disabled clients (Egel, 1982; Handleman, 1981). While the effectiveness of operant techniques for teaching responsive speech to nonverbal children is well documented (Harris, 1975), the limitations these programs demonstrate for teaching spontaneous language are less recognized (Sosne et al., 1979). Programs designed to increase a child's spontaneity attempt to reduce a child's reliance on verbal prompts and manipulate the environment to create a need for communication (Sosne et al., 1979). Many severely developmentally disabled clients demonstrate situationally specific responses and seem bound to the physical elements of the stimulus situation (Hamilton, 1966). Consequently, not only are these clients limited in their ability to initiate interactions, but also in their ability to generalize behavior from one situation to another (Handleman, 1979; Rincover & Koegel, 1975). As a result of growing interest in the problem of generalization, numerous effective strategies have been identified. For example, providing clients with a variety of teachers has been shown to facilitate their generalization to novel persons (Garcia, 1974; Kale, Kaye, Whelan, & Hopkins, 1968). Also, teaching clients in a variety of settings can assist their transfer of learning to other instructional settings either within a school (Griffiths & Craighead, 1972) or within the natural environment (Handleman, 1979; Handleman & Harris, 1980).

The assessment of spontaneity includes numerous variables. A client's reliance on verbal prompts can be assessed by simply providing the client with various stimulus materials and observing the response. For example, a client who correctly labels items when presented solely with an object or picture is responding spontaneously or without prompting. This form of spontaneous behavior can be measured with various objects or pictures. Also, the control that cues of the work situation (e.g., chairs, desks) have upon sitting and attending can be measured in the absence of verbal or physical prompts. On a more active level, the client's frequency of spontaneous requests or physical contacts can be recorded daily to provide baseline information. The various forms of generalization can be assessed by introducing varied stimulus conditions. For example, multiple baselines of performance can be established to measure behavior across teachers, settings, or stimulus materials. Chapter 7 provides a detailed discussion on assessing the generalization of responding.

Case 1: Jack

Jack was admitted to a private school for the developmentally disabled at the age of four in 1980. His primary educational classification was neurological impairment, and he was diagnosed as autistic according to Diagnostic and Statistical Manual of Mental Disorders (DSM-III; American Psychiatric Association, 1980) criteria. Jack was reported as demonstrating a severe communication disorder and as having difficulty in relating interpersonally.

During the summer of 1980, Jack received a full neurological examination at the request of the Child Study Team. While results of the examination revealed no clear evidence of neurological dysfunction, a recommendation to continue his medication for seizures, which were reported during the year, was made. Jack's parents were advised to consult with the neurologist in January, 1981. In September, 1980, the findings of a hearing screening conducted at the school indicated wax buildup in Jack's ears. A follow-up visit to an otolaryngologist resulted in successful removal of the wax and a report of no ear pathology or impaired hearing.

Everyone concerned devoted the first few weeks of the school year to assessing Jack's motivation and responsiveness and to establishing basic instructional control. On the school's intake questionnaire, Jack's parents indicated that his favorite foods were raisins and pretzels. This report was confirmed by Jack's teachers when they observed a 60% increase in his quiet sitting as the result of using primary reinforcement. Initially, he was reinforced only for an instance of unprompted sitting. By the end of the third week of school, Jack was sitting quietly with his hands in his lap for 20-minute work periods maintained only by intermittent social reinforcement.

Jack would not establish eye contact on command, as evidenced by 0% responding during a 3-day baseline. On many occasions, he would avert his gaze when asked, "Look at me." The use of a food prompt successfully increased his eye contact within a few days to 85% correct; however, an attempt to systematically fade the prompt failed. A hand shadow prompt was employed successfully next and faded completely. Within a month, Jack was consistently establishing eye contact upon hearing his name 90% of the time. Once eye contact was established, Jack was taught to follow one-step commands. Initial assessment indicated no response to directions such as "Come here," "Stand up," and "Sit down;" however, after six weeks of instruction, Jack was responding to 10 commands with 90% accuracy.

Basic instructional control skills were established quickly and maintained. An informal sound inventory conducted during the first few weeks of school revealed that Jack would occasionally vocalize a few consonants (*m, p, t, b*). These vocalizations were random, however, and not in response to statements made by others. A program was designed to reinforce each free vocalization with social praise. This program was successful at increasing Jack's rate of vocalizing by 200%. At the same time, Jack began formal instruction with nonverbal imitation tasks. He mastered 15 gross motor items relatively quickly; however, he demonstrated some difficulty with fine motor movements. He also began to identify noun items receptively. After difficulty with the initial discrimination, Jack's receptive vocabulary increased steadily. Proximity prompts were necessary when he was being taught the first four discrimination tasks and were faded successfully for successive tasks.

Shortly after Thanksgiving holiday, a decision was made to start formal verbal imitation training. This decision was based on Jack's good foundation with nonverbal imitation and his high rate of free vocalization. The *d* sound was targeted for initial training and was brought under instructional control in 7 days when Jack achieved the mastery criterion of 90%. He then took 15 days to master the *m* sound. At first, Jack experienced some difficulty with the discrimination of the *d* and *m* sounds; however, he demonstrated mastery in two weeks. His first sound combination was *m* plus *a*, and he soon was labeling a picture of his mother as *ma*. Jack's imitative and labeling vocabulary grew steadily throughout the year.

The curriculum for Jack's second year at the school focused on functional language training. Programs designed for increasing the complexity of speech and use of language to describe the function of objects, environmental actions, and spatial relationships were implemented. In addition, experiences were provided to facilitate the transfer of Jack's language to a variety of people and settings.

Jack's ability to use language to describe environmental events and to communicate needs progressed steadily during the two years. The school's records of his daily progress were confirmed by formal assessment measures. For example, Jack achieved a PPVT raw score of 3 in June, 1981 and a score of 20 the following June. His raw scores on the Expressive One-Word Test indicated similar growth from 0 in June, 1981 to 9 in June, 1982. Also, results of the Goldman Fristoe administered in December, 1982 reported that most sounds could be stimulated by the examiner. Jack's performance on the Bankson Language Screening Test reflected his growth with the functional use of language. He was able to expressively identify four body parts and five verbs. He also identified the categories of animals and toys, and the function of four objects and four prepositions.

Case 2: Ronni

Ronni was enrolled in a university-based program for developmentally disabled children at age seven after attending a public school special education class for two years. Ronni was classified as neurologically impaired and described as having a severe communication handicap. She was referred to the university program as a result of slow progress and inadequate educational resources available in the current placement.

Ronni's admission to the program included a comprehensive evaluation by the neurodevelopmental institute sponsored by the university's medical school. Reports indicated that all of her peripheral sensory systems were intact, as well as her general neurological functioning. Psychological and educational assessment found Ronni to be functioning in the moderately retarded range of intelligence. In addition, findings of the speech and language evaluation described Ronni's language as echolalic and reported a good imitative ability with all sounds, many sound combinations, and one- and two-syllable words.

During the first week of school, Ronni's teacher assessed her motivation and instructional control behaviors. Ronni demonstrated an ability to sit still in both one-to-one and two-child group situations. During 20 trial sessions, Ronni was sitting appropriately at the beginning of the teaching trials on the average of 90% of the time. In addition, she required only an average of two prompts to sit during intertrial periods. Assessment of Ronni's eye contact on command indicated a mean of 85% correct. Her spontaneous eye contact was slightly lower than when requested with a mean of 80% responding over five 20 trial sessions.

While Ronni demonstrated good sitting and attending behaviors, when presented with a toy or object, she would hold it in front of her eyes, turn it, and stare at it for an extended period. In order to accurately assess Ronni's self-stimulation, the behavior was defined more specifically as "looking at an object held by two fingers and rotated for more than five seconds where a two second pause constituted the end of an episode." The results of a 5-day time sample of three 10-minute observations revealed a mean of 15 self-stimulatory behaviors.

Ronni demonstrated an ability to follow many one-step commands, however, she experienced difficulty with multiple directions. While she seemed to enjoy praise and touch, it was observed that cookies and chocolate motivated Ronni to complete tasks that she was incapable of doing previously. For example, when asked to string 10 beads, Ronni accomplished the task with an average of four prompts. She required only one prompt when primary reinforcement was available.

Ronni experienced success with many nonverbal imitation tasks. She was able to imitate both gross and fine motor movements, in addition to most sounds, common objects, actions, and three-word sentences. Initially, she would not only imitate the target verbalization, but also the command, "Say." Through a process of systematically deemphasizing the command, Ronni began to imitate the verbalization only within 6 days. On the 10th day, the command was represented at normal volume. A raw score of 46 on the Expressive One-Word Test confirmed Ronni's imitative ability.

Ronni's language curriculum focused on improving her functional use of language. Her echolalia dominated her verbal responses. For example, when asked the function of a common object, or social question, Ronni exclusively responded with a repetition of the question. Her receptive comprehension of those concepts was good. The results of 6 months of language instruction indicated that Ronni was answering personal questions and describing everyday environmental events. On the Bankson Language Screening Test, Ronni identified all nine body parts, nine objects, and nine verbs. In addition, she identified eight of nine object functions and seven of nine prepositions.

SUMMARY

Jack and Ronni responded well to treatment and demonstrated steady growth in social, language, and cognitive areas. While many severely developmentally disabled clients learn to speak and to use language functionally, many difficulties exist during language training. Systematic assessment can guide the process.

Accurate assessment of peripheral systems is often a difficult task (Handleman et al., 1982). Due to the nature of their difficulties, many severely developmentally disabled clients are described as untestable, and specific areas of functioning remain in question. As a result of this difficulty, interdisciplinary, comprehensive evaluations are needed (Handleman et al., 1982). Sensitivity, combined with perseverance, can yield accurate assessment, medical diagnosis, intervention, and rehabilitation.

Instruction in basic instructional control behaviors can be problematic. The difficulty many severely developmentally disabled clients experience with information processing can be disruptive to programming. Also, overselective clients who respond solely to a particular aspect of a stimulus array are hampered in their ability to form basic discriminations (Lovaas, Koegel, & Schriebman, 1979). Programming efforts for these clients need to be highly systematic and based on ongoing assessment; they also need to emphasize concreteness and frequent exposure.

Clients who cannot learn to speak pose difficulties for clinicians. Once a decision is made to introduce an alternative form of communication training, the instructional environment needs to be modified to support the nonverbal system. Staff and especially family members must become familiar with the system in order to facilitate effective communication.

The literature has been convincing; many severely developmentally disabled clients can be taught to communicate. Over a decade of research and experience has resulted in a growing methodology devoted to communication assessment and training.

REFERENCES

Alpert, C. (1980). Procedures for determining the optimal nonspeech mode with the autistic child. In R. L. Schiefelbusch (Ed.), *Nonspeech language and communication*. Baltimore: University Park Press.

Altman, K., & Krupshaw, R. (1982). Increasing eye contact by head-holding. *Analysis and Intervention in Developmental Disabilities, 2*, 319–328.

American Psychiatric Association. *Diagnostic and Statistical Manual of Mental Disorders* (3rd ed.). Washington, DC: Author.

Baer, D., Peterson, R., & Sherman, J. (1967). The development of imitation by reinforcing behavioral similarity to a model. *Journal of the Experimental Analysis of Behavior, 10*, 405–416.

Banaroya, S., Wesley, S., Ogilvie, H., Klein, L. S., & Meaney, M. (1977). Sign language and multisensory input training of children with communication and related developmental disorders. *Journal of Autism and Childhood Schizophrenia, 7*, 23–31.

Bennett, C. W., & Ling, D. (1972). Teaching a complex verbal response to a hearing-impaired girl. *Journal of Applied Behavior Analysis, 5*, 321–328.

Bonvillian, J. D., Nelson, K. E., & Rhyne, J. M. (1981). Sign language and autism. *Journal of Autism and Developmental Disorders, 11*, 125–138.

Bricker, W. A., & Bricker, D. D. (1970). A program of language training for the severely handicapped child. *Exceptional Children, 37*, 101–111.

Carr, E. G. (1981). Sign language. In O. I. Lovaas (Ed.), *Teaching manual for parents and teachers of developmentally disabled children: The Me Book*. Baltimore: University Park Press.

Carr, E. G. (1982). Sign language. In R. L. Koegel, A. Rincover, & A. L. Egel (Eds.), *Educating and understanding autistic children*. San Diego: College Hill Press.

Carr, E. G., Binkoff, J. A., Kologinsky, E., & Eddy, E. (1978). Acquisition of sign language by autistic children. *Journal of Applied Behavior Analysis, 11*, 489–501.

Cook, A. R., Anderson, N., & Rincover, A. (1982). Stimulus overselectivity and stimulus control: Problems and strategies. In R. L. Koegel, A. Rincover, & A. L. Egel (Eds.), *Educating and understanding autistic children*. San Diego: College Hill Press.

Dunlap, G., & Egel, A. (1982). Motivational techniques. In R. L. Koegel, A. Rincover, & A. L. Egel (Eds.), *Educating and understanding autistic children*. San Diego: College Hill Press.

Egel, A. (1982). Programming the generalization and maintenance of treatment gains. In R. L. Koegel, A. Rincover, & A. L. Egel (Eds.), *Educating and understanding autistic children*. San Diego: College Hill Press.

Fygetakis, L., & Gray, B. B. (1970). Programmed conditioning of linguistic competence. *Behavior Research and Therapy, 8*, 153–163.

Garcia, E. (1974). The training and generalization of a conversational speech form in nonverbal retardates. *Journal of Applied Behavior Analysis, 7*, 137–149.

Garcia, E., Guess, D., & Byrnes, J. (1973). Development of syntax in a retarded girl using procedures of imitation, reinforcement and modeling. *Journal of Applied Behavior Analysis, 6*, 299–310.

Gelfand, D. M., & Hartmann, D. P. (1980). *Child behavior analysis and therapy*. Elmsford, NY: Pergamon Press.

Griffiths, H., & Craighead, W. E. (1972). Generalization in operant speech therapy for misarticulation. *Journal of Speech and Hearing Disorders, 37,* 485–498.

Hamilton, J. (1966). Learning of a generalized response class in mentally retarded individuals. *American Journal of Mental Deficiency, 71,* 100–108.

Handleman, J. S. (1979). Generalization by autistic-type children of verbal responses across settings. *Journal of Applied Behavior Analysis, 12,* 273–282.

Handleman, J. S. (1981). Transfer of verbal responses across instructional settings by autistic-type children. *Journal of Speech and Hearing Disorders, 46,* 69–76.

Handleman, J. S., Arnold, M., Veniar, F. A., Kristoff, B., & Harris, S. L. (1982). Assessment and remediation of hearing loss in an autistic youngster. *Hearing Instruments, 33,* 10–11.

Handleman, J. S., & Harris, S. L. (1980). Generalization from school to home with autistic-type children. *Journal of Autism and Developmental Disorders, 10,* 323–333.

Haring, N. G. (1982). *Exceptional children and youth.* Columbus, OH.

Harris, S. L. (1975). Teaching language to nonverbal children with emphasis on problems of generalization. *Psychological Bulletin, 82,* 565–580.

Hart, B. M., & Risley, T. R. (1968). Establishing use of descriptive adjectives in the spontaneous speech of disadvantaged preschool children. *Journal of Applied Behavior Analysis, 1,* 109–120.

Hewett, F. M. (1965). Teaching speech to an autistic child through operant conditioning. *American Journal of Orthopsychiatry, 35,* 927–936.

Hollis, J. H., & Sherman, J. A. (1967). *Operant control of vocalizations in profoundly retarded children with normal hearing and moderate bilateral loss (#167).* Lawrence, KS: Parson's Research Center.

Howlin, P. (1981). The effectiveness of operant language training with autistic children. *Journal of Autism and Developmental Disorders, 11,* 89–106.

Isaac, W., Thomas, R., & Goldiamond, I. (1960). Application of operant conditioning to reinstate verbal behavior in psychotics. *Journal of Speech and Hearing Disorders, 25,* 8–12.

Kale, R. J., Kaye, J. H., Whelan, P.A., & Hopkins, B.L. (1968). The effects of reinforcement on the modification, maintenance and generalization of social responses of mental patients. *Journal of Applied Behavior Analysis, 1,* 307–314.

Kiernan, C. (1977). Alternatives to speech. A review of research on manual and other forms of communication with the mentally handicapped and other noncommunicating populations. *British Journal of Mental Subnormality, 23,* 6–28.

Koegel, R. L., & Egel, A. L. (1979). Motivating autistic children. *Journal of Abnormal Psychology, 88,* 418–426.

Koegel, R. L., & Felsenfeld, S. (1977). Sensory deprivation. In S. Gerber (Ed.), *Audiometry in infancy.* New York: Grune & Stratton.

Koegel, R. L., & Schreibman, L. (1977). Teaching autistic children to respond to simultaneous multiple cues. *Journal of Experimental Child Psychology, 24,* 299–311.

Koegel, R. L., & Traphagen, J. (1982). Selection of initial words for speech training with nonverbal children. In R. L. Koegel, A. Rincover, & A. Egel (Eds.), *Educating and understanding autistic children.* San Diego: College Hill Press.

Litt, M. D., & Schreibman, L. (1981). Stimulus-specific reinforcement in the acquisition of receptive labels by autistic children. *Analysis and Intervention in Developmental Disabilities, 1,* 171–186.

Lovaas, O. I. (1981). *Teaching developmentally disabled children: The Me Book.* Baltimore: University Park Press.

Lovaas, O. I., Berberich, J., Perloff, B., & Schaefer, B. (1966). Acquisition of imitative speech by schizophrenic children. *Science, 151,* 705–707.

Lovaas, O., Koegel, R., & Schreibman, L. (1979). Stimulus overselectivity in autism: A review of research. *Psychological Bulletin, 86*, 1236–1254.

Marshall, N. R., & Hegrenes, J. R. (1970). Programmed communication therapy for autistic mentally retarded children. *Journal of Speech and Hearing Disorders, 35*, 70–83.

Murphy, G. (1982). Sensory reinforcement in the mentally handicapped and autistic child: A review. *Journal of Autism and Developmental Disorders, 12*, 265–278.

Newsom, C., & Rincover, A. (1981). Autism. In E. J. Mash & L. G. Terdal (Eds.), *Behavioral assessment of childhood disorders*, 397–439. New York: Guilford.

Peterson, R. (1968). Some experiments on the organization of a class of imitative behavior. *Journal of Applied Behavioral Analysis, 1*, 225–235.

Rincover, A., & Koegel, R. (1975). Setting generality and stimulus control in autistic children. *Journal of Applied Behavior Analysis, 8*, 235–246.

Rincover, A., & Koegel, R. L. (1977). Research on the education of autistic children: Recent advances and future directions. *Advances in Clinical Psychology, 1*, 113–126.

Risley, T. R., & Wolf, M. M. (1967). Establishing functional speech in echolalic children. *Behavior Research and Therapy, 5*, 73–88.

Sailor, W. (1971). Reinforcement and generalization of productive plural allomorphs in two retarded children. *Journal of Applied Behavior Analysis, 4*, 305–310.

Sailor, W., & Guess, D. (1983). *Severely handicapped students: An instructional design*. Boston: Houghton Mifflin.

Sailor, W., Guess, D., & Baer, D. (1973). Functional language for verbally deficient children: An experimental program. *Mental Retardation, 11*, 27–35.

Sherman, J. A. (1965). Use of reinforcement and imitation to reinstate verbal behavior in mute psychotics. *Journal of Abnormal Psychology, 70*, 155–164.

Silverman, F. H. (1980). *Communication for the speechless*. Englewood Cliffs, NJ: Prentice-Hall.

Skinner, B. F. (1957). *Verbal behavior*. New York: Appleton-Century-Crofts.

Sloane, H. R., Johnson, M. K., & Harris, F. R. (1968). Remedial procedures for teaching verbal behavior to speech deficient or defective young children. In H. N. Sloane & B. A. MacAulay (Eds.), *Operant procedures in remedial speech and language training*. Boston: Houghton Mifflin.

Sosne, J. B., Handleman, J. S., & Harris, S. L. (1979). Teaching spontaneous-functional speech to autistic-type children. *Mental Retardation, 17*, 241–245.

Sternberg, L. (1982). Perspectives on educating severely and profoundly handicapped students. In L. Sternberg & G. L. Adams (Eds.), *Educating severely and profoundly handicapped students*. Rockville, MD: Aspen Systems.

Stevens-Long, J., & Rasmussen, M. (1974). The acquisition of simple and compound sentence structure in an autistic child. *Journal of Applied Behavior Analysis, 7*, 473–479.

Walker, G. R., Hinerman, P. S., Jenson, W. R., & Peterson, P. B. (1981). Sign language as a prompt to teach a verbal "yes" and "no" discrimination to an autistic boy. *Child Behavior Therapy, 3*, 77–86.

Wetherby, A., & Koegel, R. L. (1982). Audiological testing. In R. L. Koegel, A. Rincover, & A. L. Egel (Eds.), *Educating and understanding autistic children*. San Diego: College Hill Press.

Wolf, M. M., Risley, T. R., & Mees, H. I. (1964). Application of operant conditioning procedures to the behavior problems of an autistic child. *Behavior Research and Therapy, 2*, 305–312.

Chapter 7

Behavioral Assessment of Academic Functioning

INTRODUCTION

The assessment of academic functioning with severely developmentally disabled clients is a complex endeavor. Not only must the behavioral and communication deficits be considered, but the assessor is presented with a wide range of cognitive difficulties. Unlike the moderately mentally retarded or learning disabled client where certain learning patterns can be predicted, the severely developmentally disabled client presents a more idiosyncratic picture.

Wing (1979) describes the severely developmentally disabled population as demonstrating pervasive cognitive deficits that influence many areas of functioning. Numerous reports suggest that these cognitive difficulties affect clients' abilities to use such skills as symbolic language, play, communication, motor organization, and imitation (Carter, Alpert, & Stewart, 1982; Cromer, 1981; Kanner, 1943, 1957, 1971). Bartak (1979) confirms the cognitive dysfunction of severely developmentally disabled clients and describes the complex array of difficulties encountered with information processing. The information processing deficits of these clients may include difficulty encoding stimuli (Hermelin & O'Connor, 1970), perceptual motor impairments (Lansing & Schopler, 1979), and visual-spatial deficits (Carter et al., 1982; Rutter, 1979). The distinctive problem severely developmentally disabled learners have with discrimination tasks is documented repeatedly (Ellis et al., 1982; Robinson & Robinson, 1976). The severely developmentally disabled client also has been described as a very inefficient learner (Robinson & Robinson, 1976).

In order to clarify the discussion of the academic difficulties demonstrated by severely developmentally disabled clients, many reports have organized academic functioning into the following areas: (a) instructional control, (b) basic skills, (c) academic readiness, and (d) academic learning. In addition to being used as academic-skill categories, these areas provide a framework for assessment and curriculum planning.

The assessor of the academic functioning of this population is faced with identifying appropriate approaches to assessment and accurate instruments. Chapter 7 presents discussions on the intricacies of assessment with a focus on these concerns. Included is a discussion on the role of educational testing. The issues of functional skill training and naturalistic instruction also is presented. A case study is provided to exemplify the various strategies outlined in Chapter 7.

EDUCATIONAL EVALUATION

The efficacy of educational testing as a tool of assessment is considered widely. In a discussion on general testing practices in education, Swanson and Watson (1982) state that "educating and assessing a child's needs in an educational setting today are ambiguous and imprecise processes" (p. 4). Educational testing has received more criticism than other educational practices (Salvia & Ysseldyke, 1978). Areas of concern include low reliability and validity; improper administration; and little usefulness for programming. Numerous psychologists and educators report a decline in the use and utility of traditional testing procedures in the assessment process (Crawford, 1979; Scott, 1980; Smith & Knoff, 1981). This decline has resulted in attempts to refocus educational testing and to modify some testing practices.

Current discussions on educational testing include a narrower focus on the goals of planning and evaluation and a devaluing of the role of testing in the overall assessment process (Swanson & Watson, 1982). This emphasis on the functional aspects of testing is more compatible with the needs of severely developmentally disabled clients. While the majority of this population is described initially as untestable with reference to test content and interfering test behaviors, there may be times in the educational careers of severely developmentally disabled students where formal testing plays an adjunctive role in assessment. For example, as a student is placed in a more normalized and less restrictive setting, standardized testing can assist material selection, programming, and establishment of a baseline measure to evaluate further learning. Combined with the criterion-referenced nature of behavioral assessment strategies, a complete performance picture can be created. For the preschool or lower functioning client, experience suggests that standardized testing may be of little value in assessment. Early assessment and training experiences focus on instructional control and basic skills, many of which are prerequisites to test taking. Table 7–1 surveys some commonly used assessment instruments according to skill area.

Table 7–1 Commonly Used Tests in Educational Assessment

Test	Skill Area			
	Ability	*Achievement*	*Diagnostic*	*Learning*
1. Bayley Scales on Infant Development (Psychological Corporation)	•			
2. Columbia Mental Maturity Scale (Harcourt Brace Jovanovich)	•			
3. Detroit Test of Learning Aptitude (Bobbs Merrill)				•
4. Developmental Test of Visual-motor Integration (Follett)				•
5. Frostig Developmental Test of Visual Perception (Consulting Psychologist Press)				•
6. Illinois Test of Psycholinguistic Abilities (University Park Press)				•
7. Key Math Diagnostic Arithmetic Test (American Guidance)			•	
8. McCarthy Scales of Children's Abilities (Psychological Corporation)	•			
9. Motor Free Visual Perception Test (Academic Therapy)				•
10. Nebraska Test of Learning Aptitude (Psychological Corporation)	•			
11. Peabody Individual Achievement Test (American Guidance)		•		
12. Peabody Picture Vocabulary Test-R (American Guidance)	•			
13. Slosson Intelligence Test (Slosson Educational Publications)	•			
14. Stanford-Binet Intelligence Scale (Houghton Mifflin)	•			
15. Wechsler Test Series (Psychological Corporation)	•			
16. Wide Range Achievement Test (American Guidance)		•		
17. Woodcock Reading Mastery Tests (American Guidance)			•	

A Model for Educational Evaluation

Maintaining that the major goals of testing are planning and evaluation (Kirk, 1972; Swanson & Watson, 1982) is consistent with the functional posture of assessment; that is, testing becomes valuable only when it is useful to programming. Of the various educational testing models proposed, the suggestions of Bateman (1965) and Lerner (1971) seem compatible with the needs of the severely developmentally disabled. A closer look at the components of the Diagnostic Process (Bateman, 1965) and Clinical Teaching (Lerner, 1971) reveals a focus that emphasizes educational programming. While both of these models were conceptualized for the learning disabled child some years ago, the consistent concern for specificity, planning, and evaluation make the following seven components potentially useful with the severely developmentally disabled population.

1. *Identify areas of learning difficulty.* When a comparison of a child's current functioning with expected performance results in a discrepancy, a learning problem is said to exist. While measures of ability and achievement are difficult to confirm with severely developmentally disabled clients, accurate information regarding these two domains can be useful in identifying learning difficulty or developmental imbalance.

2. *Obtain a present measure of achievement.* The evaluation of performance in relevant areas can provide an index of general achievement. Standardized tests along with clinical observation and informal measures can result in helpful information regarding clients' ability with basic skills, their readiness, or their aptitude in other academic areas.

3. *Assess how clients learn.* Determining how students process the information that is presented can be useful in identifying problem areas, in addition to planning programming strategies. Important areas to consider include the reception and expression of information along with an analysis of learning modalities, such as visual, auditory, and motor functions.

4. *Consider variables that influence learning.* While the exact correlates of learning problems are difficult to determine, it is useful to consider as many contributing factors as possible. Environmental, motivational, and other psycho-educational variables can all influence learning and performance.

5. *Organize data to facilitate programming.* Carefully arranging and analyzing test results can assist in accurate interpretation. Considering variables such as consistency of responding and reliability either will heighten or minimize the usefulness of the results. Often, conducting an item analysis with regard to client strengths and weaknesses will offer information crucial to programming.

6. *Create a teaching strategy.* The functional relationship between assessment and treatment is cemented when the results of testing direct educational planning. Constructing both a curriculum and methodology that clearly addresses skill deficiency aids in program individualization.

7. *Provide for continual monitoring of performance.* Ongoing assessment can ensure effective programming. The frequent evaluation of mastery can facilitate a continual fine tuning of the educational intervention.

Issues of Testing and Test Interpretation

While the testing model proposed can result in a variety of formal, informal, and observational data, the value of this information seems correlated to a sensitivity to the needs of the severely developmentally disabled. For example, the acknowledged requirement for accurate testing is heightened by the performance styles of this population. Ensuring that a client is attending to the test stimuli becomes basic to the success of testing. During the session, having a person present who is familiar with the client often can provide consistency and information regarding the client's idiosyncratic response patterns (Handleman, Arnold, Veniar, Kristoff, & Harris, 1982). In situations where testing is conducted in a novel environment, gathering information initially about the most suitable conditions for client responding can contribute to the usefulness of the session.

While the normative data generated by standardized testing is sometimes helpful for the severely developmentally disabled client, the information derived from the client's performance during testing often is more useful. Efforts should be made to maintain the sanctity of the testing protocol; however, a familiarity with the particular client and an eye toward the type of information desired become important variables. For example, if a child is inattentive or unsuccessful with items where knowledge is suspected, it could be helpful to use language and terms that are familiar to the child as opposed to the test terminology. While these discrepancies in protocol must be noted, important information regarding a child's ability will be identified. Also, conducting an item analysis of both errors and successes can result in valuable information about a child's skill level or pattern of learning.

BEHAVIORAL ASSESSMENT

Instructional Control

Two basic questions often are asked when a child's progress is being monitored. The first question concerns a client's motivation to engage in a particular task, and the second one addresses the client's prerequisite abilities with that task. The ability to sit, attend, and comply with basic environmental demands have been presented repeatedly as fundamental skills (Lovaas, 1981; Lovaas & Newsom, 1976; Sailor, 1971). Along with client motivation, these variables are viewed as important building blocks to further instruction. While motivation and instructional control concerns cross all areas of learning, their influence is stressed particularly with regard to communication training (Harris, 1975). For this reason, a detailed discussion of this area is provided in Chapter 6.

Basic Skills

One of the most pervasive learning characteristics of severely developmentally disabled clients is their idiosyncratic and inconsistent response to sensory stimulation. Most of these clients demonstrate deficits with the most fundamental information processing skill of attending. Even when clients are taught to attend, they display difficulty in noting the similarities and differences of presented information, as evidenced in such skills as discrimination and matching. While attending is considered the most fundamental skill of communication and is discussed in detail in Chapter 6, matching (Schneider & Salzberg, 1982) and discrimination tasks (Gersten, White, Falco, & Carnine, 1982) are viewed as basic skills of information processing and are often prerequisites to other forms of academic learning.

Discussions of the acquisition of basic skills by severely developmentally disabled clients typically include concern for the phenomenon of overselective responding (Cook, Anderson, & Rincover, 1982; Schneider & Salzberg, 1982). Viewed as a major contributor to information processing difficulty, overselectivity refers to an exclusive attending to a narrow range of sensory input. That is, a client responds to a particular stimulus or selective set of stimuli to the exclusion of others. For example, a child who responds to the movements of the instructor as opposed to a picture presented for identification may be exhibiting overselective responding. Descriptions of overselectivity with severely developmentally disabled clients and overselectivity effects on their learning are many (Lovaas, Schreibman, Koegel, & Rehm, 1971; Rincover, 1978; Rincover & Koegel, 1975; Schreibman & Lovaas, 1973; Schneider & Salzberg, 1982). The identification and assessment of overselective responding in a client can lead to a prescription of educational strategies designed specifically to facilitate learning (Cook et al., 1982).

Assessment of Overselective Responding

Overselectivity has been related to the degree of stimulus control exerted on a particular behavior by the environment. Initial assessment efforts can include a survey of elements in the instructional setting that can possibly encourage overselective responding. On a global level, room furnishings, such as clocks and pictures, can serve as extra input during material presentation. With regard to educational materials, page numbers or other identifying information also can attract the overselective student. Other elements to consider include the clothes of instructors or their voices. Assessment of the amount of stimulus control that particular characteristics of the training setting have on client learning usually can be accomplished by probing a cross section of skills under varied conditions. For example, a sampling of items that a child has mastered and also is learning can be presented with different setting characteristics present. While not entirely indicative of overselective responding, noting differences in performance in the absence or presence of certain environmental elements can assist the clinician in understanding a student's performance.

The overselective student's focus also can be directed to a single component of what appears to be a simple visual stimulus. For one student, a stem may be the salient feature of an apple and therefore all stems are apples. A saddle may be considered a belt by another student because of the buckle. It is difficult to identify the salient feature to which the client is attending. Often, creating a probe that presents component parts of a picture in a discrimination task can assist the clinician in assessing whether a client is overselectively responding. For example, a client can be requested to "Touch the apple" when cards with a circle, with a stem, and with a red mark are presented.

Assessment of Matching Ability

Matching is a basic ability that enables clients to detect similarities and differences of various types of information. Having a client place an object on or next to an identical or similar object exemplifies the matching task. Matching can be demonstrated at various levels with presentation of concrete, abstract, single, and multidimensional items. The following hierarchy can form a sampling for a probe to assess a student's matching ability:

- matching one pair of simple objects
- matching alternate pairs of simple objects
- matching two pairs of simple objects in fixed positions presented randomly
- matching two pairs of simple objects of varied positions presented randomly
- matching three pairs of simple objects
- matching four or more pairs of simple objects
- matching identical two-dimensional pictures
- matching according to category
- matching colors
- matching shapes
- matching letters
- matching words

The positioning sequence in the first six steps also can be used for the last six steps.

Assessment of Discrimination Ability

The ability to discriminate information is basic to cognitive, social, and communication development. Discrimination includes an awareness of both the similarities and differences of sensory stimulation and the ability to match a concept, label, or event with appropriate information. The severely developmentally disabled learner acquires this ability to discriminate in different ways. The following sequence can provide a framework for an assessment probe of a client's discrimination ability at different levels, which can lead to comprehensive programming:

- Client is requested to touch a single item.
- Client is requested to touch a second single item.
- Client is requested to touch first item in a fixed position when presented with the other item.
- Client is requested to touch first item randomly positioned when presented with the other item.
- Client is requested to touch second item in a fixed position when presented with the other item.
- Client is requested to touch second item randomly positioned when presented with the other item.
- Client is requested to touch alternately both items in fixed positions.
- Client is requested to touch alternately both items in random positions.

This sequence can be replicated with both concrete and pictorial representations and multiple pairs of items. In addition, when there exists a core of mastered items, the size of the visual array can be gradually assessed.

Academic Skills

Severely developmentally disabled clients' pervasive cognitive deficits (Wing, 1979) can be evidenced by their poor perceptual motor ability (Lansing & Schopler, 1979), their limited associative ability (Wing, 1979), and their difficulty with concepts of size, color, and shape (Lovaas, 1981). These skill areas span the academic areas of reading, writing, and math; deficiencies in these areas typically affect academic performance.

Perceptual motor ability enables students to gather information from the environment on the various sensory levels of audition, vision, and motor activity. This ability includes the information processing skills of awareness, association, discrimination, and memory. Many have questioned the relationship between perceptual motor proficiency and academic ability (Hammill, 1974; Hammill & Larsen, 1974). While this relationship is not a clear one, many of the perceptual motor or readiness abilities directly relate to the fundamental problem of attending to information that most severely developmentally disabled clients demonstrate (Ellis et al., 1982). That is, a client may either be unaware of sensory stimulation or unable to make associations or recall presented information.

While discussions regarding curriculum development for severely developmentally disabled people heavily emphasize instructional control, basic skills, and social and communication areas, academic learning is an eventual goal for many clients. Reading, writing, and math become the focus of instruction in an attempt to provide a comprehensive educational package. When considering the academic needs of a client, the literature suggests that clinicians strike a balance between traditional and functional academic instruction (Johnson & Koegel, 1982).

Assessment of Perceptual Motor Ability

Many perceptual motor skills are considered readiness activities to academic learning. Assessment of a student's ability or deficiency with perceptual motor skills is often useful when the student is encountering difficulty in some other learning area. For example, if a child is not successful with discrimination learning, considering the possible prerequisite awareness and association skills can be informative to a clinician. As part of a comprehensive assessment effort, evaluating information processing abilities can add to the total learning picture of a particular student.

The following outline can be included in a sampling probe of perceptual motor ability:

I. Visual awareness and discrimination
   A. Attends to large objects placed in visual field
   B. Attends to objects located one or two feet away
   C. Attends to objects moving slowly toward and away from client
   D. Tracks item moving slowly out of visual field
   E. Matches size, shape, color, objects, letters, and numbers
   F. Sorts simple objects/pictures
   G. Sorts objects/pictures according to shape, color, or size
   H. Discriminates between items that are grossly different
   I. Discriminates similar items
   J. Discriminates on the basis of shape, color, and size
II. Auditory awareness and discrimination
   A. Localizes sound
   B. Responds to name by orienting
   C. Identifies environmental sounds
   D. Identifies significant persons by voice
   E. Identifies similarities and differences of sounds
   F. Discriminates between loud and soft
   G. Identifies similarities and differences of words
III. Visual memory
   A. Imitates simple single actions
   B. Imitates multiple actions

      C. Recalls single item after removed
      D. Recalls multiple items after removed
      E. Reconstructs a simple block design from memory
      F. Completes an item by filling in missing parts
      G. Names objects, letter, numbers, words, and colors from memory
  IV. Auditory memory
      A. Follows simple single verbal directions
      B. Follows multiple verbal directions
      C. Imitates single and multiple vocalizations
      D. Imitates single and multiple words and phrases
      E. Supplies the missing sound of a word
      F. Supplies the missing word of a phrase
      G. Names day of the week and months of year
      H. Restates simple events in sequence
   V. Tactile awareness
      A. Accepts touch
      B. Tolerates movement of body
      C. Discriminates between various textures
      D. Discriminates between various degrees of stimulation

Assessment of Academic Abilities

Goals for varying levels of reading, writing, and mathematical ability are found in the educational plans of most severely developmentally disabled clients. Whether a student is being taught to read safety signs, such as "stop/go," or to calculate a checking account balance, instruction in basic academics is an important part of comprehensive educational planning. While the complexity of instruction and goals will vary from client to client, certain abilities are fundamental to each academic area. For instance, one-to-one correspondence is a basic mathematical concept.

Assessment of academic performance traditionally has been accomplished by samples of various areas in standardized tests. Also, the scope and sequence charts that accompany most commercial materials identify the skills involved in a particular academic area. While these resources can assist the assessment of some severely developmentally disabled clients, a sampling that is more consistent with the needs of these clients would be more useful. The following outline attempts to provide a narrow range of academic possibilities as a framework for an assessment probe. This is by no means an inclusive outline of the various abilities demonstrated by the severely developmentally disabled client.

   I. Reading
      A. Vocabulary (recognition of whole words)
        1. Identifies own name

2. Identifies labels of environmental objects
3. Identifies safety words
4. Recognizes names of other children
5. Identifies color words
6. Recognizes sight words specific to reading series
7. Recognizes Dolch words
8. Recognizes phrases

  B. Vocabulary comprehension
1. Matches word to picture
2. Follows one-word directions
3. Defines words by function
4. Categorizes words
5. Matches opposites
6. Matches phrases to pictures

  C. Word attack
1. Identifies consonants in initial, final, and medial positions
2. Identifies consonant combinations in initial, final, and medial positions
3. Identifies short vowel sounds
4. Identifies long vowel sounds
5. Identifies diphthongs
6. Identifies irregular combinations of vowels
7. Demonstrates awareness of number of syllables in a word
8. Reads aloud with appropriate volume
9. Reads silently and demonstrates comprehension

  D. Reading comprehension
1. Follows written directions
2. Matches pictures to word/sentences
3. Identifies fact
4. Identifies appropriate sequence of events
5. Identifies main idea
6. Recognizes emotional reactions
7. Determines time

II. Writing
  A. Holds writing utensil
  B. Makes scribbles
  C. Draws within boundaries
  D. Traces various lines
  E. Traces shapes
  F. Traces letters and numbers
  G. Copies lines, shapes, letters, and numbers
  H. Copies words

    I. Follows left to right progression

    J. Draws shapes

    K. Prints numbers and letters

    L. Prints name

    M. Prints words and sentences

III. Basic mathematics

    A. Counting and number identification*

      1. Counts to 10

      2. Identifies numerals to 10

      3. Creates objects in sets 1–10

      4. Matches numerals with sets 1–10

      5. Sequences numerals 1–10

      6. Reads numerals 1–10

    B. Simple computation†

      1. Recognizes symbol for addition

      2. Adds correct number of items

      3. Performs one digit addition problems

      4. Performs two digit addition problems with/without carrying

      5. Recognizes subtraction symbol

      6. Subtracts correct number of items

      7. Performs single-digit subtraction problems

      8. Performs two-digit subtraction problems with/without borrowing

    C. Mathematical concepts‡

      1. Identifies numbers on face of clock

      2. Identifies function of hands on clock

      3. Moves hands on clock in clockwise direction

      4. Tells time by hour, half hour, quarter hour, and five- and one-minute intervals

      5. Recognizes a ruler

      6. Identifies inch, half-inch, and quarter-inch ruler markings

      7. Measures according to inch, half inch, and quarter inch

Case 1: Shawn

Shawn was a seven-year-old multiply handicapped child who was referred to a center for the developmentally disabled after attending a local private school for neurologically impaired students. Shawn's primary classification was neurological impairment based on the signs and characteristics of autism, with a secondary classification of communicationally handicapped. His intake evalua-

---

*Elements 1 through 6 can apply to numbers 10–20, 20–30, and so on.

†Multiplication and division skills can be assessed with more advanced clients.

‡Measurement of weight and volume can be assessed with more advanced clients.

tion and supporting information described him as an autistic boy with echolalic speech and ability to work in an environment that combined one-to-one and two-to-one teaching. Based on that initial information, Shawn was admitted to the center for the summer session and was placed in one of the intermediate classrooms on a trial basis.

The staff of the center used the first few weeks of the program to facilitate Shawn's adjustment and to observe and assess his ability. In order to maximize reliable reporting, Shawn's teacher assisted the speech and language specialist on the communication assessment and the learning consultant and psychologist on the assessment of his academic functioning.

Throughout the intake evaluation, it was observed that Shawn demonstrated appropriate sitting and attending skills. He would sit quietly when asked and would remain seated for fairly lengthy tasks that averaged 20 minutes. During a probe of instructional control skills, Shawn established eye contact on command 95% of the time and looked at the instructor each time his name was spoken. Shawn seemed highly motivated by brief tickles. He would smile, take the instructor's hands and say, "Tickle please." Shawn also liked the jelly beans he was given for successful performance, however, social praise, touch, and tickles seemed more reinforcing.

Shawn performed well on the other instructional control items. He followed various one- and two-step commands with 85% accuracy and reliably discriminated 10 pairs of common objects (90% accuracy). He also correctly labeled 25 pictures of everyday objects and answered 10 questions about his family members and daily living.

Assessment of Shawn's ability with basic skills included a probe consisting of matching and discrimination tasks. Shawn demonstrated ease with matching numerous pairs of both objects and pictures with 100% consistency; however, he experienced difficulty when more than two items were present. His performance dropped to 40% accuracy when the visual array was increased. This pattern of performance was consistent with his discrimination ability. Shawn was successful in discriminating pictures and objects randomly positioned when two items were present (95% accuracy with 12 items). His performance deteriorated when more items were present (45% accuracy). The relative ease Shawn exhibited with simple matching and discrimination skills suggested that overselective responding was not a contributing factor.

Sampling of Shawn's perceptual motor ability indicated strength when information was presented auditorily, however, he did experience difficulty with processing visual information. For example, Shawn inconsistently tracked objects moving slowly out of his visual field (50% of 20 trials). He was also unsuccessful with the recall of single items after they were removed (20% of 20 trials).

Assessment of academic areas revealed the beginning of premath and prewriting abilities. No evidence of reading ability was apparent at that time. Shawn consistently counted to 10 and made visible marks on a piece of paper in 90% of the trials.

ISSUES IN THE ASSESSMENT OF ACADEMIC FUNCTIONING

Translating Results into Treatment

The data generated from behavioral assessment leads directly to educational planning. According to Shawn's assessment, programs can be designed, based on skill deficiencies, to focus on visual attending, on more complex matching and discrimination tasks, and on academic skills. Ongoing assessment then would generate specific behavioral levels from which to monitor his progress and to adjust and expand programming.

Sampling various areas of functioning enables a finer assessment of learning difficulty and presents a better picture of the learning and behavioral inconsistencies that severely developmentally disabled students demonstrate. The suggestion that learning proceeds according to absolute developmental progressions does not apply necessarily to this population (Sternberg, 1982). For example, Guess and Baer (1973) reveal no functional relationship between receptive and expressive skills with severely developmentally disabled children, and Handleman, Powers, and Harris (1984) question the relationship between concrete and pictorial representations of objects. Relying solely on a developmental index for assessment might not reveal to clinicians the splinter skills that a behavioral sampling could.

Materials

While a host of commercial materials are available to clinicians and special educators, often instructor-made items can be more closely aligned with the specialized needs of the students. This seems to be particularly the case with the severely developmentally disabled, where educational planning is more individualized. Cutouts from magazines, combined with pegs from one kit and pictures from another, in many cases can provide the core of materials for a particular program or assessment probe. In this case, commercial materials can augment other sources. Many clinicians will attest to how consumable seemingly durable items can become with this population. Table 7–2 outlines, according to skill area, commercial materials that may be useful for assessment or programming.

Focus of Instruction

Curricula designed to focus on developmental progression can result in age-inappropriate tasks taught in contrived situations (Johnson & Koegel, 1982).

Table 7–2 Some Useful Commercial Materials

Materials*	Basic	Academic
1. Action Verb Boards (DLM)		•
2. All Purpose Photo Library (DLM)	•	•
3. Alphabet Picture Cards (Ideal)		•
4. Association Picture Cards (DLM)	•	
5. Auditory Training (DLM)	•	
6. Beads (Playskool)	•	
7. Body Awareness Cards (Trend)		•
8. Category Cards (DLM)	•	
9. Clock Puzzles (DLM)		•
10. Coin Counting Cards (DLM)		•
11. Concept Town (DLM)	•	•
12. Color, Object, and Number Grouping Cards (DLM)		•
13. Color and Shape Bingo (Trend)	•	•
14. Colored Balloons (Ravensburger)	•	•
15. Consonant Pictures (Ideal)		•
16. Edu-sequence Cards (Educards)	•	
17. Feel and Match (Lauri)	•	
18. Form Boards (Lauri)	•	
19. Form Puzzles (Fisher Price)	•	
20. Knob Puzzles (Childcraft)	•	
21. Large Parquetry Blocks (DLM)	•	
22. Lotto Games (Educards)	•	•
23. Lower Case Letters (Instructo)		•
24. Make-A-Word (DLM)		•
25. Making Change (Binney and Smith)		•
26. Math Cards (DLM)		•
27. Miniature Traffic Signs (Playskool)	•	•
28. Moving Up In Time (DLM)		•
29. Multivariant Sequencing Beads (DLM)	•	
30. Musical Instruments (Honner)	•	
31. Nesting Cups (Gabriel)	•	
32. New Math Flash Cards (Milton Bradley)		•
33. Number Bingo (Trend)	•	•
34. Number Pegboards (Ideal)	•	•
35. Original Mini Clocks (Judy)		•
36. Peabody Picture Libraries (American Guidance)	•	•
37. Photo Number Cards (DLM)	•	•
38. Rhyming Puzzles (DLM)	•	•
39. Ring Tower (Fisher Price)	•	
40. Same and Different Cards (DLM)	•	
41. Sandpaper Letters (Philogram)	•	•

*These materials are available in most educational catalogs.

Table 7–2 continued

	Skills	
Materials*	Basic	Academic
42. Sequential Development Alphabet Cards (Ideal)		•
43. Shape Sorter (Creative Playthings)	•	
44. Singular-Plural Dominos (DLM)		•
45. Size Sequencing Cards (DLM)	•	•
46. Small Parquetry Blocks (DLM)	•	
47. Sort-A-Cards (Milton Bradley)	•	•
48. Sorting Tray (Creative Playthings)	•	•
49. Stacking Cones (Combey)	•	
50. Stacking Number Forms (Creative Playthings)	•	•
51. Taskmaster Beginning Skills (Taskmaster)		•
52. Toy Money (Milton Bradley)		•
53. Vowel Pictures (Ideal)		•
54. Wood Blocks (Playskool)	•	•

Instructional goals and objectives formulated directly from behavioral assessment and committed to blending functional and naturalistic elements with more traditional academic areas, therefore, can match more comfortably with the needs of the severely developmentally disabled. Also, efforts to plan experiences that approximate teaching and application settings can enhance the generalization and maintenance of mastered skills (Handleman, 1979; Johnson & Koegel, 1982).

Special education curricula typically reflect a flavoring of traditional instructional areas, such as reading, writing, and math, combined with a sensitivity to plan functional experiences. While this balancing of traditional and functional skill areas often is difficult, it is an important issue to consider when assessing and designing educational programs for the severely developmentally disabled client. A preliminary survey of the environment in which a client will perform learned skills can result in identifying the best matched tasks and most appropriate materials to be used.

Maintaining an eye toward the environment in which the client will be expected to use learned skills can enhance the ultimate independent functioning of the client (Johnson & Koegel, 1982). Teaching in the most natural instructional setting lessens the distance between teaching and application settings and facilitates greater transfer of learning. Often the contrived nature of the instructional environment cannot provide the relevant cues that are needed for successful performance by many severely developmentally disabled students. For example, the use of actual utensil trays and dish racks for sorting and daily living activities presents clients with real-life and naturally cued materials.

SUMMARY

The intricacies of the cognitive development of severely developmentally disabled clients necessitates an assessment strategy sensitive to their inconsistent and idiosyncratic performance patterns. Behavioral assessment provides a systematic approach to evaluation that can produce information regarding the parameters of academic behavior and the associated variables and conditions. Behavioral assessment also leads directly to educational programming by establishing ongoing measures of performance from which to monitor progress.

The intraindividual nature of behavioral assessment facilitates total individualization. This flexibility allows clinicians the continual fine tuning and ability to focus on variables specific to severely developmentally disabled clients, such as the functional and natural components of their learning. The behavioral approach to assessment also can be augmented by normative educational testing to assist in marking performance more comfortably along a developmental continuum.

REFERENCES

Bartak, L. (1979). Educational approaches. In M. Rutter and E. Schopler (Eds.), *Autism: A reappraisal of concepts and treatment*. New York: Plenum Press.

Bateman, B. (1965). An educator's view of a diagnostic approach to learning disorders. In J. Hellmuth (Ed.), *Learning disorders* (Vol. 1). Seattle: Special Child Publications.

Carter, L., Alpert, M., & Stewart, S. M. (1982). Schizophrenic children's utilization of images and words in performance of cognitive tasks. *Journal of Autism and Developmental Disorders, 12*, 279–293.

Cook, A. R., Anderson, N., & Rincover, A. (1982). Stimulus overselectivity and stimulus control: Problems and strategies. In R. L. Koegel, A. Rincover, & A. L. Egel (Eds.), *Educating and understanding autistic children*. San Diego: College Hill Press.

Crawford, C. (1979). George Washington, Abraham Lincoln, & Arthur Jensen: Are they compatible? *American Psychologist, 34*, 664–672.

Cromer, R. F. (1981). Developmental language disorders: Cognitive processes, semantics, pragmatics, phonology and syntax. *Journal of Autism and Developmental Disorders, 11*, 57–74.

Ellis, N. R., Deacon, J. R., Harris, L. A., Poor, A., Angers, D., & Diorio, M. S. (1982). Learning, memory, and transfer in profoundly, severely and moderately retarded persons. *American Journal of Mental Deficiency, 87*, 186–196.

Gersten, R. M., White, W., Falco, R., & Carnin, D. (1982). Teaching basic discriminations to handicapped and nonhandicapped individuals through a dynamic presentation of instructional stimuli. *Analysis and Intervention in Developmental Disabilities, 2*, 305–318.

Guess, D., & Baer, D. M. (1973). An analysis of individual differences in generalization between receptive and productive language in retarded children. *Journal of Applied Behavior Analysis, 6*, 311–329.

Hammill, D. D. (1974). Learning disabilities: A problem in definition. *Division for Children with Learning Disabilities, 4*, 28–31.

Hammill, D. D., & Larsen, S. C. (1974). The relationship of selected auditory perceptual skills and reading. *Journal of Learning Disabilities, 7*, 429–435.

Handleman, J. S. (1979). Generalization by autistic-type children of verbal responses across settings. *Journal of Applied Behavior Analysis, 12*, 273–282.

Handleman, J. S., Arnold, M., Veniar, F. A., Kristoff, B., & Harris, S. L. (1982). Assessment and remediation of hearing loss in an autistic youngster. *Hearing Instruments, 33*, 10–11.

Handleman, J. S., Powers, M. D., & Harris, S. L. (1984). The teaching of labels: An analysis of concrete and pictorial representations. *American Journal of Mental Deficiency, 88*, 625–629.

Harris, S. L. (1975). Teaching language to nonverbal children with emphasis on problems of generalization. *Psychological Bulletin, 82*, 565–580.

Hermelin, B., & O'Connor, N. (1970). *Psychological experiments with autistic children.* Oxford: Pergamon Press.

Johnson, J., & Koegel, R. L. (1982). Behavioral assessment and curriculum development. In R. L. Koegel, A. Rincover, & A. L. Egel (Eds.), *Educating and understanding autistic children.* San Diego: College Hill Press.

Kanner, L. (1943). Autistic disturbances of affective contact. *Nervous Child, 2*, 217–250.

Kanner, L. (1957). *Child psychiatry* (3rd ed.). Oxford: Blackwell Scientific Publications.

Kanner, L. (1971). Follow-up study of eleven autistic children originally reported in 1943. *Journal of Autism and Childhood Schizophrenia, 1*, 119–145.

Kirk, S. (1972). *Educating exceptional children* (2nd ed.). Boston: Houghton Mifflin.

Lansing, M. D., & Schopler, E. (1979). Individualized education: A public school model. In M. Rutter & E. Schopler (Eds.), *Autism: A reappraisal of concepts and treatment.* New York: Plenum Press.

Lerner, J. W. (1971). *Children with learning disabilities.* Boston: Houghton Mifflin.

Lovaas, O. I. (1981). *Teaching developmentally disabled children: The Me Book.* Baltimore: University Park Press.

Lovaas, O. I., & Newsom, C. D. (1976). Behavior modification with psychotic children. In H. Leitenberg (Ed.), *Handbook of behavior modification and behavior therapy.* Englewood Cliffs, NJ: Prentice-Hall.

Lovaas, O., Schreibman, L., Koegel, R., & Rehm, R. (1971). Selective responding of autistic children to multiple sensory input. *Journal of Abnormal Psychology, 77*, 211–222.

Rincover, A., & Koegel, R. (1975). Setting generality and stimulus control in autistic children. *Journal of Applied Behavior Analysis, 8*, 235–246.

Robinson, N. M., & Robinson, H. B. (1976). *The mentally retarded child* (2nd ed.). New York: McGraw-Hill.

Rutter, M. (1979). Diagnosis and definition. In M. Rutter & E. Schopler (Eds.), *Autism: A reappraisal of concepts and treatment.* New York: Plenum Press.

Sailor, W. (1971). Reinforcement and generalization of productive plural allomorphs in two retarded children. *Journal of Applied Behavior Analysis, 4*, 305–310.

Salvia, J., & Ysseldyke, J. (1978). *Assessment in special and remedial education.* Boston: Houghton Mifflin.

Schneider, H. C., & Salzberg, C. L. (1982). Stimulus overselectivity in a match-to-sample paradigm by severely retarded youth. *Analysis and Intervention in Developmental Disabilities, 2*, 273–304.

Schreibman, L., & Lovaas, O. I. (1973). Overselectivity responding to social stimuli by autistic children. *Journal of Abnormal Child Psychology, 1*, 152–168.

Scott, M. (1980). Ecological theory and methods for research in special education. *Journal of Special Education, 14*, 279–294.

Smith, C., & Knoff, H. (1981). School psychology and special education students' placement decisions: IQ still tips the scale. *Journal of Special Education, 15,* 55–64.

Sternberg, L. (1982). Perspectives on educating severely and profoundly handicapped students. In L. Steinberg & G. L. Adams (Eds.), *Educating severely and profoundly handicapped students.* Rockville: Aspen Systems.

Swanson, H. L., & Watson, B. L. (1982). *Educational and psychological assessment of exceptional children.* St. Louis: C. V. Mosby.

Wing, L. (1979). Social, behavioral, and cognitive characteristics: An epidemiological approach. In M. Rutter & E. Schopler (Eds.), *Autism: A reappraisal of concepts and treatment.* New York: Plenum Press.

Chapter 8

Generalization, Maintenance, and Other Related Issues

INTRODUCTION

While the severely developmentally disabled population is for the most part a heterogeneous group, there exist some common threads. Some of the characteristics that are shared by many severely developmentally disabled clients include their difficulties with social and communication areas, as well as their difficulties with developmental skills. An additional common element is the problem that many of these clients demonstrate with the generalization and maintenance of behavior. Both of these problems make the assessment process more complicated.

The ability to transfer and apply information outside the teaching environment underscores most areas of learning. Without generalization, performance becomes situationally specific and of limited use to the client. Chapter 8 discusses the problem of generalization demonstrated by severely developmentally disabled clients and the advances made toward the remediation of generalization deficits. Specific assessment strategies also are presented to assist clinicians in identifying clients with limited and restricted ranges of performance.

While clients may demonstrate a particular behavior in one environment, they may not perform the same way in other situations or maintain this behavior over time. The maintenance of behavior complements generalization by increasing the usefulness of information. The inability to maintain learned skills is also problematic for severely developmentally disabled clients and contributes to the situational specificity of their responding. Chapter 8 discusses this problem and presents assessment strategies for maintenance difficulties.

Not only do difficulties with generalization and maintenance affect basic skill acquisition, a number of other related issues are involved. The normalization and mainstreaming of severely developmentally disabled clients depends heavily on their ability to transfer learning from one educational environment to another. Also, the current argument for providing extended school year programming for these clients is based on the difficulty demonstrated in maintaining their behavior changes. Both issues are presented in Chapter 8, along with strategies for assessing clients for mainstreaming experiences and those who will benefit from a year-round program.

GENERALIZATION

The literature consistently notes that severely developmentally disabled clients may be bound to the specific physical elements of the stimulus situation, and as a result they are restricted in their ability to generalize learning from one situation to another (Egel, 1982; Hamilton, 1966; Handleman, 1981). The term generalization refers to a person's ability to employ information beyond the limits of the teaching situation. Two types of generalization are described: stimulus generalization and response generalization.

Stimulus generalization occurs when a learned behavior is emitted under stimulus conditions different from those in training (Lovaas, Koegel, Simmons, & Long, 1973) and includes transfer of skills to new settings (Wahler, 1969) as well as to new people (Stokes, Baer, & Jackson, 1974). Response generalization occurs when changes in untrained responses co-vary with changes in trained responses (Garcia, 1974). Recognition of the difficulty severely developmentally disabled clients have with both types of generalization has produced a spate of research exploring means to facilitate generalization of learned behaviors (Burgio, Whitman, & Johnson, 1980; Cuvo & Riva, 1980; Garcia, 1974; Guess, Sailor, Rutherford, & Baer, 1968; Handleman, 1979a, 1981; Redd, 1970; Sailor, 1971; Welch, 1981). Kazdin and Bootzin (1972) urge that transfer of learning be planned rather than assumed to follow as a consequence of training.

During the course of the past decade, psychologists and educators have advanced the position that generalization of behavior should be a criterion for assessing the success of intervention (Egel, 1982; Garcia & DeHaven, 1974; Handleman & Harris, 1980; Rhode, Morgan, & Young, 1983). Research in this area has been conducted primarily with severely developmentally disabled populations (Cooke, Cooke, & Apolini, 1976). Of the limited research conducted with normal clients, the consensus is that techniques that are effective with such students are not always useful when applied to the severely developmentally disabled (Cooke et al., 1976).

Much of the work investigating response generalization in severely developmentally disabled clients has focused on the formation of response classes. A generalized response class is said to exist when all responses in a particular class (e.g., grammatical structure) show an effect of a manipulation that is made in relation to only a few members of the class (Wheeler & Sulzer, 1970). Simply stated, a response class is reflected by the appearance of novel responses that have not been modeled or directly trained. The use of response classes offers an alternative to teaching the infinite number of specific responses that a client may be expected to use every day. A large body of response-class literature has focused on the use of reinforcement to facilitate generalized imitative behavior (Baer & Sherman, 1964; Baer, Peterson, & Sherman, 1967; Bringham & Sherman, 1968; Lovaas, Berberich, Perloff, & Schaefer, 1966; Metz, 1965; Peterson, 1968; Peterson & Whitehurst, 1970; Steinman, 1970; Welch, 1981).

An investigation by Guess et al. (1968) provided a starting point for experimental analysis of generative language with analysis of the productive use of the plural morpheme. After training of the plural formation, the investigators found that retarded subjects were able to form plurals with novel stimuli and labels that they were taught only in the singular form. The use of modeling and reinforcement has been effective with severely developmentally disabled clients to establish a generative language that can extend across several language classes: descriptive adjectives (Hart & Risley, 1968); productive and receptive plurality (Guess, 1969; Guess & Baer, 1973); past and present tense verb inflections (Schumaker & Sherman, 1970); generative use of "is" in descriptive sentences (Fygetakis & Gray, 1970); adjectival inflections (Baer & Guess, 1971); generative use of "is" and "the" (Bennett & Ling, 1972); generative use of plural allomorphs (Sailor, 1971); and use of singular and plural sentences (Garcia, Guess & Byrnes, 1973). These investigations report the functional role of modeling and reinforcement procedures in the formation of a generative language that produce extensive novel language and behavioral repertoires in clients who previously demonstrated little use of appropriate language.

Once behavior is established within the teaching situation, the next step is the extension of performance to other people in addition to the teacher and to other settings beyond the classroom (Harris, 1975). The necessity for generalization of therapeutic behavior change is widely accepted, but it is not always recognized that generalization does not automatically occur simply because a behavior change has been accomplished (Stokes et al., 1974). There is now an increasing awareness of the need to program the various forms of stimulus generalization with severely developmentally disabled learners (Baer, Wolf, & Risley, 1968; Handleman, 1979a; Lovaas et al., 1973; Simic & Bucher, 1980; Patterson, McNeal, Hawkins, & Phelps, 1967; Welch & Pear, 1980).

A limited number of investigations have established viable techniques for programming generalization of nonverbal behaviors across experimenters. Redd (1970) and Redd and Birnbrauer (1969) examined specific conditions under which retarded children would generalize cooperative play in the presence of training and nontraining experimenters. Analysis of generalization of the punishment of self-destructive behavior across experimenters was conducted by Corte, Wolf, and Locke (1971) and Lovaas and Simmons (1969).

Less frequently discussed in the literature is the generalization of language-related behaviors. Garcia (1974) taught a conversational speech form to nonverbal children. Results indicated that generalization to a third experimenter was demonstrated only after the children had experienced training by two other experimenters. The generalization of a greeting response across examiners was established in hospitalized schizophrenic children (Kale, Kaye, Whelan, & Hopkins, 1968). It is consistently noted that generalization of behavior to nontraining examiners can be facilitated by the use of more than one trainer.

Garcia (1974) defined functional performance in terms of the control of behavior in situations different from those in which training took place. Extrasetting generalization has not received the experimental attention necessary to establish it as a reliably scheduled outcome of training (Garcia, 1974). Initial reports indicated that newly trained speech is used by retarded children in other situations (Risley & Wolf, 1967; Sloan, Johnson, & Harris, 1968; Wolf, Risley, & Mees, 1964), but experimental evaluation and reliable documentation of such reports has not been provided. However, the issue of the transfer of treatment gains across settings has received increased attention (Adubato, Adams, & Budd, 1981; Baer et al., 1968; Birnbrauer, 1968; Birnbrauer, Wolf, Kidder, & Tague, 1965; Kale et al., 1968; Kuypers, Becker, & O'Leary, 1968; Lovaas et al., 1973; Thompson, Braam, & Fuqua, 1982; Tucker & Berry, 1980; Walker & Buckley, 1972). The above studies indicate that transfer does not usually take place without special intervention in extratherapy settings. Transfers of treatment gains to extratherapy settings were viewed as the exception rather than the rule (Kazdin & Bootzin, 1972). Griffiths and Craighead (1972) reported the facilitation of extratherapy setting generalization of articulation training in clients by the use of reinforcement in other settings. In addition, a child treated for aphonia and trained to speak with normal loudness in therapy settings demonstrated generalization to the regular classroom by reinforcement in a reading class (Jackson & Wallace, 1974).

Most empirical investigations have focused on a single setting, primarily the school, the clinic, or the home. The few studies in which clinicians have examined behavioral techniques in nonlaboratory settings prior to the mid-1970s had not provided experimental evidence documenting the success of their treatment programs (Brown, Pace, & Becker, 1969; Hewett, 1965; Wetzel, Baker, Roney, & Martin, 1966; Wolf et al., 1964). Risley and Wolf (1967) did offer information suggesting that parents can be trained effectively to modify some of the behaviors of autistic children. Risley (1968) reported experimental evidence indicating that parents can successfully apply behavioral techniques to the behaviors of severely developmentally disabled children in a nonclinical setting.

In response to the problems that severely developmentally disabled learners experienced with stimulus generalization, consideration was given to several advantages offered by home-based treatment approaches over a clinical approach: (1) cost to parents is reduced because parents, not professionals, administer the treatment; (2) treatment conducted in the home relies on reinforcers indigenous to the setting; and consequently, (3) concern for generalization from the clinic to the home is not necessary (Nordquist & Wahler, 1973). The third consideration addresses the crucial issue that successful treatment in a clinical setting is no guarantee that treatment will transfer to the child's natural environment.

An assumption of traditional forms of psychotherapy and the earlier behavioral approaches was that changes in the therapeutic situation would generalize to the natural environment (Wulbert, 1974). This critical problem received little experimental investigation, however. Initial research conducted with severely developmentally disabled populations dealt primarily with nonverbal behaviors with the consensus that their behavioral gains in the clinical setting do not generalize automatically to the home. The absence of cross-setting generalization has been observed in both directions, from the home to the school and vice versa. Birnbrauer (1968) found that punishment effects established in the clinic did not generalize to the home to suppress a client's inappropriate behavior. Findings of Wahler (1969) indicated that contingency changes in the home significantly altered a client's behavior in the home, while the level of the client's deviant behaviors remained at baseline rates in the school.

Attempts to extend speech and language training into a child's everyday environment have been reported by Risley and Wolf (1967). Techniques to extend training in these studies were reinforcement, imitation, and fading techniques employed by parents and cottage attendants. While results of these initial attempts were reported as successful, no meaningful data were presented, nor had the success been functionally evaluated (Garcia & DeHaven, 1974). A study conducted by Miller and Sloane (1976) investigated the generalization of a language behavior from the home to the school with autistic children. Results indicated that mere training of speech sounds by parents in the home was not sufficient to facilitate client generalization to the school.

The continued need for research on the facilitation of generalization of behavior from the clinic or school to the home is noted clearly in the literature (Handleman, 1979a; Sailor, Guess, & Baer, 1973; Welch & Pear, 1980). Sailor and colleagues (1973) state the need for generalization of communication skills from the controlled training setting to the client's natural environment. Garcia and DeHaven (1974) report that further research is needed to determine which conditions are the most efficient for obtaining generalization from the clinic to the home.

Recently, Handleman (1979a) reported that severely developmentally disabled children did not automatically generalize from school to home, but their verbal responding was facilitated across settings by training in various locations in the school, as opposed to a single setting. In a follow-up study, Handleman and Harris (1980) attempted to assess the impact of single versus multiple trainers on generalization to the natural setting; they confirmed the usefulness of training at varied locations.

Consistent with the recent interest in the normalization and mainstreaming of severely developmentally disabled clients, concern for ensuring that they transfer learned behaviors to novel instructional settings was raised by Handleman (1981). Results of the study indicate that children do not automatically generalize their verbal behavior from school to a local day-care center. Handleman and Harris (1983) then confirmed the influence of training clients in a variety of classrooms upon the generalization to a novel school.

Assessment of Generalization

While the deficiencies displayed with generalization are often clear to clinicians, accurate assessment of a child's ability to transfer learning can assist programming. The use of a generalization probe where novel material is presented after a client masters targeted skills is useful in tracking generalization. For example, if a client is taught that an apple and a banana are fruit, a probe of other fruit not taught can be assessed. Also, a client who is taught certain self-help skills at home can be probed to assess generalization in the school setting.

The ability to generalize conceptually is basic to social, communication, and cognitive development. Generalization probes can be designed to assess a wide variety of concepts from "roundness" to "cupness," in addition to categories such as toys and vehicles. Stimulus materials can be organized according to concept, both on a concrete and pictorial level, and presented to the client during baseline or assessment sessions. The number of items correctly identified according to category can be recorded. After each instance of a particular concept is taught, the remaining stimuli can be tested to assess generalization. Throughout this process, items can progress from probe to training stimuli until the concept is mastered.

Being able to respond consistently with various materials in the environment increases the diversity of experiences available to clients. Providing various forms of materials during assessment enables the assessor to observe a client's ability with this type of generalization. For example, if a client is observed riding a 20-inch tricycle at home, is he or she able to ride another 20-inch tricycle at school? Also, if a client can use a 12-ounce blue tumbler in the cafeteria, can the client transfer the skill to a red tumbler of equal size? While problems with this form of stimulus generalization are often idiosyncratic, clinician identification of a deficiency in this area can direct programming to focus on increasing a client's flexibility of responding.

Assessment by a novel person in an unfamiliar setting is often a test of stimulus generalization with many severely developmentally disabled clients. For this reason, having a person who is familiar with the client available to assist in the assessment can increase the value of the results. Differences in clients responding to novel persons as opposed to familiar ones can be noted in various tasks presented to them. Variations in their performances in known and unknown settings also can be seen. When an assessor establishes consistent and reliable responding from a client, extrasetting generalization can be assessed by probing a sample of the client's activities and skills in different rooms or environments. In addition, the client can be presented with directions from various people, such as the school secretary and transportation coordinator, for further assessment of stimulus generalization.

Another important form of extrasetting generalization involves the client's transfer of learning across instructional, work, and residential environments. Assessment of this type of generalization is often difficult to accomplish due to distance, transportation, and scheduling considerations. In some cases, checklists and questionnaires can be filled out by persons in the various settings to provide information about a client's differences in responding. More accurate assessment can include probing the client's behavior in these various settings.

Because of the important role generalization plays with all learning, the assessment of both stimulus and response generalization should be part of the assessment process. Record or score sheets can simply be expanded to include columns for generalization of concept, in addition to generalization of person and setting. In addition to providing initial pretreatment information, generalization probes can become an important part of ongoing assessment. During a client's training, regularly scheduled probes can assess the durability of the client's treatment gains.

MAINTENANCE

While a client's ability to maintain behavior change complements the client's ability to generalize and strengthen responding, response maintenance has not received the same professional attention. Rusch and Kazdin (1981) distinguish between acquisition and maintenance and stress the importance of ensuring that acquired skills are maintained over time. The need for programming response maintenance is documented repeatedly (Augustine & Cipani, 1982; Dunlap & Koegel, 1980; Koegel and Rincover, 1977; Lancioni, 1982; Russo & Koegel, 1977).

If a client generalizes initially and then regresses, strategies for maintenance need to be employed. The degree to which educational gains are maintained in training or extratherapy settings often is dependent upon the presence or absence of reinforcement or other contingencies in those settings (Egel, 1982; Lancioni, 1982; Marholin & Siegel, 1978; O'Leary, Becker, Evans, & Sandargas, 1969; Sowers, Rusch, Connis, & Cummings, 1980). Koegel and Rincover (1977) report the lack of response maintenance in extratherapy settings as a function of the client discrimination between the existence or absence of systematic contingencies.

Strategies for increasing the degree of response maintenance by severely developmentally disabled clients have focused on reducing the discriminability of contingencies across environments (Egel, 1982; Connis, 1979; Rusch, Close, Hops, & Agosta, 1976; Sowers et al., 1980). Many authors suggest employing contingencies in nontreatment settings as a method for reducing the discriminability of reinforcement (Marholin, Siegel, & Phillips, 1976; Russo & Koegel, 1977; Walker, Hops, & Johnson, 1975). Lancioni (1982) found similarity of training stimuli an effective variable for increasing response maintenance in developmentally disabled students. Peer instruction also has been used as a strategy for increasing performance maintenance (Solomon & Wahler, 1973; Patterson & Anderson, 1964). Other strategies that have been employed successfully to program response maintenance in clients include the use of trained parents to introduce teaching contingencies into new settings (O'Leary, O'Leary, & Becker, 1967; Wolf et al., 1964) and the switching of training schedules of reinforcement to intermittent forms during maintenance (Kazdin & Polster, 1973; Koegel & Rincover, 1977).

Assessment of Response Maintenance

Maintenance of treatment gains is related to when training occurred. Any assessment measure can confirm response maintenance if information regarding the acquisition of assessed skills can be secured. Therefore, preassessment records that include past training data can serve as the basis from which clinicians determine how well client learning has been maintained. In this sense, the results of social, communicative, and academic skill assessments can indicate current client functioning as well as client response maintenance. The older the training data, the longer maintenance can be assessed.

Like generalization, concern for response maintenance can be part of the ongoing nature of behavioral assessment. Probes can be set up on a weekly, bimonthly, or monthly basis to assess the maintenance of a client's learned skills either in the training setting or in extratherapy environments. Constructing a maintenance inventory where mastered items are continually added and reviewed according to some fixed schedule also can provide systematic maintenance data.

MAINSTREAMING AND NORMALIZATION EFFORTS

Mainstreaming efforts have been successful with many populations of exceptional students: the mildly retarded (Gallagher, 1972), the emotionally disturbed (Vaac, 1968), the physically handicapped (Rapier, Adelson, Carey, & Croke, 1972), and the learning disabled (Glass & Meckler, 1972). Difficulty, however, has been encountered when attempts to apply the mainstreaming concept to severely developmentally disabled learners have been made (Koegel, Rincover, & Russo, 1982; Russo & Koegel, 1977). Often, the nature of the learning and behavioral difficulties demonstrated by severely developmentally disabled clients precludes mainstreaming in the traditional sense of the word (Handleman, in press). Reference to mainstreaming as the integration of the handicapped learner with less handicapped learners can increase the implementation of the concept.

Most discussions of mainstreaming refer to two important variables. Many authors call for the adoption of the normalization principle as suggested by Wolfensberger (1975), as well as the design of strategies to facilitate a client's transition to more normal environments (Deno, 1973). Treatment in the least restrictive and most normal environment is prescribed by federal legislation, Public Law No. 94-142.

Wolfensberger (1975) presents two levels of the normalization principle. On the most basic level, the principle refers to normalizing the attitudes and beliefs of the general public toward the handicapped. The second level includes the physical integration of the handicapped person into a more normal mainstream. While the first level is as relevant to the severely developmentally disabled person as to any other exceptional person, the concern for physical integration is more problematic. Nevertheless, sensitivity to the need for integration is becoming more evident (Handleman, 1979b, in press; Koegel et al., 1982; Poorman, 1980).

Severely developmentally disabled clients increasingly are being served in specialized facilities designed to include treatment components such as low client/ staff ratio and behavioral technology (Handleman, 1981). This systematic approach to education has resulted, in many cases, in distancing programs from the mainstream of public opportunity. The initial dependency by these clients on one-to-one intervention often precludes the client from public educational and community activities. Creating strategies for the eventual reentry of the severely developmentally disabled into the public mainstream has, therefore, become a priority for service providers (Handleman, 1979; Harris & Handleman, 1980; Koegel et al., 1982; Russo & Koegel, 1977).

Earlier attempts at exposing the severely developmentally disabled to more normal situations were accomplished through the efforts of parent training programs (Risley & Wolf, 1967). Extending teaching experiences into the home not only facilitates generalization (Wulbert, 1974) but introduces education into more normal, nonschool situations. Recently, the growth of community-based group homes and public school classes for severely developmentally disabled clients reflect successful attempts at integration.

While behavioral intervention has been successful in teaching severely developmentally disabled clients, their problems of transferring learning to novel settings remain (Handleman, 1979b). Consequently, an essential treatment component is the eventual weaning of a student from the teaching structure to more natural environmental contingencies (Harris, 1975). Given the difficulty that many severely developmentally disabled clients demonstrate with generalization, the transition of such clients to more normal educational environments becomes an intricate task. As a result, mainstreaming efforts need to identify strategies designed to prepare clients for more normal settings.

A highly individualized and increasingly complex curriculum can set the framework for the mainstreaming effort (Harris & Handleman, 1980). Clients can progress through a carefully designed program where variables, such as reinforcement, number of staff, and complexity of curriculum are manipulated systematically (Handleman, in press). For example, in an entry-level structure, a client can be taught instructional control and basic skills in a one-to-one instructional setting, where primary reinforcement may be required on a continual basis. Upon mastering basic skills, the client can enter an intermediate structure designed to wean the client from the structure imposed by the entry level. Client exposure to small group instruction and social contingencies and reinforcers can serve to diversify learning experiences. As a final step, the client can progress to a transitional structure that approximates a more normalized, community-based placement with regard to staffing patterns and educational experiences. The following criteria can be used for assessing a client's readiness for movement from one program structure to another.

I. Transition from entry to intermediate structure
   A. Sitting: Is able to sit in a group of two for at least one 15-minute work session and can remain seated during intertrial intervals.
   B. Eye contact: Can sustain a 3- to 4-second gaze upon command.
   C. Attention to task: Can establish visual contact with various environmental objects for 3 to 4 seconds.
   D. Reinforcement: At least one primary or secondary reinforcer can establish stimulus control over behavior.
   E. Management: Life-threatening behaviors should be absent. Also, competing and disruptive behaviors should respond to special intervention.
   F. Following directions: Can respond to simple, one-step commands involving classroom activities and self-help skills.
   G. Nonverbal imitation: Can discriminate at least three gross motor and three fine motor movements.
   H. Receptive noun identification: Can identify at least three concrete objects.
   I. Verbal or sign imitation: Can imitate at least three sounds or sign movements.
   J. Functional communication: Can verbally or nonverbally indicate two basic needs.
   K. Self-help: Responds to a diaper-free toileting schedule and can assist with dressing and undressing. Also, can drink from a cup and eat a sandwich.
   L. Social skills: Will orient to a greeting by an adult.
   M. Independent skills: Can occupy self constructively for a 2-minute period.

II. Transition from intermediate to transition structure
   A. Group sitting: Can sit in a two-client work setting for 25 minutes and remain seated with no competing/disruptive behaviors.
   B. Eye contact: Consistently maintains intermediate-level criteria. Can also orient to various classroom mediums, such as blackboards and worksheets, on command for 3- to 4-second periods.
   C. Attention to tasks: Consistently maintains intermediate level criteria.
   D. Reinforcement: Is no longer dependent on continual reinforcement and can respond to the earliest stages of a token economy.
   E. Management: Displays no behaviors that require individual attention.
   F. Following directions: Can follow at least five classroom commands.
   G. Receptive noun identification: Can identify at least three pictorial representations of objects.
   H. Verbal or sign imitation: Can imitate at least two words or two signs or gestures.
   I. Expressive language: Can identify at least two nouns and two verbs of concrete objects and actions.
   J. Functional communication: Consistently indicates two basic needs.
   K. Self-help skills: Is accident free on a periodic toileting schedule. Is also able to self-feed and undress completely.
   L. Social skills: Can greet an adult and accept brief physical contacts from others without pulling away.
   M. Independent skills: Can complete a simple matching, sorting, or completion task with prompting.
III. Criteria for transition to out-of-agency placement: Criteria for transition will vary depending on the identified placement. Variables to consider include size of group; contingencies for motivation and management; and self-help and independent functioning requirements.

Transfer to a new program should be carefully planned (Handleman, 1979b, in press; Harris & Handleman, 1980). Professionals currently involved with the client are the best coordinators of the transfer. By visiting and observing various settings during a client's transition year, an initial client/placement match can be made. After a skills assessment of the new setting, requisite skills can be identified and eventually taught. This assessment can include variables such as staff/client ratio, contingencies, school-life activities, classroom organization, and physical plant. Programming efforts then can be directed toward approximating the new environment in order to facilitate the client's optimal adjustment and generalization (Handleman, 1979; Handleman & Harris, 1980; Rincover & Koegel, 1975). To ensure continuity, a comprehensive treatment plan can be made available to the new program. The current placement can facilitate the transition process further with an offer of continued consultation services after the transfer.

Professionals from the new setting also can assume an instrumental role in the transition process (Handleman, in press). Visits to the current setting can result in professionals' familiarization with current methods, materials, and techniques to help them facilitate continuity of programming. In addition, direct work with the client by new professionals can facilitate the transfer of learning. Information gathered from the visits then can be used to modify the new setting in order to approximate current interventions and facilitate generalization of client responding. The ultimate support of both the administrator and the professional can have a direct effect on the success or failure of the mainstreaming attempt (Martin, 1974).

There are additional experiences that can be offered clients to facilitate their transition. Providing exposure to a variety of instructional settings and professionals within the current placement can facilitate their transfer of learning to the new setting. Also, visits to other outside settings and ideally to the new placement before the transfer can provide clients with exposure to different curricula and additional professionals.

Preparing severely developmentally disabled clients for placements previously inappropriate due to the nature of their problems must be planned systematically. Due to individual needs, no time limit can be set for the process. As a result, transition must be considered in the total programming for each client.

TWELVE-MONTH PROGRAMMING FOR SEVERELY DEVELOPMENTALLY DISABLED CLIENTS

Recent professional, parental, and legal attention has been focused on extended year programming for severely developmentally disabled clients. A number of legal decisions have argued that there is a compelling need for year-round experiences for these individuals (*Armstrong v. Kline*, 1979; *Battle v. Commonwealth*, 1980). Also, many authors review the legal and ethical issues involved in reaching a decision about the need for a longer school or treatment year (Larsen, Goodman, & Glean, 1981; Leonard, 1981; Makuch, 1981; Stotland & Mancuso, 1981).

A discussion of the effects of summer vacation on the performance of severely developmentally disabled people must include the pervasive problem these clients demonstrate with maintaining learned skills. This issue, in its simplest form, is one of behavior maintenance in the absence of instruction.

Extended year programming is a concern for parents, teachers, school boards, and client advocates. Assessing a client's need for a 12-month program, however, is yet another difficult task. While a client may regress during vacation periods, an important variable to consider involves skill recovery time. Also, concern exists for the quantity of instruction needed during the summer to avoid disruption of programming. An additional variable to consider refers to the degree to which different skills are vulnerable in the absence of instruction. Definitive data are difficult to obtain, however, training data and reports of medical and psychological professionals can provide useful information. For example, consistent client regression data after short vacations or absences can supply needed evidence.

Examination of legal and professional reports suggests the following areas for clinicians to assess in determining the need for extended year programming.

- *Nature of the disability:* The presence of self-injurious acts or behaviors that interfere with learning, such as self-stimulation, aggressiveness, or tantrumming, are variables to consider regarding particular disabilities of clients.
- *Severity:* The degree to which clients' behaviors exclude them from normalizing experiences and the demands placed on the environment for supervision are issues relating to the severity of a particular disability.
- *Learning problems:* Overselective responding and problems with generalization and maintenance are specific learning problems to assess. Also, motor or sensory difficulties are important areas to consider.
- *Extent of regression:* Recovery time, particular skills, and quantity of instruction are possible indicators of client regression.
- *Auxiliary support to prevent regression:* Parents' or caretakers' abilities to supervise clients and availability of community services can be considered auxiliary programming.

SUMMARY

In addition to being an intricate process, the assessment of severely developmentally disabled clients is not typically completed in one or two sessions. In this regard, behavioral assessment differs from traditional normative assessment strategies that usually are accomplished within a short period of time. The situationally specific pattern of responding by these clients, combined with the demonstrated learning difficulties, makes the assessment effort a much more comprehensive process.

Concern for generalization and maintenance of responding reflects the comprehensive nature of behavioral assessment. Without consideration for the consistency, durability, and flexibility of client learning, limited and idiosyncratic results may emerge. Assessment of behavior in various settings, with different professionals and with use of a variety of materials, as well as probing performance at posttest intervals can ensure a more complete and accurate profile.

Comprehensive assessment can lead to more comprehensive planning. Assessing a client's readiness for normalizing and community-based experiences can provide the clinician with the framework for program transition. Client and program results can be analyzed to yield a client/program match. In addition, the results of behavioral assessment can provide the information to assist clinicians in making such decisions as the need for 12-month programming. Behavioral assessment strategies can help to define the parameters of the client's disability and the resultant response patterns needed for program decision making.

REFERENCES

Adubato, S. A., Adams, M. K., & Budd, K. S. (1981). Teaching a parent to train a spouse in child management techniques. *Journal of Applied Behavior Analysis, 14,* 193–205.

Armstrong, v. Kline, 476 F Supp. 583 (F.D. Pa. 1979).

Augustine, A., & Cipani, E. (1982). Treating self-injurious behavior: Initial effects, maintenance and acceptability of treatment. *Child and Family Behavior Therapy, 4,* 53–70.

Baer, D. M., & Guess, D. (1971). Receptive training of adjectival inflections in mental retardates. *Journal of Applied Behavior Analysis, 4,* 129–139.

Baer, D., Peterson, R., & Sherman, J. (1967). The development of imitation by reinforcing behavioral similarity to a model. *Journal of the Experimental Analysis of Behavior, 10,* 405–416.

Baer, D., & Sherman, J. (1964). Reinforcement control of generalized imitation in young children. *Journal of Experimental Child Psychology, 1,* 37–49.

Baer, D. M., Wolf, M. M., & Risley, T. R. (1968). Some current dimension of applied behavior analysis. *Journal of Applied Behavior Analysis, 1,* 91–97.

Battle v. Commonwealth, 79-2158, 79-2188-90, 79-2568-70 (3rd Cir. July 18, 1980).

Bennett, C. W., & Ling, D. (1972). Teaching a complex verbal response to a hearing-impaired girl. *Journal of Applied Behavior Analysis, 5,* 321–328.

Birnbrauer, J. S. (1968). Generalization of punishment effects: A case study. *Journal of Applied Behavior Analysis, 1,* 211–221.

Birnbrauer, J. S., Wolf, M. M., Kidder, I. D., & Tague, C. E. (1965). Classroom behavior of retarded pupils with token reinforcement. *Journal of Experimental Child Psychology, 2,* 219–235.

Bringham, T., & Sherman, J. (1968). An experimental analysis of verbal imitation in preschool children. *Journal of Applied Behavior Analysis, 1,* 151–158.

Brown, R. A., Pace, Z. S., & Becker, W. C. (1969). Treatment of extreme negativism and autistic behavior in a six year old boy. *Exceptional Children, 36,* 115–122.

Burgio, L. D., Whitman, T. L., & Johnson, M. P. (1980). A self-instructional package for increasing attending behavior in educable mentally retarded children. *Journal of Applied Behavior Analysis, 13,* 443–459.

Connis, R. T. (1979). The effects of sequential pictorial cues, self-recording, and praise on job task sequencing of retarded adults. *Journal of Applied Behavior Analysis, 12,* 355–361.

Cooke, S., Cooke, T., & Apolloni, T. (1976). Generalization of language training with the mentally retarded. *The Journal of Special Education, 10,* 299–304.

Corte, H. E., Wolf, M. M., & Locke, B. J. (1971). A comparison of procedures for eliminating self-injurious behavior of retarded adolescents. *Journal of Applied Behavior Analysis, 4,* 201–213.

Cuvo, A. J., & Riva, M. T. (1980). Generalization and transfer between comprehension and production: A comparison of retarded and non-retarded persons. *Journal of Applied Behavior Analysis, 13,* 315–331.

Deno, E. N. (1973). *Instructional alternatives for exceptional children.* Reston, VA: Council for Exceptional Children.

Dunlap, G., & Koegel, R. (1980). Motivating autistic children through stimulus variation. *Journal of Applied Behavior Analysis, 13,* 619–627.

Egel, A. (1982). Programming the generalization and maintenance of treatment gains. In R. L. Koegel, A. Rincover, & A. L. Egel (Eds.), *Educating and understanding autistic children.* San Diego: College Hill Press.

Fygetakis, L., & Gray, B. B. (1970). Programmed conditioning of linguistic competence. *Behavior Research and Therapy, 8,* 153–163.

Gallagher, J. J. (1972). The special education contract for mildly handicapped children. *Exceptional Children, 38,* 527–535.

Garcia, E. (1974). The training and generalization of a conversational speech form in nonverbal retardates. *Journal of Applied Behavior Analysis, 7,* 137–149.

Garcia, E. E., & DeHaven, E. D. (1974). Use of operant techniques in the establishment and generalization of language: A review and analysis. *American Journal on Mental Deficiency, 79,* 169–178.

Garcia, E., Guess, D., & Byrnes, J. (1973). Development of syntax in a retarded girl using procedures of imitation, reinforcement and modeling. *Journal of Applied Behavior Analysis, 6,* 299–310.

Glass, R. M., & Meckler, R. S. (1972). Preparing elementary teachers to instruct mildly handicapped children in regular classrooms: A summer workshop. *Exceptional Children, 38,* 152–156.

Griffiths, H., & Craighead, W. E. (1972). Generalization in operant speech therapy for misarticulation. *Journal of Speech and Hearing Disorders, 37,* 485–494.

Guess, D. (1969). A functional analysis of receptive language and productive speech: Acquisition of the plural morpheme. *Journal of Applied Behavior Analysis, 2,* 55–64.

Guess, D., & Baer, D. M. (1973). An analysis of individual differences in generalization between receptive and productive language in retarded children. *Journal of Applied Behavior Analysis, 6,* 311–329.

Guess, D., Sailor, W., Rutherford, G., & Baer, D. (1968). An experimental analysis of linguistic development: The productive use of the plural morpheme. *Journal of Applied Behavior Analysis, 1,* 297–304.

Hamilton, J. (1966). Learning of a generalized response class in mentally retarded individuals. *American Journal of Mental Deficiency, 71,* 100–108.

Handleman, J. S. (1979a). Generalization by autistic-type children of verbal responses across settings. *Journal of Applied Behavior Analysis, 12,* 273–282.

Handleman, J. S. (1979b). Transition of autistic-type children from highly specialized programs to more "normal" educational environments. *Journal for Special Educators, 15,* 273–279.

Handleman, J. S. (1981). Transfer of verbal responses across instructional settings by autistic-type children. *Journal of Speech and Hearing Disorders, 46,* 69–76.

Handleman, J. S. (in press). Mainstreaming the autistic-type child. *Exceptional Child.*

Handleman, J. S., & Harris, S. L. (1980). Generalization from school to home with autistic-type children. *Journal of Autism and Developmental Disorders, 10,* 323–333.

Handleman, J. S., & Harris, S. L. (1983). Generalization across instructional settings by autistic children. *Child & Family Behavior Therapy, 5,* 73–83.

Harris, S. L. (1975). Teaching language to nonverbal children with emphasis on problems of generalization. *Psychological Bulletin, 82,* 565–580.

Harris, S. L., & Handleman, J. S. (1980). Programming for generalization: Educating autistic children and their parents. *Education and Treatment of Children, 3,* 51–63.

Hart, B. M., & Risley, T. R. (1968). Establishing use of descriptive adjectives in the spontaneous speech of disadvantaged preschool children. *Journal of Applied Behavior Analysis, 1,* 109–120.

Hewett, F. M. (1965). Teaching speech to an autistic child through operant conditioning. *American Journal of Orthopsychiatry, 35,* 927–936.

Jackson, D. A., & Wallace, R. F. (1974). The modification and generalization of voice loudness in a fifteen-year-old retarded girl. *Journal of Applied Behavior Analysis, 7,* 461–471.

Kale, R. J., Kaye, J. H., Whelan, P. A., & Hopkins, B. L. (1968). The effects of reinforcement on the modification, maintenance and generalization of social responses of mental patients. *Journal of Applied Behavior Analysis, 1,* 307–314.

Kazdin, A. E., & Bootzin, R. R. (1972). The token economy: An evaluative review. *Journal of Applied Behavior Analysis, 5,* 343–372.

Kazdin, A., & Polster, R. (1973). Intermittent token reinforcement and response maintenance in extinction. *Behavior Therapy, 4,* 386–391.

Koegel, R. L., & Rincover, A. (1977). Some research on the difference between generalization and maintenance in extra-therapy settings. *Journal of Applied Behavior Analysis, 10,* 1–16.

Koegel, R. L., Rincover, A., & Russo, D. C. (1982). Classroom management: Progression from special to normal classrooms. In R. L. Koegel, A. Rincover, & A. L. Egel (Eds.), *Educating and understanding autistic children.* San Diego: College Hill Press.

Kuypers, D. S., Becker, W. C., & O'Leary, K. D. (1968). How to make a token system fail. *Exceptional Children, 35,* 101–109.

Lancioni, G. E. (1982). Normal children as tutors to teach social responses to withdrawn mentally retarded schoolmates: Training, maintenance and generalization. *Journal of Applied Behavior Analysis, 15,* 17–40.

Larsen, L., Goodman, L., & Glean, R. (1981). Issues in the implementation of extended school year programs for handicapped students. *Exceptional Children, 47,* 255–263.

Leonard, J. (1981). 1980 day barrier: Issues and concerns. *Exceptional Children, 47,* 246–253.

Lovaas, O. J., Berberich, J., Perloff, B., & Schaefer, B. (1966). Acquisition of imitative speech by schizophrenic children. *Science, 151,* 705–707.

Lovaas, O. I., Koegel, R., Simmons, J. Q., & Long, J. (1973). Some generalization and follow-up measures on autistic children in behavior therapy. *Journal of Applied Behavior Analysis, 6,* 131–166.

Lovaas, O. I., & Simmons, J. Q. (1969). Manipulation of self-destruction in three retarded children. *Journal of Applied Behavior Analysis, 2,* 143–157.

Makuch, G. J. (1981). Year-round special education and related services: A state director's perspective. *Exceptional Children, 47,* 272–274.

Marholin, D., & Siegel, L. J. (1978). Beyond the law of effect: Programming for the maintenance of behavioral change. In D. Marholin (Ed.), *Child Behavior Therapy.* New York: Gardner Press.

Marholin, D., Siegel, L. J., & Phillips, D. (1976). Transfer and treatment: A search for empirical procedures. In M. Hersen, R. M. Eisler, & P. M. Miller (Eds.), *Progress in behavior modification.* New York: Academic Press.

Martin, E. W. (1974). Some thoughts on mainstreaming. *Exceptional Children, 40,* 150–153.

Metz, J. (1965). Conditioning generalized imitation in autistic children. *Journal of Experimental Child Psychology, 2,* 289–399.

Miller, S., & Sloane, H. (1976). The generalization effects of parent training across stimuli settings. *Journal of Applied Behavior Analysis, 9,* 355–369.

Nordquist, V. N., & Wahler, R. G. (1973). Naturalistic treatment of an autistic child. *Journal of Applied Behavior Analysis, 6,* 79–87.

O'Leary, K. D., Becker, W. C., Evans, M. B., & Saudargas, S. A. (1969). A token reinforcement program in a public school: A replication and systematic analysis. *Journal of Applied Behavior Analysis, 2,* 3–13.

O'Leary, K. D., O'Leary, S., & Becker, W. C. (1967). Modification of a deviant sibling interaction pattern in the home. *Behaviour Research and Therapy, 5,* 113–120.

Patterson, G. R., & Anderson, D. (1964). Peers as social reinforcers. *Child Development, 35,* 951–960.

Patterson, G. R., McNeal, S., Hawkins, N., & Phelps, R. (1967). Reprogramming the social environment. *Journal of Child Psychology and Psychiatry, 8,* 181–195.

Peterson, R. (1968). Some experiments on the organization of a class of imitative behavior. *Journal of Applied Behavior Analysis, 1,* 225–235.

Peterson, R., & Whitehurst, G. (1971). A variable influencing the performance of non-reinforced imitative behavior. *Journal of Applied Behavior Analysis, 4,* 1–9.

Poorman, C. (1980). Mainstreaming in reverse with a special friend. *Teaching Exceptional Children, 12,* 136–142.

Rapier, J., Adelson, R., Carey, R., & Croke, K. (1972). Changes in children's attitudes toward the physically handicapped. *Exceptional Children, 38,* 219–223.

Redd, W. H. (1970). Generalization of adults' stimulus control of children's behavior. *Journal of Experimental Child Psychology, 9,* 286–296.

Redd, W. H., & Birnbrauer, J. S. (1969). Adults as discriminative stimuli for different reinforcement contingencies with retarded children. *Journal of Experimental Child Psychology, 1,* 440–447.

Rhode, G., Morgan, D. P., & Young, R. K. (1983). Generalization and maintenance of treatment gains of behaviorally handicapped students from resource rooms to regular classrooms using self-evaluation procedures. *Journal of Applied Behavior Analysis, 16,* 189–202.

Rincover, A., & Koegel, R. (1975). Setting generality and stimulus control in autistic children. *Journal of Applied Behavior Analysis, 8,* 235–246.

Risley, T. (1968). The effects and side effects of punishing the autistic behaviors of a deviant child. *Journal of Applied Behavior Analysis, 1,* 21–34.

Risley, T. R., & Wolf, M. M. (1967). Establishing functional speech in echolalic children. *Behavior Research and Therapy, 5,* 73–88.

Rusch, F. R., Close, D., Hops, H., & Agosta, J. (1976). Overcorrection: Generalization and maintenance. *Journal of Applied Behavior Analysis, 9,* 498.

Rusch, F. R., & Kazdin, A. E. (1981). Toward a methodology of withdrawal designs for the assessment of response maintenance. *Journal of Applied Behavior Analysis, 14,* 131–140.

Russo, D. C., & Koegel, R. L. (1977). A method for integrating an autistic child into a normal public school classroom. *Journal of Applied Behavior Analysis, 10,* 579–590.

Sailor, W. (1971). Reinforcement and generalization of productive plural allomorphs in two retarded children. *Journal of Applied Behavior Analysis, 4,* 305–310.

Sailor, W., Guess, D., & Baer, D. (1973). Functional language for verbally deficient children: An experimental program. *Mental Retardation, 11,* 27–35.

Schumaker, J., & Sherman, J. A. (1970). Training generative verb usage by imitation and reinforcement procedures. *Journal of Applied Behavior Analysis, 3,* 273–287.

Simic, J., & Bucher, B. (1980). Development of spontaneous manding in language deficient children. *Journal of Applied Behavior Analysis, 13,* 523–528.

Sloane, H. R., Johnson, M. K., & Harris, F. R. (1968). Remedial procedures for teaching verbal behavior to speech deficient or defective young children. In H. N. Sloane & B. A. MacAulay (Eds.), *Operant procedures in remedial speech and language training*. Boston: Houghton Mifflin.

Solomon, R. W., & Wahler, R. G. (1973). Peer reinforcement control of classroom problem behavior. *Journal of Applied Behavior Analysis, 6*, 49–56.

Sowers, J., Rusch, F. R., Connis, R. T., & Cummings, L. T. (1980). Teaching mentally retarded adults to time-manage in a vocational setting. *Journal of Applied Behavior Analysis, 13*, 119–122.

Steinman, W. (1970). Generalized imitation and the discrimination hypothesis. *Journal of Experimental Child Psychology, 10*, 72–99.

Stokes, T., Baer, D., & Jackson, L. (1974). Programming the generalization of a greeting response in four retarded children. *Journal of Applied Behavior Analysis, 7*, 599–610.

Stotland, J. F., & Mancuso, E. (1981). U.S. court of appeals decision regarding Armstrong vs. Kline: The 180 day rule. *Exceptional Children, 47*, 266–270.

Thompson, T. J., Braam, S. J., & Fuqua, R. W. (1982). Training and generalization of laundry skills: A multiple probe evaluation with handicapped persons. *Journal of Applied Behavior Analysis, 15*, 177–182.

Tucker, D. J., & Berry, G. W. (1980). Teaching severely multihandicapped students to put on their own hearing aids. *Journal of Applied Behavior Analysis, 13*, 65–75.

Vacc, N. A. (1968). A study of emotionally disturbed children in regular and special classes. *Exceptional Children, 34*, 197–204.

Wahler, R. G. (1969). Setting generality: Some specific and general effects of child behavior therapy. *Journal of Applied Behavior Analysis, 2*, 239–246.

Walker, H. M., & Buckley, N. K. (1972). Programming generalization and maintenance of treatment effects across time and across settings. *Journal of Applied Behavior Analysis, 5*, 209–224.

Walker, H. M., Hops, H., & Johnson, S. M. (1975). Generalization and maintenance of classroom treatment effects. *Behavior Therapy, 6*, 128–200.

Welch, S. J. (1981). Teaching generative grammar to mentally retarded children: A review and analysis of a decade of behavioral research. *Mental Retardation, 19*, 277–284.

Welch, S. J., & Pear, J. J. (1980). Generalization of naming responses to objects in the natural environment as a function of training stimulus modality with retarded children. *Journal of Applied Behavior Analysis, 13*, 629–643.

Wetzel, R., Baker, J., Roney, M., & Martin, M. (1966). Outpatient treatment of autistic behavior. *Behaviour Research and Therapy, 4*, 169–177.

Wheeler, A. J., & Sulzer, B. (1970). Operant training and generalization of a verbal response form in a speech deficient child. *Journal of Applied Behavior Analysis, 3*, 139–147.

Wolf, M. M., Risley, T. R., & Mees, A. I. (1964). Application of operant conditioning procedures to the behavior problems of a autistic child. *Behavior Research and Therapy, 2*, 305–312.

Wolfensberger, W. (1975). *Normalization*. Toronto: National Institute on Mental Retardation.

Wulbert, M. (1974). The generalization of newly acquired behaviors by parents and child across three different settings. *Journal of Abnormal Child Psychology, 2*, 87–98.

Chapter 9

Considerations for Standard Psychological Assessment

INTRODUCTION

Clinicians, especially psychologists, often are called upon to conduct standard psychological evaluations with severely developmentally disabled clients. These requests frequently emanate from directors of special education in school districts, from pediatricians, and from administrators of various child service agencies. Indeed, most states require such an evaluation for determining the eligibility of a client for special educational services. While the theme of this book is behavioral assessment, a molar perspective on this enterprise has been provided. This has involved consideration of family and community or larger system issues, as well as consideration of antecedent, organismic, and consequent events that control behavior in the severely developmentally disabled person.

The inclusion of a chapter on the standard psychological assessment of these clients is intended as a continuation of that expanded view of behavioral assessment, but alternative data sources rather than alternative systems of functioning are discussed. The authors concur with Nelson (1980) that data from intelligence tests can be valuable adjuncts to the overall behavioral assessment enterprise. Moreover, it seems that state and federal requirements for such evaluations are not likely to change soon. As a result, special methods, measures, and guidelines are needed in order to provide standard psychological assessment data that can enhance program planning for severely developmentally disabled clients.

Chapter 9 is designed to provide clinicians with an understanding of important issues in the standard psychological evaluation of clients with severe developmental disabilities. In addition, assessment devices with particular applicability to this population are described, and assessment guidelines are offered. It is anticipated that an alternative approach to the psychological evaluation of these clients can enhance the behavioral assessment process and, ultimately, the delivery of services to autistic and severely or profoundly retarded persons.

THE GOALS OF PSYCHOLOGICAL ASSESSMENT

The psychological assessment of clients with severe developmental disabilities poses particular problems for psychologists. It is now known that these people, who were once considered "untestable" for a variety of reasons (Alpern, 1967), require a somewhat different approach to assessment. This approach is characterized by three goals:

1. the observation and evaluation of repertoires of behavior using (a) traditional instruments (e.g., Bayley Scales, Stanford-Binet), (b) those designed specifically for severely handicapped populations, (c) behavioral assessment and/or assessment of the family system;
2. data analysis to yield a profile of functional strengths and weaknesses in the domains of cognitive, perceptual, motor, language, and social functioning;
3. synthesis of data from these domains for diagnosis and provision of specific recommendations for appropriate intervention strategies within a variety of systems (e.g., classroom, family, and community).

These goals require clinicians to focus on the person and to gather information directly related to the presenting problem. Moreover, the goals emphasize each client's unique status. As a result, the maintenance of standardized procedures is considered secondary to the process of accessing assessment data. Finally, numerous potential sources of data are considered, including behavioral and family assessments. In so doing, an ecological assessment transcending multiple systems of interaction is possible.

ISSUES IN PSYCHOLOGICAL ASSESSMENT

Ipsative versus Normative Use of Tests

For clients with less severe handicapping conditions, norm-referenced tests serve many useful functions. They provide information about current level of functioning, are economical, and provide an index for evaluating change within and across individuals (Sattler, 1982). With clients who are more severely handicapped, however, the potential for misuse and misinterpretation is greater. While a discussion of the cultural bias in testing is beyond the scope of this book, a different, less well-defined bias operates against clients with severe developmental disabilities. Selection of inappropriate instruments for the cognitive assessment of clients with severe handicapping conditions is as serious a problem as that which results from testing nonhandicapped children in other than their native tongue. Lack of awareness for this source of test bias, coupled with the often taxing job of evaluating such clients, leads many psychologists to follow the path of least resistance. This results in the utilization of tests without caveat or qualification. Reynolds (1981) states that test bias is a problem of test administration and utilization of results, whereby tests inappropriate to the client's particular disability are administered, scored, and interpreted in a vacuum. The authors' experiences show that many skills of great importance to program planning for severely involved clients (e.g., assessment of imitative ability) are not tapped by many tests (the Bayley is a notable exception). Thus, two problems exist. Norm-referenced tests, because the norming sample frequently excluded severely developmentally disabled people, are often inappropriate for use alone. When used in concert with other instruments, their interpretation must be qualified. Second, these tests frequently neglect skill areas of importance to the clinician planning services for a severely involved client. The resolution of these two problems can be achieved by an altered view of the assessment goals.

Psychological assessment data on severely developmentally disabled clients should be viewed ipsatively; that is, comparisons to other similarly or nonhandicapped peers is de-emphasized, and individual profiles of strengths and weaknesses are sought. An ipsative approach is useful for several reasons. The extreme heterogeneity of severely developmentally disabled children makes the development of norms fallacious (Ho, Glanville, & Brave, 1980). This heterogeneity also reduces the utility of published "standardized modifications," such as the Sattler modifications of Stanford-Binet and Wechsler Intelligence Scale for Children-Revised (WISC-R) subtests of psychological tests (Ho et al., 1980). Ipsative interpretation of test results acknowledges the clients' position on the developmental curriculum, allows for an assessment of splinter skills, and is best considered as a process of testing the limits (Newland, 1973) in the service of gathering information useful to planning habilitative programs.

This is not to imply that nomothetic comparisons should be eschewed completely. In fact, normative interpretation of test results allows the clinician to place the client on a developmental continuum, generating new assessment questions in the process. *Sole* use of nomothetic data is unwarranted, however, and is far less useful for program planning purposes (Zumberg, 1979).

The Utility of a Problem-Solving Model

The psychological assessment of clients with severe developmental disabilities is best approached using a problem-solving model (Powers, 1984b). This model respects the interactional nature of problems in developmental disabilities by integrating data from the assessment domain and system of interaction with the general problem-solving model (Comtois & Clark, 1976; Sloves, Docherty, & Schneider, 1979) in order to answer particular assessment questions. A variety of assessment methods are available, including psychological testing, behavioral assessment, and assessment of the family system. Depending upon the individualized assessment question, one or more assessment methods are applicable.

The assessment model consists of four components: (1) assessment domains, (2) problem-solving process, (3) systems of interaction, and (4) methods of assessment. For additional information on the problem-solving model, refer to Powers (1984b).

Assessment Domains

Severely developmentally disabled clients should be assessed across five domains: cognitive, perceptual, motor, language, and social. In so doing, clinicians have access to areas of strength and weakness that would otherwise be missed by unidimensional assessment. Availability of information from these domains allows for more comprehensive treatment planning (Powers, 1984b).

Problem-Solving Process

A generic problem-solving model for psychological assessment was developed by Sloves et al. (1979). This model has applicability to the assessment of clients with severe developmental disabilities because it provides a useful framework for gathering evaluative information in each of the five assessment domains.

The problem-solving process (Sloves et al., 1979) comprises six phases: problem clarification, planning, development, implementation, outcome evaluation, and dissemination. In this model, each assessment domain (e.g., cognitive and language) progresses through all six phases in the process. For example, an assessment question emphasizing social skill deficits needs to (1) be clarified; (2) have hypotheses developed regarding why the current state of affairs exists, with assessment goals framed to test these hypotheses; (3) have instruments selected to test the hypotheses and have relevant literature consulted (planning); (4) have the assessment carried out; (5) have the assessment data evaluated, analyzed, and synthesized; and (6) have results reported to a variety of sources, including interdisciplinary team members, parents, and other professionals via written or oral communication.

Systems of Interaction

Powers (1984b) describes six systems of interaction relevant to clients with severe developmental disabilities. These include:

1. individual (client's temperament, range of motor responses);
2. classroom (teacher competencies, materials available, class size);
3. family (overinvolved, enmeshed, unaccepting, underinvolved parents);
4. school (policies and procedures for similarly disabled clients);

5. community (availability of pediatricians, dentists, babysitters, summer programs, group homes);
6. suprasystems (regulations of state and federal agencies).

As part of the process of psychological assessment, each system can be assessed
for each of the five assessment domains to determine the extent to which the
system (a) interferes with resolution of problems in that domain and/or (b) can be
utilized in problem resolution for each relevant domain.

Methods of Assessment

Once the assessment question has been clarified (Step 1) and assessment goals
have been formulated (Step 2), methods and materials to address those goals must
be developed (Step 3). The methods selected are not chosen a priori; rather, they
are developed to address the particular informational needs of each client. Thus,
the authors' view is clearly opposed to the practice of giving every client a
Stanford-Binet intelligence test and an Adaptive Behavior profile, regardless of
the presenting problem.

Clinicians have three assessment methods from which to choose (Powers,
1984b). These can be used singly or in combination depending upon the assessment question posed in Step 2. They include (1) psychological testing, (2) behavioral assessment, and (3) assessment of the family system. *Psychological
testing* encompasses assessment instruments both for traditional, nonhandicapped
populations (e.g., the Wechsler Scales, Stanford-Binet, and Bayley Scales) as
well as instruments developed for particular multihandicapped people (Hiskey-
Nebraska; Maxfield-Buchholz Social Maturity Scale for Blind Preschool Children). Several of these instruments applicable to severely developmentally disabled clients are described in Chapter 9. Sattler (1982), Ulrey and Rogers (1982),
Gerken (1979), and Mulliken and Evans (1979) provide additional information on
available psychological tests for a wide variety of handicapping conditions.

Particular assessment questions may require *behavioral assessment*. These
procedures are described in detail in Chapter 2. They involve collection of data
through direct observations, self-report scales, archival records (e.g., nursing
reports), and permanent products (e.g., audio- or videotapes). These data assist
clinicians in identifying a target behavior, determining controlling variables,
developing a program plan, and evaluating that plan.

Client interaction with family can sometimes be a focus of attention. In these
situations, *assessment of the family system* is warranted. Three family assessment
domains are relevant: (1) assessment of the family's readiness for change,
(2) structural assessment, and (3) life-cycle assessment (Powers, 1984b).

Powers (1983b) describes the importance of determining families' abilities, resources, values, and resistances relative to changing their patterns of interaction

with their severely handicapped children prior to initiation of intervention. In this assessment of readiness for change, this model provides information that allows clinicians to tailor intervention programs to families' particular resources and constraints.

A structural assessment often provides useful information regarding the role of severely developmentally disabled clients in their families. Harris (1982) describes several of these roles, their impact upon family functioning, and their implications for intervention. For example, one such role is that of "mother's little helper:" a sibling takes on parental responsibilities and roles with the handicapped brother or sister. This pattern has an impact on all family members, often reverberating through the system in less than desirable ways (Harris, 1982).

It also can be useful to consider the life cycle of the family with a developmentally disabled member (Harris & Powers, 1984). Different roles, stresses, and limitations are placed on parents and other family members depending on the age of their severely developmentally disabled child. For example, a family with a young autistic child may well be more concerned with developing basic self-help skills in the child and selecting an appropriate school. The motivation to work hard for and with the child may be high. In contrast, the parents of a 21-year-old autistic adult may be concerned about their own advancing age and future care for their child, about issues surrounding sexuality, or about alternative living arrangements for their child. These parents also may be far less motivated to do evening programming with their child, after already expending considerable energy in years past. Knowledge of such life-cycle issues permits the clinician to tailor interventions to the particular needs of the family.

The Utility of Syndromal Diagnosis

The recent appearance of the *Diagnostic and Statistical Manual of Mental Disorders* (3rd ed.) (DSM-III; American Psychiatric Association, 1980) can be seen as an advance over previous editions insofar as children are concerned (Harris, 1979; Harris & Powers, 1984; Powers, in press). While certain limitations persist for less handicapped persons, DSM-III diagnosis provides a useful adjunct to the behavioral assessment of clients with severe developmental disabilities.

The manual provides nomothetic descriptions of behavior; that is, the focus is on developing generalizations that apply to many people. Diagnostic classifications that summarize client behavior and suggest co-varying behaviors are assigned to a given client. These DSM-III diagnoses thus serve the useful function of (1) acting as a screen to assist in the identification of problematic performance; (2) assisting clinicians in determining whether or not to treat an identified problem; (3) grouping clients into relatively homogeneous groups for treatment purposes; and (4) promoting comparisons of subject samples across published studies (Hartmann, Roper, & Bradford, 1979). In contrast, idiographic (behavioral) assessment leads to an emphasis on the specifications of person, setting, event, and organismic controlling variables so that treatment planning can take on a highly individualized focus.

Syndromal diagnosis has utility to the behavioral assessment enterprise when diagnosis is used as a starting point for individualized (idiographic) assessment. The *Diagnostic and Statistical Manual of Mental Disorders'* diagnosis performs an initial, broad-band assessment function (Harris & Powers, 1984; Powers, in press). The controlling variables for individual DSM-III criteria met by the client are then determined using a SORKC analysis (Kanfer & Saslow, 1969). Clinicians then consult the literature for relevant assessment strategies for each criterion identified, leading to a functional analysis of that criterion. This in turn leads to treatment hypotheses, intervention, evaluation, and follow-up according to the generic behavioral assessment model presented in Chapter 2. Powers (in press) describes this process in greater detail.

Syndromal diagnosis can be seen as useful to the process of psychological evaluation of clients with severe developmental disabilities. While the assignment of a diagnostic label may sometimes be unnecessary, state department of education policies or insurance company practices may require diagnosis for purposes of reimbursement. In addition, the integration of findings in child psychiatry will be more feasible using a common system of classification (Kazdin, 1983). Hence, interdisciplinary communication can be fostered. For these reasons, clinicians providing services to severely developmentally disabled clients would do well to consider the utility of DSM-III diagnosis when conducting psychological evaluations with these individuals.

The Role of Screening in the Assessment Process

Under certain circumstances, it may be advantageous to screen a client initially rather than undertake a full psychological assessment. Two situations predominate here. The first concerns the very young child, referred for the first time, where a handicap is suspected. In such cases, a screening for a psychological/developmental handicap may cause less stress for the child and less cost to the parents. Significant findings then can be pursued with a full assessment, if warranted. The Denver Developmental Screening Test (Frankenburg & Dodds, 1973) or the McCarthy Screening Test (McCarthy, 1978), a short form of the McCarthy Scales of Children's Abilities (McCarthy, 1972), is useful in this regard.

The second situation concerns the client with multiple handicaps. Here the clinician may know that while a full assessment will probably be needed, the order in which the separate domains are assessed may lead to new hypotheses or obviate the need for extended evaluation. For example, the verbally unintelligible severely retarded client with cerebral palsy may be best served by an initial pediatric neurological exam, followed by an evaluation by a speech therapist. A determination that problems in muscle control due to cerebral palsy interfere with speech may assist the psychologist in selection of assessment instruments.

Linking Psychological Assessment to Instructional Programming

Earlier in Chapter 9 it is noted that one of the goals of psychological assessment with severely developmentally disabled clients is the development of instructional programs. This goal warrants elaboration. The ultimate goal of any interaction with a severely developmentally disabled client is habilitation. Whenever an assessment is undertaken, that assessment should lead to clear recommendations for compensatory programs that can be implemented realistically in the target setting. Specific instructional programs to remediate the client's needs in cognitive, perceptual, motor, language, and/or social areas should be provided as dictated by the assessment question. Moreover, consideration of multiple systems of client interaction should be included in these program plans. By emphasizing the development of specific and evaluable interventions resulting from psychological assessments, more efficient and accountable use is made of both clients' and professionals' time.

Prerequisite Skills for Client Assessment

Some clients may be trained in prerequisite test-taking skills before the assessment is undertaken. For example, several tests (PPVT-R, Columbia Mental Maturity Scale) require a pointing response. For the client lacking this mode of responding, alternative preparatory steps are required. The clinician may undertake a program to train the client to point to objects (see Harris, 1976). Once the client is trained, formal assessment can begin.

Because of the client's handicap, an alternative form of responding may be required. For example, one of the authors (MDP) trained a quadriplegic cerebral palsied boy to respond to the Pictorial Tests of Intelligence (French, 1964) by pointing to his choice of four pictures with a light beam strapped to his head. Rigid head pointers and eye glances also can be used in such cases.

In some situations, clients will not be able to follow the verbal direction, "Give me the ———," sit in a chair for extended periods, or establish and maintain eye contact with the examiner. Obviously, such deficits prevent assessment, and leave the clinician with the choice of training the client for the task or providing a less formal assessment. The former option (training) is the method of choice whenever feasible.

Some instruments allow training the client for the task as a part of standard administration. These include the Kaufman Assessment Battery for Children (Kaufman & Kaufman, 1983a); the Peabody Picture Vocabulary Test-Revised (Dunn & Dunn, 1981); the Columbia Mental Maturity Scale (Burgemeister,

Blum, & Lorge, 1972); and the Leiter International Performance Scale (Leiter, 1948). It is clear that wherever possible these allowances should be taken advantage of; however, any special procedure allowed should be described explicitly in the service of qualifying the test results.

PSYCHOLOGICAL ASSESSMENT INSTRUMENTS

The selection, administration, and interpretation of appropriate tests for severely developmentally disabled clients is the next step in the assessment process. Several tests with particular utility for these clients are presented. Each issue described above should be considered when selecting, administering, and interpreting data obtained from these instruments.

Bayley Scales of Infant Development

For clients functioning below the developmental level of three years, an accurate statement of current status, strengths, and weaknesses can be difficult to obtain. The Bayley Scales (Bayley, 1969), developed for use with nonhandicapped infants aged 2 to 30 months, provide a "developmental ruler" against which to measure mental and motor functioning of severely developmentally disabled clients.

The Bayley Scales were developed to assess current status and the extent of deviation from normalcy of young children. They are not to be used as predictors of later functioning due to the plasticity of behavior that is characteristic of young developmentally disabled and nonhandicapped children. Bayley (1969) notes that for young children it is frequently helpful to have a parent present during testing. Administration time is 30 to 60 minutes.

Composition. The Bayley Mental Scale consists of 163 items, while the Motor Scale contains 81 items. In addition, the clinician fills out an Infant Behavior Record immediately after testing, providing data on the client's responsiveness, attention, activity level, and body motion during the assessment situation. The three assessment scales function in a complementary way; each provides information useful to the interpretation of the other two.

Assessment activities are divided into "situation codes" (e.g., all items using the pegs are included in one situation code). Use of the situation codes allows the clinician to progress through various levels of task difficulty using the same stimulus materials. The clinician also can move more rapidly through the test by using these codes and can gain useful information for test interpretation. Situation code "H" provides an example of the range of item difficulty across one code. Here, the first item is scored if the client merely regards a cube. Credit for the last time cannot be attained unless the client attempts to secure three cubes.

Scores Obtained. The Bayley Scales yield a Mental Development Index (MDI), and a Psychomotor Development Index (PDI). Both are standard scores with a mean of 100 and a standard deviation of 16. The "floor" (lowest possible score) of both the MDI and PDI is 50, necessitating the notation "<50" for those severely developmentally disabled clients who score below this point. Age-equivalents also can be determined for clients scoring very low on the Mental or Motor Scale.

Standardization. The Bayley Scales were standardized on 1,262 nonhandicapped infants, ages 2 to 30 months. Subjects were chosen from all geographical regions of the United States. Norms, reliability, and validity are excellent.

Summary. The Bayley Scales are useful when assessing severely developmentally disabled clients. While they sample a wide range of behavior, the earliest items are heavily loaded motorically. Thus, when assessing clients with developmental ages below one year, an additional and more comprehensive measure of receptive and expressive language is warranted. For these clients, the Learning Accomplishment Profile for Infants and the Sequenced Inventory of Communication Development are useful adjuncts. With older clients, the principal use of the Bayley is in profiling strengths and weaknesses and in determining a level of functioning.

Columbia Mental Maturity Scale

The Columbia Mental Maturity Scale (CMMS) (Burgemeister et al., 1972) provides a nonverbal measure of general reasoning ability. These include "both simple perceptual classification tasks and higher-level abstract manipulation of symbolic concepts" (Burgemeister et al., 1972, p. 7). The client responds by pointing, and is required to choose which of several figures on a card does *not* belong. Correct responding is based upon the client's skill in rule formulation for gross-to-subtle discrimination of size, form, or color. The test includes sample items that allow the clinician to train the client for the test. Moreover, the cards are large, with considerable white space between stimulus pictures, allowing clients who possess a gross pointing response or those who depend upon a rigid head pointer or light beam the space to respond. Administration time is 15 to 30 minutes.

Composition. There are 92 stimulus cards in the CMMS. Depending on age or suspected developmental level, a given client will be administered approximately 51 to 65 items.

Scores Obtained. The CMMS yields four scores: an Age Deviation Score (ADS); a Maturity Index (MI); percentile ranks; and stanines. The ADS is a standard score (mean = 100; standard deviation = 16) that indicates the client's deviation of the obtained score from a specified chronological group. The ADS is *not* analogous to an intelligence quotient, and should not be interpreted as an estimate of intellectual ability. The Maturity Index indicates the standardization group most similar to the client in terms of test performance. Percentiles and stanines are helpful both in clarifying the ADS and in placing the ADS into a more relevant context.

Standardization. The CMMS was standardized on 2,600 children aged 3 years, 6 months through 9 years, 11 months. Reliability is good, and test validity is satisfactory.

Summary. The Columbia is particularly useful when assessing severely developmentally disabled clients with physical handicaps (e.g., cerebral palsy) because of its large stimulus cards. Unfortunately, it can be difficult to determine which errors are errors of visual perception and which are due to poor perceptual motor skills (Canter, 1956). Nonetheless, this test is a useful supplementary measure of nonverbal reasoning for severely developmentally disabled clients.

Pictorial Tests of Intelligence

The Pictorial Tests of Intelligence (French, 1964) are designed to measure the general intellectual level of handicapped and nonhandicapped children. This test requires no expressive language for completion. Clients must be able to (a) hear verbal instructions (e.g., "Find the ———" or "Point to the ———"), (b) respond to visual stimulation, and (c) produce a pointing response or a reliable alternative (e.g., eye glance). Each card has four stimulus pictures, each picture in one quadrant, with considerable white space separating the stimuli. Administration time is approximately 40 minutes.

Composition. The Pictorial Tests of Intelligence comprise six subtests designed to measure children's perceptual organization, verbal comprehension, and ability to manipulate numerical and spatial symbols. The six subtests are:

1. Picture Vocabulary—provides a measure of verbal comprehension;
2. Form Discrimination—assesses the client's ability to match forms and discriminate between shapes that are similar. Perceptual organization is the principal process measured;
3. Information and Comprehension—assesses client's general understanding of words, range of knowledge, and verbal comprehension;
4. Similarities—provides a measure of the client's ability to discriminate and generalize similarities across several stimulus pictures;
5. Size and Number—assesses "perception of size, number symbol recognition and comprehension, ability to count, and ability to solve simple arith-

metical problems'' (French, 1964, p. 6). Numerical reasoning is also assessed.

6. Immediate Recall—provides a measure of the client's ability to remember perceptions of form, space, and size relationships after the client views them for 5 seconds.

Scores Obtained. The Pictorial Tests of Intelligence yield three scores: deviation IQs, mental ages, and percentiles. The deviation IQs have a mean of 100, and a standard deviation of 16. Mental ages can be computed for the total score and for each subtest. However, mental ages for individual subtests are far less reliable and should be interpreted with caution.

Standardization. The normative sample comprised 1,830 children between the ages of 3 and 8 years. While the norms are excellent, they are over 20 years old (1962). Test reliability and validity are satisfactory.

Summary. The Pictorial Tests of Intelligence are useful as measures of nonverbal intelligence. In particular, the profile of strengths and weaknesses of clients across subtest areas aid in their educational program planning. The stimulus cards are large and the pictures well spaced, facilitating performance of clients with concurrent motor problems. This is a test that deserves more recognition for its utility with low- and nonverbal severely developmentally disabled populations.

McCarthy Scales of Children's Abilities

The McCarthy was developed to determine the strengths, weaknesses, and intellectual abilities of young children across a wide variety of areas. Task content was designed to be useful for a variety of types of clients, and test materials were selected with an eye toward sustaining client interest and having gamelike qualities. Administration time is approximately 60 minutes for nonhandicapped children. Up to 90 minutes may be required for some severely handicapped clients.

Composition. The McCarthy has 18 subtests:

1. Block Building
2. Puzzle Solving
3. Pictorial Memory
4. Word Knowledge
5. Number Questions
6. Tapping Sequence
7. Verbal Memory
8. Left-Right Orientation
9. Leg Coordination
10. Arm Coordination
11. Imitative Action
12. Draw-A-Design
13. Draw-A-Child
14. Numerical Memory
15. Verbal Fluency
16. Counting and Sorting
17. Opposite Analogies
18. Conceptual Grouping

These subtests make up six scales: the Verbal Scale; Perceptual Performance Scale; Quantitative Scale; Memory Scale; Motor Scale; and the General Cognitive Scale.

Scores Obtained. Scaled scores are obtained for each of the six scales. Each scaled score has a mean of 50 and a standard deviation of 10, with the exception of the General Cognitive Scale. This latter scale yields a General Cognitive Index (GCI) with a mean of 100 and a standard deviation of 16. The GCI describes the client's functioning at a given point in time, and represents the client's "ability to integrate his/her accumulated learnings and adapt them to the tasks of the MSCA when administered to him/her" (McCarthy, 1972, p. 5). In the absence of supporting research data, the GCI should not be considered interchangeable with IQs from the Wechsler Intelligence Test for Children-Revised or the Stanford-Binet (Sattler, 1982).

Standardization. The McCarthy was standardized on 1,032 children, aged 2 years, 6 months to 8 years, 6 months. The sample was stratified for age, sex, race, geographic location, and father's occupation. Test reliability and validity are excellent.

Summary. Due to the wide variety of skills assessed, the McCarthy is an excellent device for testing developmentally disabled young children (Ferrari, 1980; Kaufman & Kaufman, 1977). Moreover, the range of skills assessed facilitates further assessment and program planning.

Sequenced Inventory of Communication Development

The Sequenced Inventory of Communication Development (SICD) (Hedrick, Prather, & Tobin, 1975) is a language battery designed to assess various processes that contribute to a client's communicative interaction with the environment. Test items are arranged in developmental sequence and conform to other published developmental schedules. Testing begins at different levels depending upon estimated level of functioning or age. Administration time varies from 30 minutes for young children to approximately 60 minutes for older clients. While intended for nonhandicapped children between 4 and 48 months old, this inventory has great utility for severely developmentally disabled children, particularly where a language disorder coexists with mental retardation. There are numerous manipulatives (e.g., dolls, puppets, balls, cars, and so on), making this a highly interesting test for clients.

Composition. The SICD has a Receptive Scale and an Expressive Scale. The Receptive Scale assesses awareness, discrimination, and understanding. Behavior is sampled by direct observation of client responses to verbal requests, or by parental report. All items are sequenced chronologically.

The Expressive Scale assesses client imitating, initiating, and responding to motor, vocal, and verbal stimuli. Linguistic behaviors measured include (1) verbal output (mean response length, structural complexity, emergence of various parts of speech), and (2) articulation on a developmental progression. Items are scored as pass or fail.

Scores Obtained. The Receptive and Expressive Scales yield a Receptive Communication Age (RCA) and an Expressive Communication Age (ECA). Both RCA and ECA are estimated levels of functioning expressed in months.

Standardization. The SIDC was normed on 252 nonhandicapped white children ages 4 to 48 months from the Seattle, Washington area. While reliability was very good, more research on test validity is needed.

Summary. Despite inadequate norms and validity, the SICD is a useful test for clients with language impairments compounding their severe developmental disabilities. The RCA and ECA are useful descriptive indices and provide information for program planning purposes. In addition, the test materials are highly motivating.

Wisconsin Behavior Rating Scale

The Wisconsin Behavior Rating Scale (WBRS; Song & Jones, 1980) is a criterion- as well as norm-referenced instrument that contains extensive scale items for severely and profoundly handicapped clients. The WRBS is intended for use with clients functioning below the developmental age of 3 years. The WBRS can be completed in 15 to 20 minutes utilizing third-party assessment (parent or teacher as informant). Considerably more time would be required for a first-person assessment. The WBRS has psychometric properties often absent in other schedules for severely, profoundly, or multiply handicapped clients. All subtests represent an attempt to operationalize the concept of adaptive behavior described in the 1973 *Manual on Classification and Terminology* of the AAMD (Grossman, 1973). Song and Jones (1980) list four primary uses of the WBRS: (1) to determine overall level of client functioning; (2) to profile development in basic areas and to provide information on strengths and weaknesses in each area; (3) for ongoing evaluation; and (4) for program planning and remediation efforts.

Composition. There are 11 subtests within the WBRS:

1. Gross Motor
2. Fine Motor
3. Expressive Communication
4. Receptive Communication
5. Play Skills
6. Socialization
7. Domestic Activities
8. Eating
9. Toileting
10. Dressing
11. Grooming

Scores Obtained. Each item of each subtest is scored on a three-point scale (0 = does not perform; 1 = emergent skill; 2 = independent, skillful performance). Scores obtained include (1) Percentile Ranks, (2) Behavioral Age, and (3) Subscale Age Equivalents.

Standardization. The WBRS was standardized on 325 severely or profoundly mentally retarded clients below the developmental age of 3 years. All clients were residents of an institution in central Wisconsin. The WBRS standardization also included 184 nonhandicapped infants and children (age: birth to 4 years). Both interrater reliability and validity were good.

Summary. The WBRS is an excellent instrument for assessing the adaptive behavior of severely developmentally disabled clients. While its subtests are not exhaustive, it contains a reasonable number of items per age group to be useful as a criterion-referenced device. The concept of emergent behavior is an important one for severely handicapped clients; its inclusion in the WBRS is noteworthy. Most importantly, it is one of the most psychometrically sophisticated tests of adaptive behavior for severely and profoundly retarded institutionalized clients. Further research will be necessary, however, to determine whether the WBRS systematically over- or underestimates adaptive functioning of noninstitutionalized severely developmentally disabled clients. Finally, as is the case with most subtests measuring small segments of overall functioning, WBRS subtests should be interpreted with caution because of the restricted range of behavior assessed in each area.

Learning Accomplishment Profile

The Learning Accomplishment Profile (LAP; Sanford, 1974) is a criterion-referenced assessment device that allows teachers or parents to determine current levels of client skills in six areas. It is designed for children with developmental ages from 1 to 6 years. The teacher conducts the assessment, reducing the need for more highly trained professionals. The provision for teacher assessment also allows testing to take place under familiar conditions, and over time. The LAP is intended as an ongoing evaluative instrument, designed to link the assessment process to instructional service delivery more effectively. Administration time is 20 to 30 minutes.

Composition. There are six areas of functioning assessed by the LAP:

1. Gross Motor Coordination
2. Fine Motor Coordination
3. Social

4. Self-Help
5. Cognitive
6. Language

Scores Obtained. The LAP yields a Developmental Profile—a pictorial interpretation of strengths and weaknesses—across the six areas sampled. In addition, Developmental Age is calculated for each area by noting the age of the item preceding the ceiling item. Finally, a Rate of Change can be determined pursuant to ongoing assessment. Rate of Change is obtained by dividing the Developmental Age in a given area by the client's chronological age. The psychometric properties of these scores are not described in the manual.

Standardization. Reliability, validity, and normative data are not provided in the manual. While items selected were drawn from various developmental schedules, item selection procedures are not explicated.

Summary. The LAP is a helpful developmental schedule for severely developmentally disabled clients. It is most appropriate as a supplemental measure of functioning in the six areas assessed. The availability of several items at each developmental age is particularly useful. The LAP measures *present* level of functioning, and should not be used to predict future abilities or disabilities. Lack of normative, reliability, or validity data and reliance upon third-party assessment are weaknesses of the LAP.

Learning Accomplishment Profile for Infants

The Learning Accomplishment Profile for Infants (LAP-I; Griffin & Sanford, 1975) is a downward extension of the LAP (see above). It is a criterion-referenced test for infants from birth to 33 months, with items drawn from various normative developmental schedules. It is administered by parent or teacher report. The LAP-I provides parents and teachers of handicapped infants with a record of the child's present level of functioning across six areas of development. The LAP-I also identifies the next appropriate developmental skill to be achieved by the infant and provides instruction for infant training. Administration time is 20 to 30 minutes.

Composition. Six areas of functioning are assessed by the LAP-I. Behaviors within each area are presented hierarchically. The areas include:

1. Gross Motor Coordination
2. Fine Motor Coordination
3. Social
4. Self-Help
5. Cognitive
6. Language

Scores Obtained. The LAP-I yields a Developmental Age for each of the six areas above and a total Developmental Profile.

Standardization. Reliability, validity, and normative data are not provided in the manual. No procedure for selecting particular items from other developmental schedules is described.

Summary. The LAP-I is a useful supplementary assessment device for very low functioning severely developmentally disabled clients. It assesses multiple behaviors at each month, making it more comprehensive than many other tests for infants. Continued assessment over time is possible. The results of the LAP-I lead to prescriptive diagnostic teaching activities. The teaching methods described in the manual, however, may require modification for older severely developmentally disabled clients. Drawbacks to the test include its lack of norms, reliability, or validity data, and the common problems typically associated with self- or third-party reporting.

Developmental Profile II

The Developmental Profile II (Alpern, Boll, & Shearer, 1980) provides a screening of abilities across five areas in children from birth through age 9. The respondent is a person who knows the client well (e.g., parent, teacher), and the information is obtained during a structured interview.

Composition. The Developmental Profile II consists of 186 items divided into five scales:

1. Physical
2. Self-Help
3. Social
4. Academic
5. Communication

Each item is scored as pass or fail, and basals and ceilings are utilized to speed administration.

Scores Obtained. The Developmental Profile II yields a Physical Age, Self-Help Age, Social Age, Academic Age, and Communication Age. Age scores are expressed in years and months, and are determined by giving months of credit for each item passed (similar to the Stanford-Binet). While an IQ Equivalence Score can be computed, the psychometric properties and the screening nature of this test render such a score suspect.

Standardization. The Developmental Profile II was standardized on 3,008 children from Indiana and Washington. Reliability and validity are satisfactory.

Summary. The Developmental Profile II can be considered a useful screening device for clients with severe developmental disabilities. Because it encompasses a broad age range, clients with widely disparate splinter skills can be assessed. Assessing this type of client may require the clinician to ignore the ceiling cutoff procedures. As such, ipsative use of this test is most appropriate. The Developmental Profile II has only two or three items (skills assessed) per level of functioning (either six-month or one-year intervals), making it a poor criterion-reference device. Its use for diagnostic-prescriptive teaching may be limited by this fact.

Vineland Adaptive Behavior Scales

The Vineland Adaptive Behavior Scales (Sparrow, Balla, & Cicchetti, 1984) are revisions of Doll's (1965) Vineland Social Maturity Scale. The revised Vineland Scales emphasize the person's performance on age-appropriate activities, and are designed to assess personal and social adaptive behavior in clients from birth through 19 years of age. They also are appropriate for use with developmentally disabled children and adults.

Composition. There are three components to tne Vineland Adaptive Behavior Scales: (1) The Interview Edition, Survey Form, (2) The Interview Edition, Expanded Form, and (3) The Classroom Edition.

The Interview Edition, Survey Form contains 297 items and provides a general assessment of adaptive behavior as well as areas of potential strength and weakness. Data are gathered in a semistructured interview requiring 20 to 60 minutes to complete. *The Interview Edition, Expanded Form* provides a more comprehensive adaptive behavior assessment that can assist in preparing Individualized Educational Plans (IEPs) and Individualized Habilitation Plans (IHPs). Containing 597 questions, the Expanded Form requires approximately 60 to 90 minutes to administer. *The Classroom Edition* contains 244 questions and is designed to provide an assessment of adaptive behavior in the classroom. It is in questionnaire form and requires approximately 20 minutes to complete.

Each component assesses adaptive behavior across the following four domains:

1. Communication (receptive, expressive, written)
2. Daily Living Skills (personal, domestic, community)
3. Socialization (interpersonal relationships, play and leisure, coping skills)
4. Motor Skills (gross and fine)

In addition, both Interview Editions contain a series of 36 questions for the assessment of maladaptive behavior.

Items are scored as 2 (yes, usually occurring), 1 (sometimes or partially occurring), 0 (no, never occurring), and N (no opportunity for assessment). Basals and ceilings are utilized to speed administration.

Scores Obtained. The Vineland Adaptive Behavior Scales yield a variety of derived scores. These include standard scores (mean = 100, SD = 15), percentile ranks, stanines, age-equivalents, grade-based percentile ranks, and interedition scaled scores.

Standardization. The Vineland Adaptive Behavior Scales were standardized on a national sample of 3,000 people selected to represent the U.S. population according to the 1980 census. Supplementary norms are available (Interview Editions only) for mentally retarded adults in both residential and nonresidential settings and for visually impaired, hearing impaired, and emotionally disturbed clients in residential facilities. Reliability and validity are excellent.

Summary. The Vineland Adaptive Behavior Scales are excellent instruments for use when evaluating the adaptive behavior of severely developmentally disabled clients. They aptly serve a wide variety of clinical, diagnostic, educational, and research functions. A noteworthy addition to the utility of the scales is the standardization sample overlap with the Kaufman Assessment Battery for Children (K-ABC; Kaufman & Kaufman, 1983a), allowing valid comparisons of the scores obtained on the two devices. With those clients for whom the K-ABC is appropriate, this opportunity for comparison is unique among evaluation instruments.

Kaufman Assessment Battery for Children

Recently, a new assessment device, the Kaufman Assessment Battery for Children (K-ABC; Kaufman & Kaufman, 1983a), has appeared on the market. While there are no known published reports of its use with severely developmentally disabled clients, the K-ABC may be employed with some of these individuals in the future. As a result, a brief discussion of the K-ABC, and some precautions for its use with autistic or severely retarded clients are provided.

The K-ABC is designed to assess the intelligence and achievement of children aged 2½ to 12½ years (Kaufman & Kaufman, 1983b). Intelligence is defined as the client's problem-solving and information processing *style*, as well as the client's level of *skill* in using that style (Kaufman & Kaufman, 1983c). This definition represents a theoretical distinction based on recent developments in neuropsychology and cognitive psychology (Kaufman & Kaufman, 1983c). The four Global Scales of the K-ABC are:

1. *Sequential Processing:* solving problems where the emphasis is on the serial or temporal order of stimuli;
2. *Simultaneous Processing:* using a gestalt-like or holistic approach to integrate many stimuli to solve problems;
3. *Mental Processing Composite:* a combination of Sequential and Simultaneous Processing scales, yielding a global estimate of intellectual functioning;

4. *Achievement:* demonstrating knowledge of facts, language concepts, and school-related skills. (Kaufman & Kaufman, 1983b, pp. 1–2)

Each Global Scale has a mean of 100 and a standard deviation of 15. The K-ABC is an extremely well-standardized test, and has excellent validity and reliability. Most subtests are considerably different from the Wechsler or Stanford-Binet subtests, due to the K-ABC's emphasis on discriminating children with problems in sequential versus simultaneous processing. In addition to the Global Scales, the K-ABC has a Nonverbal Scale that can be administered in pantomime. Because of the emphasis on hemispheric lateralization and language disorders in autistic children, clinicians working with this population may be initially attracted to the K-ABC. Refer to McCann (1981) for a review of hemispheric asymmetry in autism.

Interest in the possible uses of the K-ABC with autistic individuals led the authors to assess several of these clients formally with the Mental Processing subtests. The cautions and suggestions offered are based on these test administrations and on clinical experience in the psychological assessment of autistic individuals. Therefore, the comments should be construed as hypotheses and as suggestions of areas for future research.

By and large, the K-ABC Mental Processing subtests require considerable receptive and "inner" language. This proved to be an area of difficulty for clients. Two subtests in particular, Matrix Analogies and Spatial Memory, required concepts that were too difficult for some clients. The K-ABC allows the examiner to "teach for the task" with the sample and the first two items, a laudable addition for purposes of examining severely developmentally disabled clients. However, even this provision did not help these clients understand what was required of them for completion of Matrix Analogies or Spatial Memory.

The tendency of low-functioning autistic or retarded clients to exhibit stimulus overselectivity (see Chapter 4) may interfere with responding on subtests with multiple stimulus components. For example, one client (age 12 years, 5 months) selectively attended to the flame on the *Photo Series* sample item, rather than to the (salient) candle length. Another client (age 11 years, 3 months) systematically did better when *auditory* cues were stressed. When confronted with a stimulus with *both* auditory and visual components, this client consistently attended to auditory components and ignored visual components. The interaction between stimulus overselectivity and various Mental Processing subtests is an important area for future research with severely developmentally disabled clients. This is particularly true for more intellectually impaired autistic and mentally retarded clients, as these groups have been shown to exhibit greater degrees of stimulus overselectivity than peers with higher IQs (Schover & Newsom, 1976; Wilhelm & Lovaas, 1976).

Some problems in interpretation of very low scores exist with the K-ABC. Clients with raw scores of zero on two or more subtests in any one of the four scales (sequential, simultaneous, nonverbal, or achievement) cannot be assigned a standard score for that scale. In addition, a standard score for the Mental Processing Composite (simultaneous + sequential scores) cannot be computed if more than two Mental Processing subtests have raw scores of zero. In these cases, the clinician must obtain a mental age-equivalent for the scale from Table 6 (Kaufman & Kaufman, 1983c) and extrapolate a standard score for the client. This can be done by selecting the table in Table 2 of the Interpretive Manual that corresponds to the client's mental age, finding a standard score of 100, and assigning the corresponding subtest score for the scale in question. Such extrapolations always must be described in the test report.

Ultimately, the utility of the K-ABC for severely developmentally disabled clients will depend on the battery's ability to assist in instructional programming. The answer concerning this important dimension will be determined empirically; lack of an answer should not deter clinicians from *considering* the K-ABC with particular clients. However, in the absence of data linking test results to efficacious instructional programming, the K-ABC is best regarded as experimental with clients who are severely developmentally disabled.

Wechsler Scales and Stanford-Binet: Cautions and Caveats

A word of caution is necessary on use of the most familiar tests of cognitive functioning: The Wechsler Intelligence Scale for Children-Revised (WISC-R; Wechsler, 1981), the Wechsler Preschool and Primary Scale of Intelligence (WPPSI; Wechsler, 1967), the Wechsler Adult Intelligence Scale-Revised (WAIS; Wechsler, 1981), and the Stanford-Binet Intelligence Scale (Terman & Merrill, 1960). Use of these tests with clients who are severely developmentally disabled entails a trade-off between the desire to compare clients to "normal" peers, and the desire to profile their strengths and weaknesses. Because psychological assessment is seen as a first step toward educational (or habilitative) program planning, the latter is prescribed. Hence, reduced value is found in these tests.

There are times when the authors will administer particular subtests from the WISC-R or Stanford-Binet to assess a particular cognitive process, but rarely will the device be used alone. There are several reasons for this. First, these tests (particularly the WPPSI and the Stanford-Binet) rely heavily on receptive and expressive language skills for task performance. Second, optimum testing conditions are required to meet standard administration guidelines (Mulliken, 1979). Third, the directions for subtests are often complex. Finally, multiply handicapped clients may have particular difficulties with some subtests on these tests. Sattler (1974) provides a table for determining physical abilities necessary for Wechsler tests. A description of functions assessed by individual subtests of the

WISC-R, WPPSI, WAIS, or Stanford-Binet can be found in Sattler (1982) Appendix C.

The critical point to keep in mind—and the reason for the authors' choice of other assessment devices over those described above—is that tests should be selected based upon clients' developmental levels rather than upon their chronological levels (Zigler, 1969). The nature of severe developmental disabilities requires the creative, careful, and judicious selection of psychological tests for use with this population.

GUIDELINES FOR ASSESSMENT OF THE SEVERELY DEVELOPMENTALLY DISABLED

The process of assessing clients with severe developmental disabilities can be enhanced by following certain guidelines (Powers, 1984a). As the variation in the behavior of these individuals suggests that procedural flexibility be the rule, these guidelines should not be followed slavishly.

Set the Stage for Assessment

In order to facilitate the evaluation of severely developmentally disabled clients, certain "preparatory" behaviors on the part of the clinician are warranted. Whenever possible, a detailed social and developmental history should be obtained prior to meeting clients and their parents or caretakers (see Chapter 3). Armed with this information, clinicians are better equipped to understand their clients' particular situation, facilitating the assessment process.

It is helpful to spend some time building rapport with the client at the onset of each evaluation session. The exact duration necessary will depend on a variety of factors, including the client's age, the client's ability to tolerate novel situations, the nature of the handicapping condition, the parent's ease with the examiner, and the examiner's experience. Initially, the examiner should assume that the client is ill at ease and should proceed slowly. For example, by allowing the client a few minutes to wander about the examination room and play with some strategically placed toys, the examiner can often reduce the client's initial anxiety in a novel environment. The examiner can interact with the parents during this time, enlisting their aid in determining the client's nicknames, idiosyncratic methods of responding, and preferred reinforcers. Examiner approach behavior (e.g., calling the client over, leading him or her by the hand, holding the young client) then can be initiated and the formal assessment begun. It is important to note, however, that a great deal of clinically and educationally relevant data can be obtained by observing the client's behavior during initial rapport building. During this unstructured time, the examiner should be observing the client just as carefully as during the formal evaluation.

Parents should be permitted in the evaluation room whenever feasible. This is especially important for very young children, and less so for older ones. By allowing a parent to be present, the examiner gains access to effective limit-setting strategies with the child. If the client is nonvocal and uses an idiosyncratic method of responding to requests and demands, parents often are excellent "interpreters" for the child. There are times, however, when the presence of a parent will interfere greatly with the process of an evaluation. To determine whether a parent's presence would be helpful, consideration of the client's age may be useful: (a) for clients under the age of five, assume that the parent's presence in the room will be a help, not a hindrance, unless otherwise notified; (b) for clients older than five years, assume that they can tolerate their parent's absence. In either case, if there is reason to question the utility of including or excluding a particular client's parents, ask the parents to help make the decision. Parents always can be asked to leave or rejoin the examiner should the need arise. They know the client best, and their suggestions often can make the difference between a successful and unsuccessful evaluation session.

It is important for the examiner to provide an atmosphere that is conducive for evaluating the client. As parents sometimes approach the assessment of their child as if they too are being evaluated, it is important to put them at ease. This can be accomplished by making an active effort to join with them initially, utilizing them as "expert consultants" on their child's behavior, and by acknowledging their anxieties and fears. In many ways, evaluations are more stressful for parents than for the client, particularly those evaluations for initial diagnosis of a young child with suspected developmental delay. It is essential that the examiner be attentive to interpersonal processes and be a supportive, caring professional to parents. Not only will this help the parents through a potentially difficult experience, but it also will facilitate the evaluation and the parents' acceptance of resulting recommendations.

Select Appropriate Instruments

Because the goals and methods of assessing the severely developmentally disabled differ from those employed with nonhandicapped clients, three issues must be considered when selecting assessment instruments for an evaluation: (1) developmental age versus chronological age of the client, (2) adaptation of test materials and procedures, and (3) use of multiskilled tests (Powers, 1984a). Each of these will be considered separately.

Zigler (1969) notes that while the mentally retarded child's development continues along the same course as a nonhandicapped peer, it does so more slowly. This observation has particular relevance for school psychologists evaluating severely developmentally disabled clients, for several reasons. First, it helps determine the appropriate level at which to begin testing (Ho et al., 1980). For example, a 30-year-old profoundly mentally retarded adult who is functioning below a 36-month-old level may be better assessed by the Bayley Scales of Infant Development (Bayley, 1969) than by the Columbia Mental Maturity Scales (Burgemeister et al., 1972), because the Bayley samples a broader range of behavior below age 3. Second, development of a profile of relative strengths and weaknesses is facilitated by basing the selection of assessment devices on developmental level. Using this profile, educational program planning can proceed more systematically by placing ceiling-level strengths on the relevant developmental continuum (e.g., motor, receptive language) and by providing instruction in progressively more difficult skills. Finally, choice of developmental over chronological age provides data that lead to evaluable educational "starting points." For many years, severely developmentally disabled clients were considered untestable because they could not respond to stimuli at the level psychologists considered "appropriate." Rather than assessing clients at their own level, psychologists began where they thought these clients should be. Attending to the client's developmental level will help prevent errors of this type.

Adaptations of standardized tests are frequently necessary due to the need to accommodate for multihandicapping conditions and different developmental levels in clients. In some cases, standardized, norm-based assessment may be appropriate for a severely developmentally disabled client. For example, both the Bayley Scales of Infant Development (Bayley, 1969) and the Vineland Adaptive Behavior Scales (Sparrow et al., 1984) may be appropriate for use with certain children. The idiosyncratic patterns of strengths and weaknesses of many severely developmentally disabled clients often makes the use of more traditional instruments difficult, however. As a result, several guidelines are appropriate when considering the adaptation of testing materials. First, when selecting tests, consider those *not* in need of adaptation first. Second, select tests created for clients with particular handicaps wherever possible. Examples include the Wisconsin Behavior Rating Scale (Song & Jones, 1980) and the Tests of Pictorial Intelligence (French, 1964). Include tests designed to assess cognitive, adaptive, communicative, motor, and social functioning. In selecting assessment devices from a wide variety of tests, psychologists gain flexibility in creating an individualized battery (Forcade, Matey, & Barnett, 1979; Ho et al., 1980).

Alternative communication formats also may be necessary. For example, nonvocal methods of communication, including language boards, rigid head pointers, Bliss symbols, or electronic voice synthesizers, may be required to enable the client to respond to test stimuli. Similarly, Sattler (1972) developed multiple choice yes/no formats for use with some Stanford-Binet and WISC-R subtests, while Levy (1982) modified the PPVT by allowing clients to hand the examiner cut-up cards rather than point to correct responses.

The client also may need to be taught to respond to the particular format of the test. For example, responding to the Columbia Mental Maturity Scale requires left-to-right scanning of the stimuli and identification of the stimulus that is different or "not the same." If these two prerequisite behaviors are not in their clients' repertoire, psychologists must consider whether they will teach to the task or select an alternative instrument.

In all cases, modifications depend on the examiner's knowledge of the client's handicap, the client's attentional limitations, and the examiner's creativity. As with all adaptations in procedure and form of administration, notation in the final report is essential.

Several tests frequently used with severely developmentally disabled clients assess only one skill. Such tests potentially underrepresent a client's abilities (Sattler, 1982). For example, the PPVT-Revised (Dunn & Dunn, 1981) provides a nonvocal measure of a client's reasoning where the input consists of figural and spatial information. This is especially a problem for clients with severe developmental disabilities because of their highly uneven profiles of mental abilities. As these clients often exhibit splinter skills, one-skill tests may fail to fully assess important areas of functioning (Ferrari, 1980). This problem becomes particularly critical when program planning decisions must be made.

One solution to this dilemma is to use multiskill tests when evaluating clients with severe developmental disabilities (Powers, 1984a). Ferrari (1980) compared the utility of the McCarthy Scales of Children's Abilities (McCarthy, 1972) with the PPVT (Dunn, 1965) with low-functioning autistic children, and found that the PPVT significantly underestimated cognitive functioning. Thus, in order to provide the child with as much opportunity as possible to gain credit for particular strengths, multiskill tests should be administered whenever possible. Examples of multiskill tests include the McCarthy Scales, the Woodcock-Johnson Psycho-educational Battery (Woodcock & Johnson, 1978), and the Kaufman Assessment Battery for Children (Kaufman & Kaufman, 1983). In the event that the use of a single multiskill test is not possible, the individualized assessment battery that is constructed should be sensitive to a broad range of areas of functioning in order to give as complete a profile of strengths and weaknesses as possible.

Attempt Formal Assessment

When the stage has been set appropriately and relevant instruments have been selected, formal evaluation begins. The client should be required to establish and maintain eye contact with the examiner, or with the test stimuli, before proceeding with that item. For some clients, this skill already will be present. For others, a certain amount of training to the task may be necessary. In the latter case, verbal prompts ("Look here"; "Look at me") or physical prompts (lightly orienting the client's face in the direction of the stimulus material or holding the item in front of the client's eyes, then gradually moving it toward the table) can be used. As a general rule, it is better to first provide a verbal prompt, and then to move gradually to more physical prompts as needed. In short, the less prompting, the better.

When evaluating clients with severe developmental disabilities, it may be necessary for clinicians to schedule more frequent breaks than when evaluating less handicapped children. While some clients will complete the evaluation with little delay, others will only be able to tolerate a brief period of assessment on a given day, necessitating a second or even a third day of testing. In either case, it will be important to attempt to gauge the tempo and timing that produce optimal results for the client, and to follow the client's lead whenever possible.

The examiner should identify the variety and range of reinforcers that motivate the severely developmentally disabled client prior to the evaluation. This can be accomplished by asking parents which verbal, physical (e.g., hugs, tickles, and backrubs), and primary (i.e., food) reinforcers are effective with their child, and by "reinforcer sampling" by the examiner before the evaluation begins. While examiners should refrain from rewarding responses to test items, other behavior—appropriate attending, sitting, eye contact, and so on—can be acknowledged and reinforced. When selecting reinforcers, examiners should begin with the least interfering (i.e., verbal approvals) and progress through to physical and then primary reinforcers only as necessitated by the client's failure to respond. In all cases, physical and primary rewards should be paired with verbal approval. Periodically during the evaluation, examiners should revert to verbal approvals alone to determine whether they have acquired motivational properties, providing important assessment data.

It is sometimes helpful to substitute materials in order to better assess a skill. For example, clients with limited vision may not be able to identify body parts on the picture of a child used in the Stanford-Binet, but can identify their own body parts. Similarly, when using the Bayley Scales for the assessment of severely developmentally disabled clients with deficiencies in motor control, the square wooden blocks from the Stanford-Binet are better than their more slippery plastic Bayley counterparts. While such flexibility can be justified when in the child's best interest, it always should be noted in the written report.

Many severely developmentally disabled clients have had no experience with the task instructions contained in assessment devices. They may not have a reliably established pointing response, or may not understand the command, "Give me the ———." In such cases, the examiner must determine whether the client can learn the required responding behavior through teaching for the task, or whether the response is beyond the client's capability. While some assessment instruments, such as the Kaufman Assessment Battery for Children, have built-in provisions for teaching the task, others do not provide for this deficit in the client's responding, and may require the examiner to undertake teaching before presenting

Exhibit 9–1 Special Considerations for Informal Assessment

---

1. Does hearing appear normal?
2. Does vision appear normal?
3. What is the incidence of seizures?
4. Is there presence/absence of gestural communication, and both gestural comprehension and usage?
5. Is generalized imitative ability present/absent?
6. Describe any incidental language.
7. Describe any functional metaphorical language.
8. Describe complexity of language expression (intonation, prosody, babbling, and so on).
9. Describe receptive language.
10. Describe type, nature, and intensity of any self-stimulatory behavior.
11. Can self-stimulation be interrupted? What are the consequences?
12. Describe type, nature, and intensity of self-injurious behavior.
13. Can self-injurious behavior be interrupted? What are the consequences?
14. What is the motivation for self-injury and/or self-stimulation (attention seeking, escape/avoidance, sensory feedback, to gain access to reinforcers)?
15. Describe understanding of cause-effect relationships.

---

the item. When teaching for the task is required, additional information on the client's learning style can be obtained.

Formal Assessment Failure

Some severely developmentally disabled persons will not be amenable to formal evaluation. Despite the most creative efforts of the examiner, the pervasiveness of the client's handicap may prevent any meaningful one-to-one interaction. In such cases, the examiner must evaluate the client on a more informal basis and rely more heavily on third-party assessments. The examiner can observe the client's general behavior, use of test materials, reactions to novel stimuli, patterns of exploration, play behavior, and interactions with others in the evaluation room. In addition, third-party assessments can be obtained from parents, teachers, or caretakers using the Wisconsin Behavior Rating Scales (Song & Jones, 1980), the Learning Accomplishment Profile (Sanford, 1974), the Developmental Profile II (Alpern et al., 1980), the Vineland Adaptive Behavior Scales (Sparrow et al., 1984), or the TARC Assessment System (Sailor & Mix, 1975). Exhibit 9–1 identifies several other important areas to consider in an informal assessment.

Note of Caution

The task of evaluating severely developmentally disabled clients requires a considerable amount of patience, creativity, clinical sensitivity, and flexibility on the part of examiners. It also may involve the violation of standardized test procedures, substitution, and the use of external rewards. While the ultimate goal is to determine clients' functional strengths and weaknesses through whatever means are feasible, all deviations from standard practice must be noted in the evaluation report along with qualified results. If this is done, the valuable information obtained by the astute examiner will be less likely to be misunderstood or misused by others who will use the information later on.

CASE STUDY

It may be instructive to consider the issues and tests described in Chapter 9 as they apply to an actual assessment case. The case report that follows (Exhibit 9–2) was selected both because it illustrates these issues and tests and because it presents a comprehensive assessment model necessary for severely impaired clients.

Exhibit 9–2 Psychological Evaluation

Name: Jack Richards	Born: 8/16/73
Address:	Seen: 10/27/81
Parents: Tom and Mary Richards	C.A.: 8–2
Referred by:	Sibling:

Reason for referral: Psychological evaluation for program planning

Diagnoses: 1. Retrolental Fibroplasia (RLF) OU—Totally Blind
                 2. Developmental Delay
                 3. Early Childhood Psychosis

Data Collected: 1. Bayley Scales of Infant Development
                 2. Perkins-Binet Tests of Intelligence for the Blind (attempted)
                 3. Wisconsin Behavior Rating Scale
                 4. Rimland Diagnostic Checklist for Behavior-Disturbed Children (Form E-2)
                 5. Parental Interview
                 6. Diagnostic Observation

Background and Observations

Jack is a slender, attractive boy who is small for his age. He is right-handed. Jack's excellent gross motor coordination was evident throughout the testing session. He was accompanied by his mother, Mary Richards, who sat in for the entire assessment and subsequently was interviewed.

The history form completed by Ms. Richards prior to the assessment reveals that Jack was born after 27 weeks gestation, weighing 2 pounds, 3 ounces. His Apgar score was 2/5. Jack was

Exhibit 9–2 continued

given oxygen immediately, spent two months in an incubator, and suffered RLF that led to total blindness. When he was 11 days old, he suffered respiratory apnea and remained very ill for three weeks. Jack was then released from the hospital without further complications. Ms. Richards noted no problems in Jack's sucking, chewing, swallowing, crying, or sleeping. At present, Jack is reported to be in good health. He has contracted none of the usual childhood illnesses (chicken pox, measles, and so on) and has no history of seizures. Parental report noted allergic reactions to pollens, but no history of asthma.

Over the years, Jack has manifested a variety of behaviors indicative of developmental disability. As a young child, Jack engaged in several autisticlike behaviors, including resistance to touch, rhythmic rocking, impaired language functioning, self-stimulation, and indifference to people. A diagnosis of early childhood psychosis was made during his early years. Jack entered the Thompson School about two years ago. He was initially enrolled in a class for young autistic children and most recently (1981–1982) in a class for older children with multiple handicaps. He began to talk at age 2, stopped at age 3, and has begun to use occasional words functionally again. Jack continues to receive speech therapy at the Thompson School; he is progressing slowly. He reportedly has several functional words, gestures, and signs. During the testing session, some of these were elicited, but none were spontaneous.

Developmental milestones were attained later than usual in all areas. Walking and self-feeding were mastered by 18 months. Independent toileting was accomplished by 3 years. Because of Jack's blindness, these delays are not surprising. Considerable training was needed to teach Jack how to dress and accomplish basic self-help skills. Jack's academic programming has focused on language and communication skills, preacademics, and self-help. Progress has been slow, but steady. He has attended special educational programs throughout the course of his school career.

Jack has been described as a child with sensory (visual), communication, neurological, and emotional handicaps. While progress in school has been made, teacher report indicates that Jack's inappropriate behavior at times interferes with his learning. In this regard, one type of behavior may be prominent, only to be replaced by another when the first one decreases. A highly structured academic and nonacademic classroom regimen has been somewhat successful in modifying these behaviors.

Jack is currently in his last year of eligibility for the Thompson School program. Ms. Richards is interested in identifying an educational placement for 1982–1983 and in obtaining an assessment of Jack's cognitive and social abilities. It is to these goals that the current evaluation is addressed.

Upon meeting the examiner, Jack readily moved to sit at a desk when Ms. Richards noted that he was "going to do some work." He was physically active during the session, becoming more and more compliant as time progressed. Jack's ability to adapt to the testing situation and to two unknown examiners is testimony to the careful instruction provided him in sitting and attending skills. During the initial phases of the assessment, Jack manipulated many of the materials in a somewhat nonpurposeful fashion. As he grew more familiar with the setting, such behavior was quickly and clearly replaced by more purposeful task interaction. Finally, as the session continued, Jack became clearly responsive to the examiner's requests for instructional control behavior (e.g., sitting properly, facing front, hands on desk, head up).

Jack responded to appropriately chosen test items with interest and perseverance. Those test items that were beyond his capabilities usually elicited a confused, perseverative constellation of behaviors characterized by noncompliance, stereotypy, and a rapid loss of interest. While Jack's frustration tolerance with individual items was difficult to assess, the mere fact that he was able to stick with a rapidly changing examination protocol is encouraging.

Exhibit 9–2 continued

Jack was receptive to the examiner and readily sought his contact and attention. He enjoyed being hugged, backscratched, and tickled and sat quietly next to the examiner after testing while a parental interview was conducted. Jack exhibited some initial noncompliant behavior relative to sitting still and giving back test items, but he gradually shifted to being extremely compliant by the three-quarter mark of the session.

Language production and comprehension were discrepant. Parent and teacher report the presence of several signs, but Jack was unable to produce these without prompting. Generally speaking, there was a great deal of reliance upon the examiner's correct anticipation/guess of Jack's desires. His receptive communicative skills were better developed, but were initially interfered with by his noncompliant behavior.

Jack's cognitive style can be described as impulsive, global, and trial-and-error based for items he was able to interact with, and generally fragmented for items that were too difficult. The consistency of his behavior in the latter two thirds of the session and his ease in relating to the examiner, coupled with his general compliance and parental report, indicated that an accurate sample of behavior was obtained.

Findings

On the Bayley Mental Scale, a basal level was established at 14 months and a ceiling attained at 23 months with Jack showing an ability to build a tower of six blocks. Numerous items were not administered because of their inappropriateness for a child without vision. For example, Jack was unable to tactually discriminate body parts on the doll, a 19-month-old task. He was, however, able to point to six different parts of his own body.

The Behavior Scale reflects Jack's tendency to be dependent upon external prompts as cues for his behavior. His responsiveness to persons tended to be accepting and demanding. A relatively contented child, Jack recovered rather easily when upset. Orientation to objects tended to be perseverative and lacking in imagination. Jack frequently mouthed new objects as they were given to him, engaged in their use for a brief period of time, and then appeared to lose interest in them. While he was active throughout the session, he generally was cooperative after an initial reaction to the newness of the situation and exhibited good instructional control. In addition, Jack was an aware, reactive child. He was vigilant to changes in structure and materials, and displayed relatively smooth fine and gross muscle movements.

On the Perkins-Binet he passed two items at year IV, one for the three-hole form board and another that required identification of four body parts. At year V, Jack passed the item requiring the identification of six body parts and the item comparing the relative size of two blocks. Because Jack's age greatly exceeds the Bayley's ceiling age, and because many items could not be administered because of Jack's blindness, all results on this test should be interpreted with caution, and further should be construed as descriptions of behavior obtained under test conditions rather than indices of intellectual ability relative to a norm group. The same caution holds for the Perkins-Binet, as Jack's communication handicap prevented the administration of the majority of items for years IV and V.

On the Wisconsin Behavior Rating Scale (WBRS), Jack showed a notable discrepancy between self-help skill acquisition and all other areas. Such skills tended to be far better developed, due in all probability to the intensive teaching effort at home and in school. In contrast, play skills were poorly developed. Here Jack presents as a child who plays only with his brother, and even then intrusively at times. Appropriate play with a variety of objects is lacking. Socialization skills are also fairly poor. While Jack seeks affection and will repeat performances that are rewarded, he has yet to learn to share or take turns. In relation to WBRS norms, Jack's socialization and play skills are roughly equivalent to those of a 1-year-old child.

Exhibit 9–2 continued

Receptive and expressive language abilities are slightly better developed, but still below the 36-month ceiling. Receptively, Jack was able to recognize several common objects (shoe, ear, eye, cup, and so on). Additionally, he was able to follow simple, one-step commands. He could not, however, identify body parts on a doll or on the examiner. Expressively, Jack was able to gesture "yes" and spontaneously produce the words "jump" and "no" but was unable to indicate the functions of objects or to put words together to form a phrase. Relative to WBRS norms, Jack's combined language abilities fall at roughly the level of 1½ years.

His gross and fine motor skills are well developed relative to the WBRS norms. Jack passed all items on the gross motor subscale with the exception of walking down the stairs with one foot to a step. He passed all items administered on the fine motor subscale giving him age-equivalents of approximately 2 years according to WBRS norms.

As noted, self-help is an area of relative strength for Jack, confirmed by his surpassing all self-help norms on the WBRS. Parental report indicates that Jack can make his bed and put a blanket on it. He can set a table, clear the table, and get out a cup of dog food to feed the dog. He knows how to put away some of his clothes and knows the location of various clothing items (underwear and pajamas) in his dresser.

Ms. Richards indicated that Jack can fill a cup and drink alone and can use a fork and spoon appropriately. While his toileting is independent, he has at times used wetting his pants as an attention-getting device. Jack can dress himself but cannot button (although he can unbutton), cannot start a zipper (although he can finish it), and cannot tie his shoes. Snapping is problematic for Jack because of poor pincer pressure. While Jack can brush his teeth when all materials are provided, he is not independent in this skill. He brushes his hair when given a brush, and can run water for a bath and wash most of his body parts.

Numerous atypical behaviors were retrospectively identified by Ms. Richards on the Rimland Diagnostic Checklist (Form E-2). Jack was described as failing to imitate or to respond differentially to loud versus soft sounds. He engaged in rhythmic rocking as a young child, often to music. In addition, Jack often would act as if people "were not there." His mother described him further as difficult to reach and rather stiff and awkward to hold as a young child. His presently identified grace and gross motor ability is evident from his early years.

Prior to age 5, Jack resisted any extensive use of his hands for long periods of time. He also engaged in rituals, becoming upset if anyone interfered with them. Characteristically, Jack was not physically "pliable" as a child. He enjoyed being left alone, was neither sensitive to criticism nor affectionate, and was aloof and indifferent. Jack began to speak a few words but stopped talking at 3 years of age only to begin again later. He has never used the word "I." Ms. Richards reports that she observed these behaviors within the first 6 months of his life. His score on the Rimland Scale was +10, which places him in neither group (autistic or otherwise behavior disordered) that the checklist is designed to diagnose.

Discussion

A serious delay in communicative ability serves to compound the problems caused by Jack's RLF-caused blindness. While Jack's performance on the various tests administered cannot be compared to any norm group, certain promising patterns were observed. Jack was a reasonably compliant child who, after engaging in initial episodes of "testing the limits" with the examiners, settled down to the testing regimen. He remained under good instructional control for the greater part of the session. Such behavior bodes well for future educational experiences of a structured nature.

On several occasions, Jack exhibited the ability to imitate the motor behavior of the examiner (e.g., clapping hands, playing xylophone). As a precursor to both communication training and prevocational training, the development of a generalized imitative ability is key.

Exhibit 9–2 continued

Jack's adherence to the examiner's structure and overall compliant, friendly, and affectionate behavior suggest the efficacy of a highly structured, consistently applied program of teaching for both academic and nonacademic skills. He has an emergent conception of cause/effect and seems to integrate and profit from prior experience that is explicitly reinforced. Jack was vigilant and sensitive to environmental changes. Relative to his vision loss, this is a very desirable attribute. There exists a tendency for Jack's behavior to become fragmented, however, when incoming stimuli are either too novel or too rapid.

Despite the high number of atypical symptoms noted, there is no justification for a diagnosis of infantile autism by DSM-III criteria. However, when compared to other RLF children, many of whom display autisticlike symptoms, the findings on the Rimland show that Jack has more withdrawn behavior. Jack presents as a multihandicapped child who is blind and mentally retarded, and who exhibits a series of behaviors that interfere with more independent functioning (e.g., eye poking, language impairment, social skill deficits, play skill deficits). He has been fortunate to have parents who are advocates for him and an educational setting that has pushed for his attainment of reasonable educational and social goals.

Recommendations and Conclusions

Jack's programs at the Thompson School and at home have been successful in developing his self-help skills to a large extent. Continued work in these areas is recommended with the added focus of training for generalization from school to home and vice versa, as well as to novel settings.

Language and communication skills training continues to be an area of major focus. Jack needs to develop a generalized imitative ability for both motor and verbal behavior as prerequisites to verbal and nonverbal communication training. Objects, actions, and relationships between objects (e.g., prepositions) should be stressed with an emphasis toward functionality. While the development of a sign language system is appropriate for Jack, it should be concurrent with training to establish his verbal behavior and should be preceded by his development of a generalized imitative skill.

Jack's educational programming should include one-to-one matching, shape and size discrimination, auditory discrimination of common sounds, following commands, concepts of "your" and "my," and relationships among objects (in, on, under, next to, through, over). Further, effectiveness in training and education will depend upon the use of behavioral teaching methods utilizing the techniques of shaping (or teaching through the use of successive approximations), fading, reinforcement, and extinction. Specific reinforcers that may be functional with Jack include physical reinforcement (tickles, hugs, backscratches), verbal praise, and, with new skills yet to be mastered, food. Whenever reinforcers are used with Jack, they should be administered quickly and contingently, and in the following rapid order: verbal praise, physical reinforcers, primary reinforcers (e.g., food or drink). As his skill proficiency develops, fading backwards along this continuum can be begun. Lastly, allowing Jack a functional reward (cookie for the appropriate manual sign) may prove to be highly effective.

As with all areas targeted for intervention, Jack's adaptation in a seeing world must be accomplished in the areas of socialization with peers and appropriate play. Jack's absence of visual sensory feedback marks these areas as difficult ones in which to operate. Nonetheless, continued exposure to peers through game playing and sharing/acknowledging others' presence in school is recommended. Such training should be planned for, implemented, and evaluated with the same emphasis and resolve as more "typical" academic behaviors (e.g., communication training). The same is true for play; objects providing sensory feedback are most appropriate to this child, and their appropriate nonperseverative use should be stressed. Jack's

Exhibit 9–2 continued

attendance at camp each summer has been of great benefit to him and should be continued by all means.

As Jack's eligibility at the Thompson School expires at the end of the 1981–1982 academic year, alternative placements should be sought. Given Jack's prior successful training and emergent understanding of the consequences of his behavior, a highly structured and specialized educational setting is recommended. In such a setting, preacademics, social skill, self-help, language and communication, and general behavior management should be emphasized. In order to further Jack's emergent abilities in all of the above areas, a consistent, contingent programming effort will be required. Ideally, this effort will include home training for both Jack and those with whom he resides in order to promote generalization.

At some point in the future, it might be useful to consider a short-term group-living experience in a small residential setting. The purpose here would be twofold: attendance at such a facility would allow 24-hour teaching of the self-help and socialization skills that are a focus of training for Jack, while at the same time preparing him for the eventual return to his family as a more fully functioning member. In addition, such placement would recognize his family's needs—working, caring for a home, socializing on the outside, and training a multihandicapped child all at once are very difficult for them.

Within a few years, it will be necessary to consider prevocational training for Jack. Plans for a training curriculum to supplement his preacademic and communication training should be considered soon. Jack will need to develop such skills as matching-to-sample and tactual discrimination, among many others.

Summary

At the age of 8 years and 2 months, Jack exhibits several multihandicapping conditions, including blindness, mental retardation, and behavioral disorders. He has benefited from his placement at the Thompson School, as evidenced by his emergent self-help skills, communicative abilities, and ability to relate to and interact with adults. While lacking a generalized imitative ability, Jack has an emergent understanding of causality suggesting the efficacy of a highly structured and carefully planned behavior intervention program for academic and social skills. Continued behavioral intervention in academic and social skills is recommended.

SUMMARY

In Chapter 9, guidelines for the psychological assessment of clients with severe developmental disabilities have been provided. Integration of behavioral assessment goals and of psychological assessment has been attempted in a way that allows maximum flexibility and accountability for clinicians, and provides data useful for planning client programs. Several tests have been reviewed in detail, with their particular utility for this population stressed. Guidelines for conducting psychological evaluations with severely developmentally disabled clients have been presented. Finally, a case example was provided to illustrate several assessment devices, as well as a comprehensive format for the standard psychological assessment of the severely developmentally disabled.

REFERENCES

Alpern, G. D. (1967). Measurement of "untestable" autistic children. *Journal of Applied Psychology, 72*, 478–486.

Alpern, G. D., Boll, T. J., & Shearer, M. A. (1980). *Developmental Profile II*. Aspen, CO: Psychological Development Publications.

American Psychiatric Association. (1980). *Diagnostic and Statistical Manual of Mental Disorders* (3rd Ed.). Washington, DC: Author.

Bayley, N. (1969). *Bayley Scales of Infant Development*. New York: Psychological Corporation.

Burgemeister, B. B., Blum, L. H., & Lorge, I. (1972). *The Columbia Mental Maturity Scale* (3rd ed.). New York: Harcourt Brace Jovanovich.

Canter, A. (1956). The use of the Columbia Mental Maturity Scale with cerebral palsied children. *American Journal of Mental Deficiency, 60*, 843–851.

Comtois, R. J., & Clark, W. D. (1976). A framework for scientific practice and practitioner training. *JSAS Catalogue of Selected Documents in Psychology, 6*, 74. (Ms. No. 1301)

Doll, E. A. (1965). *Vineland Social Maturity Scale*. Circle Pines, MN: American Guidance Service.

Dunn, L. M. (1965). *Peabody Picture Vocabulary Test*. Circle Pines, MN: American Guidance Service.

Dunn, L. M., & Dunn, L. M. (1981). *Peabody Picture Vocabulary Test-Revised*. Circle Pines, MN: American Guidance Service.

Ferrari, M. (1980). Comparisons of the Peabody Picture Vocabulary Test and the McCarthy Scales of Children's Abilities with a sample of autistic children. *Psychology in the Schools, 17*, 466–469.

Forcade, M. C., Matey, C. M., & Barnett, D. W. (1979). Procedural guidelines for low-incidence assessment. *School Psychology Digest, 8*, 248–256.

Frankenburg, W., & Dodds, J. (1973). *Denver Developmental Screening Test*. Denver: LADOCA Project & Publishing Foundation.

French, J. (1969). *The Pictorial Tests of Intelligence*. Boston: Houghton Mifflin.

Gerken, K. C. (Guest ed.). (1979). Services to preschoolers and children with low incidence handicaps. *School Psychology Digest, 8*.

Griffin, P. M., & Sanford, A. R. (1975). *Learning Accomplishment Profile for Infants* (experimental ed.). Winston-Salem, NC: Kaplan Press.

Grossman, H. (Ed.). (1973). *Manual on terminology and classification in mental retardation*. Washington, DC: American Association on Mental Deficiency.

Harris, S. L. (1976). *Teaching speech to a nonverbal child*. Lawrence, KS: H & H Enterprises.

Harris, S. L. (1979). DSM-III: Its implications for children. *Child Behavior Therapy, 1*, 37–46.

Harris, S. L. (1982). A family systems approach to behavioral training with parents of autistic children. *Child and Family Behavior Therapy, 4*, 21–35.

Harris, S. L., & Powers, M. D. (1984). Diagnostic issues. In T. H. Ollendick & M. Hersen (Eds.), *Child behavioral assessment: Principles and procedures*. Elmsford, NY: Pergamon Press.

Harris, S. L., & Powers, M. D. (1984). Behavior therapists look at the impact of an autistic child on the family system. In E. Schopler & G. Mesibov (Eds.), *The effects of autism on the family*. New York: Plenum Press.

Hartmann, D. P., Roper, B. L., & Bradford, D. C. (1979). Some relationships between behavioral and traditional assessment. *Journal of Behavioral Assessment, 1*, 3–21.

Hedrick, D. L., Prather, E. M., & Tobin, A. R. (1975). *Sequenced Inventory of Communication Development*. Seattle: University of Washington Press.

Ho, C., Glanville, S., & Brave, J. C. (1980). Challenges in evaluating young developmentally disabled children. *Journal of Clinical Child Psychology, 9*, 233–235.

Kanfer, F. H., & Saslow, G. (1969). Behavioral diagnosis. In C. M. Franks (Ed.), *Behavior therapy: Appraisal and status*. New York: McGraw-Hill.

Kaufman, A. S., & Kaufman, N. L. (1977). *Clinical evaluation of young children with the McCarthy Scales*. New York: Grune & Stratton.

Kaufman, A. S., & Kaufman, N. L. (1983a). *Kaufman Assessment Battery for Children*. Circle Pines, MN: American Guidance Service.

Kaufman, A. S., & Kaufman, N. L. (1983b). *Administration and scoring manual for the Kaufman Assessment Battery for Children*. Circle Pines, MN: American Guidance Service.

Kaufman, A. S., & Kaufman, N. L. (1983c). *Interpretive manual for the Kaufman Assessment Battery for Children*. Circle Pines, MN: American Guidance Service.

Kazdin, A. E. (1983). Psychiatric diagnosis, dimensions of dysfunction, and child behavior therapy. *Behavior Therapy, 14*, 73–99.

Leiter, R. G. (1948). *The Leiter International Performance Scale*. Chicago: Stoelting.

Levy, S. (1982). The use of the Peabody Picture Vocabulary Test with low-functioning autistic children. *Psychology in the Schools, 19*, 24–27.

McCann, B. S. (1981). Hemispheric asymmetries and early infantile autism. *Journal of Autism and Developmental Disorders, 11*, 401–411.

McCarthy, D. (1972). *McCarthy Scales of Children's Abilities*. New York: Psychological Corporation.

McCarthy, D. (1978). *McCarthy Screening Test*. New York: Psychological Corporation.

Mulliken, R. K. (1979). Evaluation of multi-handicapped children. In R. K. Mulliken & M. Evans (Eds.), *Assessment of children with low-incidence handicaps*. Stratford, CT: NASP Publications.

Mulliken, R. K., & Evans, M. (Eds.). (1979). *Assessment of children with low-incidence handicaps*. Stratford, CT: NASP Publications.

Nelson, R. O. (1980). The use of intelligence tests within behavioral assessment. *Behavioral Assessment, 2*, 417–423.

Newland, T. E. (1973). Assumptions underlying psychological testing. *Journal of School Psychology, 11*, 316–322.

Powers, M. D. (1983a). Behavioral assessment of developmentally disabled preschool children. *New Jersey Journal of School Psychology, 3*, 16–25.

Powers, M. D. (1983b). *Assessing readiness for change in families with severely developmentally disabled children*. Manuscript submitted for publication.

Powers, M. D. (1984a). *The psychological assessment of severely developmentally disabled clients*. Manuscript submitted for publication.

Powers, M. D. (1984b). Assessment of the severely developmentally disabled: The problem-solving model. Paper presented at the 92nd annual meeting of the American Psychological Association, Toronto.

Powers, M. D. (in press). Syndromal diagnosis and the behavioral assessment of childhood disorders. *Child & Family Behavior Therapy*.

Reynolds, C. R. (1981, August). Test bias: In God we trust, all others must have data. Address to the APA Division of Evaluation and Measurement, 89th annual meeting of the American Psychological Association, Los Angeles.

Sailor, W., & Mix, B. J. (1975). *The TARC Assessment System*. Lawrence, KS: H & H Enterprises.

Sanford, A. R. (Ed.). (1974). *The Learning Accomplishment Profile*. Winston-Salem, NC: Kaplan Press.

Sattler, J. M. (1972). Intelligence test modifications on handicapped and non-handicapped children, final report. San Diego. San Diego State University Foundation. (ERIC Document Service No. ED 095 673)

Sattler, J. M. (1974). *Assessment of children's intelligence*. Philadelphia: W. B. Saunders.

Sattler, J. M. (1982). *Assessment of children's intelligence and special abilities* (2nd ed.). Boston: Allyn & Bacon.

Schover, L., & Newsom, C. (1976). Overselectivity, developmental level, and overtraining in autistic and normal children. *Journal of Abnormal Child Psychology, 4*, 289–298.

Sloves, R. E., Docherty, E. M., & Schneider, K. C. (1979). A scientific problem-solving model of psychological assessment. *Professional Psychology, 10*, 28–35.

Song, A. Y., & Jones, S. E. (Eds.). (1980). *The Wisconsin Behavior Rating Scale*. Madison: Central Wisconsin Center for the Developmentally Disabled.

Sparrow, S. S., Balla, D. A., & Cicchetti, D. V. (1984). *Vineland Adaptive Behavior Scales*. Circle Pines, MN: American Guidance Service.

Terman, L. M., & Merrill, M. A. (1960). *Stanford-Binet Intelligence Scale*. Boston: Houghton Mifflin.

Ulrey, G., & Rogers, S. J. (Eds.). (1982). *Psychological assessment of handicapped infants and young children*. New York: Thieme-Stratton.

Wechsler, D. (1967). *Wechsler Preschool and Primary Scale of Intelligence*. New York: Psychological Corporation.

Wechsler, D. (1974). *Wechsler Intelligence Scale for Children-Revised*. New York: Psychological Corporation.

Wechsler, D. (1981). *Wechsler Adult Intelligence Scale-Revised*. New York: Psychological Corporation.

Wilhelm, H., & Lovaas, O. I. (1976). Stimulus overselectivity: A common feature in autism and mental retardation. *American Journal of Mental Deficiency, 81*, 26–31.

Woodcock, R. W., & Johnson, M. B. (1978). *Woodcock-Johnson Psychoeducational Battery*. Hingham, MA: Teaching Resources Corporation.

Zigler, E. (1969). Developmental vs. difference theories of mental deficiency. *American Journal of Mental Deficiency, 73*, 536–556.

Zumberg, M. (1979). Evaluating severely/profoundly retarded children and adults. In R. K. Mulliken & M. Evans (Eds.), *Assessment of children with low-incidence handicaps*. Stratford, CT: NASP Publications.

Planning and Evaluating Programs for the Severely Developmentally Disabled: An Overview

INTRODUCTION

Clinicians serving the severely developmentally disabled sometimes work in service delivery systems that fail to meet important planned goals. In such cases, clinicians may be sufficiently distressed that after a burst of fruitless effort to generate change, they will ultimately "burnout" and attempt to ignore program problems, or resign because of accumulated frustrations. Chapter 10 proposes that when situations such as these arise, another option exists for caring clinicians. This option—termed program planning and evaluation—has been implemented with a variety of special education service-delivery programs (Maher, 1981a; 1981b; 1982a; 1982b), and has applicability to the broad range of programs serving the severely developmentally disabled. The value of program planning and evaluation is that it allows programs to be made explicit and to be carried out systematically. Program planning and evaluation activities are therefore both reactive and proactive. As a reactive measure, program evaluation will help clarify and redress existing service delivery problems as perceived by program staff. As a proactive measure, program design and evaluation procedures can be used to develop clear, well-defined programs. Because these programs are being evaluated before, during, and after implementation, problems in service delivery can be confronted before they get out of control.

Institutions and agencies provide many educational and training services to clients with severe developmental disabilities. In addition, these organizations provide services to staff and engage in administrative activities designed to coordinate overall service delivery. While there are many programs for delivering these services, the efficacy and efficiency of service delivery varies both within and among agencies. Even on an informal basis, some agencies have a reputation for excellence while others would be shunned by an informed consumer. To enable professionals to deliver services more effectively, certain planning and evaluation activities can be undertaken. The purpose of Chapter 10 is to describe a generic program planning and evaluation framework developed by Maher and Bennett (1984), and discuss its application to programs serving severely developmentally disabled clients.

Chapter 10 focuses on assessing service delivery *systems*, rather than assessing *individuals*; nonetheless, this expanded view has several elements in common with "standard" behavioral assessment. First, it focuses on (system) behavior that is multiply determined, with antecedent and consequent stimuli. The processes common to all systems (e.g., sanctions for operation; boundaries between subsystems; boundary roles; homeostatic functions) can be considered as analogous to organismic stimuli in the assessment of individual cases. To follow this analogy, "organismic" systemic stimuli, interacting with environmental stimuli, affect system functioning. Second, program planning and evaluation activities focus on observable, verifiable behavior. Finally, evaluation of both system functioning and the effects of systemic interventions are emphasized in this framework.

However, the expanded unit of analysis of this model necessitates a broader view of evaluation than that for individuals, encompassing multiple methods. These include evaluation of goal attainment, collateral effects, consumer reactions, cause-effect relationships (as per single-case designs), and cost-effectiveness (Maher & Bennett, 1984).

This framework is offered as a heuristic device to guide clinicians in their thinking about planning, evaluating, and delivering a wide variety of services to clients with severe developmental disabilities. It is hoped that use of this or any other systemic model may prevent the "myopia" that so frequently occurs when individuals are assessed in a restricted context.

PROGRAM PLANNING AND EVALUATION DEFINED

Program planning and evaluation comprise activities to assist clinicians in the development and improvement of habilitative and rehabilitative services to severely developmentally disabled persons. Program planning further can be defined as the process of creating a new program or improving one already in operation. The program planning process requires a determination of (1) program need, (2) program goals, (3) resources (including staff, materials, and activities) that the program will require, (4) ways to evaluate the effectiveness of the program, and (5) ways the program can be improved (Maher & Bennett, 1984).

Program evaluation can be defined further as the process of gathering information about a program so that evaluative judgments can be made (Maher & Bennett, 1984). These judgments include (1) deciding to keep the program in its present form, (2) deciding to continue the program with certain modifications, and (3) deciding to end the program.

Evaluation activities are designed to provide information that will assist in program improvement. Five classes of information can be obtained about a program (Maher & Bennett, 1984):

1. need
2. goals
3. strengths and weaknesses of alternatives
4. manner of implementation
5. success

Once obtained, this evaluative information permits professionals to state more definitively what has occurred with a given program and why. Changes can then be introduced as needed, leading to an improved delivery of services to clients with severe developmental disabilities.

ANTECEDENT EVENTS CREATING A NEED FOR PLANNING AND EVALUATION SERVICES

The need for planning and evaluation services is readily and painfully apparent to some practitioners. Beyond clinicians' own concerns about the adequacy of care and their sense of responsibility to professional standards, at least three trends fuel this demand for skill in program evaluation. The first is due to the efforts of the judiciary in establishing standards of care and training for handicapped persons. The second is the result of budget cutting by federal and state agencies. Service delivery organizations (schools, adult activity centers, residential institutions) must demonstrate that programs receiving funds are in fact achieving promised goals. This trend toward accountability in service delivery has created a need for ongoing planning and evaluation activities. Finally, Congress has legislated the need for these services through the passage of the Education of All Handicapped Children's Act of 1975 (Pub. L. No. 94–142).

Judicial Events

In 1972, the Court held in *Wyatt v. Stickney* that institutionalized mentally retarded clients had the right to habilitation, geared toward raising levels of adaptive functioning through formal and informal education and treatment (Baumeister, 1981). In *Youngberg v. Romeo*, the Court stated that mentally retarded persons involuntarily committed to state institutions have the right to safety, freedom from restraint, and the right to reasonable training to ensure safety and freedom from unnecessary restraint. Unfortunately, the Court in *Youngberg v. Romeo* did not define in detail standards of "minimally adequate or reasonable training" (Bateman, 1982). The possibility that future definitions of reasonable training will be determined by case law are great, and this argues for a proactive effort by professionals. In this way, methods of "reasonable training" can be defined, developed, and evaluated using techniques of program evaluation prior to judicial action. Should the courts then be asked to rule on these issues, evaluation information will be available for determining the effectiveness of questionable programs.

Budgetary Events

Reduced spending for public education and training programs for the severely developmentally disabled are a reality of the 1980s. Planning and evaluation activities can address these events in several ways. Programs that are successful can be improved upon and replicated, and ineffective programs can be eliminated. Moreover, armed with evaluation data, the professional has a stronger base from which to argue against further cuts (Maher, Illback, & Zins, in press).

Legislative Events

Perhaps the most pervasive legislation affecting service delivery to handicapped school-aged clients is Public Law No. 94–142. Two requirements of this law in particular create a need for planning and evaluation services: (1) the development of Individualized Educational Plans (IEPs) with specific goals and objectives for each handicapped student, and (2) the Least Restrictive Environment mandate. Both require decisions about program options presently in operation. For example, is the least restrictive alternative (Program A) as educationally effective as the more restrictive alternative (Program B)? Another evaluation question might focus on whether the current reading program is helping the client achieve reading goals and objectives as described in the IEP. These evaluation questions require specific types of information that can be obtained using program planning and evaluation methods.

GENERIC PROGRAM PLANNING AND EVALUATION MODEL

According to Maher and Bennett's (1984) framework, four characteristics define good planning and evaluation. The planning and evaluation efforts should have *utility*. That is, they should serve the needs of those requesting planning and evaluation. Professionals accomplish this by confronting important problems, providing information in a timely fashion, documenting and recording information obtained in a clear manner, and coordinating program plans and evaluation results with the staff to facilitate utilization of information obtained.

Efforts undertaken must be *feasible*. They should be realistic, diplomatic, and frugal. Planning and evaluation efforts also should be ethically and legally *responsible*. Finally, these efforts should present *accurate* information, obtained in technically defensible ways from a variety of sources (Maher & Bennett, 1984).

Maher and Bennett's (1984) framework for planning and evaluation is presented in Exhibit 10–1. The five service delivery areas described are represented on the abscissa, while the planning and evaluation process is represented on the ordinate. This framework includes four phases: (1) problem clarification, (2) program design, (3) program implementation, and (4) outcome evaluation.

Problem Clarification

Maher and Bennett (1984) describe problems in service delivery across any one of the five areas as an undesirable state of affairs (U.S.O.A.). By interviewing multiple levels of staff (e.g., aides, professionals, program directors), professionals will find that a variety of opinions and concerns often will surface. The information obtained from each of these individuals is important to program improvement. However, without an organizing framework, the information cannot be used efficiently and may not be used effectively. The problem clarification phase is designed to organize this information. It seeks to define the type and extent of the problem so that a program can be designed to improve it. Maher and Bennett (1984) note four steps to problem clarification:

1. identification of perspectives on the problem in service delivery to investigate more extensively;
2. needs assessment designed to determine the desired state of affairs (D.S.O.A.) and compare it to the U.S.O.A.;
3. assessment of the relevant context, including the evaluator's knowledge of the system, an assessment of the system resources available for change, and an assessment of the staff's readiness for change;
4. description of the clarified problem that will integrate all information obtained in steps 1–3, and specify the group or individual experiencing the problem (the target), the target's needs, and the relevant context within which those needs are embedded.

Program Design

Once the service delivery problem has been clarified, a program to assess service delivery needs must be designed. As used here, "need" represents the discrepancy between the current state of affairs (C.S.O.A.) and the D.S.O.A. (Maher & Bennett, 1984).

Maher and Bennett (1984) note that there are three tasks when designing a program. First, a rationale for the program's existence must be developed whereby the future program's purposes, goals and objectives are specified. Second, pro-

Exhibit 10–1 Generic Planning and Evaluation Model

	Planning and Evaluation Process			
	Problem Clarification	Program Design	Program Implementation	Outcome Evaluation
Assessment Services				
Instructional Services				
Related Services				
Personnel Development Services				
Administrative Services				

Source: Maher, C. A., & Bennett, R. E. (1984). *Planning and Evaluating Special Education Services.* Englewood Cliffs, NJ: Prentice-Hall, p. 10. Reprinted by permission.

grams already in existence (either within the agency or elsewhere) that might address the service delivery need are considered. This task prevents the possible duplication of services, and can be achieved through professional consultation and literature reviews. Finally, one of the program options that was considered is selected, and a written program design is developed. The program design is essentially a procedure manual for how the program will operate, who will participate in its operation, what their responsibilities will be, and how the program will be evaluated. Exhibit 10–2 describes Maher and Bennett's (1984) components of a program design. As can be seen in Exhibit 10–2 the program design model has three parts: (1) purpose (program rationale; who will be served, in what manner, and by which staff; outcomes expected); (2) implementation guidelines (human, informational, technological, financial, and physical resources necessary; specific program activities; staff responsibilities; timeline for activities; allowable "flex" in the program); and (3) outcomes (procedures for evaluating whether the program was successful in achieving its goals and objectives).

Once the program design has been written, but prior to its implementation, Maher and Bennett (1984) suggest that it be evaluated according to five criteria. These include (1) clarity, (2) comprehensiveness, (3) internal consistency, (4) compatibility with agency policy, and (5) theoretical soundness. Once evaluated, and altered as desired, the program is ready to be put into practice.

Exhibit 10–2 Components of a Program Design

1. Purpose
   1.1 Program rationale
   1.2 Scope
       1.21 Activities
       1.22 Client population
       1.23 Staff
   1.3 Major outcomes expected
2. Implementation
   2.1 Preconditions for operation
       2.11 Human resources
           2.111 Number, type and qualifications of staff
       2.12 Informational resources
           2.121 Policies and procedures
               2.1211 Criteria for selecting program clients
               2.1212 Evaluation plan
       2.13 Technological resources
           2.131 Materials
           2.132 Equipment
       2.14 Financial resources
           2.141 Budgets
               2.1411 Developmental budget
               2.1412 Operational budget
       15 Physical resources
           2.151 Facilities
               2.1511 Rooms
               2.1512 Buildings
               2.1513 Sites
   2.2 Nature of methods and activities
   2.3 Roles, responsibilities and relationships of staff
   2.4 Sequence and timing of activities
   2.5 Amount of permissible variation across sites
3. Outcomes
   3.1 Program goals
       3.11 Objectives cross references to activities (2.2 above)

Source: Maher. C. A.. & Bennett. R. E. (1984). *Planning and Evaluating Special Education Services.* Englewood Cliffs. NJ: Prentice-Hall. p. 13. Reprinted by permission.

Program Implementation. In this phase, the evaluator provides program design information to the staff, assists them in the beginning stages of implementation, and evaluates the program during implementation so it can be improved on an ongoing basis (Maher & Bennett, 1984). This phase helps to "work out the bugs" that may not have been considered during the program design effort. It also reveals discrepancies between the program plan and actual program operations that may need to be corrected.

Human service programs only work when staff are committed to making them effective. Communication between planners and implementers therefore becomes essential. Maher and Bennett (1984) describe a useful approach for determining the extent to which a program is operating as intended. The acronym DURABLE identifies key areas to consider in order to foster communication and "ownership" of the program by staff. In addition, the DURABLE approach facilitates the ongoing evaluation of the program in operation. Each dimension of the acronym is described.

- *Discuss* the program's purpose, implementation, and expected outcomes with all personnel involved in service delivery.
- *Understand* staff concerns so that a sense of concern is communicated and possible alternative courses of action are identified before intervention.
- *Reward* staff for carrying out the program in a manner consistent with the program design. This can be accomplished with verbal praise or written evaluations to superiors.
- *Adapt* program operations on the basis of information obtained from the staff or through program evaluation.
- *Build* a sense of commitment, enthusiasm, and interest in the staff.
- *Learn* about program problems that have been roadblocks to continued effective operation.
- *Evaluate* the extent to which the service delivery program is operating as planned. This will provide written information for legal or ethical guidelines that must be adhered to (e.g., the use of appropriate assessment instruments), as well as for program improvement.

Not every DURABLE dimension will be appropriate to every service delivery problem. Consideration of relevant dimensions will facilitate program compliance, however, and failure to attend to staff needs at this level probably dooms a program to failure.

Outcome Evaluation. This phase describes program effects after the program has been in operation. Outcome assessment information can be used to revise, expand, or terminate ineffective or harmful programs (Maher & Bennett, 1984).

Maher and Bennett (1984) describe five ways to assess outcome for program planning and evaluation purposes. First, *goal attainment* can be evaluated by assessing the degree to which the program met the goals described in the program design. Second, *cause-effect relationships* can be assessed using single-case experimental designs. Third, *consumer reactions* can be assessed by surveying parents, teachers, aides, and caretakers for their perceptions of goal attainment. In addition, the social validity of the intervention and outcome can be assessed by asking these same individuals for their perceptions of the validity of the target problem, the intervention chosen, and the outcome achieved (Wolf, 1978). Fourth, *collateral effects* can be assessed, including positive and negative side effects that may have occurred as a result of the program. In the case of negative effects, this information may lead to alteration or termination of the program. Finally, *cost-effectiveness* can be assessed.

SERVICE DELIVERY AREAS

Each phase of the generic program planning and evaluation model is carried out with the specific program under consideration as noted in Exhibit 10–1. Different programs can be categorized by the target group served, as well as by program goals and objectives. It is to these various service delivery areas that attention is given now.

Maher and Bennett (1984) describe five service delivery areas that can be evaluated using program planning and evaluation methods. Taken together, these areas cover a broad range of habilitative and rehabilitative services useful to clients with severe developmental disabilities. These areas include: (1) assessment services, (2) instructional services, (3) related services, (4) personnel development services, and (5) administrative services.

Each service delivery area is comprised of specific programs. For our purposes, programs can be defined as "organized configurations of resources—people, materials, and facilities—designed to assist the individual, group, or organization to meet a specific need" (Maher & Bennett, 1984, p. 4). A need represents a discrepancy between a current state of affairs and a desired state of affairs, or between the way things are and the way it is thought they should be.

An example may be useful. One of the authors (MDP) was asked to evaluate a program designed to provide after-school recreational services to autistic children. Technically, the program constituted a *related service* because it was designed to enhance the instructional efforts provided for these children in school. It was a *program* because it consisted of resources (teachers, aides, toys, materials, classroom space) that were organized in a deliberate manner to meet the needs of parents for recreational programming for their children. Thus, the program came into being to address a need (discrepancy between an undesirable and desirable state of affairs) as perceived by parents. The program evaluator's discussions with the program staff identified their desire for an evaluation of parental (consumer) satisfaction. This led to development of a survey questionnaire designed to identify parental attitudes toward the program, including areas of strength and weakness. Receipt of this information led to a decision to continue the program, with modifications in one content area and in the timing of progress reports to parents. The consumer evaluation procedure was designed to be used on an ongoing basis (every six months).

As can be seen from the above example, program planning and evaluation activities assist administrators in making decisions about the program. The information obtained can be used to adjust the program, bringing it more into line with established or emergent goals. In addition, if evaluation seeks to measure compliance to state or federal regulations, accountability can be determined. To gain a broader perspective on the types of programs for the severely developmentally disabled that can be planned and evaluated, each of the service delivery areas is discussed.

Assessment Services

In planning and evaluating assessment services, clinicians have as a goal the provision of information for use in making decisions about individual clients. Maher and Bennett (1984) note that two types of assessment decisions can be made: (1) eligibility decisions and (2) programming decisions. As each of these decision possibilities entails specific assessment programs, they will be discussed separately.

Planning and evaluating eligibility programs is an area of great importance to clients with severe developmental disabilities. The particular needs and handicaps of these clients make preplacement evaluation a difficult enterprise (see Chapter 9). While it may appear to the outsider that eligibility evaluation is approached on the level of single-case assessments, a program does in fact exist even if it is not made explicit. Conceptualizing events in programmatic terms leads to useful modes of evaluation. There are goals, activities, resources, and timing sequences that are organized in a particular way to lead to an evaluative statement about a given client's eligibility for any services. The emphasis may range from eligibility for community placement to eligibility for nonvocal training, but the goal is always one of information gathering for decision-making purposes.

For many clients, the severe nature of their handicap qualifies them for services immediately. These individuals were identifiable from infancy, and have likely received a variety of special services already. For this group, the assessment for eligibility question is concerned with a more subtle issue: how can a comprehensive evaluation be conducted such that the client's particular needs will be identified? To answer this question, refer to the assessment model described in Chapter 9.

In applying this evaluation framework, it is useful to think of each specific eligibility decision as a program. Thus, a program exists to assess clients psychologically as in the problem-solving model presented in Chapter 9. Programs also exist to change a client's status on the unit, to determine eligibility for sheltered workshop or educational placement, to screen clients for medical or psychosocial problems, and to determine whether a client would benefit from a foster grandparent. Not all of these programs will be explicit; initially, most will not.

However, the utility of planning and evaluating assessment services is that these programs can be put in evaluative form. That is, the program can be put into a form whereby it can be evaluated against its explicit purposes, goals, and objectives. Only then can data-based decisions be rendered regarding program continuation, alteration, or termination.

Once a client has been determined eligible for a service (e.g., adult activities or sheltered workshop), habilitative programs are developed and can be evaluated. These habilitative and rehabilitative activities were identified as needs in the eligibility determination program, and became part of the client's daily routine. Periodically, they need to be reviewed for their efficacy and efficiency in meeting the client's goals as stated in the Individualized Educational Plan (IEP) or the Individualized Habilitative Plan (IHP). These review activities (IEP Annual Review) have goals, purposes, objectives, activities, resources expended, and anticipated outcomes. If viewed and constructed programmatically, these review activities can be evaluated using the generic program planning and evaluation model presented earlier in Chapter 10.

Instructional Services

Instructional services are those individual and group programs that are designed to facilitate the social, intellectual, and vocational growth of clients with severe developmental disabilities. Two types of programs make up instructional services: (1) individual programs and (2) group programs (Maher & Bennett, 1984).

Individual programs are those provided the client on the basis of strengths and weaknesses identified during assessment. If the client is of school age, these programs are listed in the IEP; for older clients they are noted in the IHP. They include programs to reduce self-injury, to teach independent toileting, to teach greeting responses, and so on. These programs exist to redress a specific need in a particular client, and can be evaluated according to their ability to achieve their stated goals. In contrast, group programs provide instructional services to a number of clients. These include foster grandparent programs, community release programs, special classes, and group homes. Group homes provide a service to many clients, and can be evaluated on the basis of their ability to achieve that goal.

A note of clarification may be needed. Newcomers to program planning and evaluation frequently confuse *group programs* with *individual programs that are implemented in a group*. An example of the latter would be a social skills group for five autistic adults, where each client had specific (and perhaps different) goals to achieve. Because the goals and objectives of each group member are individualized, they can be described and evaluated as individual programs. However, should an evaluation of the group program for "social skills training for autistic adults" be requested, different evaluative questions are operative. For example, the staff may request that the program evaluator determine whether the social skills training group met its goals of (1) meeting weekly for 40 minutes, (2) being perceived as useful by group members and staff, and (3) assisting each group member in achieving 75% of their individual goals as described in their IHP.

Related Services

The pervasiveness of severe developmental disabilities often requires the services of a wide variety of professionals. Related services exist to support instructional services (Maher & Bennett, 1984). Hence, a related service program is warranted only to the extent that it contributes in some meaningful way to the client's ability to benefit from instruction.

Severely developmentally disabled clients often require the related services of pediatric neurologists, speech therapists, occupational therapists, specialized transportation, psychological counseling, therapy for their families, or ongoing medical consultation. The service delivery program for each area consists of professionals engaging in specific goal-directed activities in order to facilitate the instructional/habilitative process for the client. The agency or organization requesting these services has specific goals for the service area, just as the service provider (e.g., occupational therapist or recreation leader) has goals for himself or herself. These goals and the activities that lead to them can be evaluated using program planning and evaluation methods.

Assessment, instructional, and related service areas are concerned with the delivery of services to severely developmentally disabled clients. Just as these programs can be evaluated and planned, the programs that exist for the staff who work with the clients (personnel development) and for the administrators who manage the entire service delivery network can be evaluated. While their emphasis is decidedly different, the personnel development and administration areas deliver services critical to the running of any organization for the severely developmentally disabled.

Personnel Development Services

Staff members need to be competent to do their jobs (Maher & Bennett, 1984). Because so many disciplines are involved with severely developmentally disabled clients, personnel development can be seen as a far-reaching task. For example, consider the diverse areas of expertise required by therapists counseling the families of young severely mentally retarded children. Therapists must be aware of etiologic, prognostic, and complicating aspects of the disability; they must be expert in the psychosocial stressors that such families experience, such as feelings of loss, mourning, or anger, and in patterns of sibling and extended family interaction. Add to this expertise in psychotherapy, assessment and intervention, and knowledge of community resources. Fortunately, it is possible to define these needs and evaluate their provision.

Persons other than the professional staff come under the purview of personnel development services. Many agencies and institutions employ paraprofessionals to supplement professional staff, thereby increasing the staff-client ratio. The variability in training staff underscores the special importance of planning and evaluating personnel development services in programs for the severely developmentally disabled. In public school programs, each state has a Department of Education that sets minimum training requirements for teachers and aides. These requirements presume a basic, entry-level proficiency in areas critical to the job. While these requirements vary, reasonable upper and lower boundaries exist. For institutional aides, however, minimum technical proficiency requirements are often quite low. It naively is expected that because these paraprofessionals are being supervised by trained professionals, the expertise of the professionals will "trickle down" to those that they supervise. This rationale has frequently proven unworkable, resulting in high rates of staff burnout, turnover, apathy, and client mismanagement. Moreover, anyone familiar with the pressures inherent in delivering services to autistic and severely/profoundly mentally retarded clients will recognize that professional staff are by no means exempt from this state of affairs.

One solution proffered by many institutions and agencies has been to provide inservice training, professional conferences, and expert consultative services to paraprofessional and professional staff (Maher & Bennett, 1984). The administrative goal of this training is generally to improve services to clients by increasing the competence of the staff. Whether such goals are achieved, however, is a question that only can be answered through evaluation activities. Thus, each component personnel development activity (e.g., inservice training) can be thought of as a program and evaluated using the generic program planning and evaluation model. When the multiplicity of disciplines that may be called upon to provide services to severely developmentally disabled clients is considered, the task of planning and evaluation takes on considerable breadth. For example, Powers and Healy (1982) describe a program to teach pediatricians about handicapping conditions of childhood. This program was developed for one group of related service providers who have frequent (and often the initial) interaction with parents and their children. The training model entailed a comprehensive evaluation component that led to ongoing modification and refinement of the training program. Efforts such as these are critically important.

Administrative Services

The delivery of administrative services should not be exempt from the evaluation process. Using Maher and Bennett's (1984) framework, this area represents the management activities that coordinate the delivery of assessment, instructional, related, and personnel development services to severely developmentally disabled clients. The task of coordinating seemingly disparate service delivery areas can be a difficult one. However, when viewed programmatically, administrative services can be seen as a configuration of separate but related programs, each designed to contribute to the overall management function. These programs include (but are not limited to) supervision of professional and paraprofessional staff; case management; recruitment of new staff; community liaison work; formal peer review and consultation efforts (utilizing, for example, the services of the Association for Advancement of Behavior Therapy); budget analysis; and conducting program evaluations.

SUMMARY

The generic planning and evaluation framework is intended as a model for assessing systems beyond the individual level. Some modifications will be necessary when planning and evaluating services for the severely developmentally disabled. These modifications will be likely to occur when clinicians develop service delivery options to accommodate the extreme types of handicapping conditions involved. The planning and evaluation process, in contrast, will probably remain intact across client groups and agencies.

Use of this framework with severely developmentally disabled clients is still in a formative stage. It is expected that, over time, continued use will generate modifications and improvements in the model, and lead to an expanded view of assessment in severe developmental disabilities.

REFERENCES

Bateman, B. (1982). Youngberg and Romeo: Analysis and commentary. *Analysis and Intervention in Developmental Disabilities, 2,* 375–382.

Baumeister, A. A. (1981). The right to habilitation: What does it mean? *Analysis and Intervention in Developmental Disabilities, 1,* 61–74.

Maher, C. A. (1981a). Developing and implementing effective individualized education programs for conduct-problem adolescents: The goal-oriented approach to learning. *Child Behavior Therapy, 3,* 1–11.

Maher, C. A. (1981b). Implementation of Public Law 94–142: Challenges and opportunities for behavior modification. *Child Behavior Therapy, 3,* 79–83.

Maher, C. A. (1982a). Making decisions in planning for delivery of school psychological services. *Professional Psychology, 13,* 309–317.

Maher, C. A. (1982b). Improving the program-planning skills of school psychologists: Use of performance feedback. *Professional Psychology, 13,* 681–690.

Maher, C. A. & Bennett, R. E. (1984). *Planning and evaluating special education services.* Englewood Cliffs, NJ: Prentice-Hall.

Maher, C. A., Illback, R. J., & Zins, J. E. (Eds.). (in press). *Organizational psychology in schools: A handbook for school professionals*. Springfield, IL: Charles C Thomas.

Powers, J. T., & Healy, A. (1982). Inservice training for physicians serving handicapped children. *Exceptional Children, 48*, 332–336.

Wolf, M. M. (1978). Social validity: The case for subjective measurement or how applied behavior analysis is finding its heart. *Journal of Applied Behavior Analysis, 11*, 203–214.

Youngberg v. Romeo, 50 U.S.L.W. 4681, 4684 (June 18, 1982).

Social and Developmental History Form*

Name of child _____ Birth date _____
If a favored nickname is used, what is it? _____

Name of parents	Address	Phone

If addresses are different, where does child live? _____

Mother: Date of birth _____ Place of birth _____
  Highest education level _____ Occupation_____
  Workplace _____
  Any handicaps or problems? _____
Father: Date of birth _____ Place of birth _____
  Highest education level _____ Occupation _____
  Workplace _____
  Any handicaps or problems? _____
Language(s) spoken at home _____
Other children in family: (if more than four, please use reverse side)

Name	Birth date	Sex	Foster or adopted?

_____

*Thanks to Joan B. Chase, EdD, Kenneth C. Schneider, PhD, and the Psychological Clinic of Rutgers University for permission to reprint this form.

Do any of the above have: School problems?_____ Health problems? _____
Other? _____
If so, please explain who and what problems _____

_____

Are there any other "extended family members" or caretakers who are living in the home? _____

_____

The following questions refer to the child to be evaluated:
Is the child natural? _____ Adopted? _____ Foster? _____
If not a natural child to you, at what age was placement made? _____
Is child in a school? _____ Where? _____

In a special program?_____ Where? _____

In day care? _____ Where? _____

With a sitter more than two hours a day? _____ Where and with whom? _____

What concerns you about your child? _____

How long have you been concerned about the above problem(s)? _____

Who referred you to this clinic? _____

What problems (health, developmental) have been identified by other professionals?

Problem	*Professional*	*Address*
_____	_____	_____
_____	_____	_____
_____	_____	_____
_____	_____	_____

When and how do you feel these difficulties developed? _____

_____

_____

In doing this evaluation, what questions would you like the evaluator to try to answer for you? _____

_____

_____

The following questions concern the birth history of this child:
Which pregnancy was this? _____
Does mother have a history of fertility problems? _____ Miscarriages? _____
    Stillbirths? _____
How was your health during this pregnancy? _____

Did you have difficulty with:

Excessive weight gain? _____	Blood pressure? _____
Bleeding or staining? _____	German measles? _____
Rh incompatibility? _____	High fever? _____
Medication? _____	Toxemia? _____

Physician used: _____
Address: _____
Hospital and town: _____
Was delivery induced? _____ Cesarean? _____
Was it a single or multiple birth? _____
Type of anesthesia used? _____
Time in labor? _____
Were there any complications during delivery? _____
Birth weight and length? _____
Was the child born prematurely? (if yes, which month) _____
Did the child have any difficulty breathing after birth? _____
Was oxygen necessary? _____
Was the child in an incubator? (if yes, for how long) _____
Apgar score, if known _____
Were there any other complications? _____
Were there any congenital malformations? If so, have they been corrected? ____

Were there any difficulties with any previous or subsequent pregnancies?
_____ If so, describe and give dates _____

The following questions refer to earliest development:
Did you breast or bottle feed? _____
Were there any problems with feeding? _____

Did the child appear to enjoy body contact, or did the child seem not to enjoy or
dislike body contact? _____

As a newborn, were there any difficulties with:

Sucking _____	Crying _____
Chewing _____	Sleeping _____
Swallowing _____	Other problems _____

The following questions refer to recent development:
Who is your child's physician? (name and address)

_____

_____

Please check which of the usual childhood illnesses your child has had. Please note when.

Chicken pox _____	Scarlet fever _____
German measles _____	Whooping cough _____
Regular measles _____	Diphtheria _____
Mumps _____	Rheumatic fever _____

Has the child had:

Seizures? _____	Tonsillitis? _____
Allergic reactions? _____	Asthma? _____
Frequent colds? _____	Frequent stomach upsets? _____

Others? _____
Has your child had any other illnesses? (type of illness and when) _____

_____

_____

What is the highest fever your child has had? _____ When? _____

_____

Has your child ever been hospitalized? (if *yes*, please include when, why, how long, where, physician) _____

_____

_____

Is your child currently on medication? (if *yes*, please give name, dosage, reason, and the prescribing physician) _____

_____

_____

Was your child ever on medication for an extended period of time? (if *yes*, please explain) _____

_____

_____

Has your child had any food cravings, dislikes, or allergies? (if *yes*, please describe) _____

_____

Has your child ever had a hearing test? (if *yes*, give details and recommendations)

_____

_____

Has your child ever had a vision test? (if *yes*, give details and recommendations)

_____

_____

Which hand does your child prefer when he/she:
Eats _____ Writes _____ Throws a ball _____

Check milestones attained and age:	*Age attained*	*Not yet attained* (check)

A. *Motor*
   1. Head held up
   2. Sat without help
   3. Crawled
   4. Stood holding on
   5. Took steps holding on
   6. Walked

B. *Feeding*
   1. Ate junior foods
   2. Ate solid foods
   3. Held cookie and chewed
   4. Chewed table foods
   5. Finger fed
   6. Held spoon
   7. Fed self
   8. Gave up bottle

C. *Toileting*
   1. Expressed desire to have diaper changed
   2. Used potty or toilet when placed
   3. Stayed dry during day
   4. Stayed dry during night
   5. Bowel control
   6. Asked to go when necessary
   7. Went independently

D. *Social*
   1. Smiled when played with
   2. Discriminated family from nonfamily
   3. Interacted (babble, play) with others
   4. Learned simple games (peek-a-boo, patty-cake)
   5. Showed shyness with others
   6. Was responsive to play of other children
   7. Separated from others

E. *Language*
   1. Babbled
   2. Mimicked sounds
   3. Understood ''no'' or other simple commands

	Age attained	Not yet attained (check)
4. Said first word	_____	_____
5. Understood more complex commands	_____	_____
6. Named objects	_____	_____
7. Used sentences	_____	_____

8. Describe current language use:

_____

_____

_____

_____

The following questions refer to the child's educational history:

Current school _____ Grade _____

Address _____

Sponsoring district _____

Teacher _____ Principal or Child Study Team member _____

_____ Classification _____

School history: list where and what type of program (e.g., special class, etc.)

	Year	Placement	Comments on Progress
Pre-N	_____	_____	_____
N.S.	_____	_____	_____
Kg.	_____	_____	_____
1	_____	_____	_____
2	_____	_____	_____
3	_____	_____	_____
4	_____	_____	_____
5	_____	_____	_____
6	_____	_____	_____
7	_____	_____	_____
8	_____	_____	_____
9	_____	_____	_____
10	_____	_____	_____
11	_____	_____	_____
12	_____	_____	_____

High school diploma: yes _____ no _____

Other schooling _____

_____

_____

_____

The following questions refer to the child's current skill status:

A. *Self-Help*   *Describe*
   1. Eating _____
   2. Dressing _____
   3. Toileting _____
   4. Bathing _____

B. *Gross Motor*
   1. Walking _____
   2. Running _____
   3. Stairs _____
   4. Jumping/hopping _____
   5. Active games _____

C. *Fine Motor*
   1. Blocks/beads _____
   2. Pencil for writing _____
   3. Use of scissors _____
   4. Art work _____

D. *Social*
   1. Play with friends _____
   2. Shopping (mail order, etc.) _____
   3. Active games _____
   4. Table games _____

E. *Language*
   1. Gestures _____
   2. Speech _____
   3. Words _____
   4. Full sentences _____
   5. Accurate parts of speech _____
   6. Conversations _____

F. *Reading Level* _____

G. *Writing Level* _____
   1. Print _____
   2. Script _____
   3. Typing _____

H. *Current Activities* _____
   _____
   _____

Please check the category that best describes your child's behavior:

	Never	Sometimes	Often	Usually
Smiles				
Rocks rhythmically				
Is a loner				
Fusses				
Is unhappy				
Startles				
Plays well with toys				
Is self-willed				
Is cautious				
Throws things				
Laughs				
Stares into space				
Fights				
Is shy				
Gets angry				
Is calm				
Wets the bed				
Plays with children				
Is moody				
Has nightmares				
Is frightened				
Is happy				
Bangs head				
Steals				
Shows no interest in toys				
Lies				
Seems tense				
Is affectionate				
Sets fires				
Is stubborn				
Cries easily				
Is overly active				
Daydreams				
Is friendly to strangers				
Is wary				
Has tantrums				

Other characteristics (specify)_____
_____

Have there been any problems in these areas? If so, please describe.

_____

_____

_____

_____

_____

Any other problems? _____

_____

Is there anything else that might help us in this evaluation? _____

_____

_____

_____

_____

Person filling out this form _____

Relationship to child _____

Signature _____

Date completed _____

Index

A

About the Authors

Michael D. Powers, Psy.D., is Director of Behavioral and Community Psychology at the Child Development Center, Georgetown University School of Medicine. Dr. Powers has been a teacher, supervisor, and consultant with autistic and severely/profoundly retarded children and adults. His publications have focused primarily on the behavioral assessment and treatment of the developmentally disabled and their families, psychological assessment of the severely handicapped, and syndromal diagnosis of childhood disorders.

Jan S. Handleman, Ed.D., is the Educational Director of the Douglass Developmental Disabilities Center of Rutgers–The State University of New Jersey. The Center is a university-based, state-operated school for the education and treatment of autistic children. His research interests include various psychoeducational issues concerning severely developmentally disabled clients.